The Nature of

ALSO BY JAMES J. FARRELL

Inventing the American Way of Death, 1830–1920
The Nuclear Devil's Dictionary
The Spirit of the Sixties
One Nation Under Goods:
  Malls and the Seductions of American Shopping

The Nature of College

How a New Understanding
of Campus Life Can Change the World

James J. Farrell

milkweed
editions

Published 2010 by Milkweed Editions
Printed in Canada by Friesens Corporation
Cover Design & Art Direction: Tonky Designs
Cover Photography: Ward Yoshimoto
Author photo courtesy of St. Olaf College
Interior design by Wendy Holdman
Interior illustrations by Jens Mattson
The text of this book is set in Arno Pro.
10 11 12 13 14 5 4 3 2 1
First Edition

Please turn to the back of this book for a list of the sustaining funders of Milkweed Editions.

Library of Congress Cataloging-in-Publication Data

Farrell, James J.
   The nature of college / James J. Farrell.
     p.   cm.
   ISBN 978-1-57131-322-5 (pbk. : alk. paper) — ISBN 978-1-57131-819-0 (e-book)
   1. College students—United States—Conduct of life. 2. Education, Higher—Aims and objectives—United States. 3. Universities and colleges—United States.
   I. Title.
LB3605.F34   2010
378.73—dc22

                                          2010031777

This book is printed on acid-free paper.

To America's College Students

The Nature of College

Web site: natureofcollege.org

Prelude

A way of seeing is also a way of not seeing.
Kenneth Burke, *Permanence and Change*

"Ordinary" is just another word for not paying attention.
Frank Gohlke and Mark Lowry, "Prairie Castles"

We have several thousand thoughts a day, and probably about 95 percent of those thoughts are the same every day.
John Adams, *Thinking Today as if Tomorrow Mattered*

Education, I fear, is learning to see one thing by going blind to another.
Aldo Leopold, *A Sand County Almanac*

I am sane only when I have risen above my common sense. . . . Wisdom is not common.
Henry David Thoreau, Journal entry: June 22, 1851

■ ■ ■ ■ ■ ■ ■

College students have a lot on their minds. A few years ago, students of mine mapped the mind of an average college student. I gave them an outline of an empty head and asked them to fill it with the everyday concerns of college life. The results were fascinating: classes, homework, grades, friends and family, sex and relationships, food and snacks, drinking and drugs, jobs and financial issues all interrelated with religious and moral concerns. They try, as one student said, "to figure out what the hell they're going to do with the rest of their lives."

As this suggests, students think about a lot at college. But what do they really learn? In the classroom they pick up some math, a little science, and a social study or two. They learn enough American history and political science to be competitive on trivia night, but they also acquire such subtle skills as how to look attentive in class while thinking of sex, relationships, and money. They discover, quickly, the social

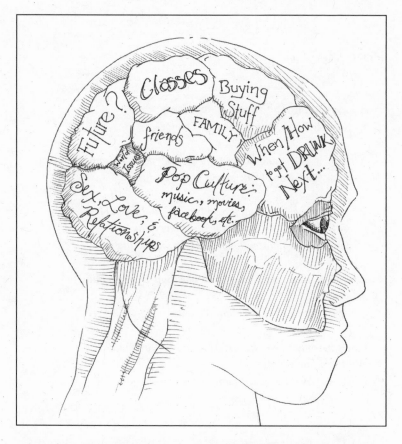

value of a major, which is why so many incoming students are premed or pre-law. If they aren't careful, students might get stereotyped by less desirable majors, like the soon-to-be-impoverished poets in English or the dreamers in the art department. By the second semester of their first year they already know which professors give an "easy A" and why they should never take an 8:00 a.m. class again. Masters at multitasking, they procrastinate, text friends, check Facebook, drink coffee, listen to music, and clean—all at once.

At college, students learn to live for the breaks and wait for the weekend. They know which fraternities throw the wildest parties. They master the fine art of drinking beer from a bong or a Frisbee or a boot, along with the more difficult lessons associated with overcoming a hangover. At parties and elsewhere, students learn how to present themselves

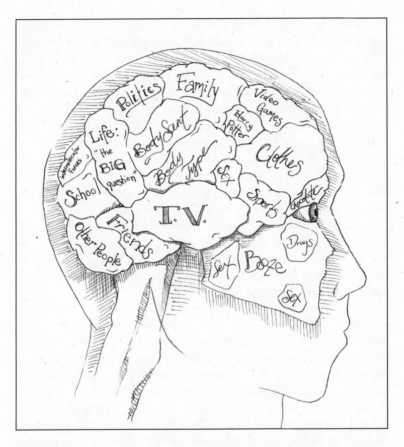

physically and socially for maximum magnetism. Once they draw someone in, students practice other arts and crafts, like the fine art of hooking
up or the subtle craft of condom use. They find the best campus places
for privacy and discover the delicate politics of "sexile."

The academic cycle of cramming for tests and forgetting a great per-
centage of the material immediately afterward becomes the cycle of
their academic life. It's the grade that's important, not what they actually
learn. Therefore many students refine their talent for bullshit: perfecting
the discussion of books they've never read, cranking out five hundred
words about anything or nothing, writing a response paper ten minutes
before class, and pounding out a ten-page expository essay (with foot-
notes) in a day. "Good students" learn what the professor wants, which
buzzwords she likes, and how to give her both in bulk.

Of course, some students learn more substantial stuff in academia. These students learn to love ideas and the art of a well-crafted sentence. They learn to work harder than they ever imagined, and to play harder, too. Some students learn several of life's important questions, and one or two of the answers. They learn a little more about the self beneath the surface, and what they're good at and good for.

Most students take a foreign language, but many discover that slang is taken more seriously by their peers. So students learn how to call out a tool, troll, nerd, slush, or *sorostitute*, and they know synonyms for "liquid courage" and "beer goggles." A lot of college slang involves natural endowments, natural functions, and the call of nature, but almost none of it enhances students' love or understanding of the natural world.

Students learn college culture (mostly from other students—certainly not professors) and pass the patterns and practices of everyday life on campus from one graduating class to the next. But as they find a place in campus culture, they also define their place in the world, both socially and ecologically.

College is a place where students could think twice about American culture and ecosystems, but most students still don't, despite the fact that people are causing climate change—transforming the good Earth into a different planet. We love to joke about global warming. Warming sounds like something familiar, and, especially in the North, it sounds good. But we're facing what Hunter Lovins calls—more accurately— "global weirding." Global weirding is radically different from anything human beings have ever experienced. Earth is not just getting warmer, it's warming *and* cooling, getting wetter *and* drier, becoming stormier and increasingly unstable. To make matters worse, "weirding" is a feedback loop, responding in ways that reinforce these problematic tendencies. As ice melts, more heat is absorbed into oceans. As tundra melts, more methane leaks into the atmosphere, accelerating the greenhouse effect. At current rates of change, in the year 2100 New York will have as many 100-degree days as Miami does now, and coastal colleges and universities may be underwater in more than just a financial sense.

Students learn a lot in college, but most students aren't learning what they need to create a restorative society, a hospitable earth, and a future with college campuses securely above water. Colleges now need to provide the knowledge and practices humans need for the future, to show in word and deed how a sustainable society might work. A college that wants to remain relevant to its students will teach them how to be leaders in the ecological transition of the twenty-first century. If it works right, a college education will teach students to develop what David Orr calls "designing minds," minds that are prepared to design a good society in harmony with nature. Orr suggests that higher education should be designed "1. to equip young people with a basic understanding of systems and to develop habits of mind that seek out 'patterns that connect' human and natural systems; 2. to teach young people the analytical skills necessary for thinking accurately about cause and effect; 3. to give students the practical competence necessary to solve local problems; and 4. to teach young people the habit of rolling up their sleeves and getting down to work." Institutions of higher education have always prepared students to succeed in the so-called real world. Our colleges and universities now need to teach students how to live responsibly on the planet as well.

Today's colleges aren't yet ready for this challenge, but students can pressure them to live up to the promise of mission statements that claim to prepare people for the future. In the 1960s, Paul Goodman challenged students: "Think about the kind of world you want to live and work in. What do you need to know to help build that world? Demand that your teachers teach you that." Much of the time, sadly, this advice is ignored. Most of us know, deep down, that we need an ecological revolution to build a new world that is sustainable—ecologically, economically, socially, and personally. Too often, however, students take courses to complete requirements instead of requiring that their courses help to build this better world. They hardly ever demand enough from their professors or their education. That's what this book is for. Uncovering the intellectual and emotional patterns that connect us to the degradation of nature, we'll discover new patterns of thinking and acting to create the world we want to live and work in.[1]

The Nature of College

Introduction: A Reader's Guide

I went to (college) because I wished to live deliberately, to front only the essential facts of life, and see if I could not learn what it had to teach, and not, when I came to die, discover that I had not lived.

Henry David Thoreau, *Walden* (amended)

Think about the kind of world you want to live and work in. What do you need to know to help build that world? Demand that your teachers teach you that.

Paul Goodman, "The Duty of Professionals"

The very least you can do in your life is to figure out what you hope for. And the most you can do is live inside that hope.

Barbara Kingsolver, *Animal Dreams*

∎ ∎ ∎ ∎ ∎ ∎ ∎

There are all sorts of books advising students how to read, but not a lot on how to engage an author in a constructive dialogue. Colleges have courses in creative writing, but not in creative reading, which is the art of reading in conversation. At its best, a book is one voice in an ongoing conversation, contributing corrections and corroborations, new ideas and insights, and waiting for a response. Because any conversation works best when the questions and conceptual frameworks are fully understood, I offer them here in the clearest form possible:

The Questions

- What are the key components of American college culture?
- Why do we act the way we do?
- What do we really value and why?
- Why do we act in ways that contradict our values?
- Why do we consume so much?
- Why isn't our common sense sensible anymore?

- How much of our lives is intentional, and how much merely habitual?
- Why is it so hard to talk about things that really matter to us?
- What are the roots of hope and change?

The Frameworks

1) The Culture of Nature

Because this book plays at the intersection of American studies and environmental studies, a basic assumption is that we always experience nature through cultural frames, that the American eye is always connected to the American "I," and that Americans grow up learning certain ways of seeing nature. One of those ways, for example, is Romantic: We see nature through the eyes of nineteenth-century landscape painters who saw nature and wilderness both as counterpoint *to* civilization, and as escape *from* it. This explains how car manufacturers can sell us environmentally destructive SUVs by advertising them in cultural landscapes that look "natural" to us, like a stunningly beautiful beach or a striking mountain scene. Because of Romantic assumptions that conflate nature and wilderness, most of us don't think that we're interacting with nature unless we find ourselves in an officially designated wilderness area.

But we are always in nature, as a second way of seeing, called "resourcism," suggests. Resourcism interprets the natural world mainly as natural resources, useful to supply human desires, but not as a living, breathing community of organisms. Surrounded by resources repurposed as products all the time, we are always in nature. The concept of "the culture of nature" doesn't mean that nature is only cultural; nature is clearly a dynamic force of its own. And it doesn't mean that people aren't nature. Despite all our cleverness and intelligence, we remain bifocal, bipedal, big-brained mammals. But we've invented a "culture of nature," so, once we're socialized, we always come to understand nature *through* culture.

This culture of nature is part of college culture, which is a subset of American youth culture, a twentieth-century development that increasingly gives young people the freedom to make sense of the world by themselves. Profs control the official curriculum, but students teach each other the hidden curriculum of college—beliefs and behavior shaped without much conscientious consideration. This hidden education is, environmentally speaking, generally more important than what is learned in classes. Students may take a few credits in environmental studies, but they *live* their environmental values every minute of every day and exemplify them to their friends. When they graduate, therefore, those practiced values, good and bad, tend to become the "culture of nature" for the next generation.

It's one of the functions of culture to teach us what's "natural"—in two ways. The first type of "natural" is what's normal, expected, routine. We think "it's only natural" to live in buildings with bathrooms, to eat three meals a day, or to party on the weekends. In this sense, the word "natural" generally means "cultural," and the word "natural" is employed because it seems less arbitrary, and therefore more compelling, than the word "cultural." If we say "it's only natural to eat meat," it's a lot more powerful than saying "it's only cultural to eat meat." In this way, culture naturalizes itself, trying to place some actions beyond the bounds of conscious and conscientious reflection.

The primary way we learn what's "natural" is through the assimilation of common sense. Common sense is everyday knowledge, what we think when we're not really thinking about things, the stuff that "everybody knows." Most of us follow common sense because it's supposed to be the accumulated wisdom of the tribe. These days, sadly, a lot of common sense is no longer wise because environmental impacts have dramatically changed the cost-benefit calculations of our normal behavior. At college, common sense is written into the cultural scripts of everyday life. Cars and computers are common sense. Air conditioning in the summer is as commonsensical as heat in the winter. TV and video games are commonsense entertainments. It's common sense to support systems—social, economic, political—that don't support ecosystems. Therefore, common sense may not be good enough for the ecological revolution of the twenty-first century.

The second way that culture teaches us what's "natural" is by defining what's nature and what's not. This is never clear or precise or consistent. Science and religion, for example, define "nature" differently, but generally speaking, in college culture the natural world is the nonhuman world. We speak of people *and* nature as if they existed in separate spheres, and we plan on "getting back to nature" over the summer, forgetting that we *are* nature *in* nature, always. This confusion has real consequences because our common cultural understandings don't remind us of our natural lives and impacts. Except in science or environmental studies classes, college students don't customarily think of nature or the environment. And that fact—that omission—is educationally important because, as one of my mentors wisely says, we are taught very well by what we are not taught.

The concept of the culture of nature, then, helps us to see the complexity of our relationships with the natural world, and our complicity with commonsense patterns of thought and behavior that don't make sense anymore. It helps us to pay attention to the *nature* of our lives, and the nature that results from our lives. It also helps us pay attention to the *culture* of our lives. And because culture is something we create collectively, it offers us real opportunities for substantial change. If the current culture of nature doesn't make sense, we can help to create a better one, and a better world.

2) Consumption, Materials, and Materialism

To parents and professors, students are people engaged in academic learning. To America's commercial interests, however, students are materialistic consumers and a major market niche. In fact, whole books have been written on taking advantage of this segment of the population. David A. Morrison's *Marketing to the Campus Crowd*, for example, notes that college students offer corporate America opportunities for "branding, selling, sub-segmenting, and new product strategies," and that, conveniently, college students can be less price-sensitive than other consumers, especially when subsidized by what Morrison calls the "Bank of Mom and Dad." College students are a profitable market, says Morrison, because of the sheer volume of their discretionary spending, along with their high concentration, rapid turnover, avid willingness to experiment, propensity for innovation and early adoption of technology, ever-changing brand loyalties, strong influence on other key consumer segments (and the mainstream marketplace as a whole), and receptivity to the right advertising, sampling, and promotions (in contrast to the average consumer). "The basic mantra behind college marketing," Morrison claims, "is to generate short-term financial gains to the bottom line and simultaneously establish long-term brand loyalties." And, as marketing consultant Peter Zollo says of younger students, "School delivers more teens per square foot than anyplace else!"[1]

If we only consumed discrete objects disconnected from the rest of the world, this might not be a problem, but in buying stuff, we buy into a *system* of stuff called materialism. Materialism is the way that Americans manage resource flows, both intentionally and unintentionally. When a student buys a computer, she thinks about its advantages for her connectedness, including (sometimes) her connection to academic resources. But while she's thinking about Internet access and word processing, she's actually *world* processing: setting off a chain of demand and supply that has far-reaching environmental consequences. She can ignore the environmental impacts of the purchase because the common sense of consumption lets her focus on her material desires instead of the material consequences of her decisions.

Locating college culture within consumer culture, then, helps us to see how American culture routinely expects us to consume stuff that consumes the world. It helps us to see how advertising pressures and peer pressures combine to make our consumption both "normal" and normative, despite its extensive environmental impacts. At the same time, however, our understanding of our consumption helps us to take control of it, so that we can change the culture of consumption to increase both our happiness and our harmonies with the natural world.

3) The Moral Ecology of Everyday Life

College culture and consumer culture aren't just sociological issues. They're ethical issues, which we can explore by examining the moral ecology of everyday life. In *Habits of the Heart*, Robert Bellah defines moral ecology as "the web of moral understandings and commitments that tie people together in community." In this book, moral ecology also includes the web of social values that ties people and the rest of nature together. To untangle this web, though, we first must understand the difference between *expressed* and *operative* values. Put simply, expressed values are the ones we *say* and operative values are the ones we *do*. Sadly, too often the operative values of our lives aren't the same as our expressed values. We say we believe in conservation and efficiency, freedom and fairness, equity and justice. But what we do is who we are, and when we look honestly at our lives, we basically buy into different values. In practice, our operative values include cheapness and novelty, fun and fashion, comfort and convenience, "cool" and conformity. When push comes to shove, we'd often rather look good than be good. We'd rather have "low, low prices" than high environmental standards. So "the good life" of American culture isn't nearly as good as it needs to be for people or the planet.

By uncovering our implicit morality, we're not only exploring the habits of our hearts, but also the more mundane habits of our days.

Environmental Values of College Culture (and American Culture)		
Individualism	Fun	Resourcism
Instrumentalism	Sociability/Friendliness	Remote Control
Credentialism	Sex-ability	Ignorance
Comfort	Materialism	Passivism
Convenience	Cheapness	*Sitizenship*
Cool	Fossil Foolishness	Presentism
Conformity	Indoor-ance	Anthropocentrism

Studies show that about 45 percent of daily behavior is habitual, which means that we don't really choose almost half of what we do. It's also true that many of our habits are things we *don't* do. Thoughtlessness is a habit, for instance, as are silence and apathy and inactivity.

This is a book of ordinary ethics. It focuses on the stuff that everybody does every day, exploring the significance of the seemingly insignificant. It investigates the culture of college by probing the underlying ideas and assumptions of student life, trying to figure out why people act the way they do and why it matters to the global community. In the process, this book creates a space for reflection and conversation about some big questions that sometimes slip under the radar. If it works, readers will get to compare their expressed values and their operative values, and decide if they're leading a good life after all.

4) Institutionalizing Environmentalism

Americans focus so much on individuals and "individual choice" that we sometimes forget the ways that systems structure choices for us. Even though we live in a world of systems—social, economic, political, intellectual, *and* natural—we often only respond to their symptoms. The price of gas, for example, is a symptom of overlapping economic, political, international, military, intellectual, and natural systems, but we usually only pay attention to the numbers on the pump. In a system that encourages externalities—the natural and social costs of production and distribution that aren't factored into the price tag—the bill for our fuel obscures deep flaws in the system that creates it.[2]

Systems structure our choices, but institutions structure our systems. Institutions are communities defined by hope and habit, stories and symbols, patterns and privileges, rules and regulations. A community—or an institution—is a way of saying "we, the people" in different settings. The family is one example of "we, the people." A church is another example, but so are colleges, corporations, media companies, and government bureaucracies. When it comes to environmentalism, college students and other Americans think that individual people choose to live "environmentally" or not. What they often forget is that institutions structure all of their individual choices. When values are institutionalized, they show up as habits, routines, peer pressure, and "common sense"—the standard operating procedures of everyday life. To most Americans, institutions are almost invisible, but their effects are profound.[3]

No matter how powerful institutions might seem, exploring their effects, including the influence they have over our hearts, can be empowering. In the 1930s, social activist Peter Maurin contended that institutions should be designed to make it easier for people to be good, and as American history repeatedly has shown, institutions *can* be changed. In this book, then, we'll consider how human systems and institutions change natural systems, and how we might change them for the better. To that end, we'll examine the inputs and outputs of natural and cultural systems and examine feedback loops in nature and culture. In the process, we can study the science and art of ecological design—the alignment of human systems and institutions with the cycles of nature—and think about perspectives and practices that make it easier for people to be good.

5) The Nature of Hope

College is not always a hopeful place. Fear of failing often animates more student activity than hope does. Fear of failing academically keeps students working on reading and research and class work, while fear of failing socially keeps students going along to get along, for fear that other students will make fun of them for their ideas and ideals. The unfortunate result is what anthropologist Michael Moffatt calls "undergraduate cynical," a way of talking tough that hides the sensitivity that could make a person vulnerable or compassionate. Such a social construction of conversation reduces the unique space a college provides for "going deep"—for thinking unconventionally about the unconventional issues of our day.[4]

If we seriously contemplate the nature of hope, however, we can replace our coping mechanisms with hoping mechanisms. Histories of hope offer a usable past for environmental activists, and stories of new hope emerging in America (often on campuses) remind us that change is possible and that our beliefs and behaviors do matter.[5]

6) Words and Worlds

Words structure our worlds. When we talk about a "good job" instead of "good work," for example, it changes the nature of the conversation and sometimes it changes nature itself. Words like "profit," "progress," "success," "cheap," and "cool"—words we don't even think of as environmental—have a lot to do with the way we treat the natural world. Paying attention, then, to how we talk about our lives, how rhetoric and persuasion work, gives us the opportunity both to understand the worlds we create through our words and how to tell the truth so that people listen. Looking deeply at language also invites us to think about new words and hybrids because, as Michael Pollan says, "names have a way of making visible [the] things we don't easily see."[6]

One such word is "ecologician," connecting ecological perspectives with the magic that can happen once we see our world clearly. And scattered throughout the text are entries from an ecologician's dictionary, defining words so that they make visible the real complexities in the moral ecology of our everyday lives.[7]

Ecologician: 1) A student of ecology, including the moral ecology of everyday life; 2) a person who practices the magical arts of regenerative design.

Wor(l)dplay: The art of using words to challenge worldviews and change the world.

The essay is a standard literary form, a useful way of arranging words to make meaning. In college, the most common kind of essay is the expository essay, a persuasive argument supported by reason and evidence. This book has many features of the expository essay—ideas, evidence, facts, endnotes—but it's ultimately exploratory. The expository essay tries to *prove* all of its contentions, while the exploratory essay prefers to *probe* connections. Exploring links between personal life, cultural patterns, and the natural world, this essay leaves space for readers to reflect on their own experience, and invites them into a conversation about the meanings of college, and the personal and institutional possibilities of a culture of permanence.

Words structure our worlds but they can also *change* the world. In *Teaching as a Subversive Activity*, Neil Postman and Charles Weingartner suggest, "We act on the basis of what we see. If we see things one way, we act accordingly. If we see them in another, we act differently. The ability to learn turns out to be a function of the extent to which one is capable of perception change. If a student goes through four years of school and comes out 'seeing' things in the way he did when he started, he will act the same. Which means he learned nothing. If he does not act the same, it means he changed his way of talking. It's as complicated as that." With any luck, the words in this book will help to change ways of seeing, ways of talking, and ways of acting.[8]

A Final Note: "Us" and "Them"

For several reasons, I've resisted writing *The Nature of College* about "them"—a group of alien beings called college students—and tried as often as possible to write about "us," learners struggling to learn how the world works so that we can make the world better. I do this, first, because even though I'm an aging college professor, I still consider myself a college student, learning from professors I know, from the students in my classes, and from the books I read and love. Second, I believe in empathy as a way of knowing, and in this book I've tried to imagine, from the inside out, what it feels like to be a college student in America today. Third, I want to invite students to take this text *personally*, to think deeply and carefully about their assumptions and intentions, their institutions and cultural patterns. And finally, many Americans (myself included) share many of the ideas and ideals of today's college students, and many of the environmental impacts as well. Still, there are times when, because of generational or historical differences, it would simply be ridiculous for me to group myself with college students. It is my great hope, however, that even when I refer to students as "they," you'll understand that we are all in this together. Of course, in all cases, you'll need to decide for yourself if you're a part of the "we" I'm describing.

1

Waking Up to Nature

To see what is in front of one's nose needs a constant struggle.
George Orwell, "In Front of Your Nose"

The obscure we see eventually. The completely obvious, it seems, takes longer.
Edward R. Murrow, as quoted in *Mad about Physics* (2001), by Christopher Jargodzki

Only that day dawns to which we are awake.
Henry David Thoreau, *Walden*

∙∙∙∙∙∙∙∙

Although some wait until afternoon, most college students wake up early in the morning to the maddening sound of an alarm clock. As the contraption beeps or buzzes, Joe College reaches out of his slumber, hits the snooze button, rolls over, and goes back to sleep. This sequence replays repeatedly until at last he throws back the blankets and gets out of bed. He's late again so he'll have to hurry if he wants breakfast before class.

Stumbling toward the bathroom, Joe begins a morning routine so well choreographed he should get a credit in dance for its flawless execution: He steps up to the urinal, relieves himself, flushes, shuffles to the sink, pumps the soap, washes his hands, dries them on a paper towel, aims a fadeaway shot toward the wastebasket, and reaches for his toiletries. Grossed out by his morning breath, he grabs toothbrush and toothpaste, turns on the water, wets the brush, spreads paste on the bristles, and begins to brush his teeth. In the mirror, his familiar face seems to be sporting a caveman wig, so today is a shower day, or at least a hat day. Spitting in the sink, Joe reels toward the showers and the dance continues.

Joe's sister, meanwhile, follows a related routine. She checks her e-mail, scans the news feed on Facebook, clicks the syllabus for Environmental Studies 101 to make sure she has the reading right, pulls up her Google calendar to confirm today's activities, and heads for the showers. She lathers up, shampoos her hair, rinses with conditioner, shaves, and enjoys a few additional minutes of hot, steamy water before she concludes.

Toweling off, she's ready to brush and blow-dry her hair, and maybe apply a little makeup.

Both students glance out the window to gauge the weather. They can't really be sure how it might feel out there because they're moving between rooms that are heated or cooled to temperatures in the seventy-degree range. Nature is burning or blowing to create this comfort zone, but they don't notice because that's just "natural." So, naturally, they check weather.com and head for the closet with today's forecast in mind.[1]

Like other college students, and most Americans, Jo and Joe College are practicing what Tim Clydesdale calls the "disengaged pragmatism" of everyday life, focusing on the tasks at hand and the day ahead, but not the meaning behind them. So far, the only time they've noticed nature was in the weather report. Waking up at college, they're waking up *in* nature, but they haven't noticed that yet. In this chapter, therefore, we'll try to wake them up *to* the nature of their mornings as well.[2]

Alarming: The Cultural Work of Clocks

It can be alarming to think deeply about an alarm clock. Normally college students notice it just twice a day, setting it at night and hearing it, regretfully, in the morning. But the time it tells transforms the whole day, and the world.

Most Americans are obsessed with time, as our language suggests: We're saving time or spending it, marking time or killing it. We have free time on the weekends—which seems to suggest that we have slave time most of the week. Many of us even feel like we're doing time, caught in a prison of work and obligations. Whatever we call it, however, all of our times are structured by clock time, the social construction of weeks and days and hours and minutes that shape our appointment books and our lives. Like many of our technical marvels, clocks and watches are machines that do the work of social construction, converting nature into culture, and in this case, nature's time into human time.[3]

Historically, human beings adjusted their life cycles to the rhythms of day and night, and slept until they were rested or until they were disturbed—often by the call of nature. It's a natural fact that human beings need sleep, and that animals, including humans, have circadian rhythms—cycles of brain-wave activity, core body temperature swings, hormone production, and cell regeneration schedules—that attune the body to the rotations of the planet. In the modern world, however, the body's circadian rhythms proved too imprecise for the demands of capitalism: People who followed natural rhythms might be late for the factory work of the industrial revolution. So the body had to be broken to the discipline of mechanical time.[4]

As early as the 1830s, Alexis de Tocqueville observed that Americans were obsessed with time, always busy with the consuming passions of individualism: "The inhabitant of the United States," he observed, "attaches himself to the goods of this world as if he were assured of not dying, and he rushes so precipitately to grasp those that pass within his reach that one would say he fears at each instant he will cease to live before he has enjoyed them. He grasps them all but without clutching them, and he soon allows them to escape from his hands so as to run after new enjoyments." This culture, in which "rush hour" might be any hour of the day, has survived and thrived in America, leading to a society plagued by what sociologists call "time poverty." In a culture of time poverty, we don't have enough time for what really matters to us, because we're too busy doing other things. Even at college, which is designed to be an interval of slow time in life, many students don't make time for meaningful work or for reflection about their hopes and dreams because there's "too much to do." Our "lack" of time has environmental impacts because it drives us to convenience, where we often accept resource-intensive solutions to our time-management problems. We believe in fast food, for example, because we lead fast lives, circumscribed by the seconds of the clock.[5]

An alarm clock tells us to get up and get to work "on time," but in focusing our attention on today's time it marginalizes other important times of our lives, like yesterday or tomorrow. Yesterday, the clock presumes, is just history, and tomorrow might as well be science fiction. Clock time is also just human time. It helps us get places on time, but it keeps us from considering natural time and—depending on our beliefs—supernatural time. By focusing our attention on the personal present, it keeps us from other temporal perspectives, perhaps until it's literally too late.

Past Time

Despite their enrollment at an educational institution designed to pass on cultural traditions from the past to the future, Joe and Jo College are not generally good at thinking in time. Most of us, in fact, don't remember—if we ever learned—the environmental history that would help us make sense of the present, so we don't know why we act the way we do. We don't understand why environmental problems have developed. We don't know about environmental successes or histories of hope. Playing by the rules of American presentism, we don't take time to think about the past—unless, of course, we're stuck in a history course.[6]

Whether we acknowledge it or not, however, we live in history, and dead men rule our lives. We inhabit the institutions dead men created and the buildings they erected. We learn from books they wrote and ideas they devised. Daily, we use the technologies they invented—amusing ourselves among the ghosts of Thomas Edison, Henry Ford, and Philo Farnsworth. Most importantly, we live in the world that they developed, despoiled, or protected. When Columbus "discovered" America, he came in wind-powered sailing ships, and encountered people who didn't use fossil fuels. But *we* use lots of fossil fuels, because dead men later discovered coal and oil and exploited them to make our lives easier and more efficient. On the other hand, dead men and women also helped to create a sublime system of American national parks, and legislative protections for wilderness and the environment. The past is always alive in our present, but, because the clock calls us to our next appointment, we rush right past it.[7]

Future Time

American presentism also keeps us from a careful consideration of the future. College is, of course, a preparation for what comes next, and—despite the immediate demands of our clocks and watches—college students worry about the future a lot. But that future is usually individual and instrumental: We're more concerned about preparation for graduate school or a career than about the quality of our communities or the fate of the Earth. Like other Americans, college students aren't very skilled at imagining the long future, or making collective plans for the world they want to live in as adults, partners, parents, and citizens. Most Americans tend not to be very mindful of future generations, and when we are, we often ask, as devout utilitarians do, "What has the future ever done for us?" This shortsightedness makes it difficult, if not impossible, to confront systemic issues like urban planning, poverty, environmental degradation, or global weirding. That's why, as Robert Paehlke says, "Time horizon may be the most important distinction between environmentalists and others."[8]

As a consequence, we don't think much about the future as something we create today, both in our activity and our inactivity. We don't notice that we are making history with each of our everyday actions. As a result, we collectively create a future that few of us really want to live in. Like it or not, what we do either reinforces ideas and institutions today, or transforms them for tomorrow. When we approach our studies as tools for civic engagement, we learn how to change the world. When we explore possibilities for environmental responsibility in our own lives, we provide possibilities for future citizens, and so we create a future with our examples as a part of its usable past. Alternately, when we settle for a present so stressful or unpleasant that it drives us to waste time with escapist TV, we create a future with more commercials and commercialism and couch potatoes, reinforcing images of people and society that often contradict our deepest values.

Nature's Time

Even if our alarm clocks located us in a stream of historical continuity, they still wouldn't connect us to biological or ecological time. Clocks ignore nature's time—the slow time of geology and evolution, the long cycles of prairies and forests and oceans. When we plan our lives only by clock time, we forget nature's rhythms and begin to assume that our time is the only time. Even though most natural rhythms are cyclical, Americans believe in linear progress with practically inevitable human improvement. In nature's time, it's progress when the sun comes up each morning, and progress again when it goes down; progress when spring sprouts every year, and once again when bright colors announce fall. In nature's time, efficiency isn't measured by speed, but by sustainability and regeneration—the ability to extend the extravagant generosity of life to another generation. When the human time line meets nature's time circle, however, it increasingly results in extinctions, which are literally killing time for other species.

In nature's time, minutes and seconds don't mean much. We think we're on time when we arrive at the appointed hour, but nature might think otherwise. It takes nature about five hundred years to make one inch of topsoil, so when we live in a way that depletes soil faster than that (and we do), we are not "on time," no matter how fast or productive we might be. When we live in a way that threatens the ecosystem services that our descendants will need, we're more out of time than on time.

Sacred Time

Whether or not gods exist, people and cultures feel a supernatural relationship to the natural world. It may be Allah or Yahweh, the Corn Mother or the Rainbow Serpent, but many people believe that something super-natural creates the world, and that our time on Earth is a divine gift in a purposeful cosmos. For example, the Bible suggests that the universe is the work of a creator, and that time is God's gift, so that an individual's time is not just hers, but God's as well. If that's true, perhaps Thoreau was right when he claimed that you can't kill time without injuring eternity.[9]

Many religious traditions structure time to point to such supernatural connections. In earlier Christian cultures, people told (and literally tolled) God's time with Angelus bells, which provided a religious frame for the day by calling people to prayer morning, noon, and night. In contemporary Islamic cultures, people orient themselves toward Mecca and pray at appointed times. All over the world, people are called to recognize the holy at traditional times in everyday life. But when bells ring at American colleges today, few students turn to prayer or contem-plation. Sacred time used to be a moment for people to consider how to "redeem the time"—how to make ordinary time extraordinary, lumi-nous with possibilities for good. Calls to prayer and holidays made time for people to listen to the sacred, and to apply the wisdom of holiness to their everyday lives. Although many religious Americans—and some college students—still take time for prayer and church services, we often see these rituals as perfunctory obligations, rather than as an opportu-nity to imagine a better world. For most college students, Sunday is just the second day of the weekend. On campus, it's the day to recover from Saturday's bacchanalian rituals and—in the evening—to start reading for next week's classes. But it could be different.[10]

We could break out of our commonsense construction of time to discover new connections between past and future, nature and culture. Alarmed by the presentism and parochialism of America's culture of time, we could begin timely conversations that would help us reshape our per-sonal and cultural perspectives on how to live sustainably for all time. Such a movement to consider time—the past, the present, the future, the natural, and the sacred—in its entirety, could literally *save* all time.

Shit Happens: The Call of Nature

In the morning, after the alarm sounds, nature calls. The bladder and bowels fill and send nerve signals to the brain, saying, "Do something!" It's one of the few times in a day that Joe and Jo College are conscious of nature's influence on their lives. So college students creak out of bed, shuffle into the bathroom, and relieve themselves. Flushing the toilet, we put nature behind us, and we don't think much of it. But the toilet is

Nature's Free Lunch: Ecosystem Services

Provisioning	Making stuff so people can make do.
Sunshine	Nature's furnace and lighting system—good for tanning, but also for photosynthesis: the conversion of sunbeams to food.
Plants	Nature's alchemists, converting sunshine to food (and spices and pharmaceuticals) by a process of photosynthesis, which also releases oxygen—a substance that is handy for our breathing. They also generate other useful materials (cotton, wood, etc.) and energy.
Animals	Nature's meatpacking plants, converting plants—some of which humans can't digest—into protein.
Rain, snow, etc.	Nature's cleanser, soft drink, and liquid recreation—also habitat for aquatic plants and animals, and a necessity for land-based flora and fauna, too.
Oceans	Nature's primary habitat—from phytoplankton to fish to great blue whales. Source of most of the seafood we eat.
Rivers	Nature's highways and a flowing source of hydropower.
Prairies, forests, wetlands	Manufacturer of biomass and biodiversity, with topsoil as a biologically beneficial by-product.
Topsoil	Keeps plants from falling over and nourishes them.
Forests	Provide food, lumber, and oxygen, limiting erosion and runoff.
Metals	For making stuff, including cars and computers and beer cans.
Air	Makes breathing easier—also flying.
Everything	Cycling (and recycling) of nutrients in system.
Regulating	Keeping biotic systems in control.
Atmosphere	Nature's screen (from ultraviolet rays).
Plants	Nature's carbon catchers, sequestering carbon dioxide and partially regulating the climate.
Decomposition	Nature's waste management, reducing the amount of garbage and shit we live in by breaking down organic wastes.
Trees and other plants	Nature's air quality control, removing pollutants like nitrogen dioxide, sulfur dioxide, ozone, carbon monoxide, and particulate matter from the air.
Trees	One of nature's sunscreens, shading people and buildings, and saving energy.
Clouds	Another natural sunscreen, and an evaporative part of the water cycle.

Continued on next page

Continued from previous page

Predators	Nature's pesticide and its population control.
Wetlands	Nature's water filter, purifying water going to groundwater.
Wind	Nature's coolant, conveyor belt for weather systems, and seed-dispersal system.
Polar regions	Nature's air conditioner.
Wetlands, plant cover	Nature's flood control, protecting coastal areas from storm surges.
Supporting	*Assisting people in their purposes.*
Atmosphere	Nature's greenhouse (maintaining temperatures to support life).
Pollination	Assisting the sex lives of plants (including crops) so that they come to fruition.
Acreage	Provides space for solid waste and sinks for gaseous waste.
Death	Nature's way of clearing space for new life.
Rain	Nature's vertical irrigation, nourishing crop growth and preventing drought.
Cultural	*Making stuff to make meanings about.*
Everything	Catalyst for curiosity, source of science.
Most everything	Stimulant for aesthetic appreciation and expression.
Landscapes	Nature's art museum and people's playgrounds.
Moon	Nature's romancer and tide pull.
Stars	Intimations of infinity, invitation to astrologers.
Animals	Totems for tribes, individuals, and sports teams.
Ecological design	A baseline for biomimicry and human cultures.
Ecosystems	Ecotourism.
Birds	Birding.
Flowers	Beauty in the wild and in the home.
Diamonds and beaches and chocolate	For romantic love.
Gold and silver	For the monetary imagination.
Preserving	*Keeping all the moving parts of the system, maintaining resilience.*
Biodiversity	Preserving more choices for natural selection.
Bioregulation	Partial stabilization of climate.

a place where the body's plumbing meets the plumbing of culture and nature, so it's a rich ecological niche.

College students talk shit all the time, but not ecologically. A superficial conversation is shooting the shit. Something obvious is "no shit!" while "bullshit!" is a standard response to falsehood. If you care, you might give a shit. If not, you might get shit-faced at a party. And if the party gets too wild, the shit hits the fan. "Shit" is on the tip of our tongues, but we need to bring it to the front of our minds, because shit isn't just a linguistic construct; it's a daily reality. Americans make about five billion gallons of waste a day without even thinking about it, but we don't *know* shit.[11]

When students need to take a shit on campus, they go to a specialized space called a bathroom. In the average college residence hall, the bathrooms seem a long way from environmental studies, but waste management *is* an environmental study. If you're a human being of average size and weight, for example, your body produces about a pound of waste, solid and liquid, every day. It's one of the few forms of production still remaining in America, one type of manufacturing that can't be shipped offshore.

The process seems simple, but it's fairly complex. When Joe College orders a cheeseburger and french fries, he chews his meal and swallows, sliding the food down his alimentary canal. There, a variety of digestive enzymes convert complex carbohydrates into simple sugars, transform fats into glycerol and fatty acids, and transmute proteins into amino acids and peptides. In Joe's small intestine, these digested nutrients are absorbed by blood and lymph vessels to be carried into the circulatory system to feed various organs. What's leftover is excremental, the waste that waits until, as the bumper sticker says, "shit happens." When it happens, we head to the toilet and drop our load into a small pool of water where it's submerged along with its pungent smell. After wiping with soft sheets of treated trees, we flush the toilet. To most of us, it's not worth a second thought.

This hasn't always been the case. Two-hundred years ago, college students disposed of their bodily wastes on campus. In the winter, people used bedpans, and then carried their waste to the outhouse. Removed from the main buildings, the outhouse was close enough for people to comprehend the problem (and the possibilities) of waste. In cities, entrepreneurs regularly cleaned "night soil" from outhouses and sold it as a fertilizer for outlying farms, providing a useful second life for what we call "waste."[12] After the arrival of indoor plumbing, however, when shit happened, it went down the drain instead of back to nature.

Most college students, like most Americans, live by what Philip Slater calls "the toilet bowl principle of American life"—out of sight is out of mind. But when the toilet flushes, shit doesn't just evaporate. It travels through sanitary sewers to a solid-waste treatment plant. At most such plants, sewage receives several different treatments. After screening and grit removal, the mixture of excrement, urine, water, paper, and other items enters a settling tank. There, solids drop to the bottom so that grease and plastics can be skimmed off the top. The water heads for secondary treatment, where microorganisms feed on bacteria, purifying the liquid. Finally—using sand filters, natural or artificial wetlands, ultraviolet light, or ozone—the water is "polished," to bring it up to legal standards, and discharged back into rivers. When we flush on campus, we're intimately (and institutionally) involved in the water cycle.[13]

Biologically, excretion can remind us of the beauties of the natural world, the ways in which our bodies are designed to manage the ins and outs of animal life. Ecologically, our bathroom break reminds us that all natural systems, including the human body, are involved in processes of consumption and return. Taking in nutrients, we expel wastes, which function in the grand scheme of nature as nutrients for other species. Culturally, however, our excretions are a mess: We treat shit like shit. As Christopher Uhl says, "We take two perfectly good resources—human manure and fresh water—and splat them together in the toilet bowl, making them both useless." But if we ever get our shit together, perhaps we'd see that human wastes aren't wasted when we use them—properly treated—as fertilizer or fuel, thus returning them to the productive and regenerative cycles of nature.[14]

The Artificial Waterfall

At some point in the day, most college students take part in a purification ritual called a shower. They walk down the hall to the bathroom carrying a plastic caddy holding soap, shampoo, conditioner, and other lotions and potions. Towel on shoulder, washcloth or loofah in hand, students look for an open shower, set their supplies on a bench, draw a plastic curtain, undress, hang up their clothes, step under the shower-head, and then open the valve to a torrent of cultural assumptions and expectations. Though turning the tap seems mechanical, it's also organic and very complex. In Northfield, Minnesota, for example, the water flowing in the shower is drawn from the Jordan Aquifer. It's pumped through a purification plant for chlorination and fluoridation, and then to water towers that provide the pressure for the whole municipal system. In a hydraulic civilization, water goes not just where it falls or flows, but where we want it.[15]

The shower gets us clean, but it also performs cultural work. Dirt is evil in our culture, and so we ritually cleanse ourselves in a sort of daily baptism, initiating us into a sect of sanitation. Early in the morning, as we're trying to wake up, a shower is cleansing and stimulating. Later in the day, after a run or a game of basketball, it's cleansing but also relaxing. In either case, a shower is a way of washing the body, but it's often also a luxury, too. The water streaming over the skin, massaging the muscles, is a sheer delight. The sound of constant flow is soothing, like a cascading creek. And the steamy heat penetrates our pores, comforting us with wondrous warmth. We bathe not just physically, but also psychologically. When we're dirty, we tell ourselves we need a shower. When we're tired or stressed, we tell ourselves we *deserve* a shower. A long shower, too, is a counterpoint to the culture of speed and efficiency so recently reinforced by our alarm clock. In a small way, a slow shower is a protest movement against a world of enforced time poverty: As we linger in the liquid tranquilizer, we're *not* quick and we're *not* efficient. This ultimately is a problem. Resisting the time pressures of our society might be a good instinct, but using fifty gallons of fresh water in the process is not so good.[16]

The Social Construction of Showers

We all understand how a shower works, and how it can work to wake us up, but we need to wake up to how it functions in the moral ecology of everyday life. Considered analytically, a shower, just like the toilet, is a way of transforming drinkable water into wastewater. The drain water finds its way (sooner or later) to an ocean, where it evaporates and circulates in clouds until it precipitates into places where we can pump it once again. In the shower, we're in the water cycle, which is affected by every turn of the tap.

We think of a shower as a private act, but when we get in the stall, we enter with a lifetime of education and expectations. Every day, ads for soaps, shampoos, conditioners, gels, and moisturizers teach us what clean really means. They teach us about feelings—about comfort and pleasure and joy and indulgence—and sometimes, for women especially, about sexiness. They teach us to get clean, but they also teach us to get that fresh, clean *feeling* that we have unconsciously learned to associate with the commodities in our shower caddy. Ads don't tell us that soap works first by bonding dirt to hydrophobic fatty acids, encapsulating the dirt in droplets of water that can be rinsed away, or that shampoos generally use detergents like ammonium lauryl sulfate to remove our hair's natural oil and phthalates to dissolve scents and thicken lotions. They certainly don't trouble us with information about the chemistry of conditioners, which not only coat the clean hair with *different* oils, but also with silicone, humectants, proteins, and quaternary ammonium compounds—primarily to make hair slick and easy to comb. We don't learn where the ingredients came from, or who was involved in manufacturing them, but that's okay, because our hair looks great, and that's what matters in the morning.[17]

Indeed, we don't learn these things because shampoo commercials aren't about shampoo: They're about cultural conceptions of beauty—about hair and the meanings of hair. Shampoo companies hire models like Cindy Crawford, Eva Longoria Parker, and Jessica Simpson—who possess what is essentially professional hair—to teach us that a woman's hair, and not the brain beneath it, is what makes her sexy and attractive. Generally these shampoo models have long, straight hair that they wave around in slow motion. Watching the ads, we might believe that the purpose of shampoo is to train hair to dance.

A guy's hair usually doesn't dance in ads. Joe College's shampoo can be stylish and scented, but for guys in TV ads, shampoo serves three putative purposes: washing hair after an athletic event, thus confirming one's manliness; getting rid of unsightly dandruff, thus confirming one's attractiveness; and convincing women to stroke the clean hair lovingly, thus confirming the gullibility of the guy who believes in such a scenario.

Shampoo ads teach us, or at least remind us, that women are meant to smell like flowers and fruit. For men, as usual, there is a narrower range of choices, and they tend not to be floral or fruity. If men smell, the ads tell us, they need to smell different from women—musky perhaps—thus confirming their independent gender identity. At the end of a shower, therefore, we can rinse off the shampoo, but it's harder to escape the images and assumptions locked in the lather of the ads. Advertisements shape our common sense of what's normal, and we respond, subtly shaping the moral ecology of everyday life.

The Natural Resources of Showers

In the shower, we get in hot water when we forget where the hot water comes from, because both water and heat come to us from nature. A toilet is basically a small pond in the bathroom, while the shower is a waterfall positioned for our convenience. While they definitely depend on plumbing and human ingenuity, they rely more basically on precipitation and the recharge of groundwater and aquifers—natural phenomena. And because water in nature is seldom warm enough for a satisfying shower, Joe and Jo College use nature to heat nature, warming water by burning fossil fuels or causing chain reactions in uranium. While we luxuriate in the shower, we also suck up the world's fresh water and generate more greenhouse gases.[18]

If a normal shower delivers three gallons of water a minute, then a ten-minute shower requires thirty gallons of water. With just one shower a day for a nine-month school year, most students will use about 8,100 gallons of water; if the average university has ten thousand students, that's more than eighty million gallons. Simple updates like low-flow showerheads could allow the university to save four million gallons of water, plus the fuels needed to warm that much water. Students would still be clean, with hair that would still glisten, but the school could easily be conserving resources.[19]

The American shower has a deeper effect, though, by impressing the planet's other people, who often emulate U.S. standards of cleanliness. "The British bath," notes Elizabeth Shove, "is in danger of being abandoned in favour of showering on a daily or twice daily basis." By itself, this English adjustment might be no big deal, but it's a small part of an energy-intensive shift in international comfort standards, and that is huge. This also suggests that standards of cleanliness are never universal or permanent. American students now expect free and unlimited water for showers in their residence halls. At one time, however, a trustee at a college in the prairies of the Midwest thought that the purchase of a single tin bathtub was an unnecessary luxury for students. The extravagance only seemed justified when he discovered that the college could charge students a nickel a bath. If today's colleges charged students for water by the gallon, it might help teach the costs incurred by lingering luxuriously in the shower, and it might be a first step toward full-cost accounting (and accountability) for all the resources in students' lives.[20]

We shower ourselves with water, in an artificial waterfall created by culture. Though our morning shower never seems like "getting back to nature," it's one place where we could wake up to nature, a place where we could practice mindfulness about our "ordinary consumption." Usually when we think about consumption, we think about buying stuff or going out to restaurants, movies, or concerts. "Ordinary consumption," on the other hand, is so routine and repetitive—like water and heat, electricity and embodied energy—that we don't normally consider it a part of our consumer behavior. In the shower, then, we can fully enjoy the comforts and convenience of the steamy stream, but we can also begin to immerse ourselves in the paradigm shift of conservation that will characterize the coming culture of permanence. .

Mirror Image: The Nature of Looking Good

After performing their cleansing rituals, Joe and Jo College usually take part in rituals of self-inspection and self-improvement in front of a mirror. The word "mirror" itself comes from the Latin root *mirari*—to admire—making a mirror, at its root, a meeting place for a mutual admiration society of one.

Yet while its smooth surface simply reflects the images of objects, a mirror also performs cultural work, reflecting the patterns of American society. It is a visual echo, and, like television, a way of seeing—and not seeing.

As a matter of physics, most mirrors reflect exactly the patterns of light and shade that hit them. But as a matter of culture, there can be significant distortions, because mirrors reflect not just the way we are but also the ways we hope (or fear) to be. For example, when we look at a mirror in the morning, we are trained by years of advice and advertising to see not just our own reflection, but also its relationship to ideal images in magazines or on TV. We are trained to focus on particulars: We don't usually see the whole picture because we're concentrating on so-called problem areas that popular culture has pinpointed for us. One student's mirror highlights his pimples and the size of his nose, while another's magnifies her worry about her makeup and hair. Mirrors permit us to objectify ourselves, to look at ourselves as others see us, rather than as we truly are. American culture teaches us to be attractive, and to dress for success, and the mirror provides the final exam to see if we have succeeded.

But mirrors can't do everything. Although they reveal the social self, they divert our attention from the natural self. Contemplating teeth, zits, facial hair, and the dark circles under our eyes, we forget to appreciate the intricacy of the organism that stands before us. We forget, for example, the marvel of our eyes, which allow us to use a mirror effectively. An immense evolutionary advantage, they provided our ancestors with the hand-eye coordination that has made *Homo sapiens* such a successful species. Containing about half the sensory receptors in the body, our eyes use about 30 percent of the brain's cortex to see that bleary face in the mirror. But we don't usually perceive the amazing ecological adaptation staring back at us. Eyeing the mirror to check out the surfaces of the self, we miss the nature of the body and the nature of its connections to the rest of nature. Although he wasn't talking about mirrors, Thoreau once wrote that he wanted to be "nature looking into nature." That's what happens in mirrors of America. But because we bring our cultural preoccupations to the mirror, we often turn out to be nature looking *away* from nature.[21]

The Student Body

The student body in the bathroom mirror is both natural and cultural. The human body is, of course, a highly evolved product of natural selection with bifocal vision, bipedal locomotion, and nimble hands with opposable thumbs. It comes with a big brain that supports complex thinking, toolmaking, communication, culture, and even college class work—not to mention autonomic functions like breathing and blood flow. It's a mammal's body in the mirror, with warm blood and temperature control, an internal combustion engine we call the digestive system, and a tangle of bloodlines and nerves that bring it all together. Right now, this animal body is brushing the teeth that make it omnivorous, able to eat both animal and plant life. But this is only the beginning. The natural body is in constant intercourse with nature.

We often speak about "people and nature" as though the body is bounded by its skin, but this is a dangerous illusion. The body in the looking glass is constantly sharing elements with its environment, amassing atoms from everywhere. As ecologist Christopher Uhl suggests in *Developing Ecological Consciousness,* "If you were to put an ink dot on a map of the Earth to designate the origins of the trillions of atoms that make up your body, the map would be covered in ink. Our atoms have journeyed to us literally from everywhere on the planet. We are a part of their cycles." We are dependent on the Earth's interdependence, and we forget it at our peril.[22]

The natural body depends on the natural world, not just abstractly, but viscerally, and not just occasionally, but constantly. For example, the body we see in the morning mirror is breathing, inhaling the oxygen that fuels the combustion of carbohydrates in the body. People can live about three weeks without food, and about three days without water, but only three minutes without air. We don't think much about that, however, because air is invisible, because it's not yet a commodity, and because it's automatic. However, if we had to buy the air we breathe, we would pay a lot more attention. If all of us needed to inhale "Perri-air" (as Mel Brooks does in *Spaceballs*) or visit an oxygen bar for our daily requirements, we'd be more mindful. If the three thousand gallons of air we take in each day were as expensive as gasoline, we'd notice. But air is still free—an ecosystem service provided by the planet—so we ignore it entirely (and allow industries to pollute it). Likewise, if we had to *choose* to breathe, we'd keep it in our consciousness, but the autonomic nervous system takes care of air for us. As Christopher Uhl suggests, "Breathing happens on its own; you are not breathing so much as you are being breathed."

Even more amazing, the body we see in the mirror doesn't just exist *in* a natural habitat, it *is* a habitat for nature, filled with microorganisms that are essential to its functioning. Recent studies show that 90 percent of the cells in our bodies aren't ours: They're bacteria. In the microbiome that is us, some bacteria are helping to convert plant sugars to usable energy for us, some are making vitamins essential to our health, some are neutralizing chemicals that could cause cancer and other diseases, and some are making food for other bacteria, including the cells that line the colon. These life-forms help shape the form of human life. Every minute of every day, we have a relationship with nature more intimate than our relationship with our families, friends, and partners. By nature, we are always in relationship with nature.[23]

The relationship, however, is not always harmonious, so we protect ourselves against microbes that have proven deadly in the past. In the United States, vaccinations are practically mandatory, so almost all college students are armed against the natural flourishing of organisms that thrive by causing disease. But we rarely stop there: On any given day a lot of the bodies seen in college mirrors are teeming with antibiotics—a word that literally means "against life"—as we try to kill the living organisms that unsettle our digestive and respiratory systems. Some of us also use antibacterial soaps and lotions to protect our skin from similar attacks. Unfortunately this defense can be counterproductive because it kills the good bacteria, leaving a body susceptible to hardier bacteria that develop resistances to our common pharmaceuticals.[24]

The natural body also absorbs the chemical elements of our culture. If we could look *into* the body, we'd see stuff we don't imagine when we look in the mirror. In "The Pollution Within," *National Geographic* writer

David Duncan recounts the chemicals that tests found in his body in 2006—polybrominated diphenyl ethers (used in flame retardants and implicated in thyroid disruptions and neurological problems in mice); DDT (used as a pesticide until it was banned in 1973); the insecticides chlordane and heptachlor; PCBs (banned in 1976); Bisphenol A (used in hard plastics like Nalgene bottles and safety goggles); phthalates (used in shampoos, car dashboards, and plastic food wrap); perfluorinated carboxylic acids (PFCAs); dioxins (used in making paper); and mercury (from coal-fueled power plants). Like most Americans, including Jo and Joe College, Duncan is poisoned by the stuff our culture uses to free us from our natural limitations: gasoline, plastics, and fossil fuels. Like it or not, the environmental impact of American culture ends up in our bodies and blood. What goes around comes around, and the outside environment comes in.[25]

We miss a lot in the mirror, but some of what we do see is also deeply related to basic biology. The culture of cosmetics, for example, may be related to our natural need for healthy mates. Many sociobiologists contend that when we're thinking about appearances we're often thinking about the appearance of health—especially the appearance of people who look healthy enough to reproduce productively. Teeth are a sign of health, so we brace them and brush them to make them more attractive. Lustrous hair is another indicator of natural health, so we shampoo, condition, and color it. Some go even further. Nature doesn't call Jo College to cosmetics, for example, but cosmetics can imitate the signs of nature. Although college girls seldom think of cosmetics in terms of evolutionary biology, they often involve biomimicry: a youthful look, with smooth skin and full lips, makes the face appear healthier to prospective suitors. In the twentieth century, a tan also became an indication of healthy outdoor activity, so many of us get tanned, if only from a bottle or a booth. We want to look well—or, as Carl Elliott says, "better than well"—and that's natural. But how we get that look is decidedly not.[26]

Right now, when Joe and Jo College look in the mirror, they're hoping to see someone beautiful or handsome looking back, because they're trying to meet social expectations. They could look for a sense of beauty that's more than skin deep, a sense of beauty that meets ecological expectations by connecting them to the biotic community. When Aldo Leopold articulated his land ethic, beauty was one of his criteria for when "a thing is right." But he clearly didn't mean scenic beauty, since he derides the shallowness of people who only like the landscapes of nature. For Leopold, beauty wasn't just what you could see, but how you might relate—beauty was functional, harmonious, whole. What if we tried to arrange our lives so that when we looked in the mirror, we would see the loveliness (and lovingness) of people who harmonized with nature? Wouldn't that be beautiful?

Waking Up to Responsibility

At college, when we wake up, we do what comes naturally, even though most of it is what comes culturally. American culture works hard to distance us from our environmental impacts and our ecological consciousness so that even though we wake up every day *in* nature, we don't generally wake up *to* nature. Our morning routine offers all sorts of cultural cues about time, busy-ness, and convenience, but very few clues about the natural world in which our harried activity occurs. We receive constant commercial messages about cleanliness and looking good, but we don't read or receive many of nature's messages—the ones sent as news about gas prices and oil wars, global weirding and habitat loss, disease and extinctions, or the simple and beautiful seasonal cycles of our campus habitat. As a result, we don't see or feel ourselves as environmental actors, participating wisely or wantonly in the rhythms and cycles of a living Earth.

When we wake up, some of us are conscious, but few of us are conscientious. Despite that fact, we all participate fully in the moral ecology of everyday life, making at least five ethical choices before breakfast. But we don't *feel* like ethical actors because we're just doing what comes culturally. We've made these choices not by our active options but by our passive participation in *systems* of choice. As this suggests, one of the most powerful things we do in life is to define normality for each other. If it's normal to flip on the lights in the bathroom, we normally think it's okay. But it might be more complicated than that. For example, when Joe and Jo College think they are just lighting a room, they're also generating greenhouse gases. If they thought about it, they might think that this is "no big deal"—and that would be true, if they only lived for a day. But Americans live a long time, so all of our "no big deals" add up to major environmental impacts. As Eric Sorensen points out in his *Seven Wonders for a Cool Planet*, "If the average North American life expectancy holds at seventy-eight years, each person can expect to produce 1,630 tons of carbon dioxide over his or her lifetime." The everyday actions of students are choices camouflaged as routines, but each of these habits is, in fact, a moral choice.[27]

Cartoon by Tom Toles. Reproduced by permission of Andrews McMeel Publishing.

Because what we do matters, we might want to wake up to more than the mere routines of the day. Mindful of the social construction of college culture and the busy-ness of campus life, we might try to set aside time for some big questions—ones having to do with the goodness of the good life or the health of the ecosystem services that we depend on. Mindful of the life-giving properties of water, we might try to conserve it for future generations. Mindful of our animal nature, we might try to be creatures who enhance habitats, instead of despoiling them. Mindful of the complexities of the human body and the other bodies that support it, we might nurture a sense of wonder for the natural world that includes us so generously.

Mindfulness: The quality of attention and care that keeps Earth in mind, so that we can mind our own social and environmental behavior. Antonym: mindlessness.

We might also begin to imagine and invent tools that literally remind us of our responsibilities for the life of the planet. Most current technologies are designed to be easy to use, and "easy" is sadly often just a synonym for "careless." The thermostat maintains the temperature in our room; the TV stands ready for instantaneous power-up; the car starts with the turn of a key. Nothing reminds us that ambient temperatures, instantaneous electronics, and automotive travel are environmental issues. Nothing tells us about the implicit choices embedded in our machines. But we can remind ourselves of our environmental impacts—and change them—by designing machines for ethical impact as well as aesthetic appeal. In *Sustainability by Design*, for example, John Ehrenfeld suggests that a dual-flush toilet disrupts the normal flow of life just enough to make us mindful of our choices. Instead of just flushing, we have to make a choice about how much water to use—and if we know anything at all, we know the choice is both environmental and ethical. Eventually, this water-saving option might become second nature to us, and we might finally establish a mindless habit that actually conserves habitats.[28]

We might also consider reinventing the habits that threaten the planet's natural (and cultural) habitats, so that our habits teach the people around us about the routines of a regenerative life. Unlike most humans in most of history, Joe and Jo College live in a segregated society, having separated themselves from the reflective experience of the natural world. Americans value "getting back to nature" on vacation, but that common phrase illustrates just how far we've removed ourselves from nature in our everyday lives. Instead of just living on the Earth, therefore, we might begin to live in the Earth's cycles and rhythms, not just as consumers of ecosystem services, but as sources of ingenuity, creating regenerative designs—social, ecological, technological, and personal designs—that make it easier to live well with nature.[29]

Fortunately, Joe and Jo College live in an environment that allows reconsideration and reconstruction of the way we live in the world: the college campus. Unlike most Americans in the workaday world, college students could easily wake up to systems thinking—to see the systems that operate beneath the surfaces of everyday life *and* to change them. In the college environment of hope and opportunity, why not practice the mapping and modeling of natural systems, including the altered stocks and flows that result from our ordinary consumption? Why not pay attention to the inputs and outputs of our natural and cultural systems, and to feedback loops in nature and culture? Why not consider the cultural resources that we have to change the systems we live in, aligning our human systems with the ecosystems of nature? Why not make our lives mean something?[30]

Academic success won't mean much in a world of ecological failures, and a college degree won't be so advantageous on a planet warmed by five degrees. The grade we get in biology won't matter that much if we compromise the planet's biological systems. Cleanliness may still be next to godliness, but it won't seem so special if it sucks up the world's fresh-water supplies. Putting on a cosmetic face in the morning may make us more attractive, but it won't matter much if the guy of our dreams is full of flame retardants or other cancer-causing chemicals. Indeed, if we're not careful *and* committed to environmental activism, we might find ourselves up shit creek without a paddle.

Our biggest environmental impacts don't usually happen before breakfast, but if we woke up to our place in the world, we would see the amazing intricacy of nature and our part in it, and the amazing damage we can do without thinking. We would begin to understand the nature of college culture, including the power of habit, the power of example, and the power of institutions. And we would begin to use this new knowledge of our culture to change the nature of our relationship with the natural world.

2

The Nature of Stuff

You can never get enough of what you don't need to make you happy.
    Eric Hoffer

Our enormously productive economy . . . demands that we make consumption our way of life, that we convert the buying and use of goods into rituals, that we seek our spiritual satisfaction, our ego satisfaction, in consumption. . . . We need things consumed, burned up, worn out, replaced, and discarded at an ever-increasing rate.
    Victor Lebow, "Price Competition in 1955"

Our secret plan is this: We're going to go on consuming the world until there's no more to consume.
    Daniel Quinn, "On Investments"

Since the earth is finite, and we will have to stop expanding sometime, should we do it before or after nature's diversity is gone?
    Donella Meadows, as quoted in *Simple Prosperity* (2008) by David Wann

■ ■ ■ ■ ■ ■ ■

Showered, shaved, and ready to take on the day, Joe and Jo College assemble what they need for class, in rooms that are overflowing with stuff: beds and desks, dressers and lamps, futons and lounge chairs, couches and carpets. The closets are crammed and the dressers are packed. Shoes are made for walking, but right now they're just hiding under the bed. Electrical devices abound—TVs, stereos, computers, game consoles, refrigerators, clocks, phones, and iPods hum around the room—while books line up on shelves and stack in piles on the floor. Easy Mac and ramen noodles are stocked on other shelves, complemented by drinks in the fridge.[1]

—move in day—

In college and elsewhere, we're stuffed. Caught in the haze of our morning routine, however, we don't think too much about any of it—it all seems natural and necessary.[2] If we asked a few questions, though, we might notice some interesting things about how we think about the things we own, and "the ways in which consumers [like us] are constructed along with the goods and services [we] are expected to require." We might note that the first lessons of college take place in dorm rooms, not classrooms, and that dorm rooms teach mainly about American material culture and materialism. We could even go deeper, tracing the environmental pathways of our possessions and exploring different possibilities for conserving the nature that's inevitably in our stuff.[3]

The Social Construction of Necessity

Most student rooms and apartments conform to the expectations of what we might call "the standard package." Though this "package" corresponds more or less to college recommendations about what to bring, it conforms even more to the expectations of college culture, a culture increasingly shaped by the marketing and ministrations of commercial culture.

In the American system of supply and demand, advertisers are the people responsible for supplying the demand, and they've recently discovered that "Back to College" is a lucrative market in several ways.[4] Marketers realize that college students socialize each other in the art of consumption, so it's important for them to teach students how to teach each other. Starting around the year 2000, therefore, retailers created "Back to College" as a fully merchandised market niche, offering American consumers another occasion for giving and getting. Retailers as diverse as Target, Wal-Mart, IKEA, The Container Store, Linens 'N Things, and Bed Bath & Beyond began to educate students with catalogs, websites, e-mails, "College Nights," and gift registries, as well as flyers advertising freebies and student discounts. This "consumer education" has been an overwhelming success: By 2006, the National Retail Federation estimated that back-to-college spending would reach thirty-six billion dollars, making it the most lucrative shopping season in America after the winter holidays.[5]

In 2007, Amazon.com offered a website for students heading to campus, calling college "the final frontier (of your education, anyhow)." They offered interactive photos of "three student habitats: the Sweet Suite, the Dude's Den, or the Study Space." The pink-and-flowery Sweet Suite was for coeds. The Dude's Den was a guy's room. And the Study Space was gender neutral. As an online shopper dragged her mouse over the pictures, pop-ups explained the accessories and necessities of college life. Laptop computers appeared in all three rooms. "You can't do college without a computer," a pop-up asserted. "How can you stretch a 2-page paper to three pages if you can't make incremental changes to the margins and font size?" Refrigerators also seemed to be part of the standard package: "Primitive peoples preserved food for later consumption by drying, curing, and salting. Good information to retain for your anthropology midterm, but we recommend a more modern method called 'a fridge.'" Amazon advised girls that it's a "new season, new school, new look, new you," and invited them to "outfit yourself in the latest, the cutest, and/or the comfiest." It reminded guys that they need video games: "Grab a couple rounds of *Big Brain Academy* on your DS Lite between classes, or slaughter your buddies in *Halo 3*. Ah, catharsis." For every consumer category, Amazon offered a variety of choices and a lot of things to buy.[6]

The whole idea is to create a space where the student feels at home—and that involves creature comforts. In America, home is where the heart is. But Americans make a house a home by filling it with things that express our lifestyle and values, and students make their new spaces homey in the same way. In the past, students made do with what the college provided, but most modern students don't. Instead, Jo and Joe College make over what the college provides by bringing in carpets, futons, beanbag chairs, lamps, electronics, curtains, comforters, and other lifestyle accessories, each creating "my space" in one of the identical rooms in a dorm corridor. In this consumer individualism, our choices reflect who we are (or who we'd like to be), but they also reflect our desire to fit in. The marketing consultants at Teenage Research Unlimited call the process "indi-filiation," a magical mix of individualism and affiliation that lets us express our uniqueness—just like everybody else.[7]

Although it's ultimately individual, off-to-college spending begins as a family affair: Advertisers tell parents that a spending splurge is the best way to express their love and mark this important rite of passage. "This is one of the largest emotional transitions people ever make," says consumer psychologist Kit Yarrow, "and shopping is a way to reduce anxiety. People feel in control when they're shopping. It's something we do really well as Americans." As a result, parents who are about to become empty nesters try hard to fill up the new nests of their offspring.[8]

There's much more to this marketing effort than a single season's sales. As Tracy Mullin of the National Retail Federation explains: "Retailers are hoping to not only boost this year's sales but also to gain customers for life." Marketers know that college students are in a position to establish lifelong brand loyalties for a new set of products. Even though current students already wield billions of dollars of discretionary spending annually in the United States, graduates will spend a lot more in the future. Student consumers are also early adopters of new technologies and artifacts—so marketers know that the latest items in today's dorm rooms will be the standard stuff in tomorrow's homes, apartments, and condos. In this way, college students foreshadow the materialism of the future.[9]

Whether or not students purchase anything at Best Buy, IKEA, Amazon, or Wal-Mart, the efforts of marketing departments shape the expectations of college consumers. Before they even get to classes, everyone learns that college is not a place apart, a reflective retreat from the everyday world—it's just another market niche with its own consumer choices. Advertisements teach "ensemble thinking," the idea that all of our things together should express a clear message about taste and values, as well as the art of comparison shopping—not comparing items to get a good price, but comparing our consumption to those immediately around us. Instead of going to college to "find themselves," students seem to be going to school to express themselves with stuff.[10]

For the past several years, I've asked students in my Campus Ecology class to audit their rooms, compiling lists of all their belongings. One such list, reproduced verbatim, includes:

CLOTHING

1 pair slippers, 2 boots, 3 mittens, 2 scarves, 1 hat, 21 pairs shoes, 6 skirts, 11 pants, 6 jackets, 2 blazers, 1 dress suit, 1 vest, 76 shirts (short, long, tank tops, etc.), 7 sweatshirts, 6 pairs sweatpants/pajama pants, 40 pairs socks (at least), 45 pairs underwear, 15 bras, 19 sweaters, 1 bathrobe, 5 pairs workout shorts, 5 belts, 1 swimsuit, 1 pair sunglasses, 7 purses

SCHOOL SUPPLIES

Too many pens/pencils to count, 33 books (many textbooks), 7 notebooks, 2 packages colored paper, 1 package computer paper, 1 package resume paper, 1 box crayons, 2 glue sticks, 1 Elmer's glue, 2 rubber cement, 1 fabric glue, 1 address book, envelopes and stamps, 3 boxes of cards, rubber bands, masking, duct, and Scotch tape, paper clips, stapler, staples, eraser, 3-hole punch, 1 pair scissors, 1 backpack, 1 box of digital camera paper, 3 boxes markers

ELECTRONICS

1 TV/DVD player, 1 iPod, 1 set speakers, 1 laptop (and case/bag), 1 CD player, 1 clock/radio, 1 wall clock, 1 cellphone, 1 digital camera (and case), 1 mouse, 2 watches, tons of CDs (music and recordable), 45 DVDs

KITCHEN SUPPLIES

1 microwave, toaster, blender, 4 bowls, 4 plates, 12 cups, 4 forks, knives, and spoons, dish towels, dish soap, 1 set knives, granola bars, Wheat Thins, tea, peanut butter

DECORATIONS

12 picture frames, 2 picture albums, 3 3-ring binders, 2 folders, 2 candles, 3 flower vases, 9 posters

HEALTH CARE

3 boxes Kleenex, shampoo/conditioner, soap, lotion, razor, bodywash scrubber, makeup, medicine for everything, hair dryer, hair straightener, 2 brushes, comb, tackle box full of earrings, jewelry, Band-Aids, 1 laundry detergent, 1 fabric softener, 1 stain remover, 2 toothbrushes, 1 floss, 2 toothpaste, 2 deodorant

BEDDING/FURNITURE

1 couch, 2 sets sheets, 3 blankets, 1 comforter, 5 towels, ottoman, 2 rugs, 2 shelves

MISCELLANEOUS

file cabinet, 1 refrigerator, 2 trash cans, 1 tool set, 4 plants, 2 spools yarn, knitting needles, 1 card, 1 laundry basket, 1 duffle bag, 3 strings of lights[11]

The quantity of commodities in the average college dorm room today is radically different from one hundred years ago. In those days a student might have three or four changes of clothes, and two or three pairs of shoes. Students took the train to college instead of arriving in cars, trucks, and vans pulling U-Haul trailers. The amount of stuff was limited, more or less, by what you could carry—or what you could fit into a steamer trunk. Furnishings were Spartan, both by necessity but also by choice: College was a place where—freed from the clutter of the material world—a student might think clearly about the purposes of life. And surprisingly enough, many of them survived their studies without lofted beds, designer lighting, or shag carpets.

All the stuff in dorm rooms today is a testament to the social construction of necessity. In a prescient 1962 essay titled "A Sad Heart at the Supermarket," poet Randall Jarrell identified the shifting nature of necessity:

> As we look at the television set, listen to the radio, read the magazines, the frontier of necessity is always being pushed forward. The Medium shows us what our new needs are—how often, without it, we should not have known!—and it shows us how they can be satisfied: they can be satisfied by buying something. The act of buying something is at the root of our world; if anyone wishes to paint the genesis of things in our society, he will paint a picture of God holding out to Adam a check-book or credit card.

Because marketers and manufacturers need us to need, they work hard to create new necessities both in college and American life, "upscaling" yesterday's luxuries into today's necessities. And so the "buyosphere" expands over time, but the biosphere, by nature, does not—and that's a problem.[12]

The Landscape of a Dorm Room

Jo and Joe College never think about it this way, but a dorm room is a natural landscape. It's not sublime, like the Rocky Mountains or the pounding ocean surf. It's not picturesque, like the winding paths in parks or the rocky outcrops on the most attractive college campuses. But it is an environment, the habitat where students spend a large part of college life. Like a landscape painting, it's also a cultural composition of nature, revealing the relationships of people to the natural world. In this landscape, we can see how people shape nature for their own ends,

Biosphere and Buyosphere	
Biosphere: Sphere of Life	*Buyosphere: Sphere of Commercial Life*
Ecosystems	Eco(nomic)systems
Ecosystem services	Business services, consumer services
Inhabitants	Consumers
Organisms	Organizations
Photosynthesis	Faux syntheses, chemical concoctions
Plants and animals in habitats	Habits in a habitat of consumption
Resource flows	Resource extraction
Gift economy	Market economy
A small world, after all	A mall world, after all
Environments intact	Environmental impacts
Evolution, natural selection	Fashion, cultural selection
Life	"The good life"
Natural cycles	"Progress"
Waste=food	Waste=waste
Commodious	Commodified
Solar-powered	Fossil-fueled
Self-sustaining	Unsustainable

The biosphere is the thin and fragile layer of air and land and water that supports all life on Earth. From space, it's a thin strip of vitality on the Earth's crust poised between an otherwise dead planet and the dead expanses of space. If the Earth were an apple, the biosphere would be no larger than the apple's skin. The buyosphere is the lively sphere of commercial life that conditions much of the consciousness in the developed world. Sometimes, therefore, it seems like it's a mall world, but the buyosphere is really just a small world inside the small envelope of the biosphere.

including aesthetic aspirations. To some extent dorm rooms are a museum of college life: Each of the artifacts on display has a story to tell, and all of the stories together add up to college culture.[13]

The Extensive Ecology of Stuff

A few of the artifacts in a dorm room make explicit allusions to nature: Posters of landscape art express our Romantic affection for nature, screensavers display natural scenes, and there are photos on the shelf from vacations to the beach or cabin. There may be goldfish or a house-plant or two, but *all* of the artifacts in the room tell stories of nature converted to culture. The textbooks are trees. The computers are silicon and hydrocarbons and metals. The clothes are cotton and leather and oil.

Everything in a dorm room is also embodied energy, which generally comes from sunshine stored in oil, coal, wood, or biomass. Embodied energy is the amount of power used to make a product and make it available, including the energy of agriculture or extraction, processing or production, distribution, and marketing. A T-shirt, for example, is made of cotton, so it embodies energy in the oil burned in growing the crop, including planting, tilling, and harvest. The shirt embodies the petrochemical energy in fertilizers and herbicides, and in manufacturing and shipping. Sooner or later, this T-shirt will be a rag—but it's always energy incarnate.[14]

There is also *dis*embodied energy in this room: Alarm clocks, TVs, stereos, coffee pots, computers, chargers, refrigerators, hair dryers, and vacuum cleaners are all grafted to the power grid. In apartments or in dorm suites, stoves and dishwashers, washers and dryers devour electricity, too. Electronic devices even consume as much as 50 percent of their electricity when they're not in use, sucking "vampire power" or "phantom load" in standby mode. Mostly, though, unless we're reading about Benjamin Franklin or Thomas Edison, we don't think about electricity because it's cheap and we've learned to focus only on its applications. Growing up in a culture of cheap energy, we have come to have what Wendell Berry calls "cheap-energy minds," with expectations of electrical appliances constantly in our lives.

Planned obsolescence: The art of designing products that don't last, either functionally or fashionably, so that manufacturers can increase sales. Disposable products are good examples of functional obsolescence, while fashion trends and the annual model change in cars are good examples of stylish obsolescence. On college campuses, new textbook editions create obsolescence as well.

Though it all seems solid and permanent, almost all of the stuff in a dorm room or apartment is also eventual junk, what some would call imminent obsolescence, some of which is planned. Laptops seem more solid than the electrical impulses that run through them, but they will be out-of-date in just a few years. Stylish new outfits will be unfashionable before the end of the year, banished to the back of the closet, the rack at the secondhand store, or the sodden mass of a garbage dump.[15]

The average American consumes more than one hundred pounds of materials a day, almost all of which is out of sight and out of mind. For instance, a fraction-of-an-ounce silicon chip resides in my computer, but the eighty-plus pounds of material involved in its production—silicon, water, chemicals, and coal or another energy source—occupy other spaces. The quarter-pounder Joe College ate for dinner is, as advertised, four ounces, but the burger's inputs include about two pounds of corn and several gallons of water, not to mention topsoil, fertilizers, pesticides, herbicides, and oil. A lot of the ingredients of our material world are immaterial to us, but not to the planet we inhabit.[16]

Many of the environmental impacts of our belongings come before they are even ours, during offshore production and global transportation. The products we buy are better traveled than we are, as one of my students noted. When closely considered, the movements of manufacturing—where raw materials from many countries are assembled in many other countries—are amazing. As another student suggested, the twenty-first-century assembly line is not confined to single factories: It spans both countries and continents, and we are the factory bosses, operating by remote control every time we swipe our credit cards.[17]

Remote control: 1) The device we use to control our TVs and other electronics; 2) The designs we use to control the world, socially and environmentally. Eating, for example, is a form of remote control.

At the store, a purchase is just a transaction: We trade money (or credit) for goods. But what happens at cash registers all over the world? When the clerk scans our purchase, it's recorded in the store's computer, which adjusts the inventory accordingly. Our simple payment drives the retailer to reorder, which drives the manufacturer to requisition more materials, which drives the farmer or miner or oil refiner to extract more from the land. As a result, the unnatural selection of the economy determines—as much as natural selection—which plants and animals will grow in which places on the planet. Human beings currently monopolize more than 40 percent of the Earth's primary productivity, so our consumer "buyodiversity"—the desire to have more things available more of the time—affects the actual biodiversity of the natural world.[18]

Educated for Ignorance

When students first encounter this "problem of invisible complexity," they're shocked and amazed. They often note that they had *no idea* that they have such far-reaching environmental impacts. This ignorance is interesting. The United States boasts one of the best systems of higher education in the world, and yet its students and graduates still don't know the basic facts about the artifacts of their daily life. To a great extent, American society socializes its kids by obscuring the true nature of their lives.[19] In part, this is the logical outcome of a system of specialization and division of labor. Following the logic of Adam Smith, Americans have embraced the efficiency of a system in which different people are responsible for different productive functions. And this is good. We get brain surgeons and rocket scientists, accountants, artists, and college professors. It's good, we think, when waste management companies collect our garbage weekly. But specialized responsibility can be a curious form of irresponsibility. In its most extreme forms, it can lead to what Hannah Arendt called "the banality of evil," in which individuals do a good job in a seemingly harmless line of work, but unwittingly contribute to systems of injustice. We can see now that American slave owners and Nazi concentration camp workers were complicit with systems of evil, but it's always harder to see the immorality of our own time. Most of us are not evil, but we're not always doing good, because our specialized cleverness keeps us from being mindful of the potentially harmful consequences of doing a good job of consumption. In our rooms, surrounded by familiar things, we feel at home, but we forget that we've also impacted the homes of people, plants, and animals around the globe, for better *and* worse.[20]

American consumer ignorance is also the result of an economic system of comparative advantage. Historically, as different cities and regions of the country specialized in the products and processes that offered advantages in the marketplace, the social and environmental impacts of those methods of manufacture moved out of sight and out of mind. Home production of food, clothes, and furnishings was supplanted by factory production, and local tailors, cobblers, and furniture makers were replaced by factory workers someplace else. As a result, people lost the local knowledge of the consequences of their consumption, as well as the local cultures of care for neighbors and neighborhoods that regulated production, consumption, and disposal of wastes. More stuff came to consumers, and it was cheaper, but its real impacts and true costs increasingly moved away.[21]

"Murketing"

Though specialization and comparative advantage play a huge role in our consumer cluelessness, our ignorance about the real story of our belongings comes mainly from the systems of misinformation we call commercial culture. Advertisers and marketers offer information about products, but they systematically screen consumers from information about their social and environmental impacts. They seduce us with stories about sexiness and sociability, cool and control, power and possibility, but they don't tell stories that don't sell—stories of extraction, production, and distribution. We see the dorm refrigerator, but not mountaintop removal mining; the laptop computer, but not the mountains of electronic waste in China. Instead of telling the whole truth, marketers often sell the half-truth (and half is a generous estimate), decontextualizing products from their real histories and recontextualizing them in fantasy worlds where costs are invisible and benefits are immediate. Thanks to such "murketing," we routinely make our consumer choices in ignorance of their actual effects and our own responsibility.[22]

> **Murketing:** 1) Promoting consumption by converting human hopes into commercial fantasies, half-truths, and lies; 2) The process of making complexity and complicity invisible.

It seems perfectly natural that companies promote the positive attributes of their products and conceal the negative implications, but if we don't know the whole truth about the goods, we can't make good decisions. It's hard to do real cost-benefit analysis when the benefits are touted in ads, and the costs are hidden from sight. In theory, the free market operates on the premise that rational people make informed decisions about consumption, so you would think that business executives, who are typically the most vocal proponents of free-market economies, would tell us everything we need to know. But in reality, advertisers operate on the belief, obviously true, that emotional promises can influence good people to make uninformed decisions about their actual consumption. In such a *system* of irresponsible consumption, it's virtually impossible for individuals to be responsible consumers, or to live sustainably. Until we change the system so that we routinely learn how our commodities and clothes are made, we'll be covering up our environmental and social shame with fig leafs and other fashions.[23]

The Really Good Life

When we furnish our rooms or fill our closets, we say "I want that," but we also tell manufacturers "make more of that"—setting in motion a whole process of extraction, production, distribution, marketing, and sales. In the process, we tell each other that this level of consumption is normal, natural, and good. We buy into a system of commercial capitalism, a story of nature converted to commodity, converted eventually to garbage. Each of our decisions, therefore, is a case study in ethics, a determination about the nature of "the good life." As we peruse the stuff available to us, we're making judgments about which goods are good for us and why. We don't think we're engaged in ethical reflection, but we are deciding what we value, and how we will embody our values in the material world. Our rooms and our belongings send messages about identity and community, but they also express our ethical sensibilities, whether we like it or not.[24]

The problem, it seems, is that we apply ethical norms almost exclusively in our face-to-face and intentional interactions. We don't feel responsible for what we don't see and don't intend. In a system of invisible complexity, we don't usually consider our inevitable complicity in this system of material goods. Consequently, we seldom think of our everyday purchases in terms of value—except, of course, when they're cheap enough to be a "good value." But style itself is a value, and the ability to keep ethics out of aesthetic judgments is also a value. The question for consumers—which is all of us—is how we can take responsibility for the systems that provide our belongings. When Chinese workers are poisoned in the process of recycling our computers, what is the moral implication for us? The answer might be as simple as paying attention to our things, but saying that it's simple doesn't make it easy.

Getting Over Stuff

Many students find the full story of their stuff to be depressing. Indeed, when we know about the implications of our consumption, shopping trips can start to feel like guilt trips. But why should we feel guilty for doing precisely what society expects us to do? Over the course of the twentieth century, American institutions—corporations, advertisers, retailers, mass media, and government agencies—worked extremely hard to shape a "morality of spending" that taught individuals how to work and spend for their own good, but also for the good of the economy, which now depends on consumer spending for two-thirds of its activity. In a consumer culture, consumption is what perfectly normal people do. And when normal people don't shop, as in times of recession, the economy suffers.[25]

Another typical response to learning the full story of our material goods is anger. We're mad about acting in ways that contradict our values. We feel trapped living in a system that expects us to be complacent while our consumption compromises the planet's life-systems. We're also angry that no one—not parents, not schools, not churches—has bothered to tell us how our habits harm our habitats. We're furious because it's so easy to be ignorant, and so hard—*systematically* hard—to be informed. Ultimately, we're mad at ourselves for being tricked into habits we hate and love at the same time.[26]

Some students have responded by cleaning and greening their rooms. Such creative individuals are choosing to buck the trend of upscaling college dorm rooms by downscaling their lives and living spaces. Downscaling is a kind of right-sizing, bringing environmentalism out of the closet and into the dorm room by getting our possessions to measure up to our deepest values. These students are starting to think twice about buying or bringing excess furniture, electronic devices, and clothing to school. When they truly need something new, they look to conscientious companies like IKEA or to Energy Star appliances and electronics. They use the Web to access secondary markets like Craigslist and Freecycle, or visit secondhand stores, extending the useful life of the embodied energy in used couches, chairs, computers, and TVs. Embracing a kind of voluntary simplicity, they make themselves at home both in their rooms and in the biosphere. More importantly, in the process, they change the character of "cool," teaching both friends and marketers a different way to think about, buy, and sell stuff. Forty-one percent of students pay attention to social messages in advertising, and two-thirds like green business practices and fair labor standards—so it's easy to see how they can begin to change a commercial culture that makes it hard to be good.[27]

Some students simply make do with less. When they learn that the most efficient dorm refrigerator has one-tenth the space of a standard-size refrigerator but uses three-fourths of the electricity, they decide that keeping their beer or bottled water cold no longer seems that cool. They practice dematerializing, looking for ways to find fulfillment without the material mess that often accompanies consumer goods. This consumer resistance involves defiance of commercial and peer pressures to consume, defiance that can be hard to sustain without a support system of like-minded friends.

At some schools, students accomplish this by going public with their concerns. While many student newspapers still sponsor contests to identify the coolest dorm rooms—following the lifestyle sections of mainstream newspapers and shows like MTV's *Cribs*—a few student newspapers are sponsoring contests to identify the "greenest" rooms and apartments, further transforming the social construction of cool on campus. Because 64 percent of college students consider word of mouth important in their purchasing decisions, creating communities of creative consumption makes a world of difference—and a difference for the world.

Many such students embrace the philosophy that less can be more fun. Owning less stuff often gives us more time because we don't have to work so much to pay for so much. Instead of getting caught up in the all-American cycle of work and spend—and the time pressures that go with it—making do with less allows time to make other choices. We have time for an evening of slow cooking and camaraderie, a saunter across campus or along the river, or a romantic evening with a special someone. We have time for those late-night conversations that mean so much and for the things (which mostly aren't material things) that offer real human satisfaction.[28]

Some colleges are even trying to encourage more stewardship in their residence halls through the construction of "green dorms." Warren Wilson College, Northland College, Pitzer College, and Emory University, among others, have built residence halls that serve human needs without compromising the environment as much as most of our buildings do. Others use their residence halls as 24/7 classrooms, posting building performance online so that residents understand the real costs of residence life. At Oberlin College, for example, students can watch energy use in campus buildings in real time. At Central College in Iowa, a new green dorm monitors energy use and allows students in different suites to compete against one another for energy efficiency. Such projects are essential because they build sustainability right into the structure of everyday life and even make it fun.[29]

College students are overstuffed, but they are learning how to get over it by changing their minds and changing the system. Advancing the ecological revolution of the twenty-first century on campus, they're assessing the real satisfactions that come with materialism, conserving the materials they do own, reducing unnecessary purchases, enjoying the extensive pleasures of things that are ecologically designed, and changing commercial systems so that they can routinely put their money where their values are.

Habits and Habitats

Eventually, however, students will need to change their habits in the public sphere, off campus, where most of American life occurs. They'll need to join a long tradition of consumer advocates and environmental activists to regulate our culture's relationships with goods so that they're better for people and the planet. From the National Consumers League to the Consumers Union, from Florence Kelley to Ralph Nader, from Henry Thoreau to Wendell Berry, conscientious Americans have reminded us that one of our consumer options is opting out of consumer conformity, and choosing the simpler satisfactions of the unstuffed life. Legislators from the Puritans to the present day have tried to reform capitalism so that it meets all our *needs*, without wasting energy on mere wants and whims. Indeed, challenging the system of consumption is almost as American as consuming itself.[30]

Changing the nature of our relationship with material goods can start here and now. If we begin to develop a real reverence for materials and their creation, reviving pre-materialist ideals of thrift, frugality, and sufficiency, we can encourage the design of products for repair and reuse, allowing us to consume materials fully before discarding them. If we practice a materialism that takes materials seriously—both individually and institutionally—we'll have a better chance of creating a culture in which we have more human satisfaction with less stuff.

Changing college culture is a way of changing American culture. When students change their lives, they change the world. When they transform their institutions, they transform the default settings of the places they live. When institutions leverage larger changes (in purchasing, in green building, in transportation alternatives) and establish new expectations, everyone begins to see the first solid evidence of the ecological revolution of the twenty-first century. And that revolution, harmonizing finally with nature's evolution, changes the possibilities for life—and the good life—both on campus and on a small and fragile planet.

3

The Nature of Clothes

My dream is to save women from nature.
   Christian Dior

*It is an interesting question how far men would retain their
relative rank if they were divested of their clothes.*
   Henry David Thoreau, *Walden*

*You don't have to signal a social conscience by looking like a
frump. Lace knickers won't hasten the holocaust, you can ban the
bomb in a feather boa just as well as without, and a mild interest
in the length of hemlines doesn't necessarily disqualify you from
reading Das Kapital and agreeing with every word.*
   Elizabeth Bibesco, as quoted in *The Virtuous Consumer*

∎ ∎ ∎ ∎ ∎ ∎ ∎

Joe College is getting dressed. He finds clean underwear in the drawer,
sorts the laundry pile to see how dirty his Gap jeans are, and searches for a
sweatshirt that passes the smell test. He slips on clean socks and his Nikes,
and he's ready to go. His sister gets dressed, too, but it takes her a little longer. For many reasons, college women are taught to worry about keeping
up appearances, so Jo has to consider issues like fit, color, and style more
than Joe does. In addition, while he's working mostly with a wardrobe of
pants, shirts, and athletic shoes, she's got more choices—pants or skirts,
T-shirts or blouses, sweaters or sweatshirts, clogs, sandals, or athletic
shoes. Today, she settles on jeans and a blue Hollister sweatshirt.

Before leaving for classes, Jo and Joe College always get dressed,
because, as Mark Twain suggested, "Naked people have little or no influence on society." Of course, naked people also have little or no environmental impact from their clothing, but nudism isn't the best method
of reducing a student's ecological footprint. Instead, most students still
dress themselves in nature, wearing fibers, petrochemicals, water, and
energy as they go about their daily business. But that's not what's on
their mind when they put on their clothes in the morning.

In general, we often don't even have clothes in mind when we get dressed; we're thinking about girlfriends, boyfriends, food, sex, or the party that we're planning. Usually we just get dressed as a matter of habit. But, like a nun's habit, our clothes are more than just fabric— they're everyday expressions of our beliefs and values, as well as implicit statements of our relationships with nature and human nature. Because any dress code is also a consumption code, we need to think about the moral ecology of clothes—and how our fashion ethic affects the world.

The Common Sense of Clothes

In middle school and high school, clothes are a kind of put-on. We put them on to try out different personas. We try on different clothes to see what they do: how they attract attention, how they affect other people's interactions with us, and how we feel when we play this part in costume. Growing up, we've learned about clothes in many different ways: from parents and relatives, neighbors and peers, and the advertisers and marketers who flak us with fashion from the day we're born. In this sartorial socialization, we learn about dress codes, formal and informal, material and mental. We learn to follow the fashion scene, whether or not we actually buy into it, and we learn to express ourselves with this second skin we wear every day. We know what's in and what's out, and we can all tell the dorks from the preppies, the geeks from the goths, and the fashionistas from the rest of the crowd.

By the time students get to college, therefore, they have a kind of clothing repertoire for the dramas of their daily lives. On campus, first-year students play again with dress and the presentation of self, each adjusting to the expectations of a new college culture and trying to craft a suitable persona. Though most colleges provide students with food and shelter, they don't supply clothes, and there's usually not an institutional dress code either. Professors are mostly clueless about fashion, so students need to learn primarily from their peers. Learning the common sense of clothes, they settle into a style of dress that's comfortable and acceptable to the people they hang out with.

The Common Sense of College Clothes

Getting dressed in the morning, we usually put on clothes that reflect and reinforce the common sense of culture. Because it's common sense, we don't have to think about it, but if we did think about it, we'd notice how complex it has become.

Like all Americans, college students value comfort, so they usually put on clothes that put them at ease. Mostly, this means cotton clothing—because cotton is soft and breathable, and because cotton trade groups have done a good job promoting their product as the "natural" choice. There's also a *style* of college comfort that's as important as the substance of comfort itself. A finely tailored three-piece suit can be perfectly comfortable, for example, but college students don't generally dress that way. Pants with elastic waistbands are very comfortable, but most college students aren't comforted by that look either. College students want the comfort that comes from familiar fashions like jeans and sweatshirts and T-shirts—clothes that signify comfort, but also informality and a laid-back lifestyle. They choose their individual look, but—in another act of indi-filiation—they tend to choose what everybody else chooses.[1]

Beyond comfort, Americans wear clothes that are functional, that regulate the air temperature near our skin. All clothes are a kind of habitat, designed to control airflow by trapping body heat in cooler weather or inviting the evaporation that cools us in warmer weather. Given such functionality, clothes could help colleges (and other fossil-fuel consumers) regulate carbon consumption by keeping indoor temperatures lower in the winter and warmer in the summer. Thermostats at sixty degrees in the winter and eighty degrees in the summer, for instance, would likely encourage a more weather-wise dress code. But Americans seem to have decided that indoor air temperatures should be standard no matter the season, and we keep temperatures at a level where we can wear T-shirts year-round. We pay more attention to fashion seasons than the natural seasons.[2]

We've also been taught by advertisers that we need specific clothes for specific occasions. These days, you need sportswear for sports, activewear for activity, and clubbing clothes for dancing. This means that most of the time most of our clothes aren't being worn, they're being closeted. In fact, many of the clothes in a college student's closet are "just-in-case" clothes, hanging around just in case they get an invitation to the ball. And some of these contingency clothes are *never* used—except as an insurance policy for remote possibilities. So most college students, like most Americans, use some clothes by not using them.[3]

Beyond comfort and functionality, we like clean clothes. Like our body-cleansing rituals, our clothing choices are a part of the American

cult of cleanliness, hammered into our heads by parents and detergent companies. We're not thinking about detergent ads when we get
dressed, but as we look for a clean shirt in the closet, we're conforming
to their model.

This expectation of cleanliness also drives a desire for quantities of
clothes. While his parents may send stuff out to the dry cleaners, Joe
College is on his own—and he doesn't want to waste money or time
on cleaning. So one reason for the considerable quantities of collegiate
clothes is laundry: The more students have, the longer they can avoid
the trip to the laundry room or Laundromat.

College clothes can look worn, but most students don't dress in
clothes that are tattered and torn. Though some people will pay for
clothes that come from the manufacturer "distressed" and defaced,
few wear clothes that have actually been repaired. In the past, most
Americans mended torn clothes, but patches and darns have gone the way
of tailors and seamstresses. In a system of low-cost labor and global out-
sourcing, it's systematically cheaper to replace a garment than to repair
it. Culturally speaking, the material we waste seems immaterial to us.[4]

When we dress in the morning, we generally want clothes that
fit—and that make us *look fit*. We don't wear clothing that is three sizes
too large or too small. And because the body often changes in college,
clothes are needed to accommodate those different possibilities. When
students gain weight, for example, they sometimes hold on to their
smaller sizes, keeping a closet of clothes for "after the diet." In any case,
most people choose clothes that flatten or flatter the body, so that it
looks like the body we *ought* to have. When we're feeling bad about having put on a few pounds, we want clothes that conceal our bulges. When
Joe College is pleased with the muscle he's amassed in the weight room,
he wants something that shows it off. When Jo College hopes to attract
the attention of that certain someone, she might dress differently than
everyday. As this suggests, the physical fit of a garment is often psychological, too. We want clothes that fit the body, but we also want them to
fit—or to alter—our different moods. Clothes can express both happiness and hopefulness, and they can provide therapy when we're in the
dumps. What we see in the mirror is important, but there's always more
to clothes than meets the eye.

Beyond the physical and psychological fits of clothing, there are
social fitness rules, too: Like our other belongings, our clothes help us
belong, so we're interested not just in how our outfits fit but how they
help us fit in. Even though we might deny it, we dress for display, and

the opinions of our friends and social groups mean a lot to us, usually even more than advertising. Acting as mannequins for each other by wearing certain styles, we're not just commercial images on the screen or pictures on the page; we're trusted friends whose opinions matter. So routine comments and compliments like "cool hat" or "cute outfit" are very good at teaching us about the substance of superficiality—the ways in which surface things like cosmetics or clothes or brand names have real impacts on our social lives. Our concern for appearances, therefore, is often a concern for "appeerances," and our desire for such social status affects both the status quo and the state of the world.

Appeerances: The way that peer pressure looks in our lives.

Though some of our clothes help us identify with the very real communities we dwell in, they also involve us in more abstract imaginative communities, the ones that are sold to us in advertising and marketing. College is a *logo-centric* world, so many students buy clothes for the logo as well as for the garment. Abercrombie shirts, Gap jeans, and Nike shoes express membership in a "consumption community"—a community characterized by common taste and values. Targeted branding strategies allow advertisers to segment the market—one kind of Converse for skateboarders, another for basketball players—but they let all of us feel like we belong to something special. Almost half of college students say that "the brands I buy say a lot about me."[5]

One of those brands is the college itself, identifying the wearer with the aspirations and values of her school. At Division I schools, a lot of the logowear expresses affiliation not with the institution's academic culture, but with its sports teams—and with the natural symbols of the institution. Collegians wear team shirts emblazoned with lions, tigers, bears, badgers, gophers, wildcats, and wolverines. Take all the collegiate mascots together, and you'd have the makings of a pretty good zoo.[6]

In describing other societies, anthropologists would call these mascots totems—animals, plants, or objects that serve as emblems for a clan, tribe, or family. Some indigenous groups, for example, have identified with plants or animals, and ritualized their relationships to them to maintain harmony with the natural world. In our mass culture, on the other hand, a totem is an animal, plant, or object that serves as a commercial emblem for a college or university, especially its athletic teams. Such symbols carry no real sense of identification with nature, no sense of interdependence, no sense of cosmic relation, except in the cosmos of fun and commercialism.

In college culture, mascots provide a symbol for sales—a brand logo that expresses fandom—but they don't give us much knowledge of nature, or affection for the natural world.[7]

Some students dress up clothes with ideas and ideals, identifying sometimes (obliquely) with nature, too. Some students sport T-shirts festooned with images of nature, logos of environmental organizations, or beliefs about nature: "Humans aren't the only species on earth. They just act like it"; "Renewable Energy—The Answer Is Blowing in the Wind." Others express their readiness for "getting back to nature" through the brands they wear. Outfitters like Eddie Bauer, REI, and Patagonia equip students for adventures in nature—presumably off campus, usually in the wilderness. In a book titled *Lifestyle Shopping*, retail consultant Martin Pegler claims that communing with nature calls for special clothes: "Companies like Eddie Bauer and The North Face cater to the nature-loving lifestyle with clothes, accessories, and even home furnishings to complete a domestic environment

in keeping with that lifestyle." Converting the outdoor life into a consumption experience, such retailers try to convince us that students can't really go hiking or camping without the proper gear. Often they also wear these clothes and accessories on campus to show that, even though they're currently here, they'd prefer to be there. "I may be an econ major," they say sartorially to people around, "but at heart I'm really a mountaineer."[8]

Lifestyle: 1) The complexity of life, reduced to the simplicity of consumption and commercial fashions; 2) A life, conceived as a collection of commodities and consumption experiences.

For all these reasons, American college students have a lot of clothes. It may not feel like so many because the closets are small, some clothes are still at home, and most students know people who have more. Compared to other cultures, however, the amount is staggering. Sometimes the reasons for this are purely practical: Different clothes are needed for different weather conditions or different occasions, and a superabundance means not having to do laundry often. But the primary reason for large quantities of clothing isn't practical—it's the American ideology of choice. When we get dressed in the morning, we want choices—of comfort, color, coverage, and communication—because those selections represent our autonomy. When Joe College slips on the same old sweatshirt and jeans, he's comforted by the fact that he could have chosen something else. When Jo College looks in her stuffed closet and bemoans the fact that "there's nothing to wear," the statement is obviously false, but it illustrates our assumptions about choice, variety, novelty, and materialistic entitlement. For many reasons, we have more clothes than we need, and each item has its own environmental impact. But that's not in our consciousness, because we have little or no information about how clothes are fabricated—how textiles are constituted from plant fibers or chemicals, and made into the fashions we think we need.

Dressing for each other—and even for our communities of consumption—is perfectly normal, reflecting the human need for affiliation and solidarity. But it doesn't always make sense on a finite planet, where this materialistic commemoration of our imagined communities has real effects on living, breathing communities of nature. As social beings, we need to celebrate our affiliations. As natural beings we need to maintain our affiliations with the more-than-human life of the planet, which begins by understanding how the Earth that sustains us becomes the clothing that defines us.

The Nature of Jeans

The average American consumer owns seven pairs of jeans, and college students practically live in them. The eighteen-to-twenty-four-year-old age group, which accounts for only 10 percent of our population, accounted for nearly 30 percent of spending on jeans in the year ending in October 2006—about $2.8 billion of the denim industry's $8.6 billion annual income. Cotton and comfortable, "cool" and common, "down home" and upscale, jeans go with everything and they can go just about anywhere. They feel natural—and, in a way, they are—but they're also cultural, and they reveal a lot about America's culture of nature.[9]

In a television commercial for Cotton Incorporated, as a camera pans over stacks of jeans in a retail store to the beat of soft rock music, captions identify, humorously, different styles of jeans: "Low Rise Jeans. Boot Cut Jeans. Skinny Jeans. Not Feeling So Skinny Jeans. Walk The Dog Jeans. Make Him Pant Like A Dog Jeans. Turns Butts Into Booty Jeans." For the 2007 "Back to College" season, Old Navy featured "New Denim/New You," with three different fits (and functions) for women— the Diva, the Flirt, and the Sweetheart. "Steal the spotlight," girls were advised, "in our show-stopping jeans." As this suggests, one of the main functions of jeans is to attract attention—primarily to the bottom of a woman's body. The Cotton Incorporated ad ends with an alleged truism, "You Can Never Have Enough Jeans."[10]

Some college students express their affection for jeans on social media sites: "Blue Jeans Are Probably the Greatest Thing Ever"; "I'm just a blue Jeans and T-shirt type of girl"; "My name is _____ and I am a blue jean addict"; "I wear my blue jeans multiple times, and I'm proud of it!"—and "My jeans are worth more than your life!" There's even a Facebook group called "I Use My Blue Jeans As A Napkin."

The rise of designer jeans has only fanned the flames. Since the debut of the company Seven for All Mankind ("Sevens") in 2000, many American women have decided that jeans capable of elongating the legs and lifting the butt are worth a lot of money. Blue Cult jeans marketed a line actually called "Butt Lifters." For genuine jean lovers, money is no object. As one Berkeley student claimed in 2005, "I don't care how much I spend on jeans, as long as they look good on me. . . . I don't mind spending three hundred dollars if they flatter my body." Her favorite brand was True Religion, a profession of faith that has more to do with fashion and the marketplace than anything spiritual. To most male collegians, designer jeans are just pricey. But to a coed in the know—and women dress for each other as much as for men—they're a mark of true distinction. True Religion's logo, for example, is "Buddha" playing a guitar, and its distinctive designs include a signature horseshoe on the pockets and thick-threaded seams. Such signs and symbols are more than a highlight for the body; they're conspicuous consumption spotlighting the size of our bank account, too.[11]

When students buy jeans, therefore, it's clear that they're also buying meanings. Some of those meanings are historical. Jeans are Western, working-class, rebellious, hippie, and hip-hop. They remind us of Levi

Strauss and California miners, generations of rugged cowboys, James Dean and fifties rebels without a cause, and Robert Moses and sixties rebels *with* a cause. As a result, paradoxically, they're both cultural and countercultural—pants for all reasons.[12]

The Impact of Jeans

With 1.5 billion pairs produced each year, and 450 million sold annually in the United States alone, jeans may be the most widely produced item of apparel on the planet. They begin with cotton, which is made with water—about two inches per week during the growing season, or about a bathtub full for each pair of jeans. Often, this water is supplied by irrigation. Rivers are redirected and aquifers depleted for crops that ultimately keep us comfortable and cool. As consumers, we think of cotton, water, and soil as renewable natural resources. And they *are* renewable, as long as producers pay attention to the regeneration of soils and the recharge of aquifers, which, generally, they don't.[13]

Because cotton is typically monocultural, it invites invasions of insects like mites, aphids, thrips, worms, and beetles. Consequently, cotton-growing demands pesticides—about 10 percent of all pesticides used on all crops in the world. Cotton-growing uses 10 percent of the world's herbicides, too, not including the defoliants used just before harvest. About a pound of chemicals is used for five pounds of cotton, and because it takes a little more than two pounds of cotton to make a pair of jeans, we're responsible for about half a pound of chemicals for each pair of jeans we own.[14] Only traces of these chemicals stay in the fiber, of course; more than 90 percent of them wash into soil, streams, lakes, and aquifers. One current strategy for reducing the use of chemicals involves genetically modified cotton. Currently GMO cotton makes up about half of the U.S. crop, so in a process we might call "jeanetic engineering," our demand for jeans has now affected the genes of cotton.[15]

The row cropping of cotton is hard on the soil, too. Plowing exposes loose soil to wind and water, leading to erosion. Tillage also speeds the breakdown of organic matter, while pesticides kill microorganisms that give soil its vitality. Irrigation waters the crop and helps it grow, but it also contributes to the salinization of the soil. Cotton may be a natural fabric, but its cultivation typically isn't kind to nature.[16]

After the harvest, cotton is ginned to separate the fiber from the seeds, bound into five-hundred-pound bales, shipped to factories, spun into yarn, woven into cloth, and cut and sewn into jeans. Each step requires fossil fuels or nuclear power, and all of the fossil fuels contribute to global weirding. Once made, the denim is dyed. In the distant past, indigo dyes came from plants and snails found around the Mediterranean Sea. Around 1900, German chemists discovered a process for synthesizing indigo, so now the raw materials for the blue in our jeans are aniline, formaldehyde, and cyanide, all of which come from petroleum.[17] Because some of us like our new jeans to look like they've been lived in, some denim is "distressed" by washing it with cellulose enzymes or perlite—a silicon rock. The process consumes a lot of water (again), plus the power needed to dry the "stonewashed" fabrics.[18]

Dyed denim is then made into jeans at factories located in low-wage markets, usually in Latin America or Asia. Manufacturing is expensive, but we don't pay for it: foreign workers do. Less than 10 percent of the retail price of jeans goes toward their production, and labor costs make up just 2 percent of that.[19] Most workers get just pennies for jeans that might retail for hundreds of times more. Some argue that exploitation is the price of economic development, or that such wages are adequate in industrial China, but cheapness isn't the only choice.[20]

Zipping up their jeans, students aren't thinking about sweatshops or the politics of free-trade zones. They're not thinking about the largely female workforce, bused into factories from rural villages, and housed in company quarters. Shopping for clothes in America can be a form of "sweatshopping," but there's no suggestion of that in our malls, catalogs, or labels. Trying on jeans in the store, customers are implicitly asked to forget the water, soil, oil, chemicals, and human labor used in their fabrication. As all Americans look for new jeans, we're asked to make environmental decisions—and ethical decisions—without any relevant information.[21]

Jeans are so common on campus that Joe and Jo College hardly ever think about them. But, like our other clothes, they help us think about our place in the global commons. If we want to think globally and act globally, jeans would be a good place to start.

The Nature of Laundry

As an artificial skin for humans, clothes get dirty. They capture spills from the cafeteria, effluents at the party, dirt from the floor, stains from the grass, and the smell of sweat. So students occasionally need to take their clothes to the laundry, where fossil fuels power machines that use chemicals to clean them. Like other consuming routines, doing the

made in Guatemala

made in Indonesia

made in China

made in Dominican Republic

made in Honduras

made in Thailand

made in Vietnam

— Made in America —

laundry is a form of ordinary consumption that we're so used to, and bored by, that we can't see the tangle of cultural assumptions spinning in the washer. We hardly ever think of ourselves as consumers in the Laundromat or the laundry room, but a significant amount of American consumption, especially energy consumption, comes from precisely such normal and unnoticed routines—forms of the inconspicuous consumption that is structured into our lives. Once again, as in the bathroom, our cleanliness dirties the planet.[22]

In the past twenty years, spurred in part by federal regulations and Energy Star standards, manufacturers have made washers and dryers a lot more efficient, but a dryer will never be as efficient as a clothesline. The clothesline was an old-fashioned technology that used solar power to dry clothes. People used implements called clothespins to attach clothes to a rope strung between two poles. On a good day, the clothes dried quickly and picked up the fresh smell of outdoor air (which is now synthesized in the scents of detergents and fabric softeners). On rainy days—or in winter, in cold climates—an outdoor clothesline was useless, so people rigged lines indoors. Still, for reasons of predictability, profit, and progress, consumers became convinced that clotheslines were "old-fashioned," and quickly opted for the mechanization of the drying process. American colleges followed suit, providing students with the appliances they had learned to expect at home.[23]

A 2006 French study examined the life-cycle costs of a single pair of jeans, and found that washing, drying, and ironing accounts for 47 percent of their environmental impact, using about 240 kilowatt hours of electricity a year—equal to the energy used to power four thousand sixty-watt light bulbs for an hour.[24]

Thankfully, reducing resource consumption in college laundry rooms is no harder than changing habits of body and mind. Practically speaking, colleges and universities could buy or lease the most efficient washers and dryers, and complement them with clotheslines and drying racks. Culturally, students could also begin to change their expectations. Students like Joe and Jo College have grown up with a rising tide of TV commercials for whiter, brighter, cleaner clothes, but they could choose to remember that cleanliness wasn't always next to godliness until members of the Cleanliness Institute—funded by Procter & Gamble, Colgate-Palmolive, Armour & Company, and Unilever—realized that, as association executive Roscoe Edlund said in 1930, "The business of cleanliness is big business," and that cleanliness was a great way to sell soaps and detergents. Students could resist this brainwashing by washing clothes—especially outerwear— less than current cultural expectations demand. They could embrace the smell test, as well as the sweet smell of clothes dried in fresh air. Less laundry, too, would extend the life span of clothes—agitation and tumbling result not only in clean, dry garments but also in lint, the common name for the fluff that used to be clothes. In short, saving rivers of water, acres of cotton, and pounds of chemicals is as simple as asking one question at the end of the day: "How dirty are these jeans?"[25]

Making New Clothes

In a 2005 essay that won the Elie Wiesel Prize for an undergraduate essay in ethics, Yale University student Sarah Stillman argued that while our clothes may be made in China, our clothing system is made by us. Focusing on young women, sweatshops, and the ethics of globalization,

Stillman wrote how "teenage girls [in other countries] are increasingly bearing the burdens of globalization while reaping relatively few of its tremendous rewards." Taking an inventory of her own room, she found that she was complicit with labor practices that she opposed.

1 Nike T-shirt: Made by company that employed Martha for five cents a shirt.

1 Adidas soccer ball: Made by company notorious for anti-unionism, low wages, and abuse of young women workers.

1 Barbie doll, legs missing: Made in China by Mattel, in factory much like Li Chunmei's. Average worker age = 14.

2 pairs New Balance sneakers: Chinese workers there are paid 18 cents an hour and forced to live in crammed 12-person dorm rooms.

"Somehow," Stillman noted, "we've become submerged in a system that genuinely repulses our ethical sensibilities." Alarmed by the gap between her expressed values and her operative values, Stillman joined students and other activists to protest the Free Trade Area of the Americas, a neoliberal trade agreement that limits labor rights, human rights, and environmental protections in the interest of free trade. As a woman, she chose to do her part to protect other women—and the Earth—from the destruction that can come with the creativity of capitalism.[26]

What Stillman and other activists are up against is the systematic ignorance fostered by globalization, and the misinformation marketers present to consumers. But what if we countered the half-truths of ads by requiring a full-cost accounting on our clothes? A new system could require retailers to reveal on garment tags not just where products were made, but who made them and how much these workers earned. It might also demand that retailers post pictures or videos of their factories so we could understand the ways our consumption affects the production process. With this sort of information we could make the simple decision to buy our jeans at places that pictured the environmental costs of cotton, and from companies that offered organic goods. We all know that feedback affects how we act in the world, so why not insist on truth in our feedback loops, instead of the glossy promises of deceptive advertising? Why not let us see the connections between social justice and environmental justice? Informed consumption is the foundation of good capitalism, so who could deny the logic of such a demand? By lobbying our legislators to pass just one law to require such

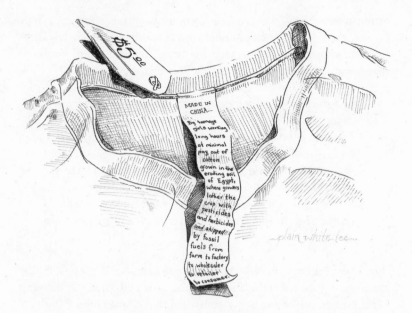

information, we could take real responsibility for our remote control of
the social and environmental impacts of clothing.[27]

Economist Juliet Schor suggests a deeper way to think about our
system of clothing, pointing directly to an ethics of dress, a morality of
jeans. Acknowledging that there is real pleasure in wearing clothes that
are creative and expressive, Schor argues, gives us the choice to prefer
quality over quantity, to take delight in the cut, color, and craft of fewer
clothes. If we discard the planned obsolescence of the fashion system,
searching for greater quality in classic styles, we would both look good
and do good. If we bought our clothes locally, we would shrink our
carbon footprint, and reward the craft and productivity of our neighbors. More importantly, Schor suggests a new standard of beauty that
includes fair trade and environmental responsibility. As a character in
the movie *Gandhi* says, "There is no beauty in the finest cloth if it makes
hunger and unhappiness." And the logical extension of owning clothes
we truly care about is that we will care for them more carefully. Once
we have purchased good jeans, for example, we will wear them until
they're worn out, making creative patches and repairs a symbol of pride,
resourcefulness, and fashion. When we grow out of things, we would be
less likely to throw them in the trash, and more likely to resourcefully
extend their useful life through donation. We might even start clothing

exchanges like libraries, which would enable us to share and wear more clothes than we actually own.[28]

Fortunately, a lot of hard work has already been done to make these possibilities a reality. Along with a politics of environmental justice, college students have also begun to invent a politics of sartorial justice. In 1997, conscientious collegians established United Students Against Sweatshops (USAS), an organization designed to make sure that college logowear is produced and traded fairly. In 2000, USAS created the Workers Rights Consortium to investigate working conditions in factories worldwide, and in 2007, they invited colleges and universities to join the Designated Suppliers Program to make sure that factory workers producing college apparel get living wages and the right to unionize.[29] Students in USAS also organize boycotts of companies that violate fair employment practices and exploit global ecosystems in order to provide cheap clothes. Because the most valuable possession of any international company is its good name (the technical term for this is "brand equity"), students and other concerned citizens can leverage reforms fairly easily. According to BrandZ.com, a source on international brand ranking, the name Nike, for example, is worth $12.5 billion—the highest brand equity of any apparel maker. That's the value of the brand— not the value of the shoes, clothes, ads, or anything tangible—and it's a value that Nike can't afford to lose if consumers learn of unfair labor practices or environmental degradation in its manufacturing processes. When consumers pressure companies and publicize their efforts, even multinational corporations need to respond—and even Nike has. If they know how to use it, college students and other consumers do have some power over powerful corporations.[30]

Boycott: A way of putting our money where our values are, a protest withdrawing business from merchants who have withdrawn from the moral ecology of the culture. "We boycott," said Martin Luther King, Jr. during the Civil Rights Movement, "not to put people out of business, but to put justice into business."

Buycott: A way of putting our money where our values are by buying from companies that improve their social and environmental impacts by promising and practicing environmental justice and regenerative design.

Students have also responded to the sweatshopping of the Earth, the ways in which the global textile trade exploits ecosystems in order to provide low-cost clothing to Wal-Mart and other U.S. retailers. As with cheap labor, the environmental cost of this production is high. But some students are changing their consumption, looking to companies like Patagonia for organic cotton, sustainable wool, or recycled fabrics. Some students are looking for alternative fibers, like hemp, corn, and bamboo, and others are buying fewer clothes and using their money for more important things.[31]

Responding to consumer demand, some blue jeans have begun turning green. In 2006, Levi Strauss introduced Eco jeans, an organic cotton line. Del Forte Denim manufactures jeans in the United States that are made entirely of organic cotton, and other niche companies are following suit. Such green jeans add another level of design, one that fits not just the human form but nature's designs as well. And the future might see additional design factors, too—fair wages and better treatment for the workers who make our clothes. U2's Bono sponsors Edun jeans, which promise fair trade practices in addition to environmental responsibility. If you wear Del Forte jeans, you can participate in Project Rejeaneration, sending your jeans back to the company for a 10 percent discount on your next pair of jeans, or make a contribution to the Sustainable Cotton Project.[32]

Such activity—personal, interpersonal, and political—offers hope for a sustainable clothing trade. If we can combine a passion for our clothes with compassion for people who make them, we can create a system that embodies our best intentions. When our passion for clothing includes compassion for the planet, we can wear it as a sign of right relationship with the Earth. And that would really be dressing for success.

4

Food for Thought

The day is coming when a single carrot, freshly observed, will set off a revolution.
Paul Cezanne

Grass is the original solar technology.
Michael Pollan, from "Michael Pollan on What's Wrong with Environmentalism" at e360.yale.edu

Look at those cows and remember that the greatest scientists in the world have never discovered how to make grass into milk.
Michael Pupin

How we eat determines how the earth is used.
Wendell Berry, "The Pleasures of Eating"

■ ■ ■ ■ ■ ■ ■

After getting up and getting dressed, Joe and Jo College head for the cafeteria, a place they usually visit three times a day. At breakfast, Jo eats a bowl of cereal with a banana. Joe goes for eggs, toast, bacon, and a glass of milk. Coffee and juice complement many of these morning meals. At lunch, Joe picks up a burger and fries, while his roommate piles up a lunch-meat sandwich. Jo looks over the soup and salad bar, and a couple of hot entrées. Coffee is still a staple, but the juices are often replaced by soft drinks. And there's definitely dessert.

Dinner is the main meal of the day. Most nights, there are numerous entrées: meat and potatoes, hamburgers (again), a pasta dish, pizza perhaps, along with a soup and salad bar—and dessert. There's a lot to choose from, but in many college cafeterias a student doesn't have to select just one. Some respond by overeating, perhaps also in part to save money on between-meal snacks. They can take anything that looks good to them because it's no big deal if they don't finish. For most students the cafeteria is an everyday occurrence, but for billions of people, past and present, it's an unimaginable feast.

Even though there's lots of food in the cafeteria, students also eat elsewhere. In fact, there's hardly anyplace they don't eat. On campus, as in America at large, eating is no longer restricted in space and time. The library is sometimes off-limits, but that's about it. Many colleges operate snack bars or a convenience store, and larger universities often feature fast food outlets in student unions. Virtually all colleges also have lucrative vending machine contracts, so there are snacks and soft drinks available at all hours. At night, after studying, Joe and his friends might order a pizza or go barhopping, with salty snacks as a complement and catalyst to the beer. The easy availability of food on campus often contributes to the phenomenon known colloquially as "the freshman fifteen."

Eating occurs almost everywhere, but food isn't always the focus of attention. Sometimes meals are just a break from the boredom of the day. Students almost always approach the cafeteria with a crowd of friends, with teammates, or with a boyfriend or a girlfriend. There are stories to tell, and ideas to share. Someone needs to bitch about Professor Pointless or ask about a reading assignment. And of course, everyone is there to scope out potential dates, catch a glimpse of a "caf crush," or see who's sitting with whom. We consume food in the cafeteria, but we also produce community.

When the eating is over, trays disappear through a window to the dish room. There, the dishes and silverware are washed, and the food scraps and napkins become trash. By the end of each week, the average student produces a pound or two of garbage.[1]

Most of us don't think much about eating, and we seldom pause to really savor the food. Students rarely analyze the cafeteria, but it's amazing if you think about it. It's one of the few places on campus where all of the senses are stimulated. The food comes in a cornucopia of shapes, colors, and textures, while meats, sauces, and french fries emanate mouthwatering scents. The clink of silverware, the buzz of conversation, the sizzle of the grill, the slurp of coffee and pop machines, the occasional crack of dropped dishes combine to create a din of white noise. Students don't always touch their food, but they experience what food technologists call "mouthfeel" every time they eat it. These tactile sensations complement their sense of taste, including the familiar flavors of favorite foods or the spicy novelty of a new ethnic entrée. All of these stimuli make the cafeteria a center of sensuality, but most miss this amazing appeal to our sensual human nature.

What does all this cooking and eating mean? On one level, it's pretty simple: Students need food. College students who don't eat generally don't graduate. The cafeteria, then, is a place where they come into contact with their animal nature, the basic need for sustenance. Eating is one part of a process of making nature into human nature, as our digestive system transforms plants and animals into *us*—our body tissues as well as the energy we need to function. Like other animals, college students are solar-powered organisms because all food is stored sunshine. When they eat Cheerios in the morning, they're eating the fruits of living oats. When they order eggs, they're looking forward to eating the reproductive cells of chickens. When they ask for a side of bacon, they're requesting a portion of a pig that's no longer breathing and snorting. Food is the nature we define as edible, one important part of our social construction of nature.

If we are what we eat, what are we?

Glibly, I am Bon Appétit's daily chore (today, I am an omelet, mushrooms, onions, etc.). But what are these things that I am eating? I am the sun's energy slowed down, I am the water of countless rivers, I am diesel fuel and deadly toxins, I am a GMO. As I look closer, I see that I am carbon, nitrogen, phosphorus, oxygen, and hydrogen arranged in a spectacular array. Like Joseph's technicolor coat, I am constantly shimmering with the movement of my cells, their enzymes, and the constant shivering of their constituent atoms. What am I? I am stardust. In my body are atoms that have been in existence for billions of years, moving in and out of new arrangements with those around them. I am the soil of many countries around the world. My oxygen atoms have been breathed in and out, fallen with water, and have been individually expressed in snowflakes. I am magical. I am chemical. I am what I eat.

Sam Dunn, St. Olaf Student

On another level, the alimentary world is pretty complicated because, whether it tastes good or not, the planet's on the plate. When students eat in the cafeteria—as in most homes and restaurants in America—they say, in effect, "I'd like my meal. But I'd also like an entrée of family farm with a gravy of global warming. Give me a side of topsoil with a pinch of pesticide, a spray of fertilizer, and a smidgen of genetic modification. Pour me 50 gallons of water and a cup of petroleum. And for dessert, I'd like a slice of yellowcake, topped off with dollop of delusion." Though they often don't realize it, students' forks, knives, and spoons are all agricultural implements. Consuming cafeteria fare, they help to produce a food system with environmental effects that change the world. So even though Joe and Jo College only eat when they're not in class, the cafeteria is another classroom, and it can teach a lot about the common sense we all consume with our food.

The Hidden Curriculum of the Cafeteria

The first lesson of Cafeteria 101 is that food is a social construction, which doesn't just mean that there's a recipe involved. Different cultures define food differently, teaching us what counts as edible, how to prepare and present it, how to serve it, and how to eat it. Eating seems so natural that we often forget how many cultural rules we follow without thinking. We could eat dogs and cats, but we don't, because we adhere to cultural conventions. We might eat all our food raw, but we don't, because cooking is the cultural process we've chosen for making our food more digestible. We might eat without utensils, scooping up food with our hands, but we don't, because we see forks, knives, and spoons as signs of civilization. We are what we eat, and not just physically, because diet defines human community. Different peoples eat differently, and culinary identities are the basis of what we call "ethnic" cuisines. In the cafeteria, students eat Chinese, Mexican, Italian, and French, but all with an American twist. Taken together, cultural rules about food determine both what we can eat and how we get our food from the earth.[2]

Another lesson in the cafeteria curriculum concerns privilege, because the cafeteria reinforces both American affluence and the ideology of choice, the idea that we deserve options in our lives. It simply seems "natural," but the standard college cafeteria is cornucopian, implicitly assuring students of the fertility of the world and the fertile ingenuity of the people who convert nature's bounty to all this food. In circumstances like these, even though we're not at Burger King, we feel deep down that we can "have it our way."[3]

Still, some students are perpetually dissatisfied with cafeteria food, carping about "the same old crap" being served week after week. But the "crappiness" of cafeteria food isn't usually a statement of quality: It's a statement of expectations and entitlement, and a statement of American values. One of the most common college complaints, for example, is that "there's nothing to eat" in the cafeteria. As a literal statement, this

is demonstrably false. But as a statement of our American expectations, it's delectably illuminating. This complaint isn't a statement about food or scarcity, but about individualism and novelty. We want food that satisfies *our* tastes, and we want it at every meal.

Cafeteria food, then, is an example of what historian Sidney Mintz calls "a taste of freedom." The free choices—of pizza, pasta, or chicken patties—make students feel good, both in the choosing and in the eating. As Mintz suggests, "The employment of food to achieve a feeling of well-being or freedom is widely felt and understood. The satisfactions seem modest; the meal one eats confirming that 'you deserve a break today' may be neither expensive nor unusual. And yet this act of choosing to consume apparently can provide a temporary, even if mostly spurious, sense of choice, of self, and thereby of freedom." The french fries really are, as congressional Republicans said in 2003, "freedom fries."[4]

In addition to its lessons about affluence and options, the modern cafeteria teaches ignorance and indifference. As currently constituted, most cafeterias screen students from relationships with the people, land, and ecological communities that produce and process the food eaten each day. Like most Americans, most college students don't know where their food comes from, and most don't care. In this way, the cafeteria exemplifies the problem of invisible complexity because it shows how institutions working in our name put our money where our mouths aren't. Colleges tell their food service administrators, either explicitly or implicitly, that they want good food for a low price. These administrators, in turn, look for dependable suppliers whose economies of scale allow them to provide economies of sale. When cafeterias buy food, then, they reinforce some American values and marginalize others. College food purchasing policies are always institutional expressions of value, which often contradict the values of individual eaters.

While money doesn't always change hands in the cafeteria, meals there do eventually cost something, reinforcing the assumption that food is a commodity. Even though food there is a sign of freedom, it's not free.

If students don't pay, they don't eat. Millions of Americans suffer from hunger because a culture of commodification considers the freedom of markets to be more important than the nutritional needs of citizens. In 2006, almost one out of every twenty-five people in the United States, many of them children, experienced chronic hunger. Everybody pays for food, of course, and we do have food stamp programs in this country. But the food system of the richest country in the history of the world leaves some people foraging in dumpsters and lining up at food shelves. And the situation is worse in developing nations. The United Nations Food and Agriculture Organization estimated that more than a billion people—about a sixth of humanity—suffer from malnutrition, and more than thirty thousand people a day die of hunger. There's plenty of food in the cafeteria, but plenty of other places where there's not, and those two realities are not unrelated.[5]

The cafeteria curriculum also teaches lessons about the culture of labor in America. Cafeteria food is a classic example of interdependence and specialization. Other people feed students so that they can focus on their academic work. Even though they provide one of life's necessities, cafeteria workers (often women and immigrants) don't make much money because American fast-food companies keep their costs down by lobbying Congress for the most minimal minimum-wage laws. "Caf" workers enjoy some flexibility in their hours, but they receive few benefits for their labor. In this way, poor workers subsidize the appetites of the affluent. They take care of student's emotions, too, as line workers are often programmed to process each and every customer with the "commercial smile," the compulsory friendliness of service workers in the American economy. How we choose to eat, therefore, affects how other people bring home the bacon.[6]

As this suggests, the cafeteria is also a classic example of our unconsidered power and privilege. Through the machinery of the market, we decide what will be planted and harvested on farms worldwide. Our tastes determine whether farm workers will plant subsistence crops for themselves or market crops for us. Our institutional preference for cheap fare determines how food gets produced and processed in this country and as far away as China. When we open our mouths to eat, we are expressing an opinion that is taken very seriously in farm fields and food factories around the world. Students at college haven't generally considered the consequences of that power, and so their choices don't always reflect their deepest values.

It's not common sense to think so, but the cafeteria is a classroom, and the curriculum of Cafeteria 101 is as important as any other class at college, reflecting earlier socialization in food rules and dining etiquette, affluence and the ideology of choice, entitlement and expectations, work and class, ignorance and indifference. Students digest these lessons as much as they digest the food, learning a lot when they think they're not learning: lessons about culture and nature that carry over into the rest of life. But there's still more to discover before the final exam.

The Agriculture of the Cafeteria

The cafeteria is where most students encounter agriculture. Even at land grant universities, which were designed to offer civic instruction in farming, most students don't learn about farming in classes anymore, and the major crop on campus is typically the lawn—harvested weekly and then discarded. Few students at any college grow their own food, relying instead on the work of farmers, fishers, fruit growers, and ranchers in other places.

Eating in the college cafeteria, students depend on a complex of agricultural institutions that have developed over time. When Joe and Jo College devour the contents of their plates, they eat food that is delivered to them systematically. The cafeteria is just one small part of a food system, which is an intellectual and institutional infrastructure for the production, processing, distribution, marketing, preparation, and consumption of food.

Systems of Food

The system starts with agriculture, which is, simply put, an ecological strategy whereby *Homo sapiens* replaces native ecosystems with specialized fields in order to increase food supplies. A farm is, in ecological terms, a structured habitat in which humans take advantage of solar energy and the photosynthesis of plants to feed their families and others, and sometimes to feed livestock, which in turn feed humans. And farming works. In the last ten thousand years, human population has increased from a few million to more than six billion.

The American food system developed slowly, evolving from a wide variety of Native American methods practiced at the time of European contact to the full-fledged industrial agriculture of the present.

The first American food revolution came in the Columbian Exchange. When Columbus arrived in the Americas he didn't "discover" the world that Indians already knew perfectly well. But he and his successors did find foodstuffs that they sent back to Europe, with astounding culinary and cultural effects. Potatoes sailed to Europe where they became a staple of the peasant classes. In Russia, they were distilled into vodka. In Ireland, they supported the population until the Great Famine, when the lack of food drove millions of Irish immigrants to North America. Tomatoes also traveled to Europe, where they became an essential part of southern Italian cuisine. Any college student who eats a pizza topped with tomato sauce is eating one of the results of this first food revolution.[7]

On this side of the Atlantic, the Columbian Exchange created a whole new world. It brought new crops like wheat, oats, and barley, and a barnyard full of domesticated animals—cattle, pigs, goats, sheep, horses, and burros. European colonists adopted maize, a native plant, and added it to their inventory of grains. More importantly, they also brought their assumptions about agriculture (that land wasn't improved or productive unless it was under constant cultivation) and private property (that land could be owned by individuals instead of shared by tribes). Most devastatingly, they brought disease, which decimated Native American populations and ecological traditions. The result was a radical remaking of the American landscape, from cultivated wildness to cultivated domestication.[8]

The second American food revolution came in the nineteenth century, with the transportation revolution and the development of national and international markets for commodities like corn, wheat, beef, and pork. Chicago became the hub of a new food system that included ranches in the West, farms in the Midwest, grain elevators along everextending railroad lines, stockyards and slaughtering plants in the city, and a Board of Trade that stimulated the flows of commodities from farm to fork. For consumers, the result was a diet of great variety, delivered via steamship and steam engine from the four corners of the world. By the end of the nineteenth century, as historian William Cronon suggests, "The Iowa farm family who raised corn for cattle purchased from Wyoming and who lived in a farmhouse made of Wisconsin pine clothed themselves with Mississippi cotton that Massachusetts factory workers had woven into fabric, worked their fields with a plow manufactured in Illinois from steel produced in Pennsylvania, and ended their Sunday meal by drinking Venezuelan coffee after enjoying an apple pie made on an Ohio stove from the fruit of a backyard orchard mixed with sugar from Cuba and cinnamon from Ceylon." In a short period, local people learned to expect global trade that offered such delectable results that few people worried about any possible side effects.[9]

One of the significant side effects of the emerging American food system was distancing. Railroads overcame the vast distances of the continent, but at the same time they distanced urban consumers from the sources of their sustenance. In meatpacking, for example, the new system kept the killing of animals far from the ultimate consumers, who increasingly bought their meat in branded packages. "In the packers' world," says Cronon, "it was easy not to remember that eating was a moral act inextricably bound to killing. Such was the second nature that a corporate order had imposed on the American landscape. Forgetfulness was among the least noticed and most important of its by-products." This forgetfulness was an essential part of the American food system, and of the moral ecology of everyday life. We still inhabit this moral landscape of ignorance and forgetfulness. And sometimes our ignorance is not just what we don't know, it's what we know and choose to ignore.[10]

The third revolution in the American food system occurred after World War II. Left with an excess of wartime manufacturing capability, scientists converted wartime research on munitions into research on chemical fertilizers and studies of nerve gas to studies of pesticide production. So the "chemicalization" of farms quickly complemented the mechanization of agriculture. The result was huge monocultures of crops and animals, planted and cultivated by tractors and other machines, protected from natural predators by chemicals, and refined and reassembled by processors into what we call food. The number of farmers declined as the size and specialization of farms grew, with destructive effects on rural communities and culture. In the process, Americans reduced the biodiversity of farms and the biodiversity of their diet, so that almost two-thirds of our calories now come directly or indirectly from four crops: corn, soybeans, wheat, and rice. As a result, when we sit down to eat, we're consuming several centuries of food revolutions, reflecting radical and largely unsustainable changes in our relationship with nature, from seeds and soil to the food we pile on our plates.[11]

Global Foodshed

Today, we can't really see the sources of our food, so we need to imagine an enormous global network called a "foodshed." A foodshed is the area affected by our eating, encompassing the land whose nutrients flow in our direction. In the past, educational institutions depended mainly on local food, available at certain seasons of the year, and many colleges even operated their own farms. Now our foodshed is global because everything is in season somewhere on the planet and we want to eat it all.[12]

In many ways, this is wonderful. Despite their dietary reliance on corn, soybeans, wheat, and rice, Jo and Joe College can eat a diet of great variety. We think nothing—absolutely nothing—about exotic foods and foods out of season. We don't think twice about Ecuadorean bananas for breakfast, Chilean grapes with lunch, or New Zealand apples in our dessert. We enjoy what Michael Pollan calls the "transcontinental strawberry: five calories of food energy that use 435 calories of fossil-fuel energy to get to a supermarket near you." Sadly, most of us take no particular delight in strawberries in January, melons in the Christmas buffet, or lettuce throughout the year. In supplying these delicacies year-round, our food system has made the extraordinary ordinary, and even boring. Eating the world where and when we want it—which is usually here and now—we've diminished the seasonal pleasures of eating.

This worldwide web of agriculture means that we consume oil with every bite we eat. Until the turn of the twentieth century, agriculture was a solar-powered process. But the invention of tractors and synthetic fertilizers—along with long-distance shipping of produce and commodities—added ancient sunlight, in the form of crude oil, to the food chain. This gradually transformed farms to rural factories in which the energy of the sun is converted to starches in plants that are consumed or converted to meat for sale in exchange for goods or money. In this way, nature's capital is converted to human capital, and nature's economy is converted to capitalism. Like the local supermarket, the college food service now depends on the fossil fuels used to plant crops, fertilize fields, harvest crops, and bring food from the fields to students' tables. Americans invest about ten calories of fossil fuels—in farming inputs, processing, packaging, and transportation—for every calorie of food energy we produce. So a diet of two thousand calories a day is also a diet of twenty thousand fossil-fuel calories. Though students often complain about greasy food in the cafeteria, they don't generally notice the oily ingredients that don't affect the taste or stain the napkins.[13]

When we fork food into our mouths, therefore, we participate in the cycles of modern American agriculture, which is a technological success and an environmental disaster.[14]

Cartoon by Tom Toles. Reproduced by permission of Andrews McMeel Publishing.

The Nature of Hamburgers

Let's get more specific and think about the nature of some favorite foods to consider our sustenance not just as stuff on the plate but as a set of relationships to the planet. A hamburger, for example, is a cultural creation that usually consists of a cooked meat patty presented artfully in the clutches of a white-bread bun. A simple sandwich weighing about a quarter of a pound, a hamburger is a quick meal, but its natural and cultural complexity makes it a challenge to digest—at least intellectually.

Indeed, even before a hamburger disappears down the digestive tract, it's virtually invisible to most of us. Common sense tells us, for example, that eating a hamburger is no big deal. But a burger is just one small portion of the problem of invisible complexity. When we consume a hamburger, we consume the all-beef patty, the bun that is carefully sized to make the small burger seem big, the ketchup, mustard, onions, pickle relish, and other condiments. But we are also indirectly eating other resources. The meat of the matter is, of course, meat. As we chomp our hamburger, we are devouring the meat protein that defines the American diet. Despite the rise of vegetarianism, ours is still a meat-and-potatoes culture. Indeed, the average North American devours more than twice the daily protein requirement—about 178 pounds of meat a year. In addition, we are consuming the resources that cattle consume in the process of becoming meat. In eating one pound of hamburger, we are, for example, consuming the two hundred gallons of water it takes to make the beef. We are also swallowing the five pounds of grain—usually corn—that it takes to make that pound of burger.[15]

When Joe College eats a hamburger, he also eats dirt. He doesn't eat it directly, of course, but he does eat dirt because the grain that farmers grow depends, like the cotton in our shirts, on agricultural practices that cause soil erosion. In 1997, the Natural Resources Conservation Service estimated that American farmlands lose 1.9 billion tons of topsoil a year, which is twenty-five times faster than nature can replace it. Mining the soil, we extract its minerals and nutrients in the form of plants we feed to people and other animals. But when we don't add back what we subtract, our food and farming don't add up to sustainability.[16]

Amazingly, a few other things we consume are even less appetizing than dirt. Usually, for example, when we eat a hamburger, we get some grease, because ground beef is generally made from fattier cuts of beef. But we are also guzzling oil, which is used to make fertilizers and pesticides for crops, and to fuel the tractors that cultivate the grain fields. And though the fertilizer helps a lot on farm fields, it's hard to keep it there. In fact, fertilizer runoff from farmland creates a dead zone in the Gulf of Mexico that doesn't have enough oxygen to support aquatic life. The nutrients that flow into the Mississippi River watershed feed phytoplankton in the Gulf, which die and decompose at the bottom of the water. Because this process takes virtually all the water-borne oxygen in the area for decomposition, the shrimp, fish, and other marine organisms that need oxygen for survival are asphyxiated. If your burger tastes a little fishy, then, this might explain it.

On a social level, we also ingest images of the good life with our hamburger, images that are sold to us through ads for fast food, images that promise family feeling and friendly fellowship if we eat under the golden arches. We are swallowing peculiar concepts of quickness and convenience, saving time in a society running at such a breakneck pace that fast food is an attractive option. Even though the cafeteria isn't branded like Burger King or Subway, it's a part of a fast-food culture in which the speed of eating often supersedes culinary pleasures.[17]

You Want Fries with That?

Students know how to eat french fries before they come to college. Americans learn to love them early in life, usually at McDonald's and

 other fast-food outlets. Kids learn that the correct answer to the question, "Do you want fries with that?" is "Duh!" And we learn that all french fries should approximate the McDonald's ideal. The average American eats about thirty pounds of french fries a year, and American college students certainly keep pace.

The nature of french fries begins with the nature of potatoes. The potato is a member of the nightshade family of plants, and is usually cultivated for its tuber, a large packet of starch that develops underground. Almost 80 percent of potatoes used for french fries in the United States grow in Idaho and western Washington. The Idaho Potato Commission has branded "Idaho potatoes" so well that we tend to think of them as a force of nature. But, in fact, they're a force of culture, and specifically agriculture, as potatoes are not native to Idaho. Settlers unsettled the original landscape by uprooting the native vegetation and planting more than four hundred thousand acres of Idaho in tubers. When you look at a field of Idaho russets, what you're seeing is affirmative action for potatoes.[18]

Before the industrialization of potatoes, Americans raised several different strains of the plant. These days, the variety of potatoes is less important than their predictability, and so just a few types of tuber provide most of our french fries. The star of spuds is the Russet Burbank, which grows in huge irrigated fields that suck water from the Snake and Columbia rivers. Damming the Snake for potatoes and power means that most of its riparian habitat has disappeared, sturgeon populations have declined, and salmon can no longer swim and leap up the river. Our french-fried potatoes ruin rivers, but no one can taste that in the cafeteria.[19]

In order to achieve "perfect-sized" potatoes, and because potato pests, weeds, and fungi love massive monocultures, growers spray potato fields regularly with chemical fertilizers and toxins like Bravo and Monitor. To reduce spraying, Monsanto briefly marketed disease-resistant, genetically modified potatoes under the NewLeaf label. Consumer worries about the genetic modification of foods caused McDonald's and Pringles to suspend purchases of this biotech brand in 2001, however, and Monsanto discontinued sales.[20]

The transformation from tuber to tater, from nature to culture, begins immediately after harvest. The first three weeks are dedicated to the curing process. Newly harvested potatoes are too sugary, and need time to convert their sugars to starches. After this brief rest, they are shipped to the processing plant, where samples are inspected while the bulk of the crop is cleaned, peeled, scrubbed, and visually inspected for rot and disease. Machines then slice potatoes and cut them into strips, electronically inspect them for defects, and shake out smaller pieces. The spuds are next blanched to remove natural sugars, stabilize enzymes, and create a uniform texture. After time in a gas-powered dryer, the potato strips are immersed in a fryer for a minute or two. Precooled to zero degrees Fahrenheit, they are then fast frozen at forty degrees below zero. At that point, they're ready for branding and bagging, and the long trip to restaurants, supermarkets, and college cafeterias across America.

Frozen potatoes—like other frozen foods—require ten times more energy than fresh fruits and vegetables, energy provided partially by the dams on the Snake and Columbia rivers. Freezing today also requires hydrofluorocarbon coolants, which don't deplete the ozone like the chlorofluorocarbons of the past, but still add greenhouse gases to the atmosphere. But because they're convenient, Americans now eat more frozen french fries than fresh potatoes.[21]

Frying the frozen potatoes is another step in the acculturation of nature. Cooking is the process of converting raw nature into culture, specifically food. It's one way that humans make nature more palatable. One common way to make carbohydrates more appetizing is to slather them with fat. We eat bread *and* butter, macaroni *and* cheese, baked potatoes *and* sour cream, mashed potatoes *and* gravy. French fries conform perfectly to this culinary rule, transforming potatoes into a "delivery vehicle for fat."[22]

When potatoes are french fried, they're submersed in boiling oil, which causes the starch inside the fry to puff up and soften, while the water inside turns to steam and heads for the surface. The moving steam blocks the oil from penetrating the potato, and causes the potato's surface to fry up crisp and golden. In the process, a potato, which is a decent nutritional package, becomes a weighty issue, with half of its fat coming from the oil it's fried in.[23]

The oil used for french fries is literally the fat of the land, since it's extracted from plants—like corn—that transmute sunshine into caloric packets of energy. Even though vegetable oils are a "healthy" alternative to animal fats, they still transform a few ounces of potatoes into a fat-filled finger food. But "we like fries not in spite of the fact that they're unhealthy but because of it." We know that if food is bad for you, it often tastes good. And there may even be evolutionary reasons for these peculiar tastes. Over time, human beings have evolved with a set of tastes and culinary preferences retained for their survival value. We seem to have developed a "thrifty gene" which helps the body store fat against the vicissitudes of nature. In hunter-gatherer cultures, people often experience seasons of want amid seasons of plenty, and fat helps them survive the starving times. American college students no longer live in such a culture of scarcity, but human bodies are still built with that biology. So the sugar of a soft drink and the fat of french fries both offer us neurobiological rewards that may contradict our better judgment.[24]

Every time Jo College eats french-fried potatoes in the college cafeteria, she's participating in this food chain. Each french fry embodies soil and sunshine, water and the health of rivers, chemicals and electricity, fossil fuels and fat. The ideas and institutions that feed us hamburgers and fries are part of the moral ecology of everyday life. They are ecological because they tie us to a web of relationships. They are moral because they are concerned with questions of the good life and questions of justice. The beliefs and behaviors that are cooked into a cafeteria meal are emblematic of the "invisible complexity" of our lives; we do not see them any more than we see air, but they structure our lives and relationships every minute of the day. Every time we stuff a french fry into our mouths, we're voting for a food system that keeps us distanced from the real consequences of our consumption. But it doesn't need to be this way.

Eating as if Nature Mattered

In *The Nature of Design*, David Orr summarizes the shortcomings of the American food system:

> We take great pride in being the best, and most cheaply fed
> people in history. But we are fed by a ruinous fossil-fuel-powered
> industrial system that contributes to climatic change, water pol-
> lution, biotic impoverishment, depletion of groundwater, and
> soil loss. It exploits labor and rural communities and undermines
> future productivity of the land. The system encourages obesity,
> cancer, and heart disease—all signs of a national eating disorder.
> Given its scale and complexity, it cannot work responsibly, nor

can consumers, ignorant of how it works, eat responsibly. The system dominated by large agribusiness firms, petrochemical companies, and seed companies undermines democracy. In fact, it works only to the extent that real democracy does not work and people do not know these things or do not see them as part of a larger pattern or fail to see opportunities to create a better food system.[25]

Extensive pleasure: The pleasure derived from living in right relation to the world. Eating is one example. Good food tastes delicious, but when you know that food has been carefully and conscientiously prepared, from farm to fork, it tastes even better. Stylish clothes are cool, but they're even better when they're cool to the people who make them and for the planet as well.

In "The Pleasures of Eating," Wendell Berry suggests that industrial agriculture has produced industrial eaters, people who, like most of us, eat meals of processed foods without consideration of the food's connection to land and water and sunshine, or to the work of cultivation and care. "The passive American consumer," Berry notes, "sitting down to a meal of pre-prepared or fast food, confronts a platter covered with inert, anonymous substances that have been processed, dyed, breaded, sauced, gravied, ground, pulped, strained, blended, prettified, and sanitized beyond all resemblance to any part of any creature that ever lived. The products of nature and agriculture have been made, to all appearances, the products of industry. Both eater and eaten are thus in exile from biological reality."[26]

Berry distinguishes between two types of pleasure in eating: intensive and extensive pleasures. Most of us focus on the intensive delights of eating—the sight and smell of food as it moves from our plates to our mouths, and its taste and textures as we eat. We focus on sensual pleasures—and this is good. But we also need to embrace the *sensible* pleasures of food—the ones that make sense of the complexities of farming and the future—learning to taste not just with our tongues, but also with our intelligence, imagination, and spirit. And that's the extensive pleasure: When our food comes from good places, good work, and good sense, it can be fulfilling as well as filling.[27]

Along with others, Berry suggests that good food is not simply the same as food that tastes good. Good food is eaten by people who

The Pleasures of Eating

Intensive Pleasures	Extensive Pleasures
Taste	Test (of right relation)
Texture	Context
Temperature	Global temperature
Spice	Space (for other plants and animals)
Epicurean	Ethicurean
Consuming food	Producing a food system
Oral	Moral
Sensory	Sensible
Personal choice	Systematic choice
Variety	Biodiversity
Plate	Planet
Mouth	Mind
Individuality	Solidarity
Ending my hunger	Ending world hunger
Here	Here and there
Now	Now and forever
Nutritious	Regenerative, nurturing the earth
Filling	Fulfilling

acknowledge dependence on farmers, soil, sunlight, water, weather, cooks, and healthy communities. Good food comes from good growing, from cultivation that produces grain and meat and vegetables in a respectful relationship to the Earth. Good food doesn't just come from the good Earth—it perpetuates the good Earth.

Eating with farming and the future in mind, we can produce a good food system. In making wise dietary choices, and in supporting changes in institutional food practices, students are changing the world of food, creating a new system that feeds people well, operates on solar power, conserves biodiversity, returns nutrients to the soil, and produces a harvest that can last forever. Fortunately, some of the components of a better food system are in place on America's college campuses. And luckily, when it comes to food, there are many different ways of doing things right.

Vegetarianism and "Vergetarianism"

On many campuses, the first course of a new food system includes vegetarianism and "vergetarianism." More than 10 percent of college students are vegetarians, and nearly a fourth of students like seeing vegetarian options in the food line. In *The Consumer's Guide to Effective Environmental Choices*, Michael Brower and Warren Leon try to help people understand which environmental choices matter most, and which choices aren't worth worrying about. For common American consumers, the most beneficial change we could make in our everyday activity is driving less. The second is eating less meat. Livestock farming worldwide generates 18 percent of greenhouse gas emissions—more than all transportation technologies combined. The fact that more grazing land typically means a decrease in forests, which sequester carbon, and that the manure and other exhalations of the world's livestock generate nitrous oxide and methane—with almost three hundred times and twenty-five times the warming effect of carbon dioxide, respectively—only makes things worse.[28]

Vegetarianism used to be, at its worst, the bland feeding the bland. But "vegetarian cuisine" is no longer a contradiction in terms, and vegetarian entrées are increasingly delectable. The National Association of College and University Food Services (NACUFS) regularly features vegetarian menu-planning workshops at their conferences and reports that many college dining services now offer vegetarian menus. Some of the food services even offer vegetarian focus groups, where students can weigh in on the types of vegetarian offerings they'd like to see served.[29]

Another good eating option is "vergetarianism." Vergetarians (people on the verge of vegetarianism) include small amounts of protein-rich meat in a diet that's high in grains, legumes, and other vegetables. They maintain the pleasures of eating animal flesh, especially responsibly raised livestock like grass-fed beef and free-range chickens, which can flourish on land that's not well suited to tilling or cultivation. Scientists estimate that if every American reduced meat consumption by 20 percent, it would reduce greenhouse gas emissions as much as if we all switched from normal cars to hybrids, so vergetarians could make a significant difference in the world.[30]

Locavores

Local foods solve some of the problems of the American food system. Fresh, humane, and affordable, they reduce energy costs for freezing, refrigeration, and packaging, as well as fuel costs for shipping. They also call us to think about the nature of our place, about biodiversity on farms, and the benefits (and costs) of eating seasonal foods. They reduce the role of intermediaries, and keep money in the local economy, instead of shipping it out to agribusiness conglomerates and multinational corporations. They allow us to be "locavores."

When we eat locally, we often eat fresh. In the American food system, the word "fresh" has been completely redefined. In most contexts, it means "recently made, produced, or harvested; not stale, spoiled, or withered." But in the supermarket and in restaurants, "fresh" means anything that advertisers can imagine. It sometimes means not canned, frozen, or preserved, but even those products can be advertised as "packed fresh."

When we eat locally, we also eat seasonally. Ever since fossil fuels entered the American food chain in the nineteenth century, we have eaten a diet determined by what we want, not by what's growing here this season. While some older people wait patiently for seasonal foods—asparagus in the spring, strawberries in June, sweet corn in August, apples in the fall—many college students don't even know when different fruits and vegetables are in season because they're always in season in the supermarket or the cafeteria. Americans believe that variety is the spice of life, and in the past century we've increased the variety in our meals by shipping it from elsewhere, even another hemisphere. In the twenty-first century, however, we might not be able to afford the environmental costs of such global consumption. If we eat locally, our variety will need to come from our culinary imaginations, and not as much from the cornucopia of food we can ship or fly across oceans and continents.[31]

Organic foods

Another course in a new college food system is organic food—crops cultivated without industrial inputs like pesticides, herbicides, antibiotics, hormones, or chemical fertilizers. Students who prefer organic foods are concerned not just with the consumption of food, but the production of food as well. They are concerned that the chemicals that poison weeds and pests also eventually poison people and ecosystems. They know that the fertilizers that maximize midwestern crop yields also maximize the size of the dead zone in the Gulf of Mexico. And they know that one of the major harvests of pesticide use is pesticide-resistant pests.[32]

In 2001, the organic food movement on college campuses got a major boost when Alice Waters, co-owner of Berkeley's Chez Panisse, helped

Yale develop its Sustainable Food Project. Focusing on food, agriculture, and sustainability, the project's organizers hoped to offer students both the understanding and the experience of sustainable eating. "The way we eat every day is a moral act," says Josh Viertel, codirector of the project. "Serving organic food can be part of a greater educational experience here." Bates College is another leader in organic experimentation. In 2008, an anonymous donor gave $2.5 million to help the Bates food service add organic options to the menu.[33]

Farms are also cropping up at colleges across the country. At St. Olaf College, for example, a sophomore named Dayna Burtness returned to school in the fall of 2004 from a summer working on a community-supported agriculture (CSA) farm. Inspired by the experience, she proposed a small farm at St. Olaf—which had its own farms until the 1960s. The answer was a resounding "no." It didn't make sense. Who would run the farm in the summer? Who would eat the produce? How did this make sense at all for a liberal arts college?[34] Undeterred, Dayna went to the college food service, Bon Appétit, and asked if they might buy any produce from a farm she didn't yet have permission to start. "Sure," they said, "we'll buy all of it!" With a willing buyer, Dayna and her collaborator Dan Borek went back to the college, and the St. Olaf Garden Research and Organic Works (STOGROW) started the next summer. In 2007, the students grew twenty thousand pounds of vegetables. That same year, STOGROW received a three-thousand-dollar award from Bon Appétit as one of the five best farms it works with nationally. All along, the student farmers have taught other students not by the book, but by example. "Most students know that St. Olaf has an organic farm," Burtness notes, "and while they might not know the finer details of what it means to be organic and why local foods are better for the environment, words like 'organic' and 'local' are entering the dialogue on campus." That's no small feat. Sometimes small experiments yield large harvests.[35]

Permaculture

Permaculture is one name for a new agriculture whose practitioners seek to supply human needs within the boundaries of nature. According to Bill Mollison, who coined the term, permaculture is "the conscious design and maintenance of productive ecosystems that have the diversity, stability, and resilience of natural ecosystems. It is the harmonious integration of landscape and people providing their food, energy, shelter, and other material and nonmaterial needs in a sustainable way." It's a design system based in biomimicry, trying to adapt nature's "pattern language" to a culture's need for food. The idea is to establish communi-ties of plants that can produce food permanently by working with na-ture instead of against it. And unlike most kinds of industrial agriculture, permaculture sustains the Earth by *creating* topsoil and dynamic habi-tats, instead of using them up.[36]

Permaculture: 1) The agriculture of forever, cultivating plants and animals in perennial, closed-loop systems; 2) The culture of permanence, cultivating human beings in cultures rooted in the land and in an ethic of ever-after, practicing regenerative design in all aspects of living.

One of the most prominent proponents of permaculture is Wes Jackson of the Land Institute in Kansas. Jackson and his research team are trying to design an agricultural system patterned on a naturally functioning midwestern prairie—a perennial polyculture of complementary plants that should be both more resilient and more sustainable than the an-nual monocultures of industrial agriculture. Researchers, therefore, are working to breed annuals like wheat, sorghum, and sunflowers into perennials, while simultaneously trying to transform productive peren-nials like the Illinois bundleflower into a harvestable plant. Compared to the monocultures of mainstream agriculture, perennial polyculture would increase biodiversity, reduce soil erosion, and cut back inputs of fossil fuels, fertilizers, and pesticides.[37]

One of the best examples of permaculture is Polyface Farm, featured in Michael Pollan's book, *The Omnivore's Dilemma*. On one hundred acres in Virginia, "grass farmer" Joel Salatin raises cattle, pigs, rabbits, turkeys, chickens (and eggs), as well as sweet corn, tomatoes, and berries—with a far greater yield per acre than any industrial farm. In a normal year, the small farm produces 360,000 eggs, 10,000 broilers, 800 stewing hens, 25,000 pounds of beef, 25,000 pounds of pork, 1,000 turkeys, and 500 rabbits. Unlike those who run factory farms, where plants and animals are forced to produce by any means possible (including chemicals, hor-mones, and confinement), Salatin pays close attention to the nature of his plants and animals, rotates them to minimize stress on the land, and tries to understand how he can work best with the animals he is asking to produce for him. He speaks, for example, of the "chickenness" of his chickens, and tries to structure their days so that they're engaged in the pleasures of playing chicken, instead of being cooped up their entire

lives. Rather than engage in the radical simplifications of industrial agriculture, Salatin celebrates the complexities of natural systems. As a
result, in his pastures he produces not just meat, poultry, and fodder,
but topsoil, beneficial bugs, and beauty, too. Unlike most farms, which
undercut the natural capital they depend on, Polyface Farm shows that
food production can be good for people and for nature.[38]

There aren't yet many examples of such permaculture on college
campuses, but few institutions are better placed than colleges to begin
the experiments that point in the direction of sustainable agriculture
in this century. At small colleges like St. Olaf or urban campuses like
Yale, the experiments would likely be small—or contracted to farmers with more land. But the nation's land grant colleges, which have
been leaders in industrial farming, might begin to turn their attention
instead to the complexities of an agriculture of permanence—farming
not just for the present, but for the future as well. Few lessons are as
important for the curriculum of the twenty-first-century ecological
revolution.[39]

Mindfulness

Some culinary activity in the cafeteria is consciousness-raising. At a solidarity meal, for example, students eat a meal common to some of the
world's poorest peoples—often rice and beans and water—and reflect
on issues of hunger and justice, and the hunger *for* justice. These simple
meals remind students that a college cafeteria is exceptional and that
most of the world's people never see such an assemblage of food. In
fact, in a world context, under-consumption is a more pressing problem
than overconsumption. Sometimes students collect the money they
would have spent on a normal meal, and send it to a group working on
worldwide hunger issues, like CARE or Heifer International. Almost
always, they think about food and justice. As LaDonna Redmond says,
"If sustainable food isn't for everyone, then it isn't sustainable." For most
students, what they eat in the cafeteria is "just food." But the "same old,
same old" of the college cafeteria could, in fact, become *just* food, food
that nourishes justice in the world.[40]

Grace, in its many different religious and cultural incarnations, is another practice of mindfulness, a blessing and thanksgiving occasioned
by eating. For Jo College, it's a personal ritual. But grace is also a cultural
pattern, a small act of considerable significance that situates food not

just on the plate, but in the cosmos. It's a way, too, of acknowledging the connectedness of things, the interdependence of peoples. A good grace acknowledges the giftedness of the universe, the contingency of existence, and the sheer joy of being alive. It's a way of acknowledging the miraculous nature of everyday life. We say grace at meals, but we can *experience* grace all day long.

Such mindfulness isn't limited to religious people because all of us can honor the gifts of good land and human interdependence. All of us depend on processes that we don't entirely control—like photosynthesis and weather and health. And we depend on plenty of people we never see. I don't farm, but I eat. I don't make clothes, but I wear them. I don't make music, but I love it. We each have gifts we can give, and mindfulness (whether grace or not) helps us remember what we do share with each other, and what we *ought* to share.

A meal is a good time for mindfulness and grace, because it is at least potentially a time for transformations. A meal represents a place where sunshine becomes sustenance, where the free gift of photosynthesis comes home, where nature becomes culture. Grace is thanks for nourishment. But mindfulness is also nourishment for soul *and* society. It is a private practice of commitment, a habit that keeps both head and heart in the whole web of life. And if we act on our understandings, such mindfulness can help us think about how to heal the wounds of industrial agriculture.

Composting

When Joe College places his tray on the conveyor belt to the dish room, it moves out of sight and out of mind, and the leftover food generally moves to the garbage dump. In the cafeteria, by an interesting cultural alchemy, this perfectly edible, untouched food is made into garbage, which is essentially the result of a lack of imagination. It's what David Orr calls a "social trap." We don't want a lot of garbage, but we live in a society organized to produce it, and designed *not* to produce a wiser way of dealing with it. And so, as individuals, our only rational option is to throw it out. Maybe that's why we call it refuse—because it is our way of refusing to deal with the consequences of our consumption.

Some colleges, however, are turning the problem around by turning garbage over. At St. Olaf in 2004, for example, students collected garbage for a week to gauge the full weight of their waste. Their work allowed the college to buy a composter that converts all food waste—including meat, dairy, and even napkins—to mulch and fertilizer in three to four weeks. When school is in session, the college composts about one thousand pounds of organic material every day, keeping 190,000 pounds of garbage out of the landfill every year, and creating tons of free fertilizer to feed the flower beds and agricultural lands. As William McDonough says in *Cradle to Cradle*, "Waste is food."[41]

The Politics of Food

Some students have changed their diets or their culinary practices. Some have pressured their food service to offer ecologically edible options. But even when they nibble away at the cultural dimensions of agriculture on campus, the systemic problems persist because they are bigger than a single college's consumption. So some students have also tried to change the food system itself. They note that everyone inevitably takes part in the politics of food, in which decisions about what to plant at the farm and what to eat in the cafeteria are almost always influenced by what is spent by the government. The politics of food in America dates back to colonial times, when governments placed bounties on wolves that were attacking livestock. In the nineteenth century, the politics of food involved battles over railroad regulation and credit policies. These days, unfortunately, most food politics are camouflaged in legislation typically called a farm bill instead of a food bill. So college students and other consumers typically don't know how government spending shapes our choices about what's for dinner tonight.[42]

The main goals of U.S. farm policy are to increase the yield of food and profits that can be harvested from American fields. Farm legislation tries to keep commodity prices low, in order to keep consumers and processors happy. Though the plight of the family farmer is often invoked, bills are really intended to increase agricultural exports, both for the benefit of farmers and agribusinesses like Cargill and Archer Daniels Midland (ADM). Farm bills tend to promote free trade on the assumption that it increases efficiency. At the most basic level, they are designed to keep those farmers in business who adapt to the demands of modern industrial agriculture. Politically speaking, U.S. farm policy persists largely because it secures votes in important farm states like Iowa. It gives us plenty to eat, but also plenty to think about.[43]

The side effects of American agricultural policy include the near-extinction of farmers, more factory farms, more farmers working second and third jobs, a less robust rural culture and economy, increased fossil-fuel inputs and greenhouse-gas emissions, environmental degradation—including loss of topsoil, pollution of rivers, and depletion of groundwater supplies—and fatter consumers.[44]

Despite the efforts of groups like the National Sustainable Agriculture Coalition and the Institute for Agriculture and Trade Policy, Congress wrote a new farm bill in 2008 that was pretty much like the old one, thus missing an opportunity to rethink the politics of food. On the margins, it did extend the Conservation Reserve Program, the Conservation Stewardship Program, and the Organic Agriculture Research and Extension Initiative. The bill also added a Biomass Crop Assistance Program, new programs to make conversion to certified organic production a little easier, as well as small incentives to help young people get into farming, and to encourage farmers' markets and community food projects. But these were all dwarfed, as usual, by the commodity-support programs and a system of deregulation and subsidies that work to the advantage of food conglomerates. In the past thirty years, advocates of sustainable agriculture have made inroads into government programs, with legislation like the 1990 Organic Foods Production Act and programs like the Alternative Farming Systems Information Center in the Department of Agriculture. And yet entrenched interests, which include consumer demand for cheap food, have prevented any real systematic changes to the way we farm.[45]

Farm policy is only one element of the politics of food, however. Lobbying and sponsorships by the food industry also shape our thinking, our cafeteria choices, and, ultimately, our bodies. Lobbying prevents government agencies from telling the truth—in the food pyramid, for example—because food companies make more money when people eat more. Often, food companies place business interests above public health, sponsoring scientific research, journals, and professional societies, and publishing "fact sheets" that are routinely used in schools to educate students about "healthy" eating. They also take advantage of the underfunding of U.S. schools by offering payments for sponsorships. Soft drink companies, for example, pay schools for "pouring rights," and reward schools if soda sales increase. By the time that students come to college campuses, therefore, their tastes and food preferences have been thoroughly politicized. We may have had some cursory instruction in nutrition, but we still don't know much about the kind of eating that might be healthy for bodies, families, friends, communities, and the Earth.[46]

As this suggests, the most powerful politics of food is not narrowly political; the most powerful politics of food is the politics of common sense. When common sense tells us that we should eat what's served in the cafeteria or fast-food restaurants without considering ecological impacts, that's a powerful political achievement. When common sense tells us that a supermarket is the best place to get our food, that's political. When food companies distract us with "nutritionism" and images of sociability, they get to shape the real politics of food. And when we sit down to eat uncritically, we help to reproduce the politics of a food system that eats ecosystems for breakfast—and lunch and dinner and snacks. Until we conquer the politics of consciousness—until we craft a more conscientious common sense—we'll be on the losing side of the politics of food.[47] But when we see food as a set of relationships instead of a menu of edibles, when we pay attention to the sources and resources involved in our food, when we decide to enjoy the extensive pleasures of eating, and when we vote as if the health of the planet was at stake, then there's a chance for a more complex and sustainable agriculture.[48]

When we sit down to eat we're impacting the environment whether we know it or not. We're also practicing our environmental values, whether we intend to or not. Sitting at the table with our friends, we're changing the world, for better or worse. But we always have choices.

The dinner table is where each of us is nourished by the bounty of the Earth, where we can experience the intensive pleasures of food—its tastes and textures, its colors and aromas. It is where we can see what happens when nature meets culture in the form of food, and where we can use our power as consumers to choose not just what we eat, but the food system we eat in. It is a place where we might also experience the delectable—and extensive—pleasures of good food that nourishes people who nourish the Earth.

5

The Nature of Cars

I think that cars today are almost the exact equivalent of the great Gothic cathedrals: I mean the supreme creation of an era, conceived with passion by unknown artists, and consumed in image if not in usage by a whole population which appropriates them as a purely magical object.
Roland Barthes, "The New Citroen"

The car has become a secular sanctuary for the individual, his shrine to the self, his mobile Walden Pond.
Edward McDonagh, "Lincoln and Modern America"

Crap, I'm a problem.
St. Olaf student, reading an early version of this chapter

■ ■ ■ ■ ■ ■ ■

Most college students come to school in cars. On move-in day each year, they use more and more horsepower to carry the couches, chairs, carpets, TVs, video-game consoles, stereos, lamps, and other "necessities" of college life to campus. Parents and hometown friends usually depart at the end of move-in day, but many cars stay along with the students. For Americans, automobiles are something we believe we need. In a 2009 Pew Research Center survey, 88 percent of the population ranked cars as a necessity—higher than any other item. Even though humans lived meaningful lives for thousands of years before cars were invented, today it seems we can't live without them.[1]

Though most college campuses are relatively compact, 86 percent of collegians embrace America's belief in cars, saying that having one is crucial. Sixty percent actually owned cars in 2006. Students think about a number of things when they buy cars—appearance and styling (96 percent); design and quality (96 percent); and value for the money (96 percent)—but environmental concerns don't surface overtly in the data. Costs are, of course, a significant factor for "poor college students," but—as with other Americans—Jo and Joe College don't usually think much about the environmental costs of cars.[2]

This isn't entirely surprising, because advertisers help us *not* think about the nature of cars. In 2004, students spent almost $15 billion purchasing 1.5 million cars. Knowing that brand loyalty begins early, manufacturers market directly to students in the hopes of cornering a huge group of buyers. They do so by placing their cars in the TV shows, video games, and music videos young people like to watch. Toyota even used a modified Scion xB as a podium for DJs in dance clubs. When it's time to graduate, companies try to seal the deal with special offers for the seniors, who are perfectly seasoned to choose the "right" car.[3]

Because few professors teach anything about cars, these ads—along with parents, friends, consumer reports, and Internet forums—form the bulk of American automotive education. Even though cars aren't in the curriculum, they still drive environmental and social patterns at U.S. colleges and universities, which tacitly conform to the main tenets of automotive culture. Celebrating the life of the mind in classrooms, students are usually not mindful of the vehicles parked and passing outside. Although cars and SUVs are radically changing the natural world, they seem perfectly natural, almost part of the campus landscape.

Even at small colleges, cars make a big environmental difference. In 2004, my Campus Ecology class calculated the total miles driven by faculty and staff in getting to school from their homes: The total for 763 people for a single day was 19,778 miles, nearly four-fifths the circumference of the Earth. Individually, commuting is just a minor nuisance, but collectively it's a major contributor to greenhouse gas emissions.[4]

Cars are a solution to many American "problems," but they're a major problem for the planet. So we need to rethink the American "auto motive"—what moves people to drive cars—to imagine a campus and a culture where cars might be more than just an afterthought. If we understand how they work, culturally and ecologically, we might consider how to go about transforming cars and the car culture so that we actually get where we want to go.

Growing into Cars

In the United States, cars are conveyances, but they are also meaning machines. They transport passengers and freight, but also carry a crowd of assumptions and ideas. American students come to college already knowing what cars mean. While they are not usually a part of formal education, cars are still a required course in the hidden curriculum of American life.

Across the country, people grow up expecting that if they want to get anywhere in the world, they need to go by car. As a result, students come to college with an automotive mind-set. But this mind-set isn't simply logistical. In childhood, a car is associated with Mom and Dad, and takes on the deep emotional resonances you might expect from what we call "the family car." For children, 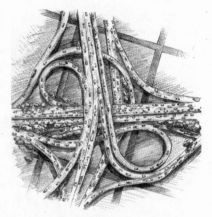 the family car is a safe space, a place for falling asleep to the rhythms of the road. In adolescence, when parents are often stressed and over-scheduled, driving time is often the best time for family conversations. When you're sitting in the car with Mom or Dad, it's easier to share stories, because, after all, this isn't "a talk"—it's just a drive. And you're not face-to-face, so somehow the words come easier. Many students also have pleasant memories of car trips: camping vacations, weekend visits to relatives, the time the family drove to Disney World.[5]

For most American kids today, cars are probably more natural than nature, the highway cloverleaf more common than clover leaves. Unlike children historically, they travel more miles by car than by foot. And with more and more families installing video systems in cars, kids may not even look out the windows anymore. They traverse a landscape without experiencing it; they may see it fleetingly, but otherwise they're senseless, missing out on the sounds and smells of the out-of-doors. Outside the car, away from the TV, the natural world doesn't seem natural anymore: It seems strange.[6]

A little later in life, cars are part of one of the most important rites of passage in our culture: getting a driver's license. For many students, the driver's license is what makes sixteen so sweet because cars enable a more active social life in high school. And since cars are among the gods of American culture, the driver's test is often more important than religious rites of passage like confirmation or the bar mitzvah.

A rite of passage is a ritual conceived by a culture to mark the transition of individuals from one status to another. Birth and birthdays, baptism and bar mitzvahs, weddings and funerals are among the rites of American culture. Coming-of-age—or proving oneself as an adult—is

a common rite of passage in all human cultures, usually involving train-
ing, preparation, purification, some kind of test, and a conclusive communal ritual in which the person's new status is recognized. The whole
process usually acquaints young people with the most important virtues
and values of the culture, along with a set of practices considered to be
crucial to thoughtful adulthood in the community.[7]

In America, we practice rites of passage, but we don't ritualize
coming-of-age very well. And driving a car doesn't teach the best
virtues and values of American communities; it teaches individualism and mobility, technological fundamentalism and environmental
obliviousness. We think that cars increase responsibility—we're responsible for the rules of the road, car payments, gas and insurance,
and chauffeuring ourselves to all the places we go—but driving a car
doesn't tell us much about responsible adulthood in the community
or on the planet.[8]

As young people are initiated into the cult of "carhood," automobiles become an essential part of the curriculum of high school—
not just the official driver's education, but the driver's education
that students teach each other. "In high school," recalls one student,
"I drove to and from school every day. I would also drive to stores
and to friends' houses in the evenings. On weekends, it was pretty
common to spend a night simply driving around with friends for a
couple hours with no target location in mind." Many high-school
students personalize their cars with styling and accessories such as
thumping new sound systems. In high school, the official curriculum
often becomes secondary to the social learning that revolves to a
great extent around cars.

Two years after they get a driver's license, about half of American
kids take part in a second rite of passage: going to college. By the time
they arrive on campus, most college students already understand the
common sense of cars—the essential assumptions all drivers have in
common. "Everybody knows" that Americans depend on their cars.
"Everybody knows" that Mom and Dad drive to work and to the mall,
to schools, supermarkets, sports events, and doctor appointments.
"Everybody knows" that everybody's kids will drive when they grow
up. It's just common sense. But this common sense keeps us from seeing and understanding the complexity of car culture, because common
sense is only what *everybody* knows—and there's a lot more to know
than that.

The Common Sense of Cars

The common sense of cars consists of ten interrelated ideas:

1. Cars represent autonomy, a mechanical declaration of independence, Emersonian self-reliance on wheels, and Whitman's song of the
open road. As vehicles for individualism, cars allow students to craft a
schedule without thinking about other people in their community. In
America's culture of time poverty they help college students, individually, to cope. Freed from the slow-motion of pedestrianism, from the
childishness of bicycles, from the rigid schedules of public transport,
they give students time for other pursuits of happiness.[9]

2. Cars represent mobility. They get us where we want to go and
away from where we are. According to sociologist Zygmunt Bauman,
Americans equate immobility with "social deprivation and degradation"; we love movement, and scorn stopping and stasis. So American
teenagers think nothing of driving five or ten miles to a movie, ten or
twenty miles to the nearest shopping center, or a hundred miles to a
campground instead of having a good time where they already are. Many
mammals are territorial, but not *Homo automotivo*—this animal prowls
a vast range limited not by the body's ability but by the car's.[10]

3. Cars represent power. They empower people who can run roughly
ten miles an hour on their own to go seventy miles an hour while barely
moving a muscle. Still, we don't often consider the physical power embodied in cars. We think more about the social power of cars because
they convert horsepower into social prowess. In a recent survey, more
than half of respondents claimed that they could tell what someone is
like from the kind of car he or she drives. In *Fast Cars, Cool Rides*, teenagers told Amy Best how cars allow us to perform ourselves, to try on
identities to see how we fit in by conforming to the automotive practices
of the group.[11]

Cars promise to power the transformation of the self. In automobile
ads, the nerd that buys a muscle car also purchases a new personality.
The woman who drives a sports car looks more adventurous, while in an
SUV anybody can be king of the road. And a luxury car screams financial success. Instead of developing our skills and talents, our character,
and our characteristic ways of engaging our communities—instead of

cultivating the values and virtues that might make us a person worth knowing—we can just slip behind the wheel of a "new and improved" stereotype and drive away with a mechanical personality.

On campus, having a car gives a student a certain cachet. A person's popularity depends on lots of factors—personality, talent, looks, interests, abilities, and congeniality, for example—but one of the factors is what we might call "caracter." More than the peons we call pedestrians, a car owner clearly possesses power—power to drive people to their destinations as well as power to loan a car. Often, there's an exchange involved: Riders pay for gas or do other favors for the driver. So sharing cars and sharing rides is part of an informal system of exchanges that can cement relationships on campus as well as strain them.

If your car happens to be "cool," so much the better. A Jeep Cherokee is better than the old Oldsmobile your parents drove for years. A Pontiac Vibe is better than a minivan. These rankings aren't just imposed on us by car ads—they're produced and reproduced by our own comments and compliments everyday.[12]

4. It's common sense that cars represent portable privacy and non-pharmaceutical stress relief. This small room on wheels allows college students to get away from annoying roommates and prying friends, and to listen to their own music at their own choice of volume, something that's not always permissible in a dorm room. In the personal space of a car, we can be selfish, going our own way, and thinking our own thoughts. We can also travel to anonymity—to a place where nobody knows our name. For one college student, driving is "my own personal way of dealing with stress, by myself, to 'get away from it all.'" And she's not alone. When the Pew Research Center asked Americans to say what they liked about driving, the largest number replied that they liked it for relaxation and quiet time, for being alone, for time to think or to unwind from a hectic day. Because we inhabit a frenetic and stressful culture, because we're "connected" almost everywhere else, we use our cars for "carcooning."[13]

Beyond this singular privacy of cars, there's also a shared privacy, especially for lovers. As early as 1905, the second verse of "In My Merry Oldsmobile" linked cars and courtship:

> They love to "spark" in the dark old park
> As they go flying along
> She says she knows why the motor goes
> The "sparker" is awfully strong

Each day they "spoon" to the engine's tune
Their honeymoon will happen soon
He'll win Lucille with his Oldsmobile
And then he'll fondly croon . . .

As historian Beth Bailey suggests, cars historically moved courtship from the front porch to the back seat. These days, in the car, college lovers can escape the school's gossip mill. Lovers can make out without being outed, enjoying intimacy independent of the judgment of others.[14]

5. Cars represent freedom. As one of my students says, "[My car] gives me the freedom to go where I want, when I want, no questions asked." Cars, we think, allow us to be spontaneous—and spontaneity, for college students, is associated with authenticity. Because cars take students away from authority (parents, priests, professors, and college staff), they also free them from the watchful eye of the older folks who have been restricting them all of their lives.[15]

One form of freedom is the escape. Cars are the getaway vehicle from a life of boredom and routine. Sometimes it's an escape to nature. From the very beginning cars have been sold as a technology that can bring urbanites into the countryside, offering access to the outdoors and to the virtues that nature offers. Henry Ford famously said, "We shall solve the city problem by leaving the city." And SUV advertisements often sound like Thoreau on the virtues of solitude in nature.[16]

One of the most popular escapes in college is "the road trip," a car odyssey with friends, with no serious purpose, one that involves driving quite a distance. Going to the city for a concert isn't a road trip, even if you stay overnight. On a road trip, the travel is as important as the destination—and sometimes there's no particular destination at all. The important elements are driving, music (sometimes singing), companionship, and the intensity of conversations that develop when compatible human beings are confined in a small space for a long time.[17]

6. It's common sense that cars are fun. Almost all cars are recreational vehicles, and almost all car ads represent recreational uses of cars. We seldom see the parental chauffeur, the driver running errands, the shopper in supermarket parking lots, or the commuter stuck in traffic. Instead we see the couple out for a date, the family on vacation, the SUV parked on a remote mountaintop. Despite the fact that these fun

scenes represent a small segment of driving time, the college-market research firm Student Monitor reports that 79 percent of college students
simply "enjoy the experience of driving." A recent Pew Research Center
poll shows that, within the last week, about a quarter of Americans have
taken a joyride, driving "just for the fun of it." Driving is, for most of us,
one of life's little pleasures.[18]

As this suggests, cars aren't just for driving to work; they're also
for driving to play. Cars get us where the action is—which implies, of
course, that there's not much action where we are. Cars get Joe and Jo
College to the dance club or the bar, and back again. They get students
to the Cineplex or the cool restaurant—the one that's too far from campus for just anybody to go. On Friday nights, the number-one question
at college is, "What are we going to do?" and the frequent follow-up is,
"Who can drive?"

7. Cars are sexy. In 2007 and 2008, for example, Volkswagen advertised
its cars by asking, "When you turn your car on, does it return the favor?"
In a weird way, cars are like lingerie for guys. With the right model, the
car's body can complement the man's body, adding muscle and hardness
to his image.[19]

Women's sexiness doesn't seem to depend on automotive props
as much. Sometimes SUVs and pickups add to a woman's sex appeal.
When SUVs became popular, for example, people expected that the
primary purchasers would be sporting men. But women also liked the
behemoths because they gave them a sense of power.

8. Common sense about cars definitely includes their convenience. As
one student says, "We want to be able to go anywhere WHENEVER we
want to go there." So the driver's seat is also the easy chair. At college, for
example, cars transport people, but they also serve as trucks, transporting stuff to and fro. Students need cars because they need so many other
things. Jo College needs a car to go to the grocery store. Her roommate
needs to borrow Jo's ride for a shopping run to Wal-Mart, K-Mart, or
Target. Joe needs a car to make the beer run, and he definitely needs a
car to go get gas. Cars are beasts of burden, and drivers consume them
getting to the places where they consume other stuff.

One of the conveniences of cars is saving time and human energy.
As one student suggests, "Cars speed up everything and also allow us to
pack more into our day.... What remains constant is that there are only
24 hours in a day. Cars make it possible to jam an extra run to the coffee

shop or grocery store into our day." Reducing travel time and increasing time for other activities, cars are a form of time travel.[20]

9. Cars represent comfort. With soft seats, increasingly made of leather, they embrace the human body with affection. With heating and air conditioning, drivers can control the temperature, creating the micro-climate in which *Homo automotivo* thrives. Car owners also comfort themselves in their cars by stocking them with food and drink, candy and coffee, baseball gloves and Frisbees, CDs and cell phones. We buy leather wraps for the steering wheel and accessories to play the iPod, which provides a soundtrack for the ride.

10. Cars are a form of technology, and they model our relationship with machines. Amazingly responsive, more than almost any other American artifact, they heed our wishes in ways we can really feel. Soon after you drop bread in the toaster, you get toast—but you don't get a visceral sense of toasting, unless you burn your hand. After you put warm beer in the refrigerator, you eventually get cold beer—but you don't actually feel it cooling. When you drive a car, however, you get a kinetic kick. Turn the key and the engine roars into action. Press the accelerator and feel the pistons pulsing. Floor it, and you can really feel the gravitational pull. All this power is at your command—and you *feel* it. When you move, the machine moves. It's not magic, but it feels that way.[21]

This sense of control is part of the attraction of cars. In a world that often seems out of control, our cars offer reassurance. More than any other technology of our lives, cars tell us that we can make machines that respond to our wishes. Cars are a tool for getting places, but they're also a tool for thinking—and they help us to think that technology is good for us.[22]

"Most college students," says one student, "do not see any reason not to use a car if it is available." This is common sense. Like other Americans, college students see cars as a technological fix for important aspects of the human condition. Americans have real needs, and cars fulfill a lot of them. That's why so many love cars, and why we depend on them so much. It's also why cars are such a difficult environmental problem.

The Uncommon Sense of Cars

Cars were created as a technological fix for problems in American so-ciety. They reduced urban congestion and the excremental solid waste that accompanied horse-drawn vehicles. They freed people from the fixed routes and schedules of public transportation, gave farm families access to the culture of cities, and helped urbanites get to suburbs with spacious yards and to the scenic wonders of the rural landscape. But as cars provided a solution for some twentieth-century problems, they drove us right into a twenty-first-century technological fix—a huge environmental problem caused by the solutions that came with cars. In order to get out of this mess, we'll need to question our common sense and complexify the mythology of cars to create new stories and images of transporting and transforming ourselves.

As noted earlier, cars represent autonomy, and they reinforce American values of individualism and independence. Autonomy, though, can express itself in troubling ways. As one student observes: "Driving a car is a selfish act. [Driving] inflicts externalities on society and the environment: pollutants in the form of carbon monoxide, VOCs [volatile organic compounds], CO_2, etc. Students and other drivers do not pay for the damages—asthma, climate change, smog—that these pollutants cause when they operate their vehicles." Cars are a driving force for the self, but also a driving force of selfishness.[23]

Cars offer college students autonomy, but they also engage them in an institutional gridlock that quietly controls "control" of the car. Though autonomy literally means "independence," the autonomy of cars is accomplished through a vast web of *inter*dependence. When we drive our cars, we're on our own, but we're not independent: We depend on manufacturers and mechanics, on gas stations and garages, on state road-building and repair, on traffic signals and police, and on all the other drivers. On an interstate highway, we depend even more on a complete system of engineering and traffic control. As author Jay Griffiths suggests, "The faster the traveler, the less autonomous they are, the more reliant they must be for safety on strict, exterior laws and the directions of systems. Speed fosters passivity. Driving at speed, the individual is *driven* by roads."[24]

Even though cars almost always operate on public infrastructure, they still reinforce American individualism. Protesting taxes, we forget that taxes pave the way for our mobility. Enjoying the private benefits of cars, we forget the public (and planetary) costs. And if paying those costs involves economic sacrifice or major changes to our lifestyles, we're likely to engage in "system justification"—a psychological motivation in which our "good" life justifies the status quo, and vice versa. A nation on wheels, therefore, is not always a nation concerned with commonweal. Cars help us to forget the health of the commons we always depend on.

Cars represent mobility, but they can also be roadblocks. Sometimes we really do just want to cruise, but most of the time we drive to gain access to people we want to see and places we want to be. We buy cars because we want to get somewhere. But then eventually we create more distant "somewheres" that are only accessible by car. And, as more and more somebodies need to get to those somewheres, more and more cars fill the road, forcing everyone in them to move very slowly. According to a 2005 report of the Texas Transportation Institute, the average delay in traffic for each American driver in 2003 was forty-seven hours—more than a full-time workweek. The total annual delay was 3.7 billion hours, wasting 2.3 billion gallons of fuel, and costing about $63 billion. Cars get us from one place to another eventually, but it's also the case that they just get in the way of other cars, and, ultimately, humankind.[25]

Cars reinforce our assumptions about mobility—that we should be able to go where we want when we want—but, ideologically and institutionally, they leave us in the same place: in a culture virtually immobilized by automobiles. We might like to drive to a cleaner future, but we've created a system that's friendly to cars and hostile to all other options. We've made it harder to walk, bike, bus, and travel by rail. Cars, therefore, leave us clutching individual freedoms that ultimately undermine other human freedoms—like the freedom to breathe clean air or to inhabit a stable climate system.

Cars definitely empower the individuals who drive them, but they also empower the companies who make them and the industries that service them. These powers, in turn, threaten the public's power to stop, or even alter, our driving. Whenever Congress considers a law that might threaten the corporate power of the car industry, lobbyists and campaign contributions speed from Detroit to the Capitol. Even though the results have been counterproductive to their success as businesses, the Big Three car companies (Ford, General Motors, and Chrysler) long exercised their political power to prevent more efficient forms of power for cars.[26]

Cars can give us social influence, but they require military influence to maintain the flow of gas to our tanks. Cars keep us importing oil, and exporting a foreign policy driven by that importation. Even though presidents and politicians don't like to say it, cars have twice helped drive us to war in Iraq. In a 2007 report titled "The Hidden Costs of Oil," the National Defense Council Foundation noted that the total external costs of importing oil—including direct and indirect economic costs, disruptions in supply, and military spending to protect oil supplies—rose from $305 billion in 2003 to $825 billion in 2005. If these costs were included in what we pay for gasoline, the pump price would rise by $8.35 per gallon. From this perspective, military and civilian casualties in Iraq aren't just a human tragedy; they're roadkill.[27]

Cars do provide privacy and at times that's just the right thing. But they also contribute to a pattern of privatization that may not be good for the social nature of human beings or the actual nature of the planet. "Carcooning" keeps us from public transportation, from simply walking through our communities, and from mixing with people who are different from us. The private pleasures of cars—*my* schedule, *my* route, *my* air conditioning—*my* music—reinforces American *my*opia, and may make us less tolerant of sharing and less concerned about the common good. The fact that many of our drives take us back to the residential segregation of the suburbs may also hinder our understanding of American diversity, and our ability to work with the diverse people who make up our country.[28]

Cars and car ads may reinforce our sense of freedom, especially our sense of personal liberty, but they also reduce our freedom by making us work longer hours to pay for them, for insurance, gas, gas taxes, and repairs. They are bounded freedom, and at times they impinge on the freedom of others. Although we consider them perfectly natural, cars restrict the freedom of pedestrians, who need to be alert not just to the nature around them but to the dangers of cars. "Look both ways," we tell our kids. Or else.

Our car culture also compromises our freedom *not* to have a car. Because America's infrastructure is designed for cars, it's not designed for people who don't want one or can't afford one. If Congress ever mandated cars, Americans would revolt at the infringement on our rights. But we submit willingly to a culture that essentially mandates a car for full participation in society and commercial culture.

On a deeper level, today's cars also tragically compromise the freedom of future generations to breathe clean air, inhabit a planet of biodiversity, and live in a world without global weirding.

Cars provide us with joyrides, road trips, and great escapes from the humdrum of daily life—but they can also restrict our imagination. In a time before automobiles, people learned to make do with the people near them. They created social occasions that didn't necessitate money or mobility, like cards, music, games, or even conversation. When you own a car, though, it's easier to go somewhere else for your satisfaction than to make it where you are. It's easier to go to the movies than to stay the course of a conversation that demands interpersonal engagement. It's easier to drive to commercial entertainments than to invent and engage in communal fun. Cars can drive us to distractions, but they can also drive us away from some of the central issues in human life.

Cars may sometimes seem sexy, but most of the time they don't. If you think about it, the comparison of automotive performance and sexual potency is preposterous. As Gregg Easterbrook says in *The Progress Paradox*, "Somehow Americans and Europeans have come to believe that a listless activity—sitting in a seat and pressing a pedal—represents virility. What could make a stupider metaphor for human self-expression than a car? Nothing is more demeaning than the idea that our cars say something about us." And nothing would be more refreshing than noticing the active sexiness of self-propelled people like bikers, joggers, swimmers, and pedestrians.[29]

Cars definitely reinforce our general thoughts on convenience. Joe and Jo College complain about parking at school because the lots are remote and it takes time to walk to and from their car. Coming from the land of private driveways and attached garages, most students are used to the car being convenient. They don't want to have to walk in order to drive. But some of us will drive to the gym in order to walk on a treadmill, and on breaks and vacations, of course, we often drive long distances just to walk in the wilderness.[30]

In college, the convenience of cars sometimes gets mixed with the consumption of alcohol, with disastrous results. Sometimes there are "designated drivers" or "sober cabs," but often drivers who've been drinking feel invincible and take chances under the influence that they wouldn't take when sober. Heavy drinkers are ten times more likely than other students to drive after drinking and seventy-four times more likely to drive after five drinks or more. According to a Harvard study of college drinking, 40 percent of college drinkers reported riding in a car with a driver who was drunk or impaired. And car accidents are still the number-one cause of death for young Americans. That's not exactly convenient.[31]

Cars seem convenient, but it is an inconvenient truth that convenience has costs, both social and environmental. Cars may minimize time spent in transport, but they increase time *paying* for transport because it takes time to make money for car payments, insurance, gas, and repairs. Adding to this factor, we often spend more time getting places by car than by other forms of transportation. Cars are convenient, but only because we define convenience so narrowly, seldom considering the whole cost.[32]

In *Walden*, Henry David Thoreau calculated that "the cost of a thing is the amount of what I will call life which is required to be exchanged for it, immediately or in the long run." By this standard, college students and other Americans exchange a lot of life for our automotive habits. In 2003, for example, the Bureau of Transportation Statistics showed that, on average, American households committed 19 percent of their spending to transportation, almost all of it in cars. This means that Americans exchange almost one-fifth of their time at work for their driving passions.[33]

Even though drivers move faster than walkers or bicyclists, cars haven't really reduced time spent in transport. As John Whitelegg says, "People consume the benefit of speed by spending it on distance." Marchetti's Constant (a term for the average amount of time spent traveling each day) suggests that, throughout history, human beings have spent about ninety minutes a day in movement. What's changed isn't the time, it's the distance. We cover more ground than our ancestors, but in part that's because we've created more space to cover. Today's commuters seem more modern than our ambulatory ancestors, but whether or not traffic congestion is progress is still an open question. In some ways, our travel—including car travel—has expanded to fill the time available.[34]

Cars do reinforce our commitment to comfort. With cushy leather seats, our butts become accustomed to these mobile thrones. With climate control at the touch of a button, our bodies become used to a bubble of good weather. With radios, CD players, and iPod converters, cars comfort us with our own choice of music. Unfortunately, our individual comforts are making the planet's climate system unpredictable, leading to storms, floods, droughts, and other difficulties that are decidedly *un*comfortable. Doubters claim that human influence on these changes is unproven, but insurance companies, the experts of risk, are reassessing the probabilities of environmental catastrophe, and car companies are weighing their liability risks in lawsuits like the ones that bedeviled the tobacco industry—proving the seriousness of the situation. As both businesses and governments begin to calculate the real costs of cars, everyday drivers will likely need to get comfortable with the idea of a world with fewer cars or less driving—or both.

Cartoon by Andy Singer. Reproduced by permission from the artist.

Cars model many of our relationships with technology, but—like many of our tools—they also mask important relationships and beliefs. The annual model change reinforces our sense of obsolescence and our sense of progress. The technical virtuosity of cars also keeps us thinking in the mindset of the technological fix, assuming that we can invent our way out of our environmental problems. We know cars are a major environmental menace, but we don't care to imagine life without them. So we dream about hybrids and "hypercars" and hydrogen fuel cells, imagining that a future technology will provide a quick fix for a careless culture of automobility.

In the twentieth century, people embraced the technology of cars because it was an improvement on the technology of horsepower. This technology was adapted to fit human needs, but now we have additional needs. We still want to travel using a cheap and flexible form of transportation, but we can't afford the so-called "side effects" of cars. So we need something new and improved. In the long run, we need regenerative design.

Comfearth: The amount of comfort that's consistent with sustainability.

In the twenty-first century, it's our task to reinvent cars and car culture so that they serve both human and natural communities. In the twentieth century, we adapted cars to our purposes and they worked. But in a process that we might call "reverse adaptation," we also began to adapt our culture to our cars. It's time now to think carefully about deeper human purposes, and to see what technologies might actually serve our best intentions for our lives and all life.

The Real Cost of Cars

College students pay a lot for cars, but—like other Americans—they aren't capable of seeing the real price tags. When they hop in the car to go to the movies or the liquor store, they're thinking more about the convenience than the cost, which is exactly what they're taught to do. But there are other very important costs to cars, especially in a culture where they're so common. Early in the twenty-first century, the number of registered cars in America surpassed the number of drivers. Today, 89 percent of the American population has a driver's license and most Americans use a car on most days. Our car trips total about six trillion miles every year. Whether we're making the beer run or taking a road trip, we're impacting the planet, mile after mile.[35]

Money

The cost we're most conscious of is gas, because we pay for it frequently. Fluctuations in the price of gas are among the few factors that actually affect our automotive behavior. As one collegian says, "Time and time again I hear students say that they don't want to drive somewhere because gas prices are so high, not because pollution levels are so high."

When gas prices rise, we drive less and think about smaller cars. When they drop, we don't think twice about driving, and we settle for the creature comforts of our turbo-powered SUVs.

But gas isn't the only energy we use in our cars. The car itself is "embodied energy": the total energy needed to extract, manufacture, and transport the car's raw materials—iron, steel, lead, aluminum, platinum, rubber, glass, and plastic—plus the energy needed to assemble it and truck it to a dealership. The World Carfree Network cites a 1990s German study estimating the environmental cost of producing one car: 26.5 tons of waste and 922 cubic meters of air pollution in the extraction and production of materials like iron, steel, zinc, lead, aluminum, copper, and platinum; 12 liters of crude oil leaked in the ocean and 425 cubic meters of polluted air in transporting the raw materials; 1.5 tons of waste and 74 million cubic meters of air pollution in producing the car. Historian Mark Foster estimates that "fully one-third of the total environmental damage caused by automobiles" occurs *before* they are sold and driven. Even though manufacturers have recently focused on achieving environmental efficiencies, cars still consume a lot of resources before we consume them.[36]

When we stop to fill up with gasoline, we're also paying state and federal taxes, usually about forty cents a gallon. Usually these taxes are dedicated to road repair and improvements, and might therefore be considered a "user fee." Sometimes they can *only* be used for maintaining roads and, therefore, maintaining a transit system in which mass transit and other alternatives are underfunded. Because gas taxes are charged at the pump, they also can have a useful effect on our driving habits. For instance, if we ever decided to give people incentives to drive less, a gas tax or carbon tax would be an effective motivator.

Another large monetary cost for cars is depreciation. As soon as it's manufactured, a car begins to deteriorate and depreciate. And it depreciates whether or not it actually deteriorates, because Americans are willing to pay a premium for the novelty of cars. On average, cars lose half their value every three years. The twenty-thousand-dollar car that Joe College bought sophomore year will be worth ten thousand dollars at graduation, making it a less-than-stellar investment. But we don't usually calculate that cost when we're picking up the pizza.

Insurance, especially for college students, is another big cost. Insurance rates are based on age, residence, driving experience, and driving history, which includes tickets, accidents, and license suspensions. For most college students, the critical variable is age. Young drivers are the worst risk for insurance companies—and males are worse than females. Just 7 percent of licensed drivers, teens from the ages of fifteen to twenty were involved in 18 percent of crashes and 14 percent of fatal accidents in 2003, making insurance costs for this age group very high. Even with a "good student discount" for high grades, it costs a lot to insure a car for a year. Sometimes parents pay the insurance for college cars, so the cost doesn't actually affect the driver's behavior. In either case, insuring a car is associated more with writing checks than actual driving. Because it's a more-or-less fixed cost, younger drivers don't consider insurance when they think about driving to the dance club.[37]

Road Kill

Another significant cost of cars is life. Each year, about forty thousand Americans die in car accidents, and even more are injured or incapacitated. Car accidents are the leading cause of death for drivers aged fifteen to twenty, and many college students have friends or classmates who have died. Death, therefore, is the ultimate price of an automotive way of life. We have high-profile panels to fight all sorts of diseases, but we take this human road kill for granted.[38]

Road Kill: A popular form of animal sacrifice in which we take life (including human life) to drive wherever we please.

In addition to human life, millions of animals die because of the environmental impact of a car bumper. Motorists—not hunters—kill about forty thousand deer a year in just one state—Ohio. The number is about sixty-five thousand in Pennsylvania. In the United States, there are about 1.5 million collisions with deer each year, with 150 human deaths, and $1.1 billion in property damage. And that is just one species.[39]

At the same time, polar bears are becoming another kind of road kill. Because of global warming, ice packs are melting in the Arctic Ocean, and polar bears drown trying to swim longer distances in the water. Even though our cars don't actually drive anywhere near the big bears, their environmental impacts do. And so our driving is driving some species to extinction.

Places

Cars transform places and the way we think about them. They affect the food system because automobile-fueled sprawl eats up 1.2 million acres of farmland every year, and they fragment habitats and ecosystems with roads, replacing ecological communities with automotive communities. With the associated homogenization of roadside architecture and services—the fast-food joints, motels, and roadside attractions—cars help blur the difference between a unique place and anyplace, supplanting local business with national chains.[40]

Most American college campuses are engineered for cars. The college website gives directions to prospective students, based on the assumption that they will arrive in cars. Maps—by which Americans generally mean road maps, as opposed to contour maps or hiking maps—show people how to get to campus with a car. Signs are placed on streets, but not so much on sidewalks. The admissions department is almost always near a parking lot, and these parking lots include spaces for "visitors," or more precisely, the cars of visitors.

These parking lots are one example of an automotive landscape. Parking places are important on college campuses because parked is the normal state of cars. Americans like to believe that automobiles are for mobility—and indeed, they are—but most automobiles are going nowhere most of the time. And colleges increasingly have to accommodate the cars of their students with parking lots and parking decks—dormitories for cars. This increases the area of impermeable surfaces on campus, which increases the water runoff. The asphalt surfaces affect water quality and watersheds by adding leaking fluids, road salt, and tire rubber to rivers and streams, increasing water flow, river erosion, and sediment loads, and decreasing the photosynthesis of aquatic plants. The Center for Land Use Education estimates that 55 to 75 percent of American impermeable surfaces are car habitat, and these habitats affect the quality of life for species other than humans. In addition to the physical effects of pavement, there is also a boundary effect, as roads and parking lots fragment habitat for animals, reducing the viability of an ecological niche. Our automotive landscapes seem natural to us, but they don't usually harmonize with nature.[41]

Cars transform places physically, but they also affect the way we think about places and inhabit them. Cars cover ground, but they don't really ground us in an experience of that ground. Most college students prefer driving to walking because they have places to go. But driving puts us in a peculiar relationship with the Earth. In a car, we're insulated—by cushy seats, suspension, and steel-belted radials—from the Earth, and we experience it fleetingly. In a car, at high speeds, the Earth is a blur. But even at slow speeds it's not something to savor sensually—to hear, touch, taste, and smell the natural world. Cars reduce drivers' and passengers' experience of the Earth to a single sense: sight—unless the car happens to hit a skunk. In some ways, cars make us displaced people because they make it harder to establish the intimate relationship with a place that comes from staying put and paying attention.[42]

People in a car culture are different from those in pedestrian cultures because we live in a landscape that might accurately be called a "carscape." We grow up thinking of driveways and attached garages as natural. We expect pavement to connect our homes to work, and to all the places we spend our time and money. We assume that we'll spend most of our lives in sight of streets and highways, and we think nothing of the strip malls and signage that are a large part of our visual environment. We expect lots of parking lots, even though we find them aesthetically offensive. Without cars, the landscape would be completely different. And we would be different, too.

American cars also affect the world's landscapes, and the landscape of people's minds across the globe. Cars made in the United States are an example for the world, and the world seems to want to become a car culture. In 2006, car manufacturers worldwide added sixty-seven million vehicles to the roads, and China increased its production by 30 percent, surpassing Germany as the third largest car producer in the world. In India, the new affordable Tata Nano promises to put hundreds of millions of middle-class people on the road. This seems like a real problem, but if Americans keep driving like there's no tomorrow, how can we ask the world's developing countries to park their automotive aspirations?[43]

Pollution

Cars pollute the visual and aural landscapes of our campuses, but most people don't notice because we're so used to it. They also pollute the air and eventually the soil, but these effects are invisible, so we don't notice them either. And though we experience the immediate effects of car exhaust on campus, its environmental impact changes the whole world.

Most cars run on internal combustion engines, like people do. We inhale oxygen, which helps us burn the caloric energy we eat. Depending on the capacity of our lungs, when we exhale we emit a few ounces of carbon dioxide. But a car is more capacious than we are. Our cars also inhale oxygen, and use it to burn the carbon in gasoline. So when we're driving, we're operating an iron lung on wheels.

After inhaling and burning gasoline, cars also exhale gases, as people do. A normal car exhales carbon dioxide and carbon monoxide. It emits nitrous oxide, which is three hundred times more powerful than carbon dioxide as a greenhouse gas, as well as hydrocarbons, which help to create the ground-level ozone we call smog. Indeed, car exhaust is basically one long, silent-but-deadly fart. Some of the gases in this chemical car fart can be handled by catalytic converters, but the rest of them end up in the gas chamber we call the atmosphere.[44]

CAR EXHAUST

Cartoon by Andy Singer. Reproduced by permission from the artist.

Like most Americans, Joe and Jo College don't think much about the environmental impact of their cars. It's out of sight and out of mind—part of the nature of cars. But the fact that we have created a system that allows drivers to alter the air that all of us breathe means that it's also part of the culture of cars. We wouldn't let people dump garbage into our yards, but we don't mind if they dump gaseous garbage into our air. It's not the only choice: If regulations required exhaust pipes to terminate in the passenger compartment of the car, requiring each of us to breathe our own gaseous production, we'd come up with more creative solutions for pollution and greenhouse gas emissions.[45]

Climate

The final cost of cars is climate change. "American energy consumption has climbed by fifty percent since 1970," notes James Speth, "accompanied by major growth in carbon dioxide emissions. The United States in 2007 consumed about twenty-one billion barrels of oil a day, about the same as Japan, Germany, Russia, China, and India combined." For Americans, a large portion of our ecological footprint comes from our cars. By weight, gasoline is about 85 percent carbon. So when it burns in our car engines, each gallon produces about twenty pounds of carbon dioxide. If you count the fuel burned in getting gasoline to the pump, an average American car produces about twenty-five pounds of carbon dioxide per mile of driving, and more than its own weight in gases every year. We may think that running out of oil is a problem, but it's more of a problem that we're running out of places (like oceans and forests) to store all that carbon.[46]

Cars, therefore, get us from here to there, and from here to global weirding. Most technologies that humans have devised to influence the weather have been utter failures, but the automobile actually works. It doesn't help us put rain in a particular place, but it can increase the number of tornadoes, hurricanes, floods, droughts, and other catastrophic events that we will experience in the future. Insurance companies may still call them "acts of God," but they are increasingly also acts of the god we call the car.

Driving to a Sustainable Future

Critics claim that a lot of our driving is just carelessness, and they're right. But Americans are still not likely to choose "carlessness." Instead we might consider the possibilities of a carefulness that could help us get places without driving the world to global weirding and extinction.

Colleges are perfect places for the practice of such carefulness. Because most campuses reflect nineteenth-century, pre-automotive designs, they're perfectly adapted for twenty-first-century innovations. Even in the age of suburban sprawl, most colleges and universities have preserved relatively compact campuses. Instead of housing students in vast tracts of single-family homes, they've created dense residential communities in dormitories and apartment buildings. Even where colleges accommodate students' cars, they have also kept landscapes that are friendly to pedestrians and bicyclists. The population densities of the dorms and apartments make possible a wide variety of stores and services, bars and restaurants, in close proximity to each other. Students often look back on college as one of the best times of their lives, but they forget that some of the fun came from the true convenience and conviviality of a well-planned community. Remembering the good times could help students to reimagine how other communities might be improved as well.

In addition to maintaining these historic ways of creating access to goods and services (and human fulfillment) without driving people crazy, today's colleges are taking steps to curb car use, and to encourage alternative forms of transportation. Some colleges are equipping their own fleets with efficient or alternative-energy vehicles, or both. Others are investing in mass transit, offering discounts on transit passes, and trying to substitute buses for cars. Many colleges promote ride sharing and carpooling, exploring car-sharing programs like HOURCAR and Zipcar, and beginning to charge students (and sometimes faculty and staff) the full costs of parking, which otherwise are shared by students who don't drive to campus. Some even offer preferred parking places to drivers of hybrid cars and other fuel-efficient cars, and to carpools.[47]

Unfortunately, few colleges are yet considering the cultural changes that might really provide freedom from cars. If motor vehicles reflect and affect American values, do these values need to change? Can our new-and-improved values help us to drive beyond cars? Can we rate community as highly as individualism? Can we value climate stability as much as personal mobility? Can we hold all life—and the life of plants and animals—to be as important as our "good life"? For the most part, the typical college curriculum has little to say about these questions. But some students are engaging them anyway, experimenting with car-free living both before and after graduation. Reading books like Katie Alvord's *Divorce Your Car!,* and Chris Balish's *How to Live Well Without Owning a Car,* they're learning to "save money, breathe easier, and get more mileage out of life."[48]

On campus, too, some religious groups are considering what might be called a theology of cars. In the United States, we usually make our automotive purchases without divine intervention or ethical considerations. We need a car, and that's that. But recently a group of Americans has asked, "What Would Jesus Drive?" The question shows the pervasiveness of America's car culture, assuming that Jesus would want to drive. The historical Jesus walked, rode beasts of burden, or traveled by sailboat—all of which would seem to suggest a pedestrian or bicycle choice for today's Jesus. Still, "What Would Jesus Drive?" is a good question, asking adherents to think about the operative values of modern Christianity. If the Earth was created and it was good, then by what authority can we drive machines that drive its creatures to extinction?[49]

Some students are joining organizations that pay attention to the politics of cars, groups trying to mobilize the voice of the people to change the habits of the people. They're learning about the ways that government policy is complicit in the sprawl of America's car culture, both physically and psychologically. They're learning that there's no way that private markets can drive the radical changes that will be necessary for creating new modes and meanings of transportation. So they support public policy that constrains carbon emissions by including the environmental cost of cars in the price of transportation. They support carbon taxes or cap-and-trade systems; they're willing to pay for land-use planning and the infrastructure of a new transportation system. And they're willing to subsidize governments that subsidize research into eco-cars and alternative fuels. They know that other countries move people much more efficiently than ours does, and they are willing to learn from examples of enlightened public policy.[50]

Right now, it's hard to imagine the United States—or its college campuses—without cars. But the essence of the nation isn't cars—it's a set of values that appeared in history long before the internal combustion engine. And it's a reconsideration of those values that might make us more responsible drivers, and more responsible citizens of a small and fragile planet. Such rethinking might lead to a twenty-first-century transportation revolution centered not on technologies like the car, but on human geographies like the village. Instead of assuming the perpetual existence of cars and designing for sprawl, we might design human settlements for the pleasures of proximity and pedestrianism, with densely populated clusters of housing, retail, and services. Instead of plopping single-family homes in the middle of the monocultures we call lawns, we might locate our homes close together, and preserve extensive public parks, community gardens, and green spaces instead. We might place clusters of settlement along high-speed rail lines that could be supported by concentrated communities instead of locating sprawling suburbs along interstate highways. Instead of constructing huge McMansions with bars, movie theaters, and playgrounds built-in, we might save our money to make parks, gardens, bars, restaurants, and civic centers into our living rooms. In such spaces, we could revive the practices and the pleasures of neighborliness, getting to know the people we see in our shared spaces instead of waving to them from behind the steering wheel of a car. Already, cities like Portland, Oregon, and the Twin Cities in Minnesota are designing for such "smart growth," and planners elsewhere are embracing what visionaries call New Urbanist design. These changes won't come fast, but they might help to reduce the environmental impact of cars and increase the daily pleasures of human community.[51]

■ ■ ■ ■ ■ ■ ■

Our cars are on a collision course with Earth. The number of motor vehicles on the globe is increasing three times faster than the human population. Greenhouse gas emissions from these cars clot the atmosphere and change the climate. And we know this. "More and more students are becoming aware of how detrimental car emissions are to our environment," says a student, "[but] the majority either are still unaware, or simply don't care." "I see what I am doing as damaging to the environment," says another knowledgeable college student, "but it doesn't bother me in the least when it is twenty below out and I need to make a beer run." This is just common sense. In this case, environmental impacts seem remote, and the need for beer is now. "I have taken numerous classes that repeatedly stated how bad automobiles are for the environment," notes another student, "but I seldom think about this when the time comes to make my monthly Target run with friends. It is hard to break habits and I think for many college students, driving is one of those bad habits." And so our habits continue to harm our habitat.

In Buddhism and Hinduism, karma is the whole effect of a person's intentions and actions during the different phases of the person's spiritual and physical existence(s), an effect expected to shape the person's destiny. In the moral ecology of American life, "carma" might be said to be the whole effect of a person's (auto)motives and actions during a driving, or a driven, life, an effect expected to shape the destiny of the planet. Karma is also a distinctive aura, atmosphere, or feeling—places are said to have "good" or "bad" karma. In America, good "carma" might come with living in right relation with the world by questioning the common sense of cars and designing a culture that is no longer so driven by automobiles.

6

The Nature of Screens

*Our inventions are wont to be pretty toys, which distract our
attention from serious things. They are but improved means to
an unimproved end....*
   Henry David Thoreau, *Walden*

*If you are mesmerized by televised stupidity, and don't get to
hear or read stories about your world, you can be fooled into
thinking that the world isn't miraculous—and it is.*
   Anne Lamott, *Grace (Eventually): Thoughts on Faith*

We are all computer people now.
   Sherry Turkle, "How Computers Change the Way We Think"

*Only a flicker
Over the strained time-ridden faces
Distracted from distraction by distraction
Filled with fancies and empty of meaning
Tumid apathy with no concentration.*
   T. S. Eliot, "Burnt Norton"

Nothing says, "Leave me alone," like an iPod.
   Marija Knudson, St. Olaf student

Can we Google our way to wisdom?
   Maggie Jackson, *Distracted*

· · · · · · ·

Like their peers on campuses across America, Joe and Jo College are
electronically connected—and they have been for most of their lives.
American kids are immersed in media: They spend more time each week
connected to media than their parents spend at work—an average of
fifty-three hours. The daily average is seven-and-a-half hours, but media
multitasking raises the total to ten hours and forty-five minutes.[1]

It's not surprising, then, that Joe College furnishes his room with a flat-screen HDTV, laptop computer, Xbox 360, cell phone, and an iPod. On TV, he watches live sports when he can and *SportsCenter* when he can't. During election season, he watches Fox News. When he needs a break and there's nothing on, Joe takes in an episode or two of an older show on DVD. TV is one of the habits of his heart. Jo watches TV, too, but she's more likely to gather with friends in front of the screen.

They're both gamers. Joe often boots-up *Halo* or *Call of Duty* when classes end for the day. When they're feeling laid-back, both of them play *Mario Kart* or *Guitar Hero*. Sometimes Jo plays *FreeCell* while she waits for something else to happen, and they both have second lives in *Second Life* and *FarmVille* that they can attend to.

Both Joe and Jo keep their computers on most of the day, just in case. He downloads music to assemble a good playlist on his iPod, while Jo checks out YouTube for funny videos and Overstock.com for sales. She consults her sociology syllabus on Blackboard, and googles concepts that aren't clear to her. Facebook is their main online passion and they both update their profiles regularly. College wouldn't be college without electronic connections. It's just common sense.[2]

Joe and Jo also use their cell phones in a variety of ways. At least once a week, they have the sibling catch-up conversation. Jo calls Mom most days, and Joe occasionally checks-in with his high-school brother in the evening. At parties and other fun occasions, they take pictures of their friends for Facebook. Joe has an iPhone, so he has additional applications. Sometimes they watch TV or YouTube videos. But mostly the phones are social GPS units, connecting students who are planning to connect later.

Electronic communication technology has transformed the college experience. Television crept into the corners of campus in the 1950s, and computers invaded in the last half of the twentieth century. Just fifty years ago, the only computers on campus were mainframes, and students had virtually no access to them. The first IBM personal computer came out in 1981, the Apple Macintosh in 1984, and PCs and Macs began to show up on college campuses shortly thereafter. But the personal computer is just one of many computers that connect college students to friends, music, and the world. The iPod premiered in 2001, with iTunes coming two years later. Cell phones have been around for a long time, but the integrated models that serve as personal computing devices—like iPhones—are relatively recent. And things are changing so fast that this chapter may be obsolete by the time it's published. In all of these technologies, college students have been trendsetters, making college culture a good place to look for the future of American life. It's also a good place to look at the implications of our electronic life for the broader life of the planet.

This generation of college students has been called everything from "screenagers" to "the Net Generation," and they live on-screen almost as much as anywhere else. Screens are *the* place to define the self, connect to others, and find validation, belonging, meaning, and entertainment. As Michael Snider suggests, "For most Gen Y kids—those born in North America after 1979 (about sixty million at last count)—technology is second nature. It's as if they come into this world with a game controller in one hand and a mouse in the other." This chapter explores that second nature, and how it relates to nature itself. With screen time overtaking face time on campus, it's definitely time to think about how the cyberspaces of college life relate to the other spaces and natural places. In doing so, we can probe some of the common assumptions about our relationships to technology and the natural world.[3]

When Americans use the word "technology," we usually mean specific tools and gadgets that we use to make life easier and more enjoyable. But, as Langdon Winner points out in a beautiful book called *The Whale and the Reactor*, technologies often do more than we expect. Although he rejects the idea of technological determinism, Winner contends that our technologies "provide structure for human activity," inevitably influencing the way we think and act in the world. "Technologies are not merely aids to human activity," he reminds us, "but also powerful forces acting to reshape that activity and its meaning." There's a politics of television, computers, and widgets, and it's wired not into the devices themselves, but into the standard operating procedures we create while using these tools. In this way, our visible technologies become "invisible technologies," channeling our beliefs and behavior in ways we may not fully intend.[4]

Invisible technology: A tool so familiar that we forget that we're using it—and now it's using us. Grades are an invisible technology, a tool designed to communicate evaluation to students, but one which also naturalizes our ideas of authority, hierarchy, standardized excellence, quantification (the GPA), and the identity of the self ("B student").

Television: A Way of Seeing the World

By the time they enter college, students already know how to watch TV—they've had a lot of practice. Indeed, most American kids have spent more time glued to television than they've spent in a classroom, making TV—not school—America's primary educational system. Seventy-one percent of those aged eight to eighteen have TVs in their bedrooms. Less than half have any parental limits on how much they watch. So normal kids grow up with more TV than parental supervision, and they see the world that way. Children don't have X-ray vision like Superman, but they do have *tele*vision and it affects everything in their lives.[5]

TV watching changes in college, but not much. Even though it seems like books take up all their free time, college students also watch a lot of television—sometimes on TV, but on Hulu, YouTube, cell phones, or MP3 players as well. Ninety-eight percent of students watch TV during an average week. According to Nielsen, this comes out to an average of about three hours a day, and about six hours total peering into pixilated screens. "How we spend our days," says Annie Dillard, "is . . . how we spend our lives."[6]

In 2008, according to Student Monitor, college students' favorite networks were MTV, ABC, Comedy Central, FOX, ESPN, and HBO. The favorite college shows were *Family Guy*, *SportsCenter*, *House*, *Grey's Anatomy*, *CSI*, *The Office*, *The Hills*, *The Simpsons*, *Heroes*, *South Park*, *Gossip Girl*, and *Lost*. There are lots of idiosyncratic reasons to watch a favorite show, but there are broader cultural reasons for watching as well, reasons that constitute the common sense of TV.[7]

The Common Sense of TV

Why *do* we watch TV? To some extent, we tune in to kill time and overcome boredom. We grab "guilty pleasures" in the privacy of our own rooms, watching "the plug-in drug" to relax, procrastinate, or just take a break. TV is a tool for doing nothing, a method of justifying inactivity in a culture of busy-ness. We watch to control our moods, with stimulating shows to relieve boredom and familiar favorites to counter stress. We watch to spend time with friends, and to be ready for all the conversations about TV the next day. Watching TV is almost as natural as breathing.[8]

Watching TV, Joe and Jo College generally feel relaxed and passive—which is, of course, one of the reasons they watch. Students often describe TV time as "vegging out," and characterize TV watchers as "couch potatoes"—both interesting metaphors in an ecological age. Students are mammals with higher-order intelligence (at least most of them), but for about ten to twenty hours a week (on average) they prefer to think of themselves as vegetables. Why? Because thinking is hard, and vegetables don't think. Because vegetables don't have moral responsibilities. Because vegetables don't act, so they are blameless. Students seem to forget that vegetables don't have much emotional range, and that few potatoes seem really happy. So perhaps vegging out has unintended implications. In fact, a 2008 study shows that television viewing is one of the things that happy people don't do as much as unhappy ones. For that reason, perhaps, many respondents tell Gallup pollsters that we watch too much TV.[9]

Why do we continue to do something that doesn't increase our happiness? Students think that watching television is a free choice, but there are many forces conspiring to get them in front of the tube. It is a choice to watch, but it's not by chance that they end up doing it. Watching television, college students are watching ads *for* TV, as promos pump next week's episode, the shows of the new season, the new "must-see TV," or TV stars making guest appearances on talk shows. Retailers like Best Buy, Circuit City, Target, and Wal-Mart feature televisions in their ads and weekly newspaper supplements. News sources report the Nielsen ratings, entertainment news, and trends in TV technology. *TV Guide* is one of the most popular magazines in America, and most newspapers publish their own television schedules. Peers also apply pressure to watch TV, with invitations to "chill out" in their room, and with conversations premised on their watching the same shows. Even when they're not watching, they are constantly caught in its networks of promotion and marketing—and in conversations *about* television. Watching is an individual choice, but our society makes it a systematic choice—which comes naturally in a television *system*. Ninety-eight percent of us watch television, not because the shows are so good, but because that is what normal people do.

For the most part, college students get the same gratifications from television that other Americans do, and the same environmental impacts, too. The television in the college dorm room or apartment is made of the same materials as other TVs, uses the same electrical current, and imparts the same sort of environmental perspectives. They know that Discovery Channel and National Geographic feature nature shows, but forget that all the other channels broadcast environmental content, too. From CBS to TBS, from MSNBC to MTV, virtually all television offers viewers a vision of the human presence in the natural world. And unlike

Television: The Anti-College	
College Mission	**TV Mission**
Know thyself	Amuse thyself
Education: how the world works	Entertainment: how the world plays
Engagement	Escape
Honor tradition	Mock tradition
Tried and true	New and improved
Consciousness	Semi-consciousness
Community	Audience
Communities of memory and hope	Living in the now
The good life	The goods life
Scholars	Dollars
Humanization	Human interest
The best we can be	The best we can buy
Improving time	Killing time
Learning to serve	Learning to be served
Mentors	Celebrities
Complexification	Simplification
Creativity	Passivity
Soul	Sold
Proof, empiricism	Opinion
Truth	Credibility
Ideas and ideals	Images and irony
Classic/lasting	Periodical/fleeting—"And now, this."
Reflective	Affective
Discipline(s)	Diss-ipline(s)

Professor Ponderous, who drones on in a monotone, TV knows how to get its messages across.

The Lessons of TV

When we think about television, we think mainly about what scholars call "uses and gratifications," what it does *for* us. But television also does something *to* us. Sometimes it affects our behavior, but it also affects our perception and imagination. In what's called "cultivation theory," scholars suggest that watching TV trains us to watch the world—and to act in it—in ways we're not always aware of. People who watch a lot of television tend to be infected by impressions of the world that skew reality. TV junkies are often affected by the "mean-world syndrome," the perception of a world more violent and dangerous than it really is. There's likely a "men's-world syndrome" because men are overrepresented as TV protagonists, and a "young-world syndrome" because TV characters are disproportionately younger than most viewers. There's also a "sexy syndrome" and a "body-image syndrome," coming from all of the good-looking hunks and babes. An "affluent-world syndrome" results from all the upscale ads. And, of course, there is a "commercial-world syndrome," since most TV exists not to entertain or educate but to sell us stuff. We live in the real world, but that world is socially constructed, in part, by the worlds of television. And we can pick up lots of cues and clues about the nature of the real world on TV.[10]

As we watch TV shows, we also quietly study the range of human nature, seeing how characters respond to life's situations. How do sports figures deal with victory or defeat? How do detectives deal with evil, or judges with justice? How do housewives or doctors deal with temptation? How do men and women feel about their bodies? How do they approach sex and gender? As with fiction and theater, we enjoy character development and plot twists, but there is a lot more on our minds than simple enjoyment. When we watch TV we're engaged in "observational learning," picking up the social scripts and common sense of our culture. Along with the models of our everyday life—parents, pastors, teachers, bosses, friends—television affects our visions of who we are and who we should be.[11]

Deeper still is the implicit epistemology of television. Epistemology is how we know what we know—and in North America, a lot of what we know about ourselves comes from TV. In *Amusing Ourselves to Death*, Neil Postman contends that "all public discourse increasingly takes the form of entertainment. Our politics, religion, news, athletics, education and commerce have been transformed into congenial adjuncts of show business, largely without protest or even much popular notice." Eventually, we come to expect *everything* to be entertaining. This epistemology of TV has also helped to transform the meaning of truth in our country, as credibility increasingly substitutes for verifiability. While language deals in propositions that are testable, television deals mainly in images that just *are*. You can criticize the claims made in a television commercial for a "green" oil company or a nature-loving SUV, but it's almost impossible to erase the image and clever associations created by the ad. In a culture of television, our vision of the world is different than ever before.[12]

The Nature of TV

In the common sense of college culture, nature is outside, out *there*. But nature is also inside, and it's always on television, which is increasingly where students interact with and learn about it. And yet, they're not really thinking about the nature of this learning process. If television were intended for critical thinking, after all, it would be as popular as college lectures. And who watches lectures on TV? Television educates students so well precisely because they don't think it's educational. But what do they learn about *nature* on TV?[13]

Nature Channels

On TV, a lot of nature is channeled into nature channels—National Geographic, Discovery Channel, Animal Planet—and sometimes PBS. When we're paying attention, the shows on these networks teach us about the grandeur of Mount Everest, the African savanna, and the Amazonian rain forest. They offer basic lessons in geography, climate, food chains, and animal behavior. As one student said, "Without PBS when I was little, I would probably have thought lions came from zoos." Such shows also teach us about environmental threats—about deforestation, habitat loss, global weirding, and threats to biodiversity. "Without Al Gore and thermal images of the earth," another student confessed, "I wouldn't know about global warming." The shows' deeper lesson, however, is that nature is something separate from other aspects of life. Even though nature is the foundation for all markets worldwide, nature is just a niche market on TV.[14]

One reason that nature is just a market segment is that many viewers find the documentaries dull and dreary. Growing up with the quick cuts of *Sesame Street* and MTV, many of us find nature shows incredibly slow. Producers have responded, therefore, by presenting much more animal action in their documentaries than is natural. On TV, we see lion chases over and over again, even though lions spend more time digesting their dinner than pursuing it. As a result, television teaches us a lot about the hunting practices of lions, but it doesn't encourage the patience we need to really see the nature of our own habitats. It increases the entertainment value we expect from the exotic world, and decreases our ability to enjoy the beauty around us. The more we experience the world through fast cuts and engaging visuals, the more we expect the same sort of action in our lives. When TV gives us a new stimulus every few seconds, it assures that our attention spans will be brief. Television affects the eye and the "I," cultivating patterns of perception that affect our relationship to the natural world.[15]

Sometimes the explicit messages of nature shows are undermined by their proliferation. Documentaries that focus on endangered species, for example, air so frequently that it's hard to believe in the species' extinction—even after their demise, it seems, we'll still have plenty of film of them. These elegiac extinction documentaries feel like Edward Curtis's nineteenth-century photographs of the "vanishing Indian," eliciting a mournful emotion that does nothing to stop the process. And because they emphasize the beauty of nature, such documentaries reinforce an aesthetic (but not a functional) sense of nature. We should save these beautiful beasts and scenic places, the films suggest, not because they're a critical component of the biosphere but because they're pleasing to the human eye. Such TV jeremiads also tend to reinforce the problematic dichotomy between people and nature, and a definition of nature as remote, scenic, and sublime. Shows like *Planet Earth*, for example, show us a nature that's not much connected to our everyday lives. In fact, as one student said, nature on TV is most beautiful when it's uninhabited. Or, as another suggested, "Nature is where people are not,"—except, of course, for film crews.[16]

Nature shows are filled with wonder, but they're only a tiny part of a truly environmental imagination. As Bill McKibben suggests, "Even at its very best, TV covers only a small slice of the natural world. There are perhaps ten million (some say thirty million) species on Earth; of those that we know about and have cataloged, only a few meet the requirements for extensive television coverage—cuteness (or grotesqueness so complete it borders on the cute), great amiability or ferocity, accessibility (it lives on grassland plains or beaches, not in the deep ocean, badly lit caves, or rain-forest canopies), correct size to show up well on camera, and so forth. . . . The upshot of nature education by television is a deep fondness for certain species and a deep lack of understanding of systems, or of the policies that destroy those systems."[17]

There's another immense irony in these networks of nature programming, of course: The people watching these shows aren't engaged with nature itself. Providing visual pleasures and auditory sensations, the nature channels offer a vision of nature that's sublime and inspiring. But the pleasures are always vicarious, and nature is always distant, framed by the camera's eye. Screening nature, therefore, the nature channels might be screening viewers *from* nature, convincing them that they can really love nature from the living room.

Nature Channeled

When we were children, our parents may have tuned us to the nature channels, but most college students are too sophisticated to watch them now. Instead, they watch cable networks like MTV and Comedy Central, or the programs that show up online. Unlike the nature networks, the most popular TV shows tell almost nothing about nature, unless it's human nature. The world of television seems almost extraterrestrial, since the flora and fauna of the planet are almost invisible, except for pets and potted plants. TV is relentlessly anthropocentric, with most of the action taking place in hospitals, courtrooms, and other workplaces, or in cars, apartments, and coffee shops. There's some anatomy on *Grey's Anatomy*, but there's not much ecology anywhere.

Specific shows have natural implications, of course, as trivial as they may be. Among my students, a fan of *Grey's Anatomy* suggests that she learns that "it rains a lot (or all the time) in Seattle." She knows there are lots of fish in the Northwest, that the forest is close to the city, and that nature is a place to "get away," especially for male bonding. A fan of MTV's *The Hills* finds that it reinforces stereotypes of the nature of southern California—always sunny, with neatly manicured lawns and landscaping, and beaches for human recreation and flirtation. A news junkie notes that the weather in Iraq is hard on American troops. Another notes that she learned that bears and sharks attack people a lot—even though that's not true. Multiplied a million times, these are some of the unintended environmental lessons of TV.

Survivor and other reality shows are an exception to TV's rule of indoor setting, placing people in the wild, in exotic locations. Highlighting a less-loving nature than the documentaries of sublime scenery and charismatic megafauna, these shows feature struggles between contestants, but also a struggle of "man versus nature." They reinforce a crude version of Darwinism, and an even cruder culture of competition.[18]

In any case, except for the weather, it seems like nature is optional on television. It might be there on our favorite shows, but it doesn't really matter if it's not. And, again, except for the weather, there's hardly any local nature on TV. Television shows us nature everywhere in the world but near us, with nothing local or bioregional. If you wanted to know about your own habitat, unless you lived in a national park, you'd probably need to read a book or go outside.

The Nature of News

While nature is generally in the background on prime-time television programming, it does show up on the news, usually as weather, but sometimes as the subject of debate among humans. In an ideal world, the news might help us understand our relationship to the natural world. But today's televised journalism doesn't help much, for several reasons.[19]

We think of television as a medium for news and entertainment, but we forget that American news *is* entertainment—with the same demands for commercial sponsorship and audience share as other entertainment programs. In our system, news is infotainment, a way of selling an audience to advertisers by telling stories. And television stories help determine what we pay attention to. In 2008–2009, the national news implied by its coverage that the rapid collapse of the economy was more important than the slow collapse of the ecosystems that support any economy. The local news tells us that murders, burglaries, and house fires are more important than the extinction of biodiversity. Both local and national news present "decontextualized information" in a quick succession of stories strung together by the disjunctive conjunction, "And now, this." The news shows us lots of stories, but it often obscures the big story, the ongoing structures and patterns that drive daily events.[20]

Even when environmental stories make news, they usually comply with the "normal media-driven attention cycle whereby a particular issue or event enters the public's awareness, stays there for some time, and then gradually fades." The news focuses on what's ostensibly new, of course, on the daily events that can capture the attention of an audience that will also watch the ads. Television news fails when it comes to explaining long-term processes, like the slow accretion of carbon dioxide in the atmosphere, the melting of glaciers, the daily starvation of thousands of people, or the ongoing extinction of species. Those things are normal. If a glacier caves into the sea, and if there are pictures of it, it might make the news for a day. But global weirding usually makes the news only when the abnormal happens. And when the abnormal becomes normal, when the planet is melting, it's just too bad—unless it's both frightening and photogenic.[21]

Environmental reporting on TV also usually complies with the need for "balance," even when reporters end up balancing truth and falsehood. Ross Gelbspan, among others, has shown how networks and other news media "balanced" scientific, peer-reviewed reports of global weirding with assertions by skeptics financed by the carbon lobby, including major oil and coal companies (like ExxonMobil and Western Fuels). Even though our knowledge of global climate change comes from "the largest and most rigorously peer-reviewed scientific collaboration in history—the findings of more than 2,000 scientists from 100 countries reporting to the United Nations as the Intergovernmental Panel on Climate Change," journalistic "balance" pretended that it was still a closely contested question.[22]

The one place that there's no balance is in the absence of criticism of consumer capitalism. Because of the demands of sponsorship, TV news can't afford to report *systematic* critiques of American consumption and its consequences. This means that even the vocabulary of the news is slanted toward consuming. We routinely hear about the developed world and the underdeveloped world, for example, but we never hear about the overdeveloped world. We routinely hear about measures of consumer confidence and the rise and fall of same-store sales in the retail industry, but we don't hear the word "overconsumption," nor do we learn much about the systematic environmental impacts of our consuming passions. Consumer capitalism can make the news in "whistleblower" segments and in the TV versions of *Consumer Reports* that help us with our purchasing. But critiques of the system are systematically excluded. The news on TV is that the system is normal and normative, even when it isn't working well.

The Nature of Weather

Nature on the news is most prevalent not in environmental stories but in the weather report, which reveals many of our underlying assumptions about nature. "Good" weather, for example, is warm and sunny, calm and controlled, and bad weather is cold, wet, and unpredictable. "Good" weather allows for easy driving and outdoor recreation, while "bad" weather inhibits our recreation and automobility. In this case, the weather teaches us, as one college student said, that "nature is only notable when it directly affects humans."[23]

Weather shows up daily on the local news, but it only makes the national news when it's dramatic and dangerous. In a perverse way, weather coverage suggests that we *like* watching hurricanes, tornadoes, mud slides, and forest fires—at least at a distance. We enjoy seeing the ruthless power of nature in a place—our homes—where we seemingly have power *over* nature. When nature is wildly destructive, one student noted, "the screen protects us."[24]

In the rare instances that environmental problems are depicted on TV news, there's not much audience response. Television demonstrates that "everyone knows about global warming and the environmental state we're in, but few people do anything." Activists try to raise consciousness about environmental hazards, but consciousness seems to be the end of the line. Instead of watching the news to change how we act in the world, we watch as voyeurs, curious about the trials and tribulations of people in other places. Like the rest of TV, environmental news generally leaves us impassive and inactive.

The Nature of Advertising

The one television show that inspires us to action is the one we don't think is a show at all—the commercial. Common sense tells us that TV is a medium in which our shows are interrupted by commercials. But in the television system, advertising *is* the show, and programs like *Grey's Anatomy*, *Family Guy*, and *SportsCenter* are just there to keep the ads from bumping together. We don't usually think about it, but television teaches us that almost nothing is too serious for commercial interruption. It seems natural for programs—even "serious" shows like the news—to be segmented with commercial breaks. Ads interrupting the news implicitly tell us that the events of the day aren't any more important than the need to market antacids or appliances, fast food or fast cars. On TV, our needs and our lifestyles are always more important than the life of the planet.[25]

Television is a system designed to sell our eyes to advertisers. Although college students and Americans see TV as an escape from reality, marketers see TV as the way *to* the reality of commercial culture. Lolling in front of the television, we see ourselves as taking a break, but it would be more accurate to say we're at work. In *Consuming Environments*, authors Steve Craig and Clay Steinman suggest that "viewing commercials is 'work' performed by audiences in exchange for 'free' news and entertainment." Because there is simply so much advertising, however, we have a hard time seeing the cultural work it calls us to. In *The Age of Missing Information*, Bill McKibben wonders, "What happens when you see an ad, over and over, for small Ritz crackers pre-smeared and stuck together with peanut butter and sold under the slogan 'No assembly required?' What habits of mind and body does this, in concert with a hundred other messages, help produce? And how do these habits differ from the habits, the attitudes that people [formerly] got from the natural world?" It's a good question. If, as the authors of *Consuming Environments* suggest, "the most important effect of TV may be one that no one intends—accelerated destruction of the natural environment, caused by the consumption commercial television fosters," then we need to think more deeply about this system of entertainment.[26]

Television ads use the standard cultural conventions of nature to sell products from food to shelter, clothes to cars, cleansers to cosmetics. The "buyodiversity" of these ads is incredible, using different images of nature for different products and sales pitches. There are seven natures in TV advertising: three Romantic, one Darwinian, one domesticated, one corporate, and one "resourcist." In each of these variations, nature is used to add value to the product being sold, or to justify the purchase of the product. In this commodified naturalism, we get back to nature by buying manufactured goods.

One type of ad offers us a Romantic view of nature as a nurturing presence and a calm counterpoint to the stresses of everyday life. In these ads, nature is restorative and regenerative. Using some of the same conventions as paintings of pastoral and picturesque landscapes, they invite us to associate a product with the simple beauty or simple truths of nature. The serenity of nature, for example, is often the backdrop for perfume ads, so you can apparently get the serenity in a bottle.[27]

A second set of ads draw on the conventions of the Romantic sublime, and associations with wilderness, where you can get away from it all, going into the self by going into the mountains or forest. The "commercial sublime" invites us to call up a "wilderness mind-set," in which getting back to nature—even commercially—frees us from our everyday interactions with the materials of the natural world. Because our everyday lives are boring, and we need to get away, travel ads are especially good at playing up the commercial sublime. Other ads connect the Romantic sublime to the technological sublime, as in the SUV sublime, where motorized monsters cavort in remote wilderness settings.[28]

In TV ads, therefore, getting back to nature is almost always seen as a leisure or adventure experience. There are few depictions of people working in nature or relating directly with nature in any other manner. Just as pastoral and picturesque painters rarely depicted people at work in their work, the commercial sublime's focus on remote wilderness helps to hide the fact that resourcism is our dominant relationship with nature.[29]

The Romantic association of the natural with the good also affects the advertising of product attributes. Some ads, for example, feature products with "natural" ingredients, implying that nature's chemicals are intrinsically better than culture's chemicals. In cosmetic and shampoo commercials, we're invited to imagine that botanical ingredients or scents increase our own "natural" essence or aura. We're encouraged to forget that all products, even petroleum-based products, are derived from natural ingredients.

But Romantic nature isn't the only nature in commercials. Other ads offer a Darwinian view of nature as an adversary to be conquered or controlled. SUV ads are especially good at framing nature as the enemy. One Jeep ad contends, "It's your classic man-versus-nature struggle." Another challenges us "to get out there and show Mother Nature who's boss." And as crocodiles slither away from a Lexus LX470, a commercial advises, "Let nature worry about you for a change."[30]

When it comes to our relationship with nature in our own habitats, too, TV mostly teaches us that nature should be controlled. Ads for furnaces and air conditioning offer promises of "climate control." We learn about lawn care and landscaping, bug sprays and biocides. We learn about the domesticated nature of cats and dogs, and how to keep them happy with the likes of Kibbles 'n Bits. In the Midwest, we learn about corn hybrids and powerful herbicides to protect farm crops. Nationwide, we learn about pharmaceuticals that can overcome nature, and cosmetics that can cover it up. We master the art of the makeover, conquering the body in the name of beauty and popularity. Commercial culture, it seems, is designed to channel the effects of nature.

In addition to Romantic and Darwinian nature in ads, there's also domesticated nature. These ads show us that instead of going out to nature, we can bring it into the Great Indoors in the form of pets, houseplants, decorative touches, scents, posters, and photographs. We like nature, but we seem to like it more in *our* domestic habitat than outdoors. We have nature posters on our walls, and landscape screen savers on our computers. We have floral prints on clothes and Kleenex boxes. Air fresheners boast "natural scents" that mask dorm odors with extracts of outdoors. With houseplants, we value nature not as a system, but as a sign, showing that we like the look of it, but maybe not much more than that.[31]

A sixth type of television commercial capitalizes on our cultural affiliation with nature and the environmental crisis of the twenty-first century by showing us how corporations are "greening" their products and processes. These environmental advocacy ads try to associate companies with environmental preservation, or "earth-friendly" practices. In 2006, Ford enlisted Kermit the Frog to "green" its image. A 2010 Toyota Prius ad set in a stylized nature assured us that here was a car representing "harmony between man, nature, and machine." Apple is now touting "the greenest family of notebooks," ExxonMobil, which funded climate-change debunkers for years, now advertises its renewable commitments, and coal producers are touting "clean coal." Some of these ads are true, some half true, and some just greenwashing.[32]

This recent (and relentless) promotion of "green" products on TV generally keeps us ignorant, if not blissful, about our relationship with nature. Virtually all of these ads suggest that the cure for environmental problems is more consumption. None of them even hints that one of our primary problems is overconsumption. Instead they sell us the idea that new and improved "green" consumption is how we can participate in the ecological revolution of the twenty-first century. Ads never tell us that the greenest product is the one that isn't made, because that's one you can't advertise. So TV commercials raise our environmental consciousness, but only to the level of consumption, and the ads virtually guarantee that we'll stay focused on the symptoms of environmental degradation rather than the systems that created it.[33]

While the final convention of commercial naturalism is implicit, not explicit, it remains as powerful as all the other natural appeals combined. For the most part, television reinforces American "resourcism"—the idea that, as one student says, "nature can be converted to the things we need." For the vast majority of products on TV, we learn nothing at all about their natural origins or environmental impacts. In most ads, products are decontextualized from their earthly origins and impacts, and re-contextualized in fantasies of human satisfaction and happiness. All of the ads—Romantic and Darwinian, domesticated and corporate—work to help us forget that every product is nature commodified, and that every product has environmental impacts. Advertising tells us simple stories of nature to keep the actual complexities of our lives out of sight and out of mind.[34]

When we watch TV, each ad has a tiny impact on us; most of them don't affect us very much because we've mastered the art of selective attention. But all the ads together add up to what Michael Schudson calls "capitalist realism," the systematic assumption that human problems are solved by consumption. Television is the mouthpiece of consumer capitalism, and nothing that might subvert the efficacy of the ads makes it into programming. A vice president of programming for ABC revealed that "program-makers are supposed to devise and produce shows that will attract mass audiences without unduly offending those audiences or too deeply moving them emotionally. Such ruffling, it is thought, will interfere with the ability to receive, recall, and respond to the commercial message. This programming reality is the unwritten, unspoken [assumption] of all professional members of the television fraternity." If you want to have ads with significant impact, you need to have trivial and insignificant programming to frame them.[35]

Television is, therefore, a catalyst for American materialism, with virtually all ads imploring us to increase our environmental impact by buying more stuff. And it works. Boston College economist Juliet Schor has demonstrated that the more we watch TV, the more we spend. For each additional hour Americans watch weekly, we average an extra $208 in annual spending. Over a year, for an average college student watching twenty-one hours a week, that's more than four thousand dollars. And the more we spend, generally, the more we affect the natural world.[36]

The Nature of Consciousness (and Conscience)

The overall effect of television programming (including the ads) is a "normal-world syndrome," suggesting that—despite the dire warnings we occasionally hear on the news—the planet can still support all of the ordinary activities of Americans. Both dramas and comedies show normal people with minimal environmental consciousness engaged in the normal American behaviors, without ever showing the environmental complexities behind the social interactions. People on TV eat food, drive cars, breathe air, and use resources. They seldom deal with wastes, especially not their own, and they virtually never think about their environmental impacts. Their insensitivity to the environment reinforces our desensitization, as we see few examples of environmental awareness or activism. In general, television characters don't do politics—and they certainly don't do environmental politics, because it's too controversial. And ads affect the character of TV. Advertising requires a certain kind of show, a certain kind of setting. Even though the climate is changing, even though our mass culture systematically degrades the environment, most television tells us that the main changes we need to make in life are to buy better products than the ones we have now. These "new and improved" products will improve our lives, and that's all that counts. A lot of the stuff in our rooms, it seems, comes from this consumptive view of the world "as seen on TV." On both sides of the screen, consumption is perfectly natural. It's just common sense. It's the nature of TV.[37]

Watching TV—Really Watching It

Americans watch television: That's what we do. We use up half our leisure time watching the tube, spending more time with TV than any other activity except work and sleep. In early 2009, Americans were averaging 151 hours a month of television viewing, which is almost four full forty-hour weeks. Included in our TV time is an hour of commercials a day. At this rate, an American who lives to age seventy-five spends nine years watching television. Students spend thousands of dollars on a college education, but the cable bill pays for an education, too. Because it's so pervasive, it's probably more educational than most college classes. TV is a major part of the moral ecology of campus life, and yet students hardly ever think about it.[38]

We say we watch television, but most of us don't really watch at all. At its root, the word "watch" means "the act of keeping awake and alert, in order to look after, protect, or defend." Of course, this means that most of us who are "watching TV" are *not*, in fact. When we assume the couch-potato position, we are not really on guard even though there is plenty to guard against. We really need to *watch* TV, and we especially need to *watch* the ads.

We need to watch television, not just as a series of programs, but as a system. CBS, the Columbia Broadcast *System*, is just one part of an interlocked system of communications that fails to communicate effectively about environmental issues. The television system—designed to sell stuff to a people of plenty—isn't adequate for the twenty-first century. We'll always have a chance to watch mindless entertainment, but it's now time to create a system that can increase our mindfulness as well.

We also need to remember that television is never free, even on the broadcast networks. There's the cost of the equipment—TV, DVD player, video consoles, surround-sound systems. There's the cost of cable or satellite reception if we're not satisfied with basic broadcast channels. There's the cost of Netflix or other movie rentals. There's the cost of pay-per-view. There's the opportunity cost of our time, and the time that others have invested in the infrastructure of this audiovisual array. There's the material cost of plastics, glass, and toxic elements (like lead, cadmium, mercury), as well as the by-products of electronic components and computer chips. There's the cost of electricity to power the TV and its peripherals, and the embodied energy in the materials. There's the cost to America's moral and spiritual resources. And there's the cost—including the environmental cost—of our increased consumption.

Watching TV, we also need to remember that, on television, "good news" isn't always a good thing. When the GDP grows, the number of housing starts increases, or consumer confidence trends upward, it's good news on TV because, well, because that's the common sense of TV culture. The growth of the GDP really would be good news if it were connected to human fulfillment on a flourishing planet. But too often it's not. It would be good news if we were building more houses, as long as our houses keep our ecological footprint small. But few of them do. It would be good news if consumers were feeling more confident, if we knew that they would only spend their money on sustainable products. But mostly we don't. Even on the weather, it's good news if it's sunny, even though forests or farms may need rain. We need to be able to tune in to programming that's really tuned into the planet.

We also need to consider the question that Thoreau posed implicitly in *Walden*: what are communications for? In practice, *our* answers include connection, entertainment, information, profit, procrastination, disinformation, distraction, and diversion. In contrast, for Thoreau, the purpose of communications was "mutual enlightenment, not diversion, profit, or the spread of ever more information." Like Wendell Berry today, Thoreau thought that the purpose of communication was to tell the truth. And on the other end, the purpose of communications was for people to shape the truth into wisdom, and then into a life worth living.[39]

Finally, we need to consider the possibility that what we watch on TV is not as important as what we don't watch in the world around us. Every hour that we watch television is an hour we're not watching nature—keeping awake and alert in order to protect and defend a planet that's being harmed primarily by people in the developed world who see the world through television. Instead of being screened from nature, we might set down the remote controls and go out and experience places where we're *not* in control. Like Thoreau at Walden, Mary Oliver in Provincetown, or Bill McKibben in the Adirondacks, we might see what wisdom we might find in contemplating our particular part of a blue-green planet teeming with life and death, community and complexity, majesty and mystery.

It probably won't be televised.

The Nature of Computing

Television is pervasive on campus, but, more than any other recent invention, computers have fundamentally changed the college experience. On campus, Joe and Jo College interact with their electronic devices every day, and they connect virtually with friends and family and anonymous strangers all the time. Both use their computers for research and writing academic papers, but those uses tend to be sporadic, dependent on the deadlines of classes and professors. Even though computers are a recent invention, it's now hard to imagine college life without them.

Most college students today have grown up with electronics. Eighty-six percent of American homes with kids aged eight to eighteen have a computer, 74 percent have Internet connectivity, and 83 percent own a game console. Sixty-four percent of children spend recreational time with a computer every day, and they average two hours and nineteen minutes at this (versus sixteen minutes for schoolwork). As a result, computers are embedded in the lives of college students. Ninety-seven percent of college students own a computer, and many carry laptops almost everywhere. Ninety percent have high-speed Internet access in their dorm room or apartment, and 94 percent own a cell phone. This is the first generation since the 1950s to spend *less* time in front of the TV, but this doesn't mean less screen time. College students average nearly two hours a day playing video games, and nearly three hours a day on the Internet. Almost a third are bloggers, and 44 percent read blogs for about an hour a week. Students also excel at e-mail. In one semester at St. Olaf in 2007, students sent and received more than ten million e-mail messages, more than twenty-five hundred per account. A hefty majority of college students use instant messaging, and users average about eighty minutes a day. Even as communications go wireless, this generation is more connected than any other in the history of the world.[40]

The word "computer" comes from Latin roots that mean "to think with," and scientists and other researchers think with computers to model phenomena—natural, social, and economic. With their incredible search capabilities, computers help students think along with great minds, dead and alive. As text and image processors, computers also help us to share ideas with millions of other people who have access to the Internet. Computers can be good for us. But it's not clear that they have made us any more thoughtful, or that access to infinite information has made us any wiser. Nor is it clear that computers have made us better stewards of the Earth.

The Nature of Facebook

If college were to have a single textbook for life beyond the classroom, Facebook would be it. A page-turning thriller, a flashy romance novel, a political pamphlet, and a diary pulled from under the mattress and displayed for all to see—college students hit this book like no other. Drawn into its plotlines for an average of twenty minutes a day, more than 85 percent of college students use this textbook of culture and cool, flipping through its billions of photographs and studying its countless pages as if preparing for a midterm exam—except that this material includes socially significant things like a friend's new favorite YouTube video and the status of that cute guy who sits in the first row of biology class. If the Bible was the most read and referenced book of the last twenty centuries, Facebook seems to be scripture for college students in the early twenty-first century. And this cyberspace community has real-world environmental impacts.[41]

Social networking on places like Facebook and MySpace has roiled like a thunderstorm on a humid summer day. Mark Zuckerberg, a Harvard student, developed Facebook.com in 2004. Originally offered just to Harvard students, it gradually expanded to all colleges—and then to anyone with an e-mail address. Six years later, there are more than four hundred million users, who spend more than fifty-five minutes a day on the site. Each day thirty-five million people update their profiles or add to their news feeds. At the University of Illinois in 2006 and 2007, about 75 percent of students logged in to Facebook one to four times a day, and some students kept it continually open in a browser on the desktop.[42]

As with any pervasive cultural phenomenon, Facebook is a lot of different things to different people. Some use it as a blog, some as an e-mail inbox, and others simply to catalog their tastes. Some use it for self-reflection and self-expression, while others wax nostalgic, keeping up with friends from the past. It's a way to get a taste of a person's taste, as well as a way to check out people you find attractive. Facebook helps us meet with friends who are near at hand, and to connect periodically to others far away. It's a tool to satisfy the innate curiosity we have about other human beings. Indeed, Facebook is so popular because it has so many varied functions. It's the town square of the virtual village. If given fifteen minutes of spare time, more college students would spend it browsing a social network than watching television or playing a video game. With user-created pages that are constantly evolving and expanding, social sites like Facebook are often the first destination for college students in the morning and a popular late-night hangout as well.

"People treat Facebook as an authentic part of their lives," Facebook reminds advertisers, "so you can be sure you are connecting with real people with real interest in your products." With all of our "friending" and reading of news feeds, it's easy to forget that Facebook, like television, is in the business of selling eyes to advertisers. The ads aren't as intrusive as those on TV, but the Facebook website assures advertisers that they can "reach over 400,000,000 active Facebook users," "attach social actions to [their] ads to increase relevance," and "create demand for [their] product with relevant ads." And it works. Founder Mark Zuckerberg is the world's youngest billionaire because unpaid Facebook members happily create the content for a site that then targets them for advertising.[43]

Profile

Facebook claims to be a "social utility that connects you with the people around you." Anyone with an e-mail address can sign up for free. Once signed up, we're asked to craft an Internet profile. To do this, we provide extensive contact information—e-mail address, Web address, AIM screen name, postal address, and multiple telephone numbers. We also fill out information describing us—our interests and activities, favorite TV shows and movies, defining books, and music. There's a blank labeled "About Me" where we give our best attempt at self-definition. And don't forget the picture, face shot optional. As much as we'd like to insist that our profiles don't really matter, the information and images we provide make a real difference in a Facebook culture.[44]

This doesn't mean that we're always honest, however. Facebook is a place to fashion one's identity as a friend or potential mate, as a consumer or comedian. It's a place for the presentation of self in certain ways, for reputation management. But even the best crafted "About Me" doesn't tell everything. Indeed, the word "profile" implies a flattening, a dimensional reduction—etymologically it's a mere outline, more about surfaces than depth. As we fill in the blanks, we systematically reduce our sense of self to the categories appropriate for acquaintanceship and small talk, a prefab product to be consumed by our friends. Facebook is open to everything, but some activities just don't come across there. The social conventions of Facebook limit our choices—and eventually also our perception of college culture and reality.[45]

As this suggests, a lot of information is missing from Facebook. It shows the self in relation, but not in relation to much. Social networks are a good place for the friendly self, and a perfect place to foreground our commodity self—the self that is defined by consumer goods and media tastes. Yet the self as defined by family, community, skill, vocation, and nature recedes into the background. As Jean Baudrillard has noted, "We live in a world where there is more and more information, and less and less meaning."[46]

Friends and Connections

Once we have our profile perfected, or at least presentable, we're ready for interaction. On Facebook, we update where we are or how we are feeling. We offer diary entries or craft one-line jokes. Sometimes we find elementary-school friends. Some students might score a date for the weekend, but more often they look at the profiles of crushes and *imagine* scoring a date. There is a convenient birthday calendar, so we post birthday greetings on each other's walls, being sure to diversify the wording to avoid clichés that hint at the superficiality of the salutation. There is a personalized news feed, so sometimes we learn about momentous events in our closest friends' lives through Facebook. A graphic of a broken heart flashes on our news feed the moment a couple ends their relationship. So we console each other on Facebook. And we gossip.

Friendship has always been at the core of college life. And Facebook helps students connect with friends near and far. It's a social network that can build social capital. But it also advances its own peculiar conception of friendship. College students believe the old adage that "the friends you make in college are as important as the classes you take." And they know that friends come in many varieties: There are best friends and just friends, good friends and not-really-friends-at-all friends. But on Facebook, where the average user has 130 friends, virtually everyone you know is "just a friend."[47]

Robert Bellah argues that friendship has three components: "Friends must enjoy one another's company, they must be useful to one another, and they must share a common commitment to the good." None of these criteria necessarily applies when "friending" someone on Facebook. Sometimes Facebook friends enjoy each other's company, but seldom is there a common commitment to a good society or a good Earth. Students are generally sociable with their Facebook friends, but a close relationship is hardly necessary. Emerson thought a friend was rare, "a masterpiece of nature." On Facebook, friends are expected to be much more ordinary. In a situation of "networked individualism," author Maggie Jackson suggests, "wired folks have bigger networks of weaker ties."[48]

Despite all of our "friending," we still know that most of our Facebook pals are less important than our real friends, and that an hour on Facebook is less fulfilling than an hour in person. Few of us would rather look at our friends in cyberspace than be with them in some real place. That's why our photo albums show parties and adventures, friends hugging each other, and significant others kissing—not pictures of people scrolling up and down Facebook walls and "poking" each other. And Facebook is far too big to stay on a seventeen-inch LCD screen, so naturally it spills over into the rest of our life, changing how we speak and act. Everything from political canvassing to ending a relationship may now be done on a social network. With the new territory comes limitations and peculiar patterns of behavior. In real life, you usually don't simply ask, "Will you be my friend?" but on Facebook that is normal and expected. If you wanted to know if two of your friends already knew each other, you would normally have to ask one of them. On Facebook, a simple click will suffice. Conversation starters now range from, "Did you see what she wrote on Pat's wall?" to "Did I tell you Kris poked me twice last week?" A strangely timed friend request makes you wonder if the requester even *likes* you. The hilarious comment Sam made at lunch is praised with a, "*That's* going on Facebook!" Worthy stories are Facebook stories.[49]

The Nature of Distraction

Distraction: The act of paying attention to the wrong thing. In the early 21st century, Americans live in a culture of distraction, designed to keep us thinking about white teeth and sexy hair, beer and big breasts, junk food and giant cars, fun and fashion, instead of liberty and justice (or a sustainable future) for all.

In a society of disconnection, social networks make valuable connections between people separated in space or time. In a world of increasing individualism and the disintegration of local communities,
Facebook can help us cope with our decreasing sociability. Certainly
something has changed about how we experience friendship. The flash
of the screen has replaced the flesh of the body. As Maggie Jackson
suggests, "We take the faceless at face value now." In our attempts to
converse with more people—more often, more quickly, more easily—
we have fewer face-to-face conversations, reducing our communicative
dances to flat exchanges of 12-point font on virtual walls. The language
of screens lacks the language of the body. We can splash yellow, grin-
ning emoticons all we want, we can type "lol" until our fingers fall off,
but something is lost.[50]

The most profound effect of Facebook, beyond its effect on our
perception of ourselves and our communities, is what it keeps us from
doing. In fact, Facebook is probably popular because it fits so well with
a culture of distraction and a net of interruptions. When the new e-mail
pings in the inbox, we're always tempted to look—and often we do, "just
for a minute." But one thing often leads to another. Interruption scientist Gloria Mark finds that workers in West Coast high-tech firms are
interrupted almost constantly, working just eleven minutes on a project
(on average) before moving to something else. Multitasking through
the day, workers shift between twelve different work projects, averaging just twenty seconds per open window. She also found that about
45 percent of interruptions are self-initiated, as they check their e-mail,
look at the weather, or open another window on their screen. A newly
integral part of college culture, Facebook prepares students well for this
fast and fragmented world. And it helps keep their focus away from our
environmental dilemma.[51]

All of this Facebook activity is entrancing, and we participate willingly, although we also complain (of course) about how much time it
takes to keep up. Sometimes this social network feels just like work. But
all the time, it's doing cultural work—cultural work that affects our relationship with the natural world. On a globe where the climate is changing and species are perishing, it allows us to focus instead on the soap
opera of our lives. We spend less time reading the *New York Times* these
days, and more time browsing our Facebook news feed. We spend less
time thinking about democracy and citizenship, and more time caught
up in the day-to-day jockeying of the college social world. Facebook is
good for social capital, but not necessarily for social change.

Nature on Facebook

Social networks like Facebook are fundamentally about human relationships. They can be a means for solidifying and validating our connection with people we met the night before, or just an opportunity to sustain a relationship with friends who are far away. But how do they affect our relationship to nature? What do we learn about the importance of wild places and nonhuman beings when we read Facebook?

Almost nothing, it seems. Facebook is as anthropocentric as television, a human network concerned almost exclusively with human interactions. And as Facebook connects us to other humans who aren't in the same room, we disconnect from the embodied and biological world, and that's a problem. Facebook will be Farcebook if it mainly distracts us from the environmental crisis we face.

Nature in Facebook: The Materialism of Immaterialism

We commonly talk of the world of computers as "cyberspace" or "the virtual world"—a place where some of us exist as avatars in Second Life or impersonators in chat rooms. It's common sense that computers reduce our dependence on the physical world of pens, pencils, and paper, of stores and malls, of materials of many kinds. When we're online, except for the screen in front of our face, our existence seems strangely immaterial. But it's not.

Time flows and resource flows are embedded in all online activity. On a personal level, the time we spend on Facebook is time not spent on homework or making a home in our ecological community. It might be time promoting a social or environmental cause, but more likely it's just time reading news feeds about the trivia of daily life, or the new friends that your friends have "friended." So the opportunity costs are considerable.

We can join environmental groups on Facebook, and the mobilizing potential of Web 2.0 is impressive. But even as we profess green values on Facebook, the activity itself takes place away from nature, inevitably consuming real nature through the energy expended. Facebook's style of connecting to friends—and potential political allies—cannot be done without a computer, electricity, and a connection to the Internet. All of these, of course, are not possible without coal being burned, dams being built, and turbines whirling around. A more substantive interaction could be achieved by standing up, walking out of your room, and actually talking in person with friends who are also interested in social change.

The Nature in Screens

Physically, our computing has ecological effects that are invisible at first. Even if you don't find much nature on your computer screen, it's there behind the glossy surface and humming through the wires. Indeed, a forgotten part of the nature of screens is the nature *in* screens, both as raw materials and energy flows: the quartz made into silicon, the copper mined and etched into circuit boards, the coal burned to power the hard drive, and the toxicity of the outdated and discarded computer leaking hazardous chemicals. Nature from all over the globe gets processed and pressed to form our computers, televisions, iPods, iPads, and iPhonomena. A few years from now, when these devices are already "out-of-date," nature will be impacted again as we send this obsolescence to a landfill.

We tend not to think of time spent in front of TVs and computers as an act of consumption because nothing disappears from view except images. But, in all likelihood, our electronic technologies are the most energy-intensive things we own. Tracing all the processes that are necessary for the production of a desktop computer with a seventeen-inch monitor, Eric Williams suggests that it uses at least eleven times its weight in fossil fuels and chemicals to produce (our cars have a ratio of two pounds of material to every one pound of car). If we totaled up all the nature involved in getting the computer to us, we'd find approximately 530 pounds of fossil fuels, 3,330 pounds of water, and 50 pounds of chemicals—more than two tons of material in all. Contained within each computer are dozens of tiny microchips. More than 80 percent of the energy used by a typical computer will be used in the production of these small parts. By the time the computer is shipped to a retail store, 80 percent of its total life-cycle energy costs will already have been incurred.[52]

The amount of energy used to produce a desktop computer could power an entire dorm for more than two days. And the amount of water used in production is nearly half the water an average American drinks in a lifetime. We can't possibly feel the weight that our slick RAZR phone and iPod nano have on distant and disparate places in nature, but it's likely that it would take a garbage truck full of materials and water to lug all the natural materials that go into these miniature artifacts.[53]

Wasted

The image of a garbage truck is apt in this case. Moore's Law suggests that the processing capacity of computer chips doubles about every two years, so computers come with built-in obsolescence. To some extent this is good; computers are getting quicker and more capacious all the time. But our perception that new models are needed every few years is leading to immense waste. The computers of incoming college students will be "obsolete" by graduation.

Unfortunately, unlike items that are more recyclable, computers contain hazardous chemicals. Some older televisions and CRT computer monitors contained up to eight pounds of lead. The tubes themselves contained other toxic chemicals like mercury and cadmium, materials which, when dumped into landfills, quickly contaminate groundwater. It's estimated that 40 percent of the heavy metals in U.S. landfills come from discarded electronic machines. And much of our e-waste is exported to China, where unprotected workers breathe its toxic fumes. We throw it all away, forgetting that there's really no such place as "away."[54]

The Nature of "The Cloud"

The nature that's impacted by our screens isn't just the nature neglected, not just the nature transformed in production, and not just the nature polluted after we toss it in the dump. It's also the nature we use to power it all in the meantime. Connected to the Internet, our electronic impulses slither through servers commonly called "the cloud"—a soft and fuzzy metaphor that obscures the nature in our consumption of electricity, coal, gas, and uranium. On Facebook, more than two hundred million people have uploaded more than fifteen billion photographs, and all of them reside in "the cloud" on servers that suck up an increasing amount of electricity in America and across the world. Our own computers use electricity, of course, but that's just the tip of the power cord, because our casual computing depends on server farms that keep Google, Microsoft, and Yahoo! in business.

When students "poke" a friend on Facebook or e-mail Mom, servers somewhere spring to life. When they play *Call of Duty* in the virtual world, they're really gathering in a data center somewhere in the real

world. And these servers are in the energy business—big time. In "A Smarter Shade of Green," the Technology CEO Council reports that "it can cost more to power and cool a server over its lifetime than it does to buy the server." The Environmental Protection Agency estimates that server farms and other data centers alone consume 1.5 percent of U.S. electricity, precisely because cooling the servers takes about as much energy as running them. The *Economist* reports, "Microsoft's $500m new facility near Chicago will need three electrical substations with a total capacity of 198 megawatts." Computer data centers now use more electricity than the entire country of Sweden, and consumption is increasing. So, until U.S. energy policy routinely produces green electricity, Joe and Jo College are connected not just to friends, Facebook, and Wikipedia, but to coal and uranium mines, and to natural gas fields. The immateriality of computing rests on a very material base. The *system* of computing is infinitely more complex than anything that shows up on our screens.[55]

The Virtues of the Virtual

Using energy and resources isn't by nature a bad thing. Despite the environmental impacts of making and powering our obsolescing electronics, there are positive aspects of the nature of screens. Social networks, for example, can have positive applications that supersede the chitchat and gossip of everyday use. Students can create groups that bring together people with environmental interests. Social networks can also be political networks (see chapter 10), helping users to share ideas and information. In 2008, for example, volunteers for the Obama campaign designed an iPhone application that allowed students to organize their "friends lists" by state, making it easy to contact friends in crucial swing states. But these aren't the only Internet innovations that offer positive applications.[56]

Indeed, just in environmental circles, the Web offers a lot of possibilities. Virtually all environmental organizations have a virtual presence online. There are environmental news outlets like *Grist*, *Treehugger*, and *ENN*. There's EcoGeek and RealClimate for the scientifically minded, and Ecorazzi for *People* readers. There's ClimateEthics for the conscientious and *Worldchanging* for those who want to do something about it. None of these sites get as much traffic as Facebook or iTunes, but they are available, just in case we ever get serious about the nature of our lives.

Some Internet innovations go beyond information and organizing to changing the moral ecology of material life. The materials in our screens, for example, make possible a significant amount of what some activists call "e-materialization." In *Seven Wonders for a Cool Planet*, for example, Eric Sorensen notes that microchips make possible such inventions as file sharing, in which shared electronic music files displace the individually owned vinyl and plastic of records, tapes, and CDs. If Joe and Jo College (and other Americans) can derive the same musical satisfaction from the immaterial tunes of an electronic file, then American materialism has a chance to be replaced by a process of dematerialization.[57]

In the same way, Sorensen also suggests that Internet shopping—thanks to electronic retailing (or "e-tailing")—can be an efficient and environmental alternative to driving to stores to find that perfect outfit, a Miracle Bra, or the fair-trade coffee that your girlfriend recommended. E-tailing saves not just trips to the store, but in some cases the environmental costs of the store itself. As Sorensen suggests, "[a] broader application of Internet retailing could eliminate the need for 12.5 percent of retail building space. This is the same as 1.5 billion square feet of commercial space, saving hundreds of millions of dollars in heating costs."[58]

College students also find that the Internet connects them with books—and book bargains. Instead of going to the library to see if the books they need are on the shelves, they can check online. Instead of buying new books at the college bookstore, students can search the Internet for cheaper possibilities. Instead of driving to bookstores, students can search Amazon or other online booksellers. Joseph Romm estimates that "the energy costs per book sold are sixteen times greater for a conventional bookstore than for Amazon."[59]

The Internet also helps us keep our stuff from obsolescing so fast. Online selling has allowed a remarkable resurgence of secondary markets, with eBay, Craigslist, Freecycle, and other exchanges providing people a chance to buy and sell used items, sometimes keeping them out of the garbage and in circulation.

Computer screens can also convey important information. They can serve as feedback loops for the systems of our lives, reminding us of the ways in which our ordinary consumption is wired to the web of life. At Dartmouth College, for example, students in a digital-art class worked with an environmental club to outfit two residence halls with monitors showing real-time electricity use in the buildings. On-screen, an animated polar bear responds to the level of power use. When students boot up too many computers or crank up too many stereos, the bear falls through the ice.[60]

Of course, in all of these situations, there are costs as well as benefits. Internet shopping makes buying stuff so easy that sometimes we buy more than we need. It also changes the shopping experience, substituting images and abstraction for the sensuous pleasures of a store adventure. Amazon is a wonderful tool for buying books, but it's not the same as a good independent bookstore, where you might be able to curl up with a book or converse with a knowledgeable staff member. The natural capital saved in energy and materials has to be weighed against the social capital lost in shopping in person. And the electrical energy invested in electronic polar bears needs to be weighed against the effects on our beliefs and behavior.

A Delicate Balance

Facebook and other computer applications may help to express the self, but they also affect the self. When we think of ourselves in terms of a profile, or in terms of pictures, we think of ourselves differently than we do if we think of ourselves as citizens, family members, or true friends. With screens full of images and sound, we get screened from silence, calm, and solitude. When we're accustomed to "multitasking," we can find it hard to focus. One Pittsburgh-area teen told researchers that instant messaging "kind of keeps you busy. It's kind of boring talking to one person 'cause then like . . . you can't talk to anyone else." When we outsource all our memory to devices, we find it hard to remember what's important. When we're online all the time, we're affected by the experience. We think we're just "poking" a friend or uploading pictures to our albums, but we're also adapting to the medium, conforming to the social expectations of a new technology. We imagine that a constant self signs in to Facebook, but we forget that Facebook also signs in to us.[61]

Computers, like television, also affect our sense of timeliness, reducing it from days or hours to minutes, seconds, or even nanoseconds. When we get used to the speed of computers, we become impatient with the pace of face-to-face life. We routinely complain that our computers are too slow, although they are faster than anything that existed on Earth a quarter of a century ago. Computers are also complicit in the spread of "artificial urgency," the sense that we need things done immediately, if not sooner. A *Time* ad asked, "Remember what it was like before there was overnight mail, voice mail, and e-mail? You actually had time to think." The ad, of course, doesn't contend that anybody actually *did* think, but at least there was time for it. Now, we rush to meet the deadlines artificially imposed by the speed paradigm we have created. Students e-mail a professor a question, and expect an answer immediately. This is what one critic calls "reverse adaptation," a process in which we are compelled to adapt to tools we originally adopted for specific purposes. Reverse adaptation is the situation in which the tail wags the dog. It's when inventions become the mother of necessity. As Thoreau suggested one hundred and fifty years ago, "We do not ride on the railroad; it rides upon us." And so we are called to consider, and reconsider, how to use technology that seems bent on using us.[62]

Reversing Reverse Adaptation

At college, the life of the mind is not always a life of mindfulness. Students get so focused on classes, assignments, and grades that they forget to make time for reflection. Connection to TV, the Internet, and iTunes distracts them from the fact that the mind is connected to the body, and that both the body and human technologies are connected to the Earth.

Computers are remarkable tools, and most of us these days don't even stop to wonder what we would do without them. Convenience in a box, they're good for computations, communications, and commerce, as well as for information, entertainment, and self-expression. With numerous windows on a screen, we can save time, we think, by multitasking. Most of us will depend on computers for the rest of our lives.

The computer can be a tool to use in a good life, but it isn't always good. Televisions and the Internet can help to inform us, but they also *form* us, shaping our inner lives, our character, and our conception of human nature and purpose. They can provide cheap entertainment for masses of people, but they can also cheapen entertainment and degrade the masses. They can help explain the nature of our world, but they can't do as much to help us *experience* the nature of our world. As we currently use them, computers are good tools for connecting with people and disconnecting from our environment. They also reinforce some of the contradictions of American culture, including the psychological compartmentalization that lets us believe that we are living the "good life" when we're ignoring the ecosystems that support us. Giving us a mediated connectedness, our screens are at the same time a sign of several kinds of disconnection in American culture—and American character.

One person who helps us think about such disconnections is farmer and poet Wendell Berry. In a controversial essay that appeared in *Harper's* in 1987, "Why I Am Not Going to Buy a Computer," Berry wrote that he did not want to be a blind follower of technological trends. "I do not own a TV set," he said, and "I do not see that computers are bringing us one step nearer to anything that does matter to me: peace, economic justice, ecological health, political honesty, family and community stability, good work." In his meditation, Berry offered his own standards for technological innovation:

1) The new tool should be cheaper than the one it replaces.
2) It should be at least as small in scale as the one it replaces.
3) It should do work that is clearly and demonstrably better than the one it replaces. [Berry said that he did not think his poetry would improve if he used a computer rather than a pencil.]
4) It should use less energy than the one it replaces.
5) If possible, it should use some form of solar energy, such as that of the body.
6) It should be repairable by a person of ordinary intelligence, provided that he or she has the necessary tools.
7) It should be purchasable and repairable as near to home as possible.
8) It should come from a small, privately owned shop or store that will take it back for maintenance and repair.
9) It should not replace or disrupt anything good that already exists, and this includes family and community relationships.

I disagree with Berry about buying a computer, and I currently use two, not counting all the other computers that serve me remotely. I think that computers can be an appropriate technology. But I agree with Berry's effort to provide us with some standards for technological innovation, and with his critique of the default standards we usually employ: "new and improved" products that come to us from multinational corporations and marketing conglomerates, without much consideration of the full life-cycle costs of the product, or the full lifestyle impacts on people and their communities, including their natural communities.[63]

In America, we value computers because they are fast, efficient, predictable, and—at least theoretically—controllable. But the value of computers is different, depending on context. In a task-and-time context, when we have a specific job to do quickly, computers can be invaluable. In a broader context, though, we might wonder whether computers can *make* good work as well as they *do* good work. In a social context, we would need to consider the cultural consequences of computer screening, the social costs and benefits of keyboarding in front of electronic displays. In an ecological context, we would need to think about computing in a context of resource flows. Is a machine that's efficient for word processing, spreadsheets, and databases *really* efficient, *really* sustainable? In a religious context, we might need to consider how our electronic devices help us to achieve a virtuous life in an increasingly virtual world. In a human context, we would need to sort out the ways that computers and television help or hinder our experience of wonder, our sense of compassion for fellow creatures, and our commitment to justice for people in our own time and in posterity.

More specifically, we need to use our electronic devices more carefully. In the first place, we can advocate and practice a media literacy that includes critical viewing skills, and an ability to look and think outside the boxes of TV and computers for a political, economic, social, and environmental analysis of the media. But we can also empower ourselves to power them off, especially when there's stupidity on the screen. Speaking of TV, Bette Midler revealed, "I made a pact with myself. Never watch anything stupider than you. It's helped me a lot." In a context of persistent time poverty and minimal meaning making, we would be richer if we took back some of the time we give to advertisers, TV networks, and social networks.[64]

Second, we need to watch these networks for *their* networks—the ways in which they connect or don't connect us to the natural world and to social circles where people are plotting the ecological revolution of the twenty-first century. We can really *watch* TV to make sense of its place in the moral ecology of everyday life. We can compute— "think with"—our computers, checking up on environmental news and views, and linking with other concerned citizens to pressure people in power with boycotts, "buycotts," and other political action.

"Breaking Free of Screens" courtesy of Andrew Singer. Reproduced by permission from the artist.

Third, we can engage in countercultural media practices, using new media to create a new cultural politics. Instead of simply consuming the corporate offerings on TV and the Internet, we can produce our own videos and upload them on YouTube or our own websites. We can read blogs that point to the systematic problems of a mediated culture, and we can write blogs that help connect readers to good sources of information, understanding, and wisdom.

Fourth, we can combat the sensory deprivation of TV, computers, and cell phones by leaving them behind for time in nature, both wild and domesticated. We can develop our ecological consciousness with a variety of practices. We can acknowledge the sun for its contributions to our life, and live in nature's time instead of time demarked by alarm clocks. We can begin naming the nature that we love, so that we recognize plants and animals as readily as brands and logos. We can imagine our foodsheds and ritualize our gratitude by saying grace. Planting gardens or restoring native species, we can engage in the practice of the wild in a particular place. Experiencing heat and cold, rain and snow, we can deliver our own weather report. Telling stories, old and new, of sustainability, we can create or attend seasonal rituals. We can practice ecological citizenship by speaking politically for the more-than-human-community we encounter. Refusing to be screened from the natural world, we can make connections that are deeper than anything electronic.[65]

Placebook

Finally, we might use our social networks to express and enhance our ecological networks. Facebook doesn't help with that, because _placebook_

it's anthropocentric. As founder Mark Zuckerberg said, "People are the most interesting thing—other people." But it could be different. Facebook could be a social utility useful precisely for its ecocentric eccentricity. Instead of the exclusively human networking of the current Facebook, it might express more complex networks. "About Me" might ask for home place, watershed, bioregion, and ecosystem. It might include our place in food chains and product chains, or water cycles and carbon cycles. It might ask people to calculate their ecological footprint, list ten native plants where they live, or post a picture of their garden. An environmentally useful social utility might invite members to name a totem, some animal figure that animates them and binds them together. "Favorites" wouldn't be restricted to the commercial media one consumes, but could include favorite trees, animals, seasons, and wildernesses. "Relationship Status" would still include significant others, but some of the others might be nonhuman. A person could be married to a backyard garden, engaged to the wilderness in Alaska, or seeking a long-term relationship with the prairie. Such a "Placebook" would be a space to express our deepest values, instead of our superficial consumption preferences.[66]

A new Facebook would satisfy many of the human desires that make it successful, but it would also extend the range of our care. As Kathleen Dean Moore suggests in _The Pine Island Paradox_, people have a deep desire for sustaining connections to all life:

> Human beings are creatures who are drawn to one another. We humans are born into networks of dependencies and complications, hidden connections, memories and yearnings, births and rebirths, fierce, mysterious love—a web of relationships. . . . We're born into relationships, not just with human beings, but with the land—the beautiful, complicated web of sustaining connections that Aldo Leopold calls the "biotic community." Don't I value also my connections to the natural world—the deep biological connections that create

and sustain me, the emotional connections that root me to
the land and anchor me at sea?[67]

Such a Placebook would remind us that we're on the Internet, but we're
also intimately and intricately interconnected to all the creatures that
aren't.

Computers and information technologies will shape the future. But
they will shape the future we *want* only if we design them to humanize
human beings, in part by adapting us to live harmoniously within the
limits of a bountiful biosphere. Adapting our technologies to our human
dimensions and the Earth's natural cycles, we'll be watching out for the
planet, and computing—"thinking together"—in ways that we haven't
done recently. After all, we may be on the Web, but we're *in* the web of
life.[68]

7

The Nature of Parties

Party on!
Wayne and Garth, *Wayne's World*

*I don't believe in the Republican Party or the Democratic
Party—I just believe in parties.*
Samantha, *Sex and the City*

*Most of the time I don't have much fun. The rest of the time
I don't have any fun at all.*
Woody Allen

■ ■ ■ ■ ■ ■ ■ ■

As Joe College sits in his environmental history class, he's thinking
about the 1908 conservation conference hosted by Theodore Roosevelt,
but he's also considering what he'll do when class is over. He's debating whether to shoot hoops or to play video games with the guys, and
pondering how to celebrate hump day. In her biology lab, his sister
is concentrating on the anatomy of a frog, but she's multitasking too,
making mental lists of the supplies she'll need for the football festivities
on Saturday. Both of them are waiting for the weekend. Even at work,
they're often thinking of play.[1]

To some extent, this is perfectly appropriate, since the Greek root
of "school" is a word that means leisure. The Greeks understood that it
took time to understand the world, and they knew that slaves, women,
and the working classes didn't have the free time for liberal education.
Ancient Greeks used their leisure for schooling, but American college
students—including campus "Greeks"—use their free time differently.
It's hard to imagine Socrates playing *Grand Theft Auto,* or Plato and
Aristotle playing beer pong.

When the Pew Research Center asked eighteen-to-twenty-five-year-
olds to describe their generation, they used labels like "lazy," "crazy," and
"fun." Fifty percent of teens told Teenage Research Unlimited (TRU)
that their generation is "about fun," and 69 percent claimed that they "always try to have as much fun as possible." And these attitudes definitely

don't stop when students arrive at college. According to the American Time Use Survey of the United States Bureau of Labor Statistics, full-time U.S. college students spend more time on leisure and sports than on classes and homework. If actions are a measure of values, then college students value fun more than learning.[2]

Fun-damentalism: The primary religion of American life; the idea that people are created to have fun. More popular than all other fundamentalisms combined, it explains why the great American interdenominational prayer is "Thank God it's Friday."

Anthropologists studying contemporary college students note that fun is why many young adults go to college. In his 1989 study of college life, Michael Moffatt described student perceptions of the purpose of college: "Beyond formal education, college as the students saw it was also about coming-of-age. It was where you went to break away from home, to learn responsibility and maturity, to do some growing up. College was about being on your own, about autonomy, about freedom from the authority of adults, however benign their intentions. And last, but hardly least, college was about fun."[3] Even though today's students spend immense sums for the opportunity to think critically and learn about the world, they also spend thousands of dollars in the pursuit of fun. Why? Because it's a commonsense component of the moral ecology of college life.

If we want to understand the environmental impacts of college—including the impacts of common sense—we need to study fun, including the nature of parties, the wildness of wild parties, and the assumptions that govern college playtime. We need to consider the relationship of fun and fulfillment, and their connection to the pursuit of happiness, as we engage in the ecological revolution of the twenty-first century.

The Nature of Parties

College students have fun in almost as many ways as there are students. There are intercollegiate sports and intramurals, the fun of hanging out and of hooking up. There is the quiet fun of conversations, walks hand in hand, and meals together. There is the fun of video games, board games, and card games. There are fun times at the movies, making music, and creating personal playlists. Dancing and clubbing are fun, and so is active membership in campus clubs and organizations. Especially with friends, watching TV or sporting events is fun. Road trips are a gas, and so are Spring Break and foreign travel. There's even some fun in academics, although that's not talked about as much as other kinds of enjoyment. All this said, when Jo and Joe College think of campus fun, they probably think first of parties, the quintessence of good times in academia.

A party is a social gathering for pleasure and amusement, and the college party is one of the oldest campus traditions, practiced and perfected for nearly the whole history of higher education. A *wild* party is a variation on the party theme, a cultural phenomenon composed of beer, booze, music, dancing, games, and sex. Because it's where students most often encounter the wild on campus, the rituals of a party can help us think about the meanings of wildness in college culture.

Wild parties don't occur in the wilderness, of course, although occasionally they do take place outside. They usually occur in the domestic spaces of fraternity or sorority houses, "satellite houses," or dorm rooms. Whatever the location, wild behavior is expected, but not a wilderness experience.

Beer: The elixir of college life, the fermented beverage that foments fellowship, fun, fantasy, audacity, hook ups, unconsciousness, and hangovers, among other things.

There's no such thing as a wild party without alcohol; it's even debatable whether there can be any college party without it. Even though drinking is illegal for most college students, relatively few students care. In fact, in a 2006 survey by the American College Health Association (ACHA), 48 percent of college guys reported having polished off more than five drinks at their last party, while women averaged more than three. The ACHA estimated that, on average, blood-alcohol levels at the end of a party are just under the legal limits for driving in most states. More than a third of students had downed five or more drinks in a single sitting during the two weeks before the survey, which meets the standard definition of binge drinking. Although many students started drinking well before college, everyone's expected to join the fun once they get to campus. Even adults assume it is part of "the college experience." And thus drinking and drunkenness frame this time-honored ritual of college life.

The common language of drunkenness suggests that students understand its symptoms well. They refer to getting "trashed" or "smashed," "blitzed" or "blasted," "wasted," "wiped," and even "annihilated." They know it's a waste, but for some reason semiconsciousness feels good (at least for a few hours). The hurling and the hangover come later. When college students are wild, they're only in the present, though sometimes barely even there.

At parties, students often play drinking games. The most popular is probably beer pong, a contest in which pairs of students compete by tossing or bouncing Ping-Pong balls into cups of beer in order to "force" the other team to chug their beer. But games are hardly necessary to make drinking a competition. Guys have long converted peer pressure to beer pressure, trying to match each other drink for drink. And now young women are competing, too. In recent years, college women have increased their rates of drinking, binge drinking, acute intoxication, hospitalization, and unplanned sexual activities (including sexual assault). As one woman noted, "To be able to drink like a guy is kind of a badge of honor. To me, it's a feminism thing."[4]

There's no classical music at a wild party and no "easy listening." Party music is meant to rock the soul, and, more importantly, the body. It might be rock, techno, or hip-hop, but whatever the form, it will have a strong, strident—and thunderingly loud—backbeat. This music makes conversation difficult, but nobody really goes to talk. Partygoers might shout about sports teams, entertainment, or possessions, or make bad jokes, but the rules of conversation generally discourage discussions of work, schoolwork, career, or vocation. And even in a setting in which people set out to violate taboos, you generally can't break the taboo against talking about politics, religion, or spirituality. Parties are a free space for students, but the freedom seems to be channeled pretty narrowly.

Eventually, conversation gives way to dancing. After a week of sitting in classes, it feels good to get the blood moving again. Dancing is a way to put inebriation to work, letting loose, loving music, and displaying the body in motion. Sometimes, it's a kind of choreographed foreplay in which dancers strut for the attention of those they've had eyes for. If the mating dance works, some participants may proceed to making out and hooking up. On couches, in corners, and up against the wall, couples kiss and caress each other. Occasionally, these pairings are early expressions of a deep and lasting relationship. Just as often, however, they are casual—intimate relations without real intimacy. They are a way of experiencing the surface of love without its substance. In 2006, 15 percent of men and 12 percent of women reported having unprotected sex as a result of drinking.[5]

At a *really* wild party, something should be broken. In a materialist culture, students know that one way of being wildly countercultural is to mangle the materials that make our meanings for us. In the exuberance of youth, inebriation, or idiocy, lamps are bashed, upholstery torn, carpets stained with booze and barf. Ceiling tiles get punctured, walls are punched, windows are sometimes smashed. Such acts are never expected, but they are not a violation of the norms at a wild party. It's just the beast that lurks within emerging.

Although there aren't many serious conversations at parties, they seem to serve the college community as conversation pieces. Especially in the days after, a party is a topic of gossip, a way of finding out how everyone acted, and how other people responded. *Did I really do that? Oh, God! I don't believe it! Did you see what Nicole was wearing? Didn't that look trashy? What was Eric thinking when he grabbed her like that? Wasn't Bill blasted last night? He could barely see his own eyes. What was Jason thinking when he kicked that window out? Who would have thought that Ken and Barbie would hook up like that?* These stories help students recall, or simply discover for the first time, what actually happened, but they're also a way of making memories, one of the primary purposes of college life.

The components of a wild party—alcohol, inebriation, music, games, conversation, dancing, destruction, and maybe a post-party hook up—are fun for the individuals involved. But they're not just individual. They're cultural, and they do cultural work. They reinforce the values and assumptions of college culture, and they raise many questions about student behavior.

The Cultural Work of Parties

Because most professors are clueless about party protocol, students teach each other how to act at wild parties. Increasingly, first-year students show up on campus with some party experience, but unless they live in a college town, they're still not entirely sure what college fun looks like. So they venture to fraternities and sororities for experiential education. They learn the etiquette of a kegger from the experts—how to hone their skills at beer pong, how to do a classic keg stand, how to pick up a guy or a girl. In short, they learn how to fit in, whether they eventually choose to or not. They also imbibe the lessons of American culture about the divisions between work and play, boredom and spontaneity, domestication and wildness.[6]

Besides their peers, students also have cultural models for their edification. The classic movie *Animal House* and its imitators—*PCU, Revenge of the Nerds, Van Wilder, Old School, Slackers, Road Trip, Back to School*—offer audiovisual instruction and inspiration. Beer ads teach students what's expected in most drinking situations, so they're a useful guide as well. MTV's *Spring Break* specials offer annual examples of inebriation, sexualization, and fun morality as well. Despite the variety of instruction, however, the message is pretty simple: Work is dumb, boredom sucks, alcohol is awesome, and spontaneity is the same thing as genuine creativity. If we look closer, though, it's a lot more complex than common sense.

Alcohol

The cultural work of a party begins with alcohol, the ocean in which partygoers swim. Alcohol is one of nature's ways (and the primary way in college culture) of altering body chemistry and consciousness. Like other foods, alcohol enters the mouth, and glides through the esophagus to a person's stomach. Because it's a liquid, it proceeds quickly down the gastrointestinal tract where, as Koren Zailckas says in *Smashed*, "it oozes through the walls of the intestines into the bloodstream, circulating and bleeding into body cells, making them drunk."[7]

Today, college drinking is big business, and national advertisers, local advertisers, bars, and clubs work hard to make it even bigger. Most college campuses are surrounded by bars, liquor stores, convenience stores, and restaurants that enable students to act out conventional cultural scripts for college carousing. Alcohol fuels collegiate fun *and* the local economy.[8]

Coupled with the normal mythos of college drinking, this marketing is quite successful. When Student Monitor asks college students what's "in" on their campus, beer tops the list for about 75 percent of students. In 2006, beer was briefly supplanted in the top spot by the iPod, but the brew still maintained a 71 percent rating—tied with Facebook—and was followed closely by "drinking other alcohol." At college, students experience the life of the mind, but they cherish and celebrate the mind-altering life.[9]

The cultural work of alcohol is to subvert the rational mind, creating space for instinct, urges, and desire. Students think it makes them more natural, as it releases the inhibitions of the rational brain. But in fact it makes them more unnatural, since the brain is a basic part of the human organism. Partygoers usually drink to lose inhibitions, as if inhibitions were not a part of their humanity. In the act of escape, therefore, they pose critical cultural questions: Why do college students and other Americans put up with a world that's so alienating that it drives them to drink? And why do they accept an alcoholic escape instead of insisting on a cultural transformation so that everyday life actually fulfilled their humanity?

Work and Play

This alcoholic acquiescence of college students comes, in part, from American assumptions about work and play. Fun is part of the rhythm of work and rewards at college; it's almost as natural to Joe and Jo College as the rhythm of day and night. They understand class work and homework as labor, and interpret work as most other Americans do: It's the alienating stuff we do to pay for the pleasurable parts of our lives. Whatever else work is, we don't expect it to be fun. We say, "I have to go to work," not "I get to go to work." We say, "thank God it's Friday," not "thank God it's Monday." And at a party, we work hard to escape the social construction of work.[10]

It's a peculiar construction of reality that defines reading books, taking tests, and writing essays as hard work. To people elsewhere on the planet who labor long hours just to feed themselves, Jo College doesn't seem to be working very hard at all as she muddles through two or three hours of classes, a few hours of reading, and a couple of extracurricular activities. It's also peculiar because students pay for the privilege of doing this work, instead of being paid for it. Peculiar or not, students think their lives are difficult, so they pledge to "work hard and play harder." But again, why? What in the week is so unpleasant that it must be escaped with alcohol-fueled fun that may not be remembered anyway?[11]

One possible answer is that work time is controlled by someone else's specifications—mostly professors, but also coaches, music directors, and workplace supervisors. In general, the people who govern the workweek are trying to discipline the mind, the body, or both, which is what they are paid to do. But in a world of American individualism, the mildest whiff of authority elicits a reaction. As counterpoint and as revolt, students often try to spend free time being undisciplined, creating their own expectations as a contrast to the routines of work, whether or not it's good work, or good for them. And so a party's discipline is nearly the opposite of workplace discipline. A party mandates spontaneity, sociability, laughter, and behavior that is seemingly unconstrained.

Another reason for the work-play dichotomy is hardwired into the very structures of our weeks. American kids learn the lessons of the weekend early, as early as their first Saturday morning cartoons, and by the time they get to high school, it's fully ingrained. "On weekends," notes Peter Zollo of Teenage Research Unlimited, "teens get a reprieve—albeit a temporary one—from the rigors of school, work, and, often, family. For many, it's what keeps them going during the school week." This rhythm seems natural, both because it mirrors the rhythms of American adult life and because it has been marketed to young people so effectively by national and local advertisers. And so a lot of college fun takes place on the weekend: a cultural invention for rest, relaxation, commerce, and consumption.[12]

In a way, college itself is seen as the weekend of life—an amusing interval before the disciplined world of working life. College is a time for fun because American adulthood decidedly isn't. Therefore, students plan to have as much fun as possible now, before they encounter the "real world." The same sort of life-cycle calculation influences some student responses to social and environmental problems. "If the world truly is dangerous and the future uncertain, that's all the more reason to have fun now!" There's an environmental catastrophe coming, but not so fast that it should screw up our plans for the weekend.[13]

Boredom

Boredom: 1) Mindless, listless tedium, brought on by a lack of stimulation or a lack of imagination; 2) The primary social disease of college life, often cured by TV, video games, pharmaceuticals, or fun.

Like the dialectic of work and play, the interplay of boredom and fun also fuels the party syndrome on campus. The common sense of college boredom is that it is caused by dull professors, deadly classes, and tedious texts. Except in unusual circumstances, research and writing are tiresome, too. And sometimes, of course, there's just "nothing to do." Boredom is the primary social disease of college life, and a party seems a natural cure.[14]

Boredom is experienced individually, but it's constructed culturally. Twenty-one percent of Americans confess that they are regularly bored, and researchers expect that the real number is probably higher. A 1999 Yankelovich poll detected a "boredom boom" in America, with more than 70 percent of us looking for more novelty in our lives. Pollsters found that 69 percent agreed that "even though I have so much to do, I'm always looking for something new and exciting to do."[15]

To a great extent, this boredom is a product of advertisers, because they need ennui to sell novelty and excitement. If you pay attention to commercials and commercial media, for example, you quickly learn that boredom is one of the seven deadly sins of American social life. Life is inherently uninteresting, we're taught, unless we make it otherwise— and the easiest way is to buy something. We can buy *experiences* that relieve boredom, like movies, music, travel, parties, and drinking at the bar. Or we can buy *things* that might magically transform us and our lives like iPods, cell phones, perfume, cosmetics, cars, and beer. Such artifacts are popular not just because they're better, but also because they're novelties. Many Americans—and probably most college students—are neophiliacs—people in love with the new.[16]

Luckily for marketers and producers, boredom is also a side effect of this love of novelty—the more stimulated we become, the more stimulation we need to be satisfied. Instead of appreciating what we already have, we look for something new and different. "As a society," says Mary Catherine Bateson in her thoughtful book *Peripheral Visions: Learning Along the Way*, "we have become so addicted to entertainment that we have buried the capacity for awed experience of the ordinary. Perhaps the sense of the sacred is more threatened by learned patterns of boredom than it is by blasphemies." Instead of finding the extraordinary in the ordinary, we look for it in our escapes. Bored or alienated, we escape to the landscapes of fun. And the wild party is the default option for beating boredom on campus.[17]

Spontaneity

College students go to wild parties for feelings of spontaneity, novelty, and contingency, for a contrast to the routines of everyday life. For many students, there's not much joy in the day-to-day drift between classes and cafeteria, dorms and gym, library and libations. They don't really get excited watching television or playing video games. Conversations can be fun, but gossip and small talk only go so far toward human fulfillment. So a party is like an escape from the prison of a boring life, a "good time" for students who are doing time.

Many like to think that anything can spontaneously happen at a wild party but, in fact, the action is fairly predictable. When people strip and run naked outside, it's different, of course, but it's exactly the sort of "different" behavior one might *expect* at a wild party. In fact, even though it's intended as an escape from routine, the wild party *is* a routine. Such parties, both on campus and elsewhere, evince a deep human desire to be unconstrained, but they only show us how to be wild in the most conventional ways. Parties allow attendees to violate normal, daytime norms of rationality, propriety, and control. But even for this abnormal behavior there are expectations, social rules, and sanctions. And one of the most important expectations is that wildness is only temporary. In fact, one of the unstated assumptions of a wild party is that all the participants will be tame the next day. If a party is a prison break from everyday life, everyone knows that the inmates will voluntarily return to their cells on Monday. This sort of acting wild has nothing to do with a person's character; instead it's a momentary switch from one persona to another.

While the wildness of a wild party transgresses the conventional rules of proper social behavior, it stays entirely within the rules of commercial behavior. People at a party spend time together, but they also spend money getting together. Their partying is good for beer distributors, clothes manufacturers, music companies, and condom manufacturers. It adds to the gross domestic product, so it's transgressive in just the sort of way that makes a lot of money, which is to say that it's barely transgressive at all. Economically speaking, it pays to be wild.

Students naturally want to be wild, have fun, get drunk, avoid boredom, and be spontaneous, but these activities actually reveal a fairly stark view of life: Young people hate the routines of everyday life so much that they need to escape them with booze, parties, and other distractions presented by the very corporations they work for, or work toward working for, during the week. What does this say about their lives?

Footprint

At a party, students use nature to evade the nature of day-to-day life. And like all other human activities, college parties leave an ecological footprint. Parties require materials, and are connected to material culture, materialism, and manufacturing. Partygoers expend energy, human or otherwise, for transportation, and generally don't consume everything on the premises, so there's usually a good deal of waste. And if a party hook up goes too well, there might even be another "life of the party": unintended pregnancy.

One of the essential environmental inputs of a college party is beer, a cultural product made of agricultural ingredients and water, produced by the brewing and fermentation of cereal starches, usually malted barley. In the brewing stage, the grain is mashed in hot water, converting the starches to sugars. Then the liquid is separated from the mash, and boiled to concentrate the starch sources in the liquid. At this point, too, hops are added for bitterness (to balance the sugars) and for their work as a natural preservative. Then the brew is cooled, and brewer's yeast ferments the sugars, producing the alcohol many of us crave.[18]

Beer production is an energy-intensive industry that indirectly participates in all the environmental impacts of industrial agriculture, including lots of long-distance transportation. Breweries require as much as three hundred gallons of fresh water for every gallon of beer—as Coors says, "It's the water,"—and their production processes require a lot of energy to heat and cool the brew. Aluminum cans are electricity incarnate, and glass bottles are a considerable environmental expense as well. Distribution consumes fossil fuels, in moving beer from brewery to distributor to the local liquor store. A swig of beer, therefore, is an extensive environmental activity.[19]

Because beer is brewed from grain, it's a form of embodied energy depending ultimately on the sun and the photosynthesis of plants. It's liquid sunshine extracted from agricultural commodities, which are subject to the fluctuations of commodity markets. But even though the cost of beer rises with the demand for ethanol for cars, the increases don't seem to have affected college consumption—not yet. As one student said, "Beer is like gas to college kids. Regardless of the price going up, kids are not going to stop buying it." Other items at a party also have environmental footprints—pizza, snacks, plastic cups, Ping-Pong balls, CDs, stereos, and furniture—and there are social impacts, too. The drunks who drive sometimes maim car bodies *and* human bodies. Sexual hook ups often inflict emotional hurt, and sometimes lead to unintended pregnancy, overshadowing the more mundane environmental impacts of college fun.

Wildness and the Preservation of the World

Ecologically speaking, the "wild" of a wild party doesn't do much for nature, but what does it do for *human* nature? How does the American definition of wildness, shaped by commercial interests and cultural conceptions of work, play, and *fun*-damentalism, affect our human flourishing? One person we might ask is Henry David Thoreau. Even though Harvard students were conventionally wild in Thoreau's day, Henry graduated with a very different conception of the wild than Joe and Jo College. In his famous essay "Walking," Thoreau wrote that "in Wildness is the preservation of the world." He didn't have a wild party in mind, of course, but his criticism of American life can help us think twice, both about college parties and about more productive forms of rebelling against day-to-day routines.

For Thoreau, the wild wasn't just the opposite of human society. Instead it flowed from the nature of the universe. "Wild" didn't describe how he acted at parties, but how he lived his life. In Thoreau's mind, to be wild was actually a matter of conformity—not to social pressures, but to the nature of the universe, to human nature, and to one's own peculiar nature. Joe College sees freedom as an expression of his ontological in- dividualism, but Thoreau saw freedom as correspondence with what na- ture teaches us about *its* rules—the wisdom we need to inhabit the planet respectfully and responsibly. Wildness is the preservation of the world because, according to Thoreau, wildness *is* the nature of the world.

Looking to nonhuman animals, Thoreau felt a deep respect because they instinctively lived in harmony with nature, unlike humans who submit to jobs and routines that alienate them. Indeed, he hoped that people could find the same harmony he sensed in animals, but con- cluded that "in their reaction to Nature men appear to me for the most part, notwithstanding their arts, lower than the animals." Likewise, we speak of "party animals," who aren't like most animals. These individuals exhibit what we conventionally call "animal traits," but these traits are ones that most animals don't actually have. The party animal is drunk, crass, stupid, and sometimes entertaining in ways that even the wildest of animals couldn't and wouldn't match.

Because of his love for the wild universe, Thoreau mourned the fact that humans had allowed themselves to be transformed into domesti- cated beasts. In "Walking" he suggested, in contrast to popular thought, that a person was first "an inhabitant, or a part and parcel of Nature, rather than a member of society." This mind-set freed him to think un- conventionally, because he believed that wildness was a characteristic of his mind as much as it was a description of place or behavior. In many ways Thoreau was *always* a wild party, because he didn't conform to so- cial expectations. Nature was his fraternity.

Stemming directly from this wildness of thought was Thoreau's sense of the wild as a catalyst to sensibility, because a person in touch with the wild—in nature or within—could see more clearly than a person peering through the lenses of society. Thoreau went to the woods for inspiration and for perspective, while students go to parties for inebriation. Many drink not just to lose inhibitions, but to lose consciousness of the bigger issues that confront them. Students seem to drink not just for pleasure, but to dull the pain of living in a society that offers so many material goods and so little substantial hope. Even though wild parties are all about fun, it sometimes seems that they are rooted in despair, occasions when lives of quiet desperation briefly get loud.

This despair leads students to "get drunk out of their minds," to achieve the blessed mindlessness of intoxication. As a consequence, though, collegiate wildness often leads to bewilderment and regret. Thirty-four percent of students note "doing something they later regretted" as a result of their drinking and partying.[20]

Jo College is drinking not just because she's thirsty for beer, but because she's thirsty for meaning. And American society doesn't do meaning very well. So we often drink to dull the pain. For Thoreau, the wild was not just a model of individual behavior, but a source of social criticism. He embraced the tradition of the biblical prophets, who went to the wilderness for a perspective on society that society itself couldn't provide. And Thoreau used the perspective of the wild to criticize the shortcomings of the civilized world. As a refined man himself, a Harvard-educated intellectual, he understood the attractions of a settled and civilized life. But Thoreau also understood the necessity of unsettling the complacency that confined people's bodies and souls. So he used his wicked wit to skewer the social institutions that demeaned and dehumanized the people of Concord and the wider world, and to call people—including us—to repent, or at least reform. Thoreau's words have inspired many with the idea that wildness—a principled belief in the apparently impossible—can help people heal the hurts of the world.

By contrast, at college, a wild party is seldom a source of social criticism. Instead, it's a powerful institution of social conformity. Even when students think they're taking a break from the routines of American life, they're being broken to those routines. A wild party reinforces American *fun*-damentalism—the faith that fun and entertainment are the main pleasures of life, and fair compensation for a week of alienating work. A college party reinforces the primary values of a consumptive culture. It also typically strengthens conventional gender roles as well as casual and commercial definitions of sexual purpose. The supposed nonconformity of a party conforms perfectly to the expectations of American culture because it poses no threat to the established order. In many ways, a party is an implicit protest of dehumanization. An effective protest, therefore, might be expected to result in re-humanization. But most wild parties simply substitute one form of dehumanization for another, and often end with a hangover, the residual reward for an ephemeral evening of fun.

Thoreau understood the richness of the ecological margins, the ecotones where wildness flourishes on the edge of civilization. Indeed, he said that he lived "a sort of border life" on the boundaries of cultivation and wildness. He said in *Walden* that he felt "an instinct toward a higher, or, as it is named, spiritual life . . . and another toward a primitive rank and savage one." Celebrating both of these instincts, Thoreau tried to embody both of them at the same time. He wanted to be a refined savage, a wild poet-philosopher. Joe College generally doesn't follow this example. When he's being wild—and especially at a wild party—he doesn't imagine himself as spiritual, or as a poet or philosopher. Instead of embracing the wild and the spiritual at the same time, he, like most of us, segregates them. Our wild side comes out on Saturday night, the spiritual side on Sunday morning, if at all.

In the context of campus culture, then, a wild party teaches us how college students understand and value wildness. It suggests that their on-campus language about "going wild" has little or nothing to do with untamed nature. In a complex process of peer socialization, students teach each other patterns of thinking and behavior that they are likely to take into their work and play as adults. At a party, they never think that they are expressing environmental values, but in many ways, sadly, they are. And this suggests that our environmental values might still benefit from some Thoreauvian thinking.

Wild parties happen because Joe and Jo College are so tame about their expectations. Having settled for a life lived in conformity to rules that often stifle the human spirit, a life of what Thoreau called "quiet desperation," students (and other Americans) implicitly agree to be satisfied with a weekend of drinking, dancing, and debauchery. Instead of challenging institutions that demean us, we demean ourselves in a different way. Instead of making meaning, we make out. But it is fun, isn't it?

Fun-damentalism and Environmentalism

In college, perhaps for the first time in their lives, college students get a chance to really practice the *fun*-damentalism of American culture. Students have almost unlimited opportunities for fun, and handling those gratifications is one of the essential challenges of daily life man-agement. Implicitly or explicitly, students define fun, determine its pur-poses, and fit it into life's other purposes. Like most Americans, they work to be able to afford the fun of free time and consumer spending. At school, students work for the compensation of grades, and the income that good grades often generate. Whether in school or beyond, they wait impatiently for the weekend, using designing minds to plan parties and other amusements, typically ignoring the environmental impacts of col-lege fun and the morality behind it.

When students party, as we've seen, some of the environmental im-pacts are material. On-site there is a lot of garbage—bottles and cans, cups and napkins, leftover food and pizza boxes. Off-site there are the materials used in manufacturing all these things and the energy needed to get people to and from the party, to heat or cool the room, and to light up all the good times. Even so, a lot of college fun is environmentally benign—at least relatively speaking. A party leaves waste—and people wasted—but it doesn't burn a lot of carbon or consume inordinate amounts of materials.[21]

So the primary environmental impact of college fun isn't resource consumption or waste streams. It's the mental part of *fun*-damentalism. The problem with college *fun*-damentalism is that the perpetual craving for diversion diverts students—and the adults they will become—from an environmental imagination that could help us craft a society that's substantially more fulfilling. Waiting for the weekend, anticipating the big game, planning Saturday's party, ordering a late-night pizza, students engage in fun as they disengage from the intellectual play that helps to imagine a different world or a sustainable society. A loud response to quiet desperation, the quest for fun often crowds out the kind of quests and rituals that used to make coming-of-age meaningful. We may be, as Neil Postman argues, "amusing ourselves to death,"—or, even worse, amusing ourselves to extinction.[22]

If the primary educational systems—television, commercial culture, and peer pressure—can convince young people that one of the primary purposes of life is to have fun, then corporate culture doesn't have to worry about an ecological revolution that could disturb its business model. As Thomas Pynchon says in *Gravity's Rainbow*, "If they can get you asking the wrong *questions*, they don't have to worry about *answers*." If college students focus their extracurricular lives on the question, "What can I do for fun?" instead of, "What can I do for fulfillment?" they'll enjoy their pleasures until environmental breakdown precludes them.[23]

Fun doesn't just affect what we do; it defines who we are. When we absorb a fun-seeking morality, we're *fun*-damentally different people than we were before. We see life differently, and more superficially. We focus on parties and games that, on reflection, aren't all that important to our lives, and certainly not to the life of the planet. An ethic of fun complicates a deeper ethics. But it doesn't have to be this way.

The wisest students realize that, even though a lot of fun is simply superficial, there can be deeper delights, and they sense that college fun might even have implications that could help us change the world. As Maren Gelle points out in an exploratory essay called "Facets of Fun," college fun is a way of building trust and social capital. Parties lubricate interactions between college students, but the interactions don't necessarily end at the party. The passing pleasures of the party can sometimes lead to extensive pleasures. Deep friendships sometimes develop out of substantial superficiality. Students who don't talk about serious issues at a party might feel freer to bring them up afterward with one of their party friends. Students who enjoy playing together at a party might also enjoy working together on other issues at other times. Even though the *content* of a party militates against serious issues, the *processes* of a party can create social capital that can be used in other contexts. Fun could be connected to work and to happiness.[24]

Pursuing Happiness

Unfortunately, the relationship between fun and happiness is not a common consideration in college life. It sometimes comes up in psychology classes, but there's not much fun in the core curriculum. There is, however, a budding science of happiness, which suggests that fun doesn't necessarily generate human fulfillment. The New Economics Foundation (NEF), for example, has created a Happy Planet Index to illustrate correlations between environmental impacts and human satisfaction. Asking how much energy and materials produce a unit of happiness, the crude measure of the NEF rates the United States 150th in the world, primarily because we use so much energy and materials in the pursuit of our happiness.[25]

So what does make us happy? How can we reduce the ecological footprint of our pleasures? And how can we do that on college campuses? In the last twenty-five years, social scientists have begun to investigate the sources of happiness, and their work may help designing minds to create social and environmental systems that combine fun and fulfillment with the ongoing regeneration of the Earth. Practitioners of "positive psychology" like Martin Seligman, David Lykken, Edward Diener, and Mihali Csikszentmihalyi have studied the components of human fulfillment and offered guidance that makes sense for most people. One of their ideas is to go with the flow—but not in the commonsense conformist way.[26]

According to Csikszentmihalyi, for example, "flow" describes experiences when a person—let's say a college student—is so deeply engaged in a pleasurable task that he or she loses track of time. It's an experience where everything comes together, where the person gets "in the zone," where talent and skills are perfectly matched to challenges and goals. Flow can happen in sports, in those moments when an athlete loses consciousness of what she's doing and just does it. It can happen in games, when—for a while—our skills are a precise match for the challenges before us. It can happen in reading, when a book seizes our consciousness and we can't put it down. It can happen in writing, when all of our research suddenly flows onto the page in a synthesis that we hadn't quite expected. It can happen in conversations, usually late at night, when friends are attuned perfectly to each other. Flow even happens occasionally in class, when a discussion is so engaging that an hour passes in what seems like a few minutes.

. For most people, says Csikszentmihalyi, flow includes: "1) intense concentration on the task; 2) a deep sense of involvement and merging of action and awareness; 3) a sense of control over one's actions; 4) enjoyment or interest in the activity; and 5) a distorted sense of time." The conditions of flow, whatever the activity, include: "1) engagement of activity for its own sake; 2) perceived challenges of the task are relatively high and in balance with one's skills; 3) clear proximal goals that are regarded as important; 4) immediate feedback indicating one's success at meeting these goals; and 5) highly focused, rather than scattered, attention." Flow can be fun, but it's closer to fulfillment.[27]

And, according to these psychologists, flow is a key to happiness. Happiness does not come from stuff, or from the environmental degradation that can come with stuff. As psychologist Richard Ryan says, "Aspiring for a lot of material goods is actually unhappiness-producing. People who value material goods and wealth also are people who are treading more heavily on the Earth—and not getting happier." Instead, happiness comes from deep engagement in strong social networks and commitments larger than the self and longer than now.[28]

Likewise, the new science of happiness also suggests that people often find more happiness when they're not pursuing it. Pursuing pleasure adds very little to life satisfaction. But the pursuit of flow and the pursuit of meaning do affect our fulfillment—and they enhance our happiness over time. Fun provides a spike of pleasure in our lives, but fulfillment increases the baseline.

So fun is enjoyable, but it could be more than that. In some ways, if you think twice about it, college fun provides lessons for life that the official curriculum doesn't. It shows that it's possible to find pleasure in low-impact activities. It reminds us that interacting with real people can really be a blast, calling into question the ontological individualism of American culture. It also suggests the importance of pleasure in human affairs. If we're going to join an ecological revolution, it better be fun— or at least fulfilling.

College students pursue happiness by pursuing fun. In many cases, their pursuit is pretty much post-materialist—a fun that depends more on social circumstances than on consumption of the Earth's resources. So at its best, college fun offers a way of thinking about a post-materialist culture, a culture of permanence in which people find themselves fulfilled not by filling themselves with stuff but by taking pleasure in each other, and by practicing the possibilities of good work together.

Such college *fun*-damentalism could be a catalyst for a new American environmentalism. For the most part, sadly, most of today's environmentalists don't seem like they're having fun. Many environmentalists seem attracted to doom and gloom, and to suffering and sacrifice, as the primary way of avoiding doomsday. California governor Arnold Schwarzenegger suggests that, in his experience, "Environmentalists were no fun, they were like prohibitionists at a fraternity party." Forgetting that people like fun, that fun can be substantial, and that extensive pleasures can be extended pleasures—pleasures enjoyed for time immemorial—environmentalists have missed out on an important motivational force for Americans.[29]

College students could be a catalyst for such a happiness revolution. As marketers know, Joe and Jo College are early adopters in consumer culture. They could also be early adopters in a less consumptive (and more fulfilling) culture. They could cultivate virtues and values that make life good for us and other organisms. They could be the first wave of people putting an ecological logic into practice in daily life. And celebrating this ecological revolution on Saturday nights (and other times as well) could be fun.

There's no environmental reason not to party, and lots of reasons to party hearty as we increasingly adapt our habits to our habitat. Collegians could still enjoy alcohol for social lubrication, but they might need to wildly violate the taboos against substantive conversations to get to know people in all their complexity—an activity that *actually* enhances happiness. Instead of drinking the cheapest beers on the planet, students could brew their own beer or focus on local brews, thus reducing the carbon footprint of inebriation. Instead of the "same old, same old" at parties, they could cultivate diverse party styles more imaginative than the conventional themes of drink and dance, grin and grope, pimps and hos.

But eventually, any useful fun will need to confront the demons our whole culture expects to escape from: mindless work, repetitive entertainment, and minimal expectations for human fulfillment. We'll need to change the nature of work so that it offers human satisfactions as well as a paycheck. We'll need to change our minds about boredom, and about the constant stream of entertainment that infiltrates our minds. We'll definitely pay more attention to the fun and fulfillment in other parts of our lives, taking more pleasure from other experiences and making them as "cool" as the binge behavior at our standard celebrations. And we'll use our designing minds to create lives that create real happiness wherever we are.

If we were, like Thoreau, really wild about our dreams, and if we invested our energy in plans that were truly visionary—like good work, good land, and good communities on the good Earth—then our parties might celebrate not just the end of the workweek, but the beginning of the good work we're pursuing to create a culture of permanence.

8

The Nature of Sex and (Sometimes) Love

There is a lot of sex. College is about casual sex.
Anonymous college student

Human biology depends on love.
Mary Catherine Bateson, *Peripheral Visions*

*Oh what a catastrophe, what a maiming of love when it was
made a personal, merely personal feeling, taken away from
the rising and the setting of the sun, and cut off from the magic
connection of the solstice and the equinox!*
D. H. Lawrence, *A Propos of `Lady Chatterley's Lover'*

*Love is not separable from justice. The drive to make love and
to make justice should be one; it will become one the more we
overcome the current split between private and public life.*
Dorothee Soelle, *To Work and to Love*

*We cannot win this battle to save species and environments
without forging an emotional bond between ourselves and nature
as well—for we will not fight to save what we do not love.*
Stephen Jay Gould, *Eight Little Piggies*

· · · · · · · ·

In 2002, sex educator Deborah Roffman found herself in a class of fifteen- and sixteen-year-old girls getting bogged down over a question of sexual values. Roffman asked the girls to think of the meaning that sex is supposed to have in people's lives. "Meaning?" asked one of the girls. "Sex is supposed to have meaning? What do you mean by that?"[1]

College students aren't quite as clueless as Roffman's teenagers, although one collegian told reporter Chris Harris, "Sex doesn't mean anything to anyone. . . . Sex is like nothing anymore. It's nothing. It comes right after a kiss." Evidently when college students fall in love or tumble into bed (or both), they are not always doing their best thinking. As in other areas of their lives, they are generally following the common sense of our culture—although this means different things to different students. Most students are heterosexual, but many are gay, lesbian, or bisexual, and some are transgendered. Some students are hooking up as often as they can, keeping score of conquests, while others are having sex to make friends and be a part of the college crowd. Some people hook up defensively, preferring superficial sex to a relationship that might cause emotional pain, while others are engaged in serial monogamy, enjoying the pleasures of commitment one person at a time. A few college students have taken abstinence pledges, and a third are abstinent anyway. Flirting, kissing, and holding hands, students also make out, give and receive blow jobs, and experiment with exotic positions. Some are scandalized by college sex, but most students are tolerant of the varieties of sexual practice on campus. Virtually all students gossip about their own sex lives, the sex lives of friends and peers, and the casual couplings of the "players" and "sluts" on campus. Love and sex aren't often in the formal curriculum of college, but they're core competencies in today's college culture.[2]

Sex is always—always—part of the moral ecology of college life, so an examination of campus sex will help us understand college culture, American culture, and the nature of sexuality in America. When we're looking for sex and love, we seldom think of nature or environmental issues. Sometimes we imagine that we're "doing what comes naturally," but we don't usually think about the nature in sex or the environmental impacts of our lovemaking. To a great degree, love and sex are a part of a commercial culture of distraction in which advertisers teach us how to make love by spending money. They're a part of a parental culture in which American parents find it difficult to talk with their kids about their deepest values, and part of a peer culture that offers little depth or complexity in thinking about sex or love.

Like most Americans, college students tend to do sex behind closed doors. At colleges, students communicate to their roommates that they've been "sexiled," to provide privacy for a pair of lovers. Afterward, a common question is "Was it good for you?" On campus, the conventional answers to this question concern physical pleasure and matters of technique. How does one person please another, and how do they bring her or him to sexual fulfillment? These are performance issues—not surprising in a culture of performances. But there are deeper questions, with more complex and compelling answers, too.[3]

In fact, sexual fun can be educational, a prime example of ways that learning can be pleasurable. If we're really paying attention, it teaches us about biology and anatomy, about timing and technique, about cooperation and collaboration, about patience and potency. In some instances, sex invites us to think about the human condition—about intimacy and vulnerability, ethics and intention, causes and consequences. In a few cases, when birth control proves ineffective, we get to think about conception—and our conceptions of human life. In the best instances, sex invites us to ask what is really made when we're making love.

Hook-up Culture

Until recently, most college students had a conception of sex that made it meaningful within the standard American conventions of romantic love, sexual fun, physical pleasure, and prospective marriage. But these conventions are changing, and—as with technology—college students seem to be early adopters of the new rules. In *Coming of Age in New Jersey*, an ethnographic account of college life in the 1980s, anthropologist Michael Moffatt describes the cultural context of college sex lives:

> They [college students] were heirs to the second great sexual revolution of the twentieth century, the one that took place in the late 1960s and early 1970s. They had access to modern biotechnologies that effectively divorced sex from pregnancy and childbirth. They were free from the moral supervision of their elders. And, considering the eroticized nature of contemporary American popular culture, they were fish swimming in a sexual sea. . . . Sexual fun and sexual satisfaction were at the heart of contemporary adolescent notions of fun—and hence, because these same adolescents were in college, sex was at the heart of contemporary notions of college life.[4]

Since the 1980s, a few things have changed. Students come to college with more sexual experience and more sexual stimulation. Television, movies, and magazines have taught women to be "sexy," and taught men that that "sexy" is primarily for their benefit. Peer culture has confronted parental culture, pressuring students to get on with their sex lives. As one student confessed to a researcher, "Growing up, you get these vibes that if you're not having sex, you're not cool." And if you *are* cool, of course, you probably haven't thought a lot about the implications of cool because that kind of thinking is decidedly uncool.[5]

Cultural Scripts

When students get to college, they act out the cultural scripts they have learned from parents, peers, and media. Many actually understand college as the next stage in their sexual self-development. On most campuses, the pressures to participate in sexual culture also increase. Peers, parties, fraternities, and sororities promote sexual play and promiscuity. Sex columnists in campus newspapers offer advice on tactics and technique, although they don't say much about deeper dimensions of sexuality. Most college students believe that there's more casual sex in their generation than the previous one, and they're right. And increasingly this sex isn't hooked up to love or romance. As Kathleen Bogle found in interviews for her book, *Hooking Up: Sex, Dating, and Relationships on*

Campus, "none of the men and women mentioned love as a prerequisite for sex."[6]

This moral ecology of sex is called "hook-up culture," a set of expectations and sexual practices that seems passionately committed to uncommitted sex. Intentionally ambiguous, the term "hooking up" encompasses a lot of behavior—kissing, making out, oral sex, intercourse, and other variations. Guys are pressured to be "players," so they pressure girls to play along. Drinking even before they head to fraternity and sorority parties, adherents to this culture get drunk enough to make out and make love with people they don't really know. Promiscuous sexuality is even celebrated at theme parties of "pimps and hos," "CEOs and office hos," "jock pros and sports hos" (note that the constant is "hos"). "Sexting" or "booty calls" to a prospective hook-up partner are primary forms of communication, allowing couples to keep verbal interaction to a minimum. Not everybody hooks up, of course—*many* students don't—but given all the gossip, nearly everyone thinks that almost everybody does. Hook-up culture, therefore, is the default setting of college sex life, in part because people who believe in commitment or restraint don't go public with their values, except with their closest friends. Hook-up culture is public, and other cultures are private. Except for evangelical college students and other principled dissenters, therefore, students expect that one of the purposes of college life is sexual fun.[7]

To some extent, this is because they don't have time for anything better. Like alarm clocks, hook-up culture is part of the ecology of time on campus. Given other demands, there is no time for love and commitment. As one student told David Brooks of the *New York Times*, "People don't have time or energy to put into relationships." For college students fixated on good grades and jobs, "dating is simply not a productive use of time." In college sex life, it seems, convenience is more valuable than care, impersonal physicality more important than personal intimacy. This may explain why 49 percent of hook ups are "one and done."[8]

The nature of sexual fun often flows from the nature of alcohol, with casual sex preceded by love potions like beer and other alcoholic beverages. Nobody really knows precisely why. It could be the symbolic connections of alcohol and romance promoted by the liquor industry. It could be that "beer goggles" skew perceptions, reducing inhibitions and making people comfortable doing things they wouldn't do sober. It might be that alcohol offers an excuse for bad behavior. It could be that alcohol reduces the capacity for evaluation and honest communication so that attempts to stop before intercourse aren't very successful. Finally, it may be that the connection isn't causal at all: Certain personalities—risk takers, sensation seekers, and impulsive sorts—may simply be attracted both to booze and sexual experimentation. In any case, getting drunk is one of the best predictors of hooking up—and one of the leading causes of sexual tragedies.[9]

Although college sex is supposed to be all in fun, there's still a serious double standard on campus. Even though women feel increasingly free to express their sexual desires and to act upon them, the cultural meanings of sex for Joe College are different than for his sister. As a result, sometimes, when two college students are engaged in the same act of intercourse, they're doing different things. Besides the obvious physical differences, sometimes she's making love and he's just having a good time (though sometimes it's vice versa). Studies still show that men are much more likely than women to be willing to: have sex with someone they have known less than three hours; have intercourse with two different partners in six hours; have intercourse with someone they don't love; and to have sex with someone outside a good relationship. Social research suggests that men are more hedonistic than women. Women are more contextual than men; the relationship matters more in weighing sexual intimacy and commitment and security are important factors in their sexual expression. He "needs" sex, and she needs the validation that she's sexy or appealing enough to get a guy. So he's more likely to be happy with "one and done," while she's more likely thinking about something more. At the end of the hook up, too, there's a difference. If two heterosexual students are promiscuous, he's likely to be called a "player" while she's slandered as a "slut." She takes "the walk of shame" while he struts "the stride of pride." She's more likely to feel anger, regret, or depression. And if they haven't used protection, she may be pregnant.[10]

Men are also more aggressive in relationships. In a fall 2006 survey, the American College Health Association reported that almost 10 percent of women had experienced sexual touching against their will, and almost 15 percent had been in emotionally abusive relationships. One in every twenty-five women reported attempted sexual penetration against their will, and one in fifty had been raped. Each of these acts affects the individual woman, and some can traumatize victims for life. But this aggressiveness affects others, too, creating a cold climate for college women.[11]

Similarly, pornography, a multibillion-dollar industry, shows us women and men engaged in what might be called "intercoarse." Colleges are generally too politically correct to allow public displays of pornography, but this doesn't stop students—especially guys—who are looking for sexual stimulation. A 2007 study found that one in five college men view pornography every day or nearly every day, and that heavy viewers tend to binge drink more and have sex with multiple partners. Especially online, there's more pornography than you could watch in a lifetime—and it's cheaper than a date, until you begin to consider the social costs. As Pamela Paul suggests, American youth culture is becoming "pornified," as men masturbate by themselves and as "female chauvinist pigs" try to live up to the expectations of guys who spend their time watching surgically enhanced porn stars perform professional copulation.[12]

Some critics contend that we are *de*-meaning sex in our hook-up culture as we talk frankly and impersonally about hooking up, getting laid, screwing, scoring, and finding new fuck buddies. For many American students, the common sense of sex is that it's no big deal. It's normal and healthy, and if you're not getting some, then you're the one with hang-ups. There's nothing new about this—there have always been people willing to trivialize sex. What may be new on campus is the power of this "pornification," and the lack of a countervailing cultural conversation about making love. Religion, for example, used to affect how college students approached their sexual lives, but these days, with some exceptions, religion is "completely irrelevant." Most college students, like most Americans, do think that sex has some meaning, but, sadly, don't often speak those thoughts out loud. And so the *de*-meaning and *re*-meaning of sex goes on in America, with more foreplay than forethought.[13]

For college students, sex is part of the standard package of college life. Even when they don't participate, hook-up culture affects the quality of interpersonal interactions for everyone. And students who do protest are often labeled "puritan" or judgmental, which, on many campuses is more socially damning than promiscuity. For most students, though, hook-up culture is "no big deal." In the context of college culture, where few people are thinking outside the box, "no big deal" is an apt description. Few students think or talk much about the nature of love, or the environmental impacts of hooking up. But a closer look at the ecology of sex and the moral ecology of love could lead to better love lives.[14]

The Anatomy of Sex and Love

As evolution's tool for reproducing many species, including *Homo sapiens*, sex is perfectly natural, a way of maximizing the potential of natural selection. Sex is a way for college students and others to exchange genetic information—a way for different genes to get together, and for nature to generate new combinations with different chances of survival. In nature, nothing succeeds like reproduction, and sex is one of the biological processes that enhance the life chances of a species. People are mammals, and mammals mate. We've evolved to experience physical attraction to other people, as Jo College feels with her boyfriend Jack. We're wired to flirt with "contact-readiness cues" that we're not always conscious of. We get butterflies, blush, or stutter—all signals that are part of the intoxication of love. We hold hands because that brings us close enough to pick up other sensory cues—including the smell of pheromones—and it helps our major histocompatibility complex to find us partners who complement our own immune systems. We kiss because it feels good and because kissing allows the exchange of genetic and hormonal information. When we make love, we experience an adrenaline rush and an oxytocin flood. All of these physiological adaptations help human beings get *his* sperm in contact with *her* eggs. Hook-up culture depends on basic anatomy and physiology—in short, on nature.[15]

Our brains are involved with all of this, but not always our powers of rationality. As it happens, the brain is the primary sexual organ in human beings, and it processes romance in three different regions corresponding roughly to the three dimensions of love—sex drive, romantic love, and long-term attachment. According to anthropologist Helen Fisher, the ventral tegmental area handles the sex drive and the intoxication of love, secreting dopamine to create "craving, motivation, goal-oriented behavior—and ecstasy." Prompted by these thrill signals, the nucleus accumbens adds romance, secreting serotonin (a neurotransmitter that handles obsession) and oxytocin (which stimulates affection and bonding). The caudate nucleus, which normally stores directions for motor skills and doles out the body's rewards, also produces a persistent pattern for love, allowing it to be more than a passing fancy. If we ever thought deeply about Valentine's Day, we might give each other candy brains instead of candy hearts.[16]

Other mammals, especially ungulates, go into a rut—a natural cycle of sexual excitement and reproductive activity. Humans, however, are always ready to go, so we create a different kind of rut—the routine cultural scripts of conventional sexuality. When college students are flirting and fornicating on campus, they're doing what comes naturally, but in culturally-defined ways. Sex is natural, but in many ways American sex is more cultural, so that even when we fall in love spontaneously, we usually follow the scripts provided for us.[17]

Indeed, college sex happens because of the ways that nature and culture hook up in our world. Nature establishes the age of puberty, and feeds our bodies and brains the hormones that will push us toward sexual activity. Historically, improved health and nutrition in America have slowly reduced the average age of puberty in girls from about seventeen in the 1830s to about twelve now. Kids are physically ready for sex before they are emotionally ready, and before most of the adults in their lives are culturally expected to mentor them. A few parents might provide the "sex talk" to their children, but Americans in general don't have many rituals that connect nature to culture in this critical transition to adulthood. Unlike many other human cultures, we have no ceremonial way to initiate our young people into an adulthood of fertility, sexuality, and family, or to the personal, communal, and environmental responsibilities of this natural power. By default, therefore, kids use their own resources—including peer advice, pop culture, and the consumer marketplace—to deal with the nature of sex.[18]

Romantic Love and the Market of Romance

The traditional cultural script for relationships in America is the story of romantic love. Falling in love is one of the most satisfying events of a student's life because it offers experiences that are fuller and more fulfilling than most everyday activity. Most of us love being in love because it brings us closer than we've ever been to another human. We feel the joy of vulnerability, and the intimacy that's only possible when we open ourselves to each other. Instead of our infatuation with complex technologies, we now love simple pleasures like walks, long talks, and picnics. Even though we usually don't think much about our souls, we love our new soul mate. When we're in love, we're more attentive to the other, and more attentive to life: We notice more because we want to share everything with that special someone. We find communion in eating together, and in sharing ideas that we're usually too fearful to express. We discover that interdependence can be more pleasurable than independence, selflessness more fulfilling than selfishness. And we notice that making love can be more pleasurable than just getting laid. As Tim Clydesdale says, "Nothing provides more personal validation and emotional satisfaction than being caught up in the excitement of shared romance and deep affection." Like other Americans, therefore, college students generally come to commitment through the conventions of romantic love.[19]

These romantic conventions privilege emotion over rationality, affection over instrumentalism, altruism over selfishness, and commitment over carelessness. For many of us, romantic love is an escape from the rules of everyday life, a utopia for two. The cultural scripts of love implicitly protest against the operative values of the rest of our lives, as lovers like Jo and Jack become immersed in the emotion of becoming one. The excitement of love comes in large part from its ability to free us from the constraints of common sense to be better than we normally are. Most of the time, we hedge our bets with other people because we don't know how they'll react. But when we begin to think that someone (besides our parents) loves us unconditionally, we can share our true selves with one another. We can escape the demands of individualism and competition for the pleasures of care, commitment, and collaboration.[20]

Most of us love the cultural scripts of love, even though we don't consider them very much. Sociologist Eva Illouz has undertaken the difficult task of thinking carefully about this experience, valued precisely because of its ability to supersede our rationality. In her book *Consuming the Romantic Utopia*, Illouz suggests that even though romance feels like an oasis in a desert of instrumental relationships, it's also become an essential part of the culture of commercial capitalism. During the twentieth century, in fact, both the "romanticization of commodities" and the "commodification of romance" have brought love within the sphere of the market. Love and the accoutrements of love are for sale. From Valentine cards to romantic dinners, from flowers to lingerie, from Facebook pokes to engagement rings, from date nights to romantic vacations, love is fully accessorized in the American market. Cupid's arrow is so connected to commercial cupidity that it sometimes feels like you can't express your love without buying something. So even though it's definitely different and delightful, romantic love also reinforces the status quo. Love may or may not make the world go round, but it definitely makes cash registers go "ka-ching!"[21]

Nature is an essential part of this romantic utopia, as advertisers use the conventions of Romantic art to elicit romantic feeling. Flowers—and especially roses—symbolize our affection. Ads for all sorts of products show couples outside, in picturesque settings, holding hands and enjoying the privacy of primeval spaces. Strolling on the deserted beach becomes an emblem of "natural" love. Honeymoon destinations feature nature, too. Couples are invited to escape the landscapes of everyday life for landscapes that align better with the emotions and affections of love. In these landscapes of arcadia, we're transported to a place of simple innocence, personal authenticity, the emotional fusion of lovers, and material abundance that's framed as natural. Away from our everyday inauthentic lives, we can be our "true selves" and true to each other. Seemingly distant from the constructed sexuality of civilization, we experience the "natural" primal passions. If there's a place for everything, then love's place is in nature. As the *Onion* suggests in a magnificent spoof, "Epidemiological studies have found that individuals in picturesque surroundings are eight times more likely to suffer sudden swoonings, sweepings-off of the feet, and, in some extreme cases, prolonged confinement to bed with other romance sufferers."[22]

Other commercial scripts also affect our love lives, sometimes substituting sex for love. At the same time that the physical age of puberty is falling, the sexualization of children by advertisers has taught younger kids the look and the moves of sexual attraction. In his essay "Hooking Up," Tom Wolfe writes: "Sexual stimuli bombarded the young so incessantly and intensely they were inflamed with a randy itch long before reaching puberty. At puberty, the dams, if there were any left, burst. . . . From age thirteen, American girls were under pressure to maintain a façade of sexual experience and sophistication." Increasingly, American kids inhabit "raunch culture," exposed by their many media inputs to commercial fare about the hot look of "sexy" and the cool of copulation.[23]

"Raunch culture," says Ariel Levy, "isn't about opening our minds to the possibilities and mysteries of sexuality. It's about endlessly reiterating one particular—and particularly commercial—shorthand for sexiness." Raunch culture includes MTV and music videos, breast implants and Brazilian bikini waxes, *Girls Gone Wild* and Britney Spears, pole dancing and lap dancing, thongs and T-shirts lettered "Eye Candy," fishnets and Abercrombie & Fitch, flashing and exhibitionism, pornography and Paris Hilton, *FHM* and *Maxim*, *H-Bomb* and *Boink*. Raunch culture invites college students to express their sexuality by flaunting it (or a superficial substitute for it) in public. It invites students to model themselves not on the great minds of Western culture, but on the great plots of Western pornography. Raunch culture makes sex into money, and people into objects to be consumed. It's so pervasive that sometimes it just seems natural. Coupled with the decline of dating—an old-fashioned practice of getting to know a person in social situations that aren't initially sexual—the rise of raunch culture means that a hook up is often a precursor to a romantic relationship.[24]

Raunch culture targets all Americans, but it especially affects the young because it fills a void caused by the delay, if not the abandonment, of marriage. In the United States, we've postponed the average age of marriage, which means that high school and college students are biologically ready and sexually stimulated without any imminent commitments or reproductive intentions. In part, this is because we're also redefining adulthood in America, creating a new period of life that some people call "adultescence." In the 1950s, the most common age of marriage for brides was eighteen, but that's changed radically. Currently, most Americans think that adulthood begins around twenty-six, when a person has finished school, found a full-time job, and established a family. We tell researchers that the average age at which someone should marry is twenty-five. In these circumstances, waiting for marriage can mean years of abstinence.[25]

Sometimes, marriage itself just seems like a bad idea. In addition to delaying marriages, we've altered the image of marriage so that it looks less appealing than it has at just about any time in American history. As Inge Bell suggests in *This Book is Not Required: An Emotional Survival Manual for Students*, "in the modern version, romantic love leads, after much ado and complication, to marriage and living happily ever after, a state so boring that a good story always ends at just that point." The image and reality of divorce don't help either. Many college students are reluctant to make long-term commitments because they've seen adults in their lives suffering through the end of such commitments.[26]

Along with a more liberal attitude toward sexuality, this explains, in part, the popularity of cohabitation among college students, especially those living off-campus. As Tom Wolfe notes, "Stains and stigmas of every kind were disappearing where sex was concerned. Early in the twentieth century the term 'cohabitation' had referred to the forbidden practice of a man and a woman living together before marriage. In the year 2000, nobody under forty had ever heard the word, since cohabitation was now the standard form of American courtship." In some ways, too, cohabitation is a form of consumer testing, seeing whether or not a prospective spouse has the features we're looking for in a mate. Fears of commitment have combined with a consumer mentality to make living together a standard step in loving together.[27]

On campus, the cultural scripts of consumer culture and raunch culture make sense as convenient substitutes for romantic love and meaningful commitments, but they get in the way of intimate lives and deeper relationships that might cause us to grow up and grow together as loving human beings.

The Nature of Fertility

Whether we hook up or make love, we're involved in yet another relationship with nature, a relationship to nature's fertility. In *The Unsettling of America*, Wendell Berry reminds us that, whether we realize it or not, all our sexual practices teach us about how we value fertility and ritualize it. In the twenty-first century, sexual values on campus favor futility more than fertility. College students and other Americans generally want to reproduce, but not right now—and not as much as we physically could. Some college students abstain from sex, the most effective birth control on the market. Others employ barriers and spermicides—essentially pesticides for sperm—to keep fertility from its natural path. Among college students the most popular birth control practices are condoms, pills, and withdrawal (at 36 percent, 35 percent, and 15 percent, respectively). Four percent of students used *no* birth control the last time they had intercourse. As a result, about 10 percent of college women have used the morning-after pill at least once in the last twelve months. As is always the case, though, pregnancies do happen. One out of every fifty collegians reported getting pregnant or getting a girl pregnant in the past year. Thanks to American sexual attitudes and primitive sex education, the United States has a higher rate of unintended pregnancies than most developed nations—and more than many less-developed nations as well.[28]

When fertility becomes fertilization, and when nature takes its course, sex is how we make more people and more consumers, with all of their environmental impacts. As John Ryan says, "Especially since a baby born in North America will use roughly twenty-five times more resources over the course of its life than a baby born in the developing world, population growth is a problem here at home as well as overseas." On Earth, a rapidly rising population and rising expectations of increased consumption are taxing ecosystems beyond their carrying capacity. Because of increases in human population, the world is running out of basic resources like fresh water, fisheries, and arable land. When people reproduce faster than nature does, we proliferate environmental disasters.[29]

Condoms and pills are technologies that our culture employs to control nature. And they're special: As Bill McKibben suggests, "birth control is one of the few technologies that honors that other human gift, the one we share with no other species, the gift of conscious self-restraint. It is the technology of *less*." Condoms and birth control pills—like hybrid cars and wind turbines—are environmental technologies, affecting both social and natural environments. They are tools we can use to live in harmony with the nature we inhabit.[30]

Given current levels of consumption, there are too many people on Earth. This means, of course, that birth control isn't just personal. It's a policy issue and a planetary concern. So everyone practicing safe sex needs to think about how to help other people, on and off campus, practice responsible reproduction, too. Pregnancy happens one person at a time, but there are *systems* of pregnancy affected both by public opinion and public policy. So we need to wonder why federal support for domestic family planning has decreased in recent years, at the same time as a rise in unintended pregnancies. We need to wonder why federal funding for international family-planning programs dropped by 30 percent between 1995 and 2005. And we need to vote for the kind of family-planning programs—personal and local, national and international—that we believe in. Because family planning has huge environmental impacts, it's an early form of land-use planning and resource management. If we can't control our consumption, we might need to control our production of consumers, especially materialists like us who inhabit the overdeveloped world.

In a world where population is a proxy for environmental impacts, and first world population has first-rate impacts, recreational sex on campus might be environmentally wiser than procreational sex. To some extent, birth control is also consumption control and pollution prevention. In any case, fewer children and a smaller population can mean smaller environmental impacts. In the summer of 2008, *BMJ* (formerly the *British Medical Journal*) published an editorial arguing that limiting family size is "the simplest and biggest contribution anyone can make to leaving a habitable planet for our grandchildren." Even though college students are usually hooking up to make love and not children, it's not too early to think about the world they make now for the children they may eventually make.[31]

It's also true that sex is generally a low-carbon, low-impact environmental activity. People don't need to buy much equipment to do it, because most are already well equipped. They breathe more heavily when making love, exhaling carbon dioxide, but not emitting as much CO_2 as they do by eating a hamburger, driving a car, or checking e-mail on a computer. Usually, too, there's not a lot of waste from a romantic sexual encounter. Perhaps there's a condom, or an empty birth control package, but intercourse doesn't generally affect the waste stream very much.

Nature plays an important role in the love lives of college students who are, after all, wired for reproduction. But students are also conscious and conscientious animals, and can use culture to make sense of the mating instinct. In the past, culture told us that sex was primarily for heterosexual adults in a committed relationship called marriage. Today, there are more diverse cultural messages. Our commercial culture suggests that sex is for anyone past the age of puberty, but most Americans aren't yet ready for that brave new world. Many still oppose premarital sex, but most tacitly accept it. Most college students, too, have accepted the sexual expression of gay men and lesbians, yet our laws still generally deny them the institution of marriage.

Because birth control is used in most campus couplings, students don't add too many people to the world's population. But because they use birth control, they do alter the mental environment surrounding sex and reproduction. Instead of accepting cultural constraints on sex, they've accepted technological constraints—and that's a cultural tradition, too. Altogether, our culture of sex could also be called a culture of confusion. If we could hold the nature and culture of sex consciously in our minds, however, we might find more creative alternatives.

Good Sex on a Good Planet: Making Love as if Nature Mattered

Many students get off on hook ups, but most don't find sex as fulfilling as it could be. They feel pressured into a hook-up culture where they get orgasms instead of intimacy, pleasure instead of fulfillment, and sex instead of love. Many students want love to mean something, to make a difference in the wider world. Perhaps, therefore, it's time to think differently, and to imagine a different culture of sex on college campuses. Fortunately, the primary sexual organ—the brain—is naturally adapted to this project.[32]

> **Designing minds:** Minds designed to see the designs of nature and culture, *and* to design a society that harmonizes them happily ever after.

Hook-up culture is currently the default design on campus, but "designing minds" might create a culture in which love and sex were more creative and regenerative, a culture that would help us to have good sex for a good planet. Such a transformation would require a rethinking of love, and a renewal of some traditions that might be good for us and for more-than-human others, too.

Currently, college students are casual about sex, which is no surprise, because college students and other Americans tend to be casual about most things. Casual is cool. They don't want to seem too concerned or make other people uncomfortable. So they submit to the cultural scripts of casual college sex, and keep quiet about their deeper values. It's no big deal.

As Wendell Berry and others suggest, however, people who screw around with sex are playing with a powerful force. We think we're having sex with no strings attached, ignorant of the wisdom of John Muir's assertion that "when we try to pick out anything by itself, we find it hitched to everything else in the Universe." Sex has always been a central force in civilizations, as people figure out how to deal with fertility and reproduction, pleasure and passion, body and soul, individualism and community. What we're doing when we hook up is, in many ways, a cultural version of genetic modification because we're culturally altering the ways that our genes get together. We're modifying the meanings of sex and love in American life, and we're not sure about the outcome. Perhaps practicing the precautionary principle would be wiser.

As in so many other areas of American life, we've practiced the art of disconnection. We've disconnected sex from fertility. We've disconnected our sex lives from our love lives, our community lives, and our spiritual lives. We've pretended that our individual actions don't have social and environmental impacts. But we do have resources for thinking and acting differently.

We've also practiced the art of capitulation, letting more assertive people and institutions determine our culture for us. Carol Bly suggests that we often succumb to "moral drift," adopting the attitudes of people around us instead of discerning and defending our own. In *Sex and the Soul*, Donna Freitas found that today's undergraduates generally conform to the system of sex on campus, and even support it in conversations and gossip. But she also discovered that when she gave students an opportunity to write in journals, the students expressed real reservations about the hook-up culture. Freitas discovered that a culture of silence supports the culture of promiscuity. Many of her students were looking for sex as part of a deeper relationship instead of sex *apart from* a committed relationship. They wanted genuine intimacy, mutual care and connection, conversation about hopes and dreams for acting in the world. But no one talks about deep values because the discourse of sex on campus devalues them. So, sadly, it's easier for people having casual sex to talk about copulation than it is for anyone else to talk about relationships with a richer foundation. Freitas believes, therefore, that "the beginnings of change lie in the willingness of students to openly discuss what they really desire in romance and sex and, in so doing, to break down the false belief that hook up culture is normal and what everybody likes and wants."[33]

Good Sex

At the beginning of the twenty-first century, the common sense of sex on campus isn't enough to connect the love of college students to the planet that needs our love. Just as gay and lesbian love has come out of the closet, heterosexual and homosexual love both need to come out of the bedroom. When we roll over and ask each other, "Was it good for you?" we also need to wonder what "good" really means, and we need to ask if it was good for anybody else, or for the planet that powers our love.

In her book *To Work and To Love*, theologian Dorothee Soelle offers a radical interpretation of sex and love in the world. She suggests that the project of the world's creation is unfinished and ongoing, and that we work because we need to carry on the creation. With the gift of creation, Soelle says, comes the gift of good work, cocreating the world, and tending the garden so that it tends toward higher purposes. We—as small creatures with capacities for care, consciousness, and creativity—are called to participate in the evolving creation.[34]

As such, good sex might be good not just when it's recreational or procreative, but also when it's cocreative. If we ask what gets made when we make love, the conventional wisdom is that good sex makes us feel good. But good sex might also lead to us *doing* good. If making love is part of our purpose as human beings on a living planet, then what we do in bed might reasonably affect the quality and care of the rest of our lives.[35]

This extensive interpretation of love suggests that the goals of the sexual revolution—gender equality, female autonomy, and liberation from our puritan inhibitions—were a good thing, but not good enough. The sexual revolution freed us from the hang-ups of the past, but it never quite freed us *for* the more substantial revolutions of the future. Instead sex became a goal in itself, and we settled for being connoisseurs of intercourse instead of stewards of it. As Soelle says, "[During the sexual revolution] many men and women who saw themselves as sexually liberated failed to translate their partial liberation from fear and guilty feelings into overturning the structures of injustice that make love impossible. There was liberation from inhibitions, but not liberation into a more just and free world."[36]

This limited liberation comes, in part, from the relentless privatization of romantic love, which seems to aim for the fulfillment of partners, but not generally the fulfillment of anything else. In our culture, falling in love often means falling into a smaller-and-smaller vortex of passion. Our private, apolitical romances isolate us from life all around us. So love becomes a retreat from the world instead of a path into deeper engagement. As therapy for the wounds of the world, romantic love adapts to "the real world" instead of adopting new perspectives.[37]

Instead of seeing romantic love as a private refuge from the evils of the world, we might see sexual liberation as a part of a broader cultural change, and good sex as a catalyst for a good society. "What can be said of our emotional vigor if it does not break into politics?" Soelle asks. "If our embodiment in lovemaking does not move us beyond the acute, narrow joys of our own bodies to the body politic, then it has not gone far enough." Good sex, then, could be measured not just by physical thrills, but also by the way that passion generates compassion, the way that love is shared not just with one other but with all others, and the way in which personal lovemaking might be part of some larger lovemaking. The love made in college apartments and dorm rooms, in cars and other confined spaces, could expand across the landscape of individual lives and the landscape of life itself. Unlike most Americans, Soelle finds it difficult to separate love for each other from love for the nature that sustains the other.[38]

What are people for, anyway? What are the purposes of love? What is made when we make love? Besides procreation, what is sex for, and does it have any larger purposes? What's the connection (if any) between love and commitment, between love and sex, between love, sex, and marriage? How will our college sex lives affect our love lives? How does hook-up culture affect American culture? How do our love lives affect other lives in the biosphere? How does today's casual sex affect tomorrow's children? What's the *meaning* of all this sex?

There aren't easy answers to these questions, but they're still worth pondering. In *Hooking Up, Hanging Out, and Hoping for Mr. Right*, the

Institute for American Values recommends a more thoughtful approach to college sex and courtship, one characterized by serious conversations that connect operative values to expressed values, and the present to the past and the future. They suggest that college students shouldn't be so quick to label the traditional wisdom of love and relationships "old-fashioned," as if human relationships should conform to a fashion cycle. They argue that young people should take time to share *their* hopes and dreams for relationships before conforming to the commercial dreams that are so pervasive in society. And they suggest that students should try to create a culture of care that connects their daily practices to their deepest values.[39]

Biophilia

A few people have also tried to hook up our romantic love to other loves, including biophilia, the love of life in all its forms.

Americans seem to have a hook-up relationship with nature. We love nature when we're camping or backpacking, and when we're in the wilderness. We commune with nature on some weekends and vacations. But we don't generally want a committed relationship that might demand daily care—living our love in routinely responsible behavior instead of just expressing and emoting it. We feel the sentiment of love for nature—and we can see it in our photos of sunrises and sunsets, and the sublime landscapes of the national parks—but we don't generally see the practice of that love in our everyday lives. Nature is the lover who wants a more fulfilling relationship with us. But most of the time, we want a no-strings-attached relationship with her.[40]

In *The Pine Island Paradox,* philosopher Kathleen Dean Moore offers a different way to think about our relationship to nature's places. Asking, "What does it mean to love a person?" and "What does it mean to love a place?" she finds that her answers converge:

> To love—a person and a place—means at least this:
>
> One. To want to be near it, physically.
>
> Number two. To want to know everything about it—its story, its moods, what it looks like by moonlight.
>
> Number three. To rejoice in the fact of it.
>
> Number four. To fear its loss, and grieve for its injuries.

Five. To protect it—fiercely, mindlessly, futilely, and maybe tragically, but to be helpless to do otherwise.

Six. To be transformed in its presence—lifted, lighter on your feet, transparent, open to everything beautiful and new.

Number seven. To want to be joined with it, taken in by it, lost in it.

Number eight. To want the best for it.

Number nine. Desperately.

Love is an anchor line, a rope on a pulley, a taut fly line, a spruce root, a route on a map, a father teaching his daughter to tie a bowline knot, eelgrass bent to the tide, and all of these—a complicated, changing web of relationships, taken together. It's not a choice, or a dream, or a romantic novel. It's a fact: an empirical fact about our biological existence. We are born into relationships with people and with places. We are born with the ability to create new relationships and tend to them. And we are born with a powerful longing for these relations. That complex connectedness nourishes and shapes us and gives us joy and purpose.

I knew there was something important missing from my list, but I was struggling to put it into words. Loving isn't just a state of being, it's a way of acting in the world. Love isn't a sort of bliss, it's a kind of work, sometimes hard, spirit-testing work. To love a person is to accept the responsibility to act lovingly toward him, to make his needs my own needs. To love a place is to care for it, to keep it healthy, to attend to its needs as if they were my own, because they are my own. Responsibility grows from love. It is the natural shape of caring.

Number ten, I wrote in my notebook. To love a person or a place is to accept moral responsibility for its well-being.[41]

One of my favorite students and her fiancé chose this passage for their wedding, and so did my son and daughter-in-law, expressing their connection to each other and to the ends of the Earth, the purposes of the planet. In a relationship or a ritual like this, love gets larger than a single couple, and it gets coupled to larger natural processes than human satisfaction and reproduction.

Such meditations and practices restore meaning to the *de*-meaning of sex by extending it from the dorm room or the bedroom to the wider world. Such a perspective on love and the land could also reshape our perspectives on cohabitation. Right now, for most of us, cohabitation means that a couple is living together, enjoying premarital sex, and the other joys (and sorrows) of an extended relationship. But cohabitation could have a broader meaning if it also included consideration of cohabiting with the other species of the planet. Cohabitation might mean living with a lover, but it wouldn't mean limiting our compassionate love to a single person or a single species. Cohabitation might involve the loving development of habits that might sustain the world. This cohabiting wouldn't necessarily mean living harmoniously with cockroaches, but it might mean living within the cycles and systems of nature. It might mean, too, living in right relation with each other by living in right relation to the world.

Instead of falling in love, we might consider rising in love, speaking our hopes and dreams for all our relationships out loud, and trying to create a culture that makes it easier to love extensively. This won't be easy. Commercial interests for diamonds, perfume, greeting cards, chocolates, flowers, movies, TV shows, candlelit restaurants, and romantic getaways will resist. But other organizations might approve. Religious organizations might assent to the ascent of love, care, and stewardship. Some politicians will protest that love isn't tough enough for policy, but other politicians might care to connect with people's hearts and minds. And college students, too, might rise to the occasion. American culture isn't good at deeper meanings, but college students still yearn for them. As in other areas of environmentalism, colleges might be the seedbed of an ecology of love. Then, instead of casual sex, we might experience *causal* sex, sex that causes something to happen by radiating the creative force of love to the ends of the Earth.

9

The Nature of Religion

*Feeling that morality has nothing to do with the way you use the
resources of the world is an idea that can't persist much longer.
If it does, then we won't.*
  Barbara Kingsolver, *Backtalk: Women Writers Speak Out*

*The stationary [sustainable] state would make fewer demands
on our environmental resources, but much greater demands on
our moral resources.*
  Herman Daly, "Towards a New Economics"

*The environmental crisis calls the religions of the world to respond
by finding their voice within the larger earth community. In
so doing, religions are now entering their ecological phase and
finding their planetary expression.*
  Mary Evelyn Tucker, *Worldly Wonder*

*I think it pisses God off if you walk by the color purple in a field
somewhere and don't notice it.*
  Alice Walker, *The Color Purple*

■ ■ ■ ■ ■ ■ ■

When college students like Joe and Jo College think about environmental issues, they usually approach them within scientific or political
frames. They watch movies like *An Inconvenient Truth* or *Eleventh Hour*,
and take part in political campaigns that pay lip service to environmental issues. In general, however, most students don't see environmental
issues in a religious or spiritual context, or see consumer culture as an
ethical issue, informed by religious traditions.[1]
    Americans believe faithfully that our colleges and universities are
mostly secular, and that higher education doesn't have much to do with
higher beings or higher goals. Some academics believe that religion cor-
rupts the processes of scientific inquiry and critical thinking. Others
just think it is irrelevant to the life of the mind and—in some cases—to
life period. Still others are anxious to preserve the separation of church

and state at colleges and universities funded by the state. So, for many Americans—and for many college students—college is the secular city.

To a certain extent, this is true. Colleges and universities are more secular than they were a century ago. Religion remains in the margins of the college curriculum, perceived mainly as an academic question or as an extracurricular activity.[2] In class, professors put secularization on the syllabus. As a result, they avoid sharing their religious beliefs in the classroom, and they generally reject the moral development of students as an aim of their professing. A national survey found that 51 percent of students, even at secular institutions, considered it important or essential to develop their own religious beliefs, but only 8 percent of faculty concur. As a result, 62 percent of undergraduates report that "professors never encourage discussion of religious or spiritual matters," and 56 percent claim that "professors never provide opportunities to discuss the meaning and purpose of life." As far as the college curriculum is concerned, Joe and Jo College apparently don't need to contemplate the meaning and purpose of life to succeed in "the real world."[3]

Even if college instruction is secular, though, many college students are not. Despite structural obstacles, students like Joe and Jo College have spiritual lives. The popular press focuses more on students' alcohol intake, consumption, sex lives, sports teams, fads, fashions, and foolishness, ignoring the ways that those same students sometimes go deep to probe the important questions of meaning and purpose, identity and community, often within a broadly religious context. Uprooted from their homes and familial faiths, many college students are thinking about setting down roots eventually in spiritual and religious practice, but most still see college as a period of transience, so they don't always get involved. It's a life-cycle thing: Students will think about religion when they have kids.[4]

The "lived religion" of American college students is diverse and eclectic. Some maintain the denominational affiliation and practice they learned from parents. Others drift from religious orthodoxy to para-church organizations. Many distance themselves from organized religion, resenting the rules and dogma of denominations and declaring that they are spiritual, but not religious. Some students experiment with meditative practices, New Age seeking, atheism, or agnosticism. For many students, it's a mix-and-match ensemble of religious traditions, infused with their own individual inclinations. In any case, it's optional, like other elements of American society. Nonreligious teens "describe religion as a preference they simply do not happen to share."[5]

In "OMG! How Generation Y Is Redefining Faith In The iPod Era," researchers found that American individualism increasingly inflects the religious practice of young people. For many of them, the American Dream means simply doing what they want, professing an almost religious faith in individuality and moral privatism. Accustomed to the personalization and customization of computers and cable TV, downloading and iPod music mixes, fast food and cafeterias, colleges and courses, they expect to configure their own faith as well. Many students can't identify their own faith tradition or denomination, and almost a quarter identify with no denomination at all. For the most part, collegians don't participate in traditional religious services because established rituals seem to impinge on their freedom and because they prefer to sleep in on Sunday morning. Instead, their primary religious practice often consists of casual conversations with like-minded friends. Growing up in an era of American hyper-individualism, most students negotiate their own place in the religious cosmos, but few really consider religion very important to the formation of their identity.[6]

In her research on lived religion, Rebecca Kneale Gould suggests that people today are practicing religion not just in the established ways, but in all sorts of ways that bind us back to the source of life and values. All kinds of Americans are muddling toward meaning in all kinds of ways, trying to escape from "the moral relativism and secular cynicism" that surrounds them. Many are turning to spiritual language and practice for both peace and provocation. Others are "reaching deep into our hearts to ask: what are the values that we hold most dear?" Still, on college campuses, the deepest questions and concerns of students aren't often satisfied by what is mostly secular schoolwork.[7]

The environmental concerns of college students aren't always addressed either, even within religious bodies. Historically, faith groups in the United States have operated like other businesses, treating the environment as an externality, peripheral to their central aims. Bowing to the gods of American culture, denominations have focused most on individual salvation and charity, and less on core issues like justice and stewardship. In recent years, "social issues" like abortion, gay marriage, and prayer in public schools have been more important to some Christian churches than environmental issues. For the most part, therefore, the ecological consciousness of religious people in America has remained at about the same level as the consciousness of the general public, and the environment has not been seen as an issue of conscience. But this is changing—and very quickly—both on and off campus.[8]

The Spiritual Life of College Students

A 2006 survey titled "The Spiritual Life of College Students" found that college students express very high levels of spiritual interest and involvement, as well as high levels of religious commitment and participation. About 80 percent have an interest in spirituality, and almost two-thirds consider spirituality "a source of joy." While 17 percent of students score high on religious skepticism, more than three-fourths believe in God, and about the same number feel a sense of connection with God or a higher power that transcends the personal self. Joe and Jo College and their classmates aren't, apparently, as secular as they sometimes seem.[9]

This interest in spirituality and religion isn't just theoretical. Some 80 percent of college students have attended religious services in the last year, and have discussed religious topics with friends and family. Two-thirds of them pray, including 61 percent who pray at least weekly, and 28 percent who pray daily. Four in ten students consider it essential or very important to "follow religious teachings in my everyday life." And 70 percent report being actively engaged in "trying to change things that are unfair in the world." Students say that they put their religious beliefs into practice, whether or not other people notice.[10]

While researchers didn't probe the environmental implications of students' spirituality and religious involvement, they found that four out of five students believed in "the sacredness of life." Three out of five reported having had spiritual experiences while "witnessing the beauty and harmony of nature." In another study, students also suggested a connection between their spirituality and experiences in nature. Spirituality, said one student, "is how I feel when I'm in the woods by myself." "When I picture spiritual," revealed another student, "sometimes I picture the hippie earth-loving kind of people." A third student sees spirituality as having "a connection to all life and to people and the world." There seems to be an element of nature in students' sense of the supernatural, and vice versa.[11]

The survey data on religious involvement offer some insights about collegiate religiosity, but the surveys also elicit additional questions. One important question is the nature of religious belief: What do students mean when they characterize themselves as religious, or when they say that they're spiritual but not religious? Another important question regards the practical consequences of religious belief. Are believers demonstrably different than other college students, or is the difference mainly in their minds? What are the practical consequences of religious belief in a student's everyday life and in the everyday life of an imperiled world?

In *Soul Searching: The Religious and Spiritual Lives of American Teenagers*, Christian Smith and Melinda Denton surveyed teens and found strong similarities to the data on college students. But they also probed deeper with interviews to see what the survey results meant. They found that "most teens seem simply to accept religion as a taken-for-granted aspect or presence that mostly operates in the background of their lives. . . . There is very little built-in religious content or connection in the structure of most U.S. adolescents' daily schedules and routines." When asked about religious beliefs and traditions, "the vast majority could not express themselves on matters of God, faith, religion or spiritual life. . . . They know abundant details about the lives of favorite musicians and television stars or about what it takes to get into a good college, but most are not very clear about who Moses and Jesus were."[12]

So while teenagers say that religion is important, it is largely invisible in their lives. Smith and Denton suggest that "in the ecology of American adolescents' lives, religion clearly operates in a social-structurally weak position, competing for time, energy, and attention, and often losing, against other more dominant demands, particularly school, sports, television, and other electronic media." The *OMG!* study found that when young people listed their top concerns, only 18 percent chose a relationship with God, coming after (in descending order) getting a sexually transmitted disease, finding a job, grades, friends, and parents. College students tend to worship at the Church of Saint Pillow as much as at other institutions near campus. When you're in college, one young woman noted, "going to church is difficult, to wake up on Sunday mornings. Or any other morning." Young Americans *say* that religion is important (because that's what they're *supposed* to say), but they don't seem to *do* it that much.[13]

Smith and Denton contend that the operative religion of American teenagers is "Moralistic Therapeutic Deism," and that its creed looks something like this:

1. A God exists who created and orders the world and watches over human life on Earth.
2. God wants people to be good, nice, and fair to each other, as taught by the Bible and most world religions.
3. The central goal of life is to be happy and to feel good about oneself.

4. God does not need to be particularly involved in one's life except when God is needed to solve a problem.
5. Good people go to heaven when they die.

This religion is simple. It tells us to be good and feel good, and not much else. As William Galston suggests, "the gospel of personal salvation trumps the social gospel." Moralistic Therapeutic Deism—a feel-good faith with a laid-back god—doesn't replace the faith of students' fathers and mothers, but it increasingly *becomes* the practical content of those faith traditions, even for their mothers and fathers. Therefore, even though they experience religion at several levels of their lives, none of it seems to run very deep.[14]

The *Soul Searching* study describes spiritual and religious backgrounds of students before they come to college. Picking up as young people make the transition to college, Tim Clydesdale's *The First Year Out* is also skeptical of biases in the survey data. "The real issue," he contends, "is not how many college students check off 'an interest in spirituality,' but how many actualize that interest in their everyday priorities." Clydesdale suggests that students "stow their (often vague) religious and spiritual identities in an identity lockbox well before entering college." Students are so busy managing the academic and social challenges of college that they don't have time or make time to think about the nature and purpose of the universe or their place in it. They're so busy seeking credentials for success that they seldom question the cultural definitions of success. In addition, at many institutions, religious commitments are considered uncool so that "to appear over-religious can be the social kiss of death." The student who believes in religious obligations doesn't seem to understand the freedoms of college. Many college students believe in freedom of religion, but many also believe in freedom *from* religion. Religion is theoretically important, but it just doesn't seem that relevant to the routines of daily life.[15]

Joe and Jo College often associate religion with a vague morality, and subscribe to "a popular moral culture that: celebrates personal effort and individual achievement, demonstrates patriotism, believes in God and a spiritual afterlife, values loyalty to family, friends, and co-workers, expects personal moral freedom, distrusts large organizations and bureaucracies, and conveys that happiness is found primarily in personal relationships and individual consumption." As members of this religious sect—the most populous in American culture—college students occupy "the *semireligious* middle ground." And there's not much at all about the ground of Earth in that popular morality. Compartmentalizing their lives, students "stow religious identities when in educational settings, and stow educational identities when in religious settings." For the most part, too, they keep quiet about their religious beliefs. It's a sort of "don't ask, don't tell" policy that keeps everyone from the embarrassment of expressed commitments.[16]

Some religious activity on campus occurs within the standard American denominations and their outreach programs, but a lot of it happens in interdenominational para-church organizations, like the Fellowship of Christian Athletes or Campus Crusade for Christ. These groups talk and sing often about issues of meaning, belonging, and religious identity on a secular college campus, but they don't talk as much about issues of justice, vocation, and stewardship in the natural world. Such students are still seeking wholeness, but their quest is directed more toward the self than toward the community or the biosphere. The rapid growth of para-church chapters on college campuses suggests how college students think about religious practice. Young people still want to probe at questions of the divine, but they don't want to do it in a denominational or congregational setting. They prefer instead episodic religious experiences, often just talking among friends, to the ongoing liturgical practices of America's churches. Many college students no longer find meaning in the life and work of institutional religion; instead, they find it in a weekly gathering of peers.[17]

Sometimes the spirituality of college students is the segregated spirituality of American religion—a Sunday thing, an occasional counterpoint to "the real world" instead of a foundation for it. Joe and Jo College—like other Americans—tend to think of spiritual practice as *exclusively* spiritual, disconnected from work, play, friendship, and love. There's a sphere of spirituality, but it doesn't seem to touch the biosphere. Other college students, however, practice a social gospel. And increasingly college students are looking for an ecological gospel. Some of these students are even getting to the root of religion, which is relationship. Ecology is the *science* of relationships—the study of interdependence in the natural world. Religion is an *art* of relationships—the practice of interdependence between the natural and supernatural worlds. From the Latin verb "religare," religion means "to bind together," and it's meant to bind people to divinity, to each other, and to creation. Contrary to many collegiate assumptions, the basis of religion isn't conformity to denominational doctrine. It's simply the spirit that animates life, the principles that guide action in the world, and the communities that bind inspiration and practices together. The myths and symbols and scriptures of religion locate individuals cosmologically, and tell about their moral responsibilities to nature and human nature.[18]

Religion as a Natural Resource for Environmentalism

Although most college students don't think about religion and environmentalism, religion offers resources for students who care about the natural world. With this in mind, some of America's colleges and universities are beginning to offer courses or institute programs that look at the intersections of nature and the supernatural, religious practice, and environmental crisis.

In addition, several colleges and universities have instituted special programs to focus attention on the synergies of religion and environmentalism, past and present. Starting in 1996, for example, Harvard University sponsored a series of ten conferences, "Religions of the World and Ecology," linking scholars in the academic study of religion with people and practitioners curious about the intersections of religious values and environmental impacts. Each conference focused on religion and ecology in one of the world's great religions, and the series resulted in ten volumes published by Harvard University Press. Three additional conferences in 1998 brought four other disciplines concerned with the environment—science, economics, education, and public policy—into conversation about core values. At that point, some of the organizers instituted the Forum on Religion and Ecology (FORE), arguing that "the moral force of the world's religions is needed to help shape environmental policies and to mobilize people to help preserve the environment."[19]

The University of Chicago started its Religion and Environment Initiative in 2003, explaining the reasoning behind the initiative in a set of five propositions:

1) We have an environmental crisis.
2) The crisis is at least partly a crisis of values.
3) Religious communities and organizations are prime custodians of values.
4) Many people of faith have yet to link their spiritual and environmental values.
5) University students are uniquely positioned to serve as mentors and exemplars for those seeking to combine their spiritual and environmental values.[20]

Still, most college students haven't learned about such initiatives, and most don't think about the religious implications of environmental issues. But virtually all of the American mainstream denominations have issued statements on the care of all creation, emphasizing ideas, ideals, and traditions that make religion a rich natural resource for environmentalism.[21]

Religion has its problems, of course. There's often been an otherworldliness that tells believers that this world doesn't matter as much as the next world. Some evangelical sects contend that people don't need to worry about environmental problems because God takes care of it all. Some religions have preached human humility, but failed to instill it in their members. In the mainstream Judeo-Christian tradition, for example, there's been a confusion of dominion and domination, and religious justifications have been used for widespread environmental degradation. In many churches, there's a wide divide between the statements of the national church and the sermons in the local pulpit. And, of course, as with people anywhere, there's a gulf between preaching and practice that sometimes comes off as sheer hypocrisy. Religion can also cause quiescence. Some of us assume that because someone else watches over the world, we can let that higher power deal with our environmental crises. We have our own lives to lead, after all.[22]

But imperfect people will always inhabit imperfect institutions. And even religions that have ecological cosmologies can be ignored in the practices of everyday life. Even with their imperfections, though, American religious traditions can offer college students critical intellectual resources to help them think clearly about the moral ecology of everyday life, including their own. In a world where we desperately need to consider the ethics of our extensive environmental impacts, religion can connect us to some important wisdom traditions.

Below, for example, are ten religious resources that college students might consider as they wonder how to cope and hope in an all-too-depressing context of environmental degradation. They're mostly from the Judeo-Christian tradition, because that tradition still shapes the beliefs and behavior of most of America's college students. But there are environmental resources within all the faith traditions, if only we take time to look for them.[23]

1.) Creation and Creativity

The book of Genesis, the foundational text of Jews and Christians, expresses a tradition of creativity, which is found in virtually all religions.

Genesis teaches first that the universe is created and purposeful, and, second, that humans are creatures, flesh and bone, created together with light and darkness, earth and sea, fish and fowl, bird and beast, all of which is good. Finally, Genesis teaches that humans are creative as well as created. Made in the image and likeness of God, people share the capacity for imagination and invention. In this seminal story, the Earth is explained as a garden that people are called to care for, not just because it's good for them, but because it's good in itself. A part of creation, human beings are also the part that is responsible for its care—for the creative dominion of nature.

In a provocative essay called "Creation Unplugged," Bill McKibben contends that human beings today are systematically engaged in a process he calls "decreation," driving the Earth and its teeming biodiversity to extinction. So a focus on creation spirituality could be a powerful corrective to a culture that's focused on the "creative destruction" of capitalism. It can be a way to practice an ethics that's large enough to include the rest of creation, an ethics based not just on rules and prohibitions but on harmony and aspirations. And it can be a way to consider environmental ethics not just as a specialized field of ethics but as an ethic in all of our fields.[24]

2.) Sacramentality

A second religious resource is the tradition of sacramentality, which says simply that some things are sacred. Sacramentality suggests that people and things can be visible signs of invisible grace, so they have a value above and beyond their market value and their instrumental value. In the Judeo-Christian tradition, sacramentality flows from the creation of the world. It suggests that God wasn't kidding in describing all creation, and not just humanity's natural resources, as "very good."[25]

Sacramentality: The radical idea that we all live in a holy land.

One variation of this tradition is the idea that nature is a revelation of God, a place to encounter divinity. This sacramentality suggests that people don't have to go to the Holy Land because they're already on holy ground. It reveals nature as a microcosm of the macrocosm, a full representation of the cosmos. The whole of creation is captured in any small plot, and all of it is sacred and holy and good. And there are responsibilities for this ongoing creation not just in the rain forest or the wilderness, but right here as well.[26]

Sacramentality also underlines the fact that secularism is a relative latecomer in the history of the world. Most of the Earth's peoples have believed that the world is overflowing with spirits. Writing in "Christianity and the Survival of Creation," Wendell Berry asserts that "[we] are holy creatures living among other holy creatures in a world that is holy. Some people know this, and some do not." Some do not because, for the most part, both holiness and the human place in creation are ideas obscured or compartmentalized by consumer culture and the dominant institutions of the modern world.[27]

Sacramentality also affects how individuals act in the world. A healthy sense of the holy in nature tends to invite humility and reverence. Instead of managing and modifying the planet, we might learn from nature's processes. We might curb our enthusiasm for technological experimentation on the planet and embrace the precautionary principle—delaying environmental interventions until we understand the consequences. Instead of objectifying plant and animal life, we might subjectify it. Instead of always transforming nature, we might appreciate its transformative nature.

3.) Mysticism

Connected to sacramentality is another religious resource: mysticism. Many college students feel alone in the world, isolated by American individualism, screened from firsthand experience by TV and computer screens, and cut off from nature by the technological wonders of postmodernity. While most are "connected" electronically via television, computers, and cell phones, mystics connect to the cosmos in body and soul. Instead of going to church to find God, instead of reading about God in scriptures, mystics find God face-to-face—and sometimes the face that looks back is nature. Mystics invite us to experience the beauty and the wonders of the world, and to wonder why we don't feel wondrous more often. They show how to be literally awesome, responding with awe to the majesty of creation, and using that awe and wonder as a catalyst for our own lives.[28]

Outside of social institutions and expectations, even outside of themselves, mystics experience the beauty and the wisdom of the universe. Because it gets away from everyday life and assumptions, a mystical experience is like a vacation. But because it immerses individuals in the sources of all life, it's more like a vocation. Having experienced what Thich Nhat Hanh calls the "interbeing" of the universe, mystics return to Earth ready to realize the world of harmonious possibility. They don't expect rapture 24/7, but they hope to infuse a little more ecstasy into the agonies of the world. They hope to increase our capacity for wonder.[29]

4.) Sabbath

A fourth resource is the Sabbath, a tradition of rest and restoration. In America, the Sabbath is the day when some take time out to go to church or synagogue. But this tradition of worship is one small part of a larger Sabbath. The Bible suggests that the land should also get a Sabbath—every seven years instead of every seven days—so that it can recover from our constant cultivation. Today's conception of Sabbath, then, comes from a tradition of letting fields lie fallow, and it invites people to let themselves lie fallow, too, regenerating energy for production and for continuous creativity. The Sabbath is a reminder that all Earthly productivity is rooted in the land or immersed in the sea, and that human productivity is connected to the Earth as well.

Sabbath used to be a sacred time, a time when Jews and Christians considered how to "redeem the time"—how to make ordinary time extraordinary, luminous with possibilities for good. Although many religious Americans—including many college students—still attend church services on the Sabbath, they often lack that special sense of sacred time, with its promise of changing the world. For many college students, the Sabbath is just one day of the weekend, which is more for entertainment than for enlightenment. Instead of being a day free from work, the Christian Sabbath is a day they may *return* to work after the *fun*-damentalist Sabbath of Saturday night. But the Sabbath is a religious resource that college students could use to make time to listen to the sacred, and to apply the wisdom of holiness to their everyday lives.[30]

5.) Love

A fifth environmental resource is the commandment of love. As we have seen, college students think a lot about love and making love, but not usually in a religious context. In most religious scriptures, humanity is called to love God and to love our neighbors as ourselves. In the New

Testament, Christians are even called to love enemies, and the Christian tradition can be read as a radical expansion of the boundaries of love. In the nineteenth century, for example, abolitionists expanded the boundaries of love by calling for justice—love institutionalized—for people who were enslaved. Religious love isn't romantic love, although religious people can be romantic, too. It's agape, which is selfless and sacrificial. It's compassion. Romantic love may make the world go round, but religious love, at its best, makes the world go better.[31]

In this century, the boundaries of religious love are expanding again to encompass not just human beings but the whole of creation. These religions increasingly call people to love the plants and animals that are their neighbors on the planet, as well as the planet's water and air. Stephen Jay Gould wrote, "We cannot win this battle to save species and environments without forging an emotional bond between ourselves and nature as well—for we will not fight to save what we do not love." These days, therefore, agape is evolving into biophilia. And love lives are coming to encompass a love for all life.[32]

6.) Rituals of Community

In most religious traditions, love is connected to community, a sixth significant resource that religion brings to environmentalism. Individualism is an interesting idea, but it's more American than religious. The Bible, for instance, speaks mainly to the people of God, not the individuals of God. When Christians worship, they share communion, not competitive individualism. Some religious traditions teach that everyone needs salvation, but it's not just the salvation of the self—it's the self in relation.[33]

Sometimes in religious rituals individuals see the self in relation to nature. Within the Christian tradition, the shared communion is bread and wine, a feast of food. Sharing food, Christians share the grace of sunshine, photosynthesis, and rainfall. In communion, they ritualize dependence on gifts and grace which scientists prosaically call "ecosystem services."

Another resource that religious communities bring to environmental-ism is a tradition of seasonal rituals. In America these days, we still have seasons, but we experience them differently than our ancestors did. In the commercial culture that dominates our consciousness, there are fashion seasons and shopping seasons, and the natural seasons are enlisted mainly to support the retail seasons. This commercial calendar can be counterpointed by the liturgical calendar, which connects religious practice to the seasons of natural life. In most churches, for example, there are festivals of light and festivals of darkness, of birth and death and resurrection. There are seasons of restraint and seasons of joy, seasons of sacrifice, and seasons of harvest and thanksgiving. In an increasingly indoor society, religious institutions keep people connected to the seasons of life outside their doors. So when college students do go to church, they're celebrating what comes naturally—in several different ways.[34]

At its best, worship returns people to the natural rhythms of life through these Earth-honoring rituals. The goal of religious liturgy, then, is not to tell people how they should align their human rhythms with those of the cosmos; rather, liturgy shows people the ways in which these rhythms have always been one and the same. Liturgy approaches the heart of Aldo Leopold's Land Ethic: "All ethics so far evolved rest upon a single premise: that the individual is a member of a community of interdependent parts."[35]

Religious institutions also model rituals of celebration for environmentalists. Too often, environmentalism is not a lot of fun. Truthfully, a lot of it is bad news. But some religious traditions are "gospel," which means "good news." When it works well, the gospel doesn't cover up the bad news—there's evil in the world, and it's very plain to see. But the gospel looks for the good news in the bad news, the possibilities of redemption and grace. The gospel calls for celebration, not because of blind optimism—the belief that everything will turn out all right in the end—but because it's always the right time to do the right thing. When people are doing things right in their churches—which isn't all the time, for sure—their communities can offer environmentalists exuberant examples of engagement, enthusiasm, and joy.

7.) Vocation

A seventh religious tradition that connects individuals with creation is vocation, which calls people to good work. According to theologian

Dorothee Soelle, good work is good in three ways: It expresses the self, it allows the self to serve the community, and it reconciles the self with nature. Because vocation, in the Christian tradition, is a call from God, and because God is the creator of the universe, a vocation can't be at odds with the care of creation. As it happens, though, lots of American jobs and careers *are* at odds with the care of creation. And our political candidates—especially in a recession—are more concerned with job creation than with creation itself. But vocation offers religious people— and environmentalists—a way of thinking about work that helps them see not just what in the world it's good for, but also how it's good for the world, especially the natural world.[36]

As Curtis White suggests in "The Ecology of Work," many college students define a good job in terms of autonomy, professional status, and compensation, ignoring the difference between a good job and good work. White contends that work in America is a problem for two reasons: It frequently damages the environment, and it reduces human beings to functionaries, people who perform a function in an ecologically destructive system for the compensations of consumption. When students graduate, therefore, many will be looking at jobs that pay them to ignore their ecological intelligence. In the last century, Upton Sinclair observed that "it is difficult to get [people] to understand something when [their] salary depends [on them] not understanding it," and White agrees. Capitalism, he claims, is destroying the world, and most of us are helping, excusing ourselves by saying "I'm only doing my job."[37]

Joe and Jo College already know that it's possible to change your work if you change your frame of mind about it. When students really engage with ideas, they can make even a boring professor seem interesting. But it's also true that we can change the nature of our work by changing the frame of work—by rethinking its purposes and incentives. The idea of vocation and associated ideas in the world's religions offer a different interpretation of work. Vocation gives people a way of thinking about the cosmic and communitarian aspects of work, and it invites them to think about the gift of creation, the creation of an individual's own gifts, and the ways in which those gifts might be applied to the ongoing gift of creation.

College students don't talk much about vocation, partly because students don't talk about religion, but also because the idea is really challenging. Vocation means that a person must be dedicated to cosmic projects and not just the projects of American capitalism. It demands that they think about more then *money*-theism. And if, for instance, God's main projects are justice and stewardship, then that's our job description. As theologian Thomas Berry suggests, "The Great Work now, as we move into a new millennium, is to carry out the transition from a period of human devastation to a period when humans would be present to the planet in a mutually beneficial manner." A healthy sense of vocation, then, might help us align our work with nature's work. It might make sense—and not just economic sense—of "green jobs."[38]

Another possibility is to think of our consumption as vocation, because most of us affect the world more through our consumption than through our careers. Even when we're not at work, we work great changes on the world, and we change the nature of work for people around the globe. It's American common sense that when people think about work and vocation, we think more about production than consumption, more about seriousness than fun. But we could think about these oppositions ecologically, as part of larger systems of life and meaning. Instead of thinking about work *and* consumption, therefore, we might think about the work *of* consumption and our calling to consume carefully—which is to say, to consume as a practice of caring for our communities, both human and natural. We might think about leisure not just as rest *from* vocation, but as the *rest* of vocation. We might make conspicuous frugality and simple living a part of our life's work.

In the process, we might change the nature of "making a living." For most of us in America, to make a living is to make money that supports our lives and those of our families. But making a living could also be construed as making *all* living more fruitful, for people and the planet. And that work—which Buddhists call "right livelihood"—would be a good vocation for us all.

8.) Stewardship

An eighth religious resource for environmentalism is stewardship. Stewardship is the art of taking care, and it's an essential part of all vocations. Sometimes when we leave a friend, or when we're finished talking on the phone, we say, "Take care." That advice is, whether we realize it or not, a way of looking at the cosmos. Genesis, for instance, calls Christians and Jews to take care of each other by taking care of creation, and vice versa. Stewards are called to serve God by serving God's creation and preserving it, not as a mere museum of Edenic life but as an ongoing, evolving biosphere of production and reproduction.

Stewards are accountable not for the preservation of private property or the service of personal profit—although property and profit may be methods of serving and preserving creation—but for the proliferation of the teeming life of the world. Stewards are accountable not just for individual actions, but for institutional activity, too—including the anthropocentric system of accounting that discounts the good of creation. Called to serve and preserve the Earth, stewards are commanded to exercise dominion over the world in exactly the way that God exercises dominion—lovingly, compassionately, creatively, carefully.

9.) Simple Living

A ninth environmental resource in the world's religious traditions is simple living, or asceticism. One way to take care of nature is not to take so much *from* nature. Asceticism is a process of renouncing the comforts of conventional life in order to attain the comforts of an unconventional life. People don't need to be religious to consume less, as the number of "downshifters" in American culture shows, but most of the world's religions do provide a frame in which less consumption involves more meaning.[39]

Historically, asceticism has been a practice of austere self-discipline in societies more devoted to self-fulfillment and selfishness. These days, voluntary simplicity also helps people recognize the corrosive effects of a consumer society on the human spirit. And it reminds us that living harmoniously with the Earth takes work, discipline, and humility.[40]

Voluntary simplicity invites individuals to ask if consumption is good for their souls. It raises the possibility that consumer choices actually change people, warping personalities to conform to preferences. Activities not only embody intentions, they affect intentions as well. Consumption choices like watching TV, playing video games, gambling, or shopping can become habitual, so that sometimes people find themselves becoming persons they never wanted to be—people who can be satisfied by easy pleasures, and who won't strive for more substantial satisfactions. We generally think of consumption as what we get, but sometimes a consumer mentality gets us.[41]

Asceticism makes Americans uneasy because it's about discipline and restraint. We talk a lot about discipline, especially in our schools and in sports. But we also systematically undermine discipline because it's hard to sell stuff to people who are disciplined and self-assured. So advertisers and marketers work hard to substitute a fun ethic for a work ethic, and to make "discipline" sound like a dirty word. In commercial *fun*-damentalism, college students and other Americans generally understand discipline as something that other people inflict on us, and we revolt against it as an infringement on our freedom.

Religious asceticism doesn't see discipline as an imposition. It is self-discipline, and it flows from the nature of nature and the nature of human beings. Self-discipline is the art of living up to your own high expectations. It's the ability to see the love in limits. Asceticism helps us deal with too much—and with the too little that often comes with too much. Too much stuff often results in too little joy because the stuff is the conventional expression of success rather than heartfelt happiness itself. To its practitioners, asceticism offers a richer life—without riches.[42]

So religion may also be a resource for challenging the idolatry of campus consumerism. Almost all religious traditions offer ways of understanding "the good life" that don't include profligate consumption of the world. While American commercial culture invites students to define happiness in terms of status and consumption, religious traditions offer a sharp counterpoint. For environmentalists and religious people alike, the connection between consumption and the environment is impossible to ignore. As people increase their levels and habits of consumption, we decrease the quality of life for the Earth community and its human family. Sustainable living, like religious asceticism, calls us to break the obsession with stuff and status, and calls us to individual and institutional patterns of voluntary simplicity.[43]

Asceticism has its advantages. Ascetics buy less stuff, but seem to enjoy it more. Ascetics have their hearts set on the good things of this world, but they don't assume that all goods are good. Turning away from the agitations of consumer culture, they often find quiet fulfillment in "tools for conviviality"—the things that invite us into more human relationships. Instead of fast food, they share the preparation of delectable meals of slow food. Instead of watching TV all the time, they watch out for each other. Instead of tuning in to talk radio, they actually have conversations. Instead of listening to recorded music, they make their own. Instead of buying books of landscape paintings for the coffee table, they walk in the woods, or around the local pond. Instead of buying their dreams packaged in the commodities of consumer culture, they live their dreams here and now. Instead of buying what's cheapest at Wal-Mart, they buy what's most valuable—to people and the planet. As a result, ascetics often enjoy "Zen affluence," having much by wanting little.[44]

Zen affluence: The art of having much by wanting little. The art of having your heart's desire by restraining your desire. For people who live in what William Leach calls "the land of desire," this is not an easy trick.

10.) The Prophetic Tradition

A final religious resource that's relevant to environmentalism is the prophetic tradition. Because people are imperfect, we often get things wrong. But because some prophetic people are perceptive and coura-. geous, we also hear about what's wrong and who's responsible. One way to understand many religious traditions is as a succession of prophets, people who bring anger and judgment to human hubris and institutions. These are people speaking truth to power. The rant is a religious art form. It's even named after one of the prophets: It's called a jeremiad.[45]

Where do these prophets go to get perspective on their society? Do they go to the university, to the library, to the coffee shop? No, they go to nature, typically—and most often they go to the desert. To think about their society, they often need to think outside of that society. To get a perspective on the social construction of reality, they need to experience a natural construction of reality.

The prophetic tradition responds to cultural practices that undo the oneness of the universe, and to the ideas and institutions that subdue people and the planet. Its origin is spiritual, but its outcome is worldly. Its source is love, but its mantra is justice. The prophets have a passion for compassion, and their care for the wholeness of creation causes them anguish when they see it sold piecemeal in the temple of commerce.

Prophets don't care much about individuals and their intentions, because they see that we act more effectively through our institutional arrangements. They care, therefore, about how institutions serve the poor and oppressed, the vulnerable members of our communities. Environmental prophets care about the fate of the most vulnerable members of our ecological communities, the endangered species, including endangered human beings.

This means that contemporary prophets care about environmental justice, both for people and for the Earth's other organisms. As ethicist Larry Rasmussen says, they remind us that, environmentally, "different communities suffer different consequences. The wrong side of the tracks has always been more toxic. In short, injustice is authorized. It is authorized by privilege and the way privilege organizes power. That most of the privileged are good people is largely beside the point." To us, billions of people and plants and animals are out of sight and out of mind. But the prophets remind us that they're never out of God's mind.[46]

Many American conservatives like to celebrate the benefits of "trickle-down economics" whereby the economic freedom of wealthy investors eventually results in prosperity for all. There's some merit to this position, although commercial capitalism seems to have defined "all" as "those people who can pay for their own prosperity." While asceticism reminds us that enough is better than too much, the prophetic tradition reminds us that not enough is not enough. The prophetic tradition understands that excess consumption and access to resources are interrelated issues. Overconsumption is a problem for many Americans, but under-consumption is a greater problem globally. More than a third of the world's people live on less than a dollar a day; more than half live on less than two dollars a day. Millions scrabble daily for scraps to eat, and thousands die every day of hunger and malnutrition. Diseases infect people who lack even primitive medical care. Kids grow up without growing hopeful because their families need the income from child labor, or because parents can't afford to educate them. Poverty is a human tragedy, but it's also an ecological issue because it means that the gift of creation—given to all—has not been shared fairly. The prophetic tradition looks at these injustices, and calls people to redistribute the Earth's bounty justly.

The prophets condemn the status quo, but they always call for repentance and transformation. They invite people to change their ways so that everyone can live in the land of milk and honey. Contemporary prophets care about justice for plants and animals, and they help us envision an Earth ethic that would institutionalize our care for the whole Earth community. The prophetic tradition challenges religious people to challenge the hierarchies of modern life, and to see systems and communities not as links in a great chain of power but as a single interconnected web of life. It calls for changes—big changes—in our institutional arrangements. Along with the other religious resources suggested here, the prophetic tradition helps to shape the world so that people can look at creation—and our creations—and say again, "It is good."[47]

College students can be prophets, too. Still free from the conformity of the business world, college students can speak truth to power—and to their peers. The American prophet Henry Thoreau challenged his neighbors by writing honestly in *Walden* that "[t]he greater part of what my neighbors call good I believe in my soul to be bad." But how often do we even ask ethical questions about common sense and peer pressure, about the habits and routines of our lives and of the people around us? Do we believe, deep in our soul, that what our culture calls good always is good? Do we believe that college culture makes life—all life—better? If not, what can we do about it? What kinds of prophetic actions are possible, right here and right now?[48]

A Culture of Silence

Although these resources are freely available to college students and other Americans, religious and secular, many college students, like many American environmentalists, want nothing to do with religion or spirituality. After reading Bill McKibben's "Creation Unplugged," for example, one of my students agreed with McKibben's diagnosis that "our life styles are simply unsustainable and we need to make drastic changes." This student sees American materialism and consumption as irrational, but he considers religion irrational, too, and doesn't see how additional irrationality helps at all. He sees that religion can be influential (for good and for evil), but contends, "I am interested in *truth*, not wishful thinking. Maybe everything would be better if there was a god, but that is not an argument for inventing one." He doesn't believe that scripture is a sufficient reason (or a reason at all) for environmental action. And he worries that religious people who believe in eternal life don't worry enough about the life of their own planet. Concluding, he contends that "only when we appeal to our better angels [reason], not faith, will we be able to truly have a discourse to change our world."

For students like this (and there are many), the practice of environmentalism won't be a practice of religion. But such students might still learn something from religious traditions—not on grounds of faith, but on grounds of practicality. Like it or not, these traditions wield great power, good and bad, and they can help to change the world. So skeptics might note that people resonate with stories that imbue the world with purpose and passion, and that social activists like Jesus, Mohandas Gandhi, and Martin Luther King, Jr. still inspire many of their peers. Skeptical students might even find common ground with their religious peers in creatively designing the good work of stewardship.

Without religious reasons for asceticism, they might investigate the pleasures of less consumption. And, like the prophets, they might call on a wayward and wasteful people to change their ways for the possibilities of a better world and life everlasting—which is, after all, not just a description of an afterlife. It's also a description of a sustainable life.

Whether or not we practice religion or spirituality, we will need to draw on our ethical resources to speed the ecological transition of the twenty-first century. With Joe and Jo College, we will need to speak and enact our environmental values in the world, both individually and institutionally. To do that, we'll need to develop a culture in which people feel free to "go public" with their deepest values.

Today, college culture constrains both the expression of values and the practice of virtues. A few years ago, in a class on college consumer culture, I asked my students to tell me their deepest values. Then I asked them for lists of the values of college culture and of American consumer culture. It turned out that their deepest values differ greatly from the values of their cultures. We live, in fact, in a culture that's hostile to many of our deepest values, and *we think that's normal.*

I also asked students who else knew of their deepest values. For most students, the number of people was very small—usually Mom, sometimes Dad, and then one or two best friends. I asked why so few people knew, since a better world won't happen without a lively discussion of the goodness of the good life. The answer was instructive: We don't share our deepest values because we're afraid that people will laugh at us or think us weird. We'd rather be "not too bad" than "too good." This is college peer pressure at its most powerful—the pressure to keep students silent about what they really care about. The result is an impoverished discourse of virtue, and a mind-set that keeps us from acting out our best intentions. When our deepest values are private, they have almost no public consequence. If we don't speak our values, the culture conforms to somebody else's—the people who value money more than values, goods more than goodness, sex more than love, fun more than fulfillment, and—though they would never say so—environmental degradation more than sustainability.[49]

The fact of the matter is this: Our peers *won't* laugh at us. They *won't* think we're weird. Our deepest values tend to be similar. So we're not really constrained by actual others. We're constrained by the imaginary others in our heads. The misperception of others is not unique to college students. In "Yearning for Balance," researchers found that most Americans espouse values of responsibility, family life, and friendship, but they don't think other Americans do. Most cite faith and generosity as guiding values in their lives, but only a few think that others share their values. We have a broad consensus on values, but we don't realize it because we don't talk about them.[50]

The same is true of values concerning consumption and the environment. Eighty-two percent of Americans believe that most of us are wasteful, buying and consuming more than we need. Eighty-six percent are concerned about the environment, and 51 percent believe that their own consumption has a negative effect on the environment. As a result, 88 percent of us believe that "protecting the environment will require most of us to make major changes in the way we live." If we ever discussed our deepest values, we might learn that almost all of us are ready for an ecological revolution. We *can* change an ethic of "not too bad" to "not good enough."[51]

And we can help each other do this because we can, if we choose, use peer pressure to fuel the ecological revolution of the twenty-first century. Peer pressure is often a pain, pushing us to act against our better judgment, but the up side of down is that we get to pick our peers. If we hang out with people who are cynical and hopeless, we'll inevitably be affected. But if we can find friends who share our deepest values, such good friends will make it easier to be good. Indeed, as David Wann suggests in *Biologic*, "Once a simplified, ecological design ethic is more fully evolved, our society can be powered by peer pressure alone."[52]

The world's religions offer good models for how institutions can encourage the discussion of values and the practice of virtue. They are communities where people are allowed to examine the goodness of the good life, and to imagine how it might be better. At their best, religious communities engage mystery and meaning, encourage awe and wonder, and respond with gratitude and generosity. They create an institutional space where we can bring our individual stories into contact with cosmic stories, as we discern our place in a creative universe.

"Found difficult, and left untried"

When college students think about the environment, they don't usually think about religion or even moral values. They think about global weirding and pollution or rain forests and desertification. They worry about gas prices and a world that's hostile to health and happiness. They don't think about any higher power. Some students entreat their god before a test, and some athletes pray before games, but on most campuses, God is probably invoked more for damning than for all other reasons combined. Accepting the American separation of church and state, and the practical segregation of religion and daily rituals, most college students—like their professors—approach environmental issues through the secular specializations of college departments. Religion is supposed to be about ultimate matters, but college students seem to think it matters only ultimately—when they're older, when they have kids, when they have more time.

Increasingly, however, college students and other Americans are coming to see that one of the endangered species on Earth is *Homo sapiens*, and they're debating ways to avoid or ameliorate looming environmental threats. As students convert ideals to action, their methods include individual exhortation and conscientious consumption, campus politics, and national political activism. But there are other tools available to them, and one of them might be religion.

All of America's mainstream religious traditions value the health of creation, and all advocate stewardship and sharing of the Earth's resources. Like other world religions, they teach "reverence, respect, restraint, redistribution and responsibility." The prophetic strand of these traditions provides a deep critique of consumer society and its environmental impacts. And in America, religion has institutional power. Even though science and secularism are important here, it's not clear that they have the cultural resonance needed to inspire the radical social change that's necessary in the twenty-first century. College students may or may not choose to join religious communities, but there's no ecological reason not to. And when they already belong to religious communities, it's their job to make sure they're preaching and practicing the ecological truths of their traditions.[53]

Many students think that religion has failed. Many congregations operate more like social clubs than serious centers of spirituality and social justice. Many more sermons support the status quo—and its environmental implications—than question it. And many religious Americans hide the visible evidence of their faith. But this popular religion of reassurance is not the same thing as a true religion. Early in the last century, G. K. Chesterton said that "the Christian ideal has not been tried and found wanting. It has been found difficult; and left untried." The same is true today. But if they chose to, America's college students might try to apply the lessons of care and collaboration that abound in the scriptures of our many faith traditions to the hard work of ecological and cultural resurrection.[54]

10

The Nature of Politics

The ecological emergency is about the failure to comprehend our citizenship in the biotic community.

David Orr, *Earth in Mind*

It's the economy, stupid.

James Carville, during Bill Clinton's 1992 campaign for the presidency

It's the stupid economy.

Anonymous

You are responsible not only for what you do but for what you fail to do.

Molière, quoted in *Declining by Degrees: Higher Education at Risk*

■ ■ ■ ■ ■ ■ ■

Jo and Joe College don't "do" politics in a normal day. They see the headlines and the documentaries about global warming, but none of these seem urgent for very long. Jo takes a boring political science class, and Joe guffaws at the satirical absurdities of *The Daily Show*, but neither of them do much to make political life less laughable or more fun. They have grown up, in fact, in a world where politics is a four-letter word and candidates for office routinely make campaign promises *against* public enterprises and public responsibilities. Their parents taught them habits of disengagement with the wider community: They vote every four years and honor an implicit social contract that says that people don't get political as long as the government sustains economic growth and prosperity. At college, most other students don't do politics either, because—in a culture of work and distraction—there's already too much to do. In general, "politics falls on the bottom of the list of issues that young people worry or think about."[1]

Whether or not they think of it, however, their activity or inactivity on campus affects the ecology of the planet. The campus environment is connected to the farm fields, rain forests, highways, sweatshops, and aquifers of the world, but it is also intertwined with politics and the environmental policies of government. The things students do on campus are affected, both positively and negatively, by rules set by state and federal legislatures. Unfortunately, these public policies often make it harder to do the right thing.

It's hard for Joe College to do the right thing, for example, in a system that rewards cheap-energy minds, expecting cheap gas and electricity for the comfort and convenience of everyday life. It's hard for Jo to buy organic food in a system that's rigged for industrial food products. It's difficult for Americans to institutionalize transportation alternatives in a system that's politically paved for cars. It's costly to switch to alternative energy in a system that subsidizes fossil fuels and atomic power. It's hard to plan wisely for the future in a system that's focused on the next election. It's hard because public spending affects individual and institutional priorities, as do taxes, regulations, and subsidies. "As much as some might wish it otherwise," says David Orr, "environmental protection, climate stability, and conservation of biological diversity are unavoidably political." Changing individual behavior is a good thing, but it's not nearly enough to meet the environmental challenges of this century. If college students and other concerned individuals don't learn how to do politics to shape institutions and incentives, we'll never have environmental policies that make it easier to be good—and to be good for the planet.[2]

Currently, however, American college students don't inhabit a political culture robust or resilient enough to sustain the politics of sustainability. Large majorities of college students support environmental protection, but their opinions seldom register where they count: the voting booth, representatives' offices, political organizations, or social movements. If parents loved their children the same way college students love nature through politics, they would be convicted of negligence.[3]

Because college students will provide the future leadership of U.S. government, many researchers have been worried about their patterns of political participation and civic engagement. For years, college students have been largely indifferent to politics. For most of American history, they couldn't vote until they were twenty-one. Sixties activism brought the twenty-sixth Amendment in 1971, but political participation waned shortly after student protests subsided. Today's students still inhabit this traditional culture of inactivity, but a new pattern seems possible, especially in environmental politics, because young people realize that climate change will affect their generation more than their elders', and because they're finding new ways to do politics. This chapter, therefore, explores the common sense of politics on campus, and student assumptions about political participation. It outlines the social and psychological contours of political inactivity and the promise of new activism. Environmentally, it considers the individualization of responsibility—probably the most common college response to environmental problems—and suggests how we might instead institutionalize responsibility to create a new politics of permanence.[4]

How College Students Think About Politics

Mostly, they don't. College students are good learners, and by paying attention to American culture they've learned that politics aren't a priority in everyday life. Political scientists speak of "political socialization," the process by which children grow into political adulthood by integrating political knowledge, attitudes, and practices into their lives. In today's United States, however, it's probably as accurate to speak about apolitical socialization—the process of learning how to ignore politics. As CBS News commentator Dick Meyer says, "Not many students have real role models for political engagement. Mostly it is an activity that happens on TV, often performed by buffoons." As a result, "Virtually all undergraduates think politicians are gross, television news is dumb, and government is futile."[5]

For Joe and Jo College, politics is mostly mediated. As political science professor Peter Galderisi notes, "TV is 80 percent of the way young people think. [They're] much more interested in the scandal and negativity the media [constantly supplies]." Turning the television on, they turn off to politics. Using the standard conventions of television journalism, the news obscures the essence of politics, featuring stories of corruption and scandal instead of more complex stories of political purpose or public policy. Joe and Jo College learn a lot from the media, but primarily they discover that politics happens on the other side of the television screen. In the dorm room, as in the American living room, politics becomes a spectator sport.[6]

Mediated politics aren't restricted to the news, however. On late-night television, David Letterman, Jay Leno, and the crew at Comedy Central make fun of politics and politicians all the time. They ridicule the ridiculous, which is perfectly appropriate because humor is one of the ways that societies confront the taboo topics of a culture, the "open secrets" and "conspiracies of silence" that need to be heard in civic space. But to some extent, the rule on late-night broadcast TV seems to be ridicule for ridicule's sake. The message isn't anger or action, but cynical resignation. And the daily disparagement of democracy contributes to the quiet desperation of viewers. Only 12 percent of students see politics as a way for the majority to exercise their own power. As a consequence, most college students have kept their distance from politics, saying, safely, "I'm not political."[7]

"I'm Not Political"

Students say, "I'm not political" for almost as many reasons as there are students, but there are patterns in this apolitical pride. Some of the patterns are purely political, but many of them are social and psychological as well. Students are cynical about politics, for example, not just because contemporary politics seem dysfunctional (a political reason) but also because their friends are cynical (a social reason) and because cynicism protects them from the hurt of disappointment (a psychological reason).

Cynicism and Optimism and Friendliness

Sometimes "I'm not political" is a statement of cynicism because the record of recent politics, especially on environmental issues, is hardly inspiring. Jo and Joe College understand public politics as a prime site of inauthenticity, a place where you can't really be who you are. Media reports of strategy and spin reinforce the idea that politics is about credibility and not truth, about managing impressions instead of expressions of the real self or serious positions. During recent administrations, students have watched cynical "*un*vironmentalism"—the practice of obscuring and falsifying scientific findings, appointing lobbyists for regulated industries to federal office, gutting environmental regulations, subsidizing environmental degradation, and postponing serious solutions to environmental problems. For instance, during the second

Bush administration, Andrew Card, the president's first chief of staff, came from General Motors. Philip Cooney, a lobbyist for the American Petroleum Institute, became chief of staff of the White House Council on Environmental Quality. Public relations guru Frank Luntz prepared a memo for the administration arguing that Republicans could win the support of citizens who cared about the environment by questioning scientists' view on climate change and talking about conservation and preservation, even if it was just talk. With politicians like these, no wonder students become suspicious of political involvement.[8]

Bitching: A characteristic conversational mode in the college culture of complaint. An expression of cynicism, learned helplessness, and quiet desperation. Antonym: *hoping.*

Apathy and indifference make sense in a world of senseless politics. Cynicism may even be an appropriate response to apparently dysfunctional American politics. And political cynicism fits perfectly in a college peer culture that honors cynicism in the dorm room and the classroom, and in almost all forms of casual conversation. As Michael Moffatt suggests, "Undergraduate Cynical" is "the dominant mode of discourse in the undergraduate peer group." "Undergraduate Cynical" is particularly hard on idealists, because they can be mocked for their passion and their hypocrisy. But it makes life easy for the cynics. Having no standards and low expectations—believing, essentially, in nothing—they're seldom disillusioned and never hypocritical, since they have no principles to contradict. But while cynicism protects them from disappointment, it also effectively keeps the country from environmental progress.[9]

Although cynicism fuels a lot of political indifference, some students aren't political because they're optimists. "Everything always works out," they think, "so why should I worry about it?" Placing their faith in automatic progress, such students forget that progress comes not from passivism but from participation. There's even a cynical implication to this inert optimism. Doing nothing, these apolitical students still reap the benefit of other people's activism. And if nothing is accomplished, they still haven't lost any of the time they didn't invest. Such optimism, then, is sometimes just a sorry excuse for selfishness.[10]

Another variant of being apolitical is rooted in a simplistic idea of friendship: "I have friends, and I don't want to alienate them with arguments. If we stick to small talk, the relationship will go smoother." Since friendliness is one of the primary values of college culture, students don't want to risk relationships on controversial topics. In this way, friendship gets in the way of citizenship, and, as usual, private matters take precedence over the public good. That's also why volunteering, which is seen "as a neutral activity . . . unlikely to provoke conflict," works better than politics for so many students.[11]

Purity

Cynicism and optimism cause political indifference, but so does fear of contamination. Many college students avoid politics because the system is corrupt, politics is dirty, and it might compromise their values. It's ironic, then, that the same thinking doesn't apply to other institutions: Students routinely embrace institutions with equally corrosive cultural effects. The entertainment industry, for example, thrives on TV shows and movies that feature sex, violence, sex, cynicism, sex, and the kind of political talk shows that give both politics and talk a bad name. But few turn off the TV to preserve their purity. The car companies have produced gas-guzzling, climate-changing cars, and—along with friends in the oil industry—sponsored "think tanks" designed mainly to keep us filling our gas tanks. But few of us abstain from driving. So it seems that we don't really fear contamination; we fear commitment to a cause larger than the self and longer than now.

Partisanship

Some students abstain from politics because of distaste for the bipolar partisanship it fosters. In recent years, we have all watched the extreme partisanship of election campaigns, presidential pronouncements, and congressional debates. Though some students participate in this political warfare, many prefer to distance themselves from the politics of extremes, and stay away from political organizations, too. They like to party, just not politically, and prefer to think of themselves as independents. Joe and Jo College tend to see partisan identification as impinging on their expressive individualism. Students don't like to declare themselves as Democrats or Republicans (or even members of the Green Party) because they don't want their beliefs and identity restricted by party affiliation. As one student told researchers, "If I adopt certain rigid views, then it takes away some of my personal freedom." Instead of being partisans, many students prefer to become *apart*isans—people who stand *apart* from the political struggles of our times.[12]

A 2005 poll suggests that "college students no longer believe you have to join an organization to be political." While they may believe in freedom, equality, justice, or sustainability, they're seemingly content with mere abstraction and unwilling to act on their beliefs. But being apolitical doesn't mean that politics stops; it just means that other people set the rules for everyday life. When students say they're not political, they basically agree to fight for their values with both hands tied behind their backs. The result is a society in which students and other Americans struggle to live their deepest values because other people and special interests have decided to get political and institutionalize *their* values in our lives.[13]

Irrelevance

Sometimes "I'm not political" comes from the sense that politics is irrelevant to daily life. In many ways, though, politics is like air. You don't notice it when you're breathing freely, but when you get the air knocked out of you, it's obvious that it was important all along. Virtually all students attend colleges and universities subsidized by government agencies. Many students enjoy federally-funded student aid in the form of scholarships and loans. Students who eat depend on the Department of Agriculture and the Food and Drug Administration for the safety of food. Students who want to drink alcohol are regulated by age restrictions enacted by states, and those age restrictions are tied to federal highway dollars. When Joe College flips an electrical switch, he depends on public utilities commissions for regulation. When Jo College is watching the clock in a boring lecture, she's dependent on legislation designating time zones, and standard- and daylight-saving times. Watching TV, students are connected to the Federal Communications Commission; watching ads, they're watching a tax-deductible business expense for corporations. Political participation may be optional, but political influences aren't. Even at private institutions, college life is always grounded in government and politics. As Americans learned the hard way in the economic collapse of 2008, when we stop paying attention to regulations and policies, we can get into big trouble.[14]

Sometimes the sense of the irrelevance of politics comes not just from run-of-the-mill pragmatism, but also from sheer selfishness. As a Utah State junior said about politics in 2003, "Honestly, what's in it for me?" Such a self-interested attitude shouldn't be surprising in a society of ontological individualism. And it shouldn't be surprising on campus

We the People

either. Almost no one thinks that dysfunctional politics can affect their own prospects to do well. Although this may be changing after the economic collapse, we often approach the public good through the prism of private gain. It's the politics of "me, the people."[15]

Ignorance

Sometimes "I'm not political" means "I don't know enough to form a reasonable opinion on all the issues," and it is true that, like their elders, college students don't know much about political issues or the U.S. political system. While 77 percent of Americans can name two of the seven Disney dwarfs, only 24 percent can name two of the nine Supreme Court Justices. Seventy-three percent can name all of the Three Stooges, but only 42 percent can name all three branches of government. "These results are not about how 'dumb' Americans are," claims Syracuse University professor Robert Thompson. They show that pop culture socializes people better than political culture, but they also show that ignorance is curable.

Information overload also leads to ignorance. In a world of twenty-four-hour news, blogging, talk radio, and spin, students aren't sure how to deal with multiple perspectives and media bias. In a media system that thinks that reporting "both sides" is the same as telling the truth, this discernment can be difficult. As Ross Gelbspan notes in *Boiling Point*, for more than a decade no peer-reviewed scientific articles questioned the seriousness of global warming, but 53 percent of the articles published in the popular press presented both sides of a debate that wasn't scientifically debatable. One cure for such ignorance would be better reporting; another would be finding better sources of news online.[16]

Sometimes, however, political ignorance isn't accidental: It's intentional, as college students actively ignore information and organizations that might help them become better citizens. "I don't want to know about political problems," they say, effectively. In 1972, almost half of college-age Americans read a daily newspaper, but in 2004 only 21 percent did. And, despite claims of an Internet "Information Age," students aren't substituting better sources of information. According to David Mindich, only 11 percent of eighteen-to-twenty-four-year-olds list news as a major reason for logging on: "The Internet is a great source of news for some, but for most it is a way of avoiding the news, to be used for e-mail, instant messaging, and other personal information." College culture creates a campus bubble that ignores politics, and college students consequently find that they don't know enough to get engaged even if they wanted to.[17]

Intentional or not, the "ignorance excuse" for political passivity ignores the fact that you don't need to know a lot to do good politics. Lots of ignorant people participate in American politics, and there's no reason why students should disenfranchise themselves while other uninformed people vote. Ignorance isn't ideal, of course, but people who know their values and their aspirations probably know enough to participate intelligently in politics by joining good organizations and voting for parties and politicians who share their basic values. In the Civil Rights Movement, for example, not all participants knew the arcane legal codes of Jim Crow segregation and racial disenfranchisement. But they understood the values articulated by Martin Luther King, Jr., and they placed their faith in the legal abilities of NAACP attorneys like Thurgood Marshall who won cases like Brown vs. Board of Education of Topeka, Kansas. Instead of practicing political leadership, therefore, college students might also practice the fine art of political "followership."

Efficacy

Some students aren't political because they are afraid of failure. They shy away from politics simply out of fear of public speaking as the result of an impoverished political socialization. Lacking institutions where free speech is practiced, arguments are honed, and consensus is reached, Americans fear raising their voices. So the voice of the people—and the effective voice of many college students—is silence. The world is melting, and we don't say a word.[18]

This block of political "passivists" paradoxically form a silent majority, which, by default, gives power to whichever minority cries the loudest. This silence says what silence always says: "I'm happy with the world just the way it is. The status quo is the best of all possible worlds."

Silence says, "I don't care what happens, because I'm not concerned about the world my children will live in." And yet, of course, we never say that out loud, because we don't really mean it. We *do* care; we just act as if we don't.

For some students, it's not fear of failure that keeps them from politics, but rather a broader belief about efficacy. Students believe that their one vote isn't enough to change anything, and they view voting as a "symbolic gesture." Few American elections have been decided by one vote or less, of course, but recent history directly contradicts these beliefs about a lack of efficacy. Until recently, college students reflected American cultural trends that discounted the impact of individual votes and political action. But that may be changing. In 2006, one-fifth of entering first-year students still told researchers that "realistically, an individual can do little to bring about change in our society." But 63 percent of students in 2006 and 2007 believed that they could make a difference in solving problems, and 92 percent thought that people working together could be effective. In the election of Barack Obama, this trend of greater involvement fully expressed itself, with 52 percent of students voting, tipping the balance in several states toward a major change of leaders in Washington—hardly an ineffective display. "Yes we can" was a campaign slogan, but on a deeper level it was a statement of belief in efficacy.[19]

Time Poverty

The issue of efficacy is also tied up with the issue of time. Some students really do want to make a difference and change the world. But they want to do it without it taking too much time. A Princeton student told researchers that "people in our generation grew up getting really used to immediacy. You know, video games, everything coming at you all the time. . . . Here [in college] I had one friend who just worked her butt off in the 2004 election. She worked so hard and then the side she was working for lost, and she just became really disenchanted with politics after that." As this suggests, today's talented college students *expect* success immediately. They don't understand the usefulness of failure in preparing for success. In a culture of instantaneous feedback and instant gratification, students find it difficult to endure the incrementalism and the ups and downs of effective reform movements.[20]

Mostly, however, students simply have no time for politics, given their other choices and responsibilities. Students report, in fact, that the time bind is the number-one reason for not getting involved in politics. As one student said, "There are so many other things that you have to deal with and you can't ignore them." Or as another suggested starkly, "I have more pressing things on my mind that interest me more than a bunch of dishonest men." This is what Richard Flacks calls "motivated disengagement," the choice to spend time on some things and not others. Over the course of the twentieth century, Americans chose to engage with the pleasures of private life and to disengage from all kinds of public life. We are, as Flacks says, making life, not history. But, of course, in the process we are making history, too, spending our time on Earth without thinking twice about what it costs the future.[21]

Maybe even more than most Americans, college students are short-term thinkers, taught to think more about this generation than about generations yet to come. Even though students take history courses, they don't usually get a deep sense of history, or an awareness that everybody makes history in their everyday habits and routines. Like other Americans, they have no sense of posterity, and few examples of long-term thinking. Americans and their college students are here-and-now people. But the politics of now will never lead to a sustainable society or a sustainable future.

"I'm not political," then, is a political statement rooted in ineffective political socialization by parents, peers, and politicians. By the time they come to college, students have learned the individualism and privatism of their culture. For most of them, politics is mediated, so they see some of the worst examples of the political process, including extreme partisanship and political spin. Such dispiriting examples of politics drive them to cynicism, avoidance, and indifference. Even if they do maintain an interest in politics, they're not sure that they know enough to be effective, or have time enough to do politics and class work—and parties—at the same time. And so most students sit on the sidelines watching other people craft their future. And higher education doesn't always help.

Higher Education and "Sitizenship"

Whatever the particular meaning of "I'm not political," politics aren't part of daily life for most students. Students note that "political arguments at meals are rare, political topics seem not to be considered intellectually interesting or, despite a war where people their ages are being killed, urgent." America's college students—like many Americans—have opted to act as "sitizens" instead of citizens. A "sitizen" is a person who sits on the political sidelines and then bitches about the results. A citizen is a republican in the root sense of the word, a person concerned about "res publica," the public things. When we celebrate America's myriad histories of hope, we recount the story of such citizens, inspired by leaders and organized into movements. From the Revolution to the Civil War to the Cold War, citizens mapped out American ideals worth fighting for, and citizen soldiers died for them. From abolitionism to the Civil Rights Movement, from unionism to the Women's Rights Movement, citizens have gone public with American possibilities, and realized them in law, in institutions, and in the hearts and minds of the American people. So when we practice our "sitizenship" on the couch in front of the TV, we betray those earlier citizen idealists.[22]

Sitizen: A person whose civic engagement consists of sitting around and bitching about the state of the world, the gridlock in Washington, the environmental crisis, and media bias, without ever doing a damn thing about it. Antonym: *citizen.*

In his book *The Good Citizen,* Michael Schudson shows how and when Americans have changed their ideals (and practices) of citizenship. Schudson contends that Americans have jettisoned the ideal of "the informed citizen"—which was always preached more than practiced—for what he calls "monitorial citizenship." In this "postwar charter" of public life, citizens don't pay attention to politics unless it impacts them personally or threaten the economic growth that might threaten their lifestyle expectations. Monitorial citizenship is the citizenship of "me, the people," the citizenship of the easy chair.[23]

Jo and Joe College share this impoverished political culture with other Americans, but they are also confronted by campus cultural norms like the "bubble effect" that further isolate them from political engagement. As a Princeton student told interviewers, "Once I got to college I have been really disconnected from the world at large." For most students, college isn't the real world; it's a bubble, an airy interval after adolescence and before adulthood. It's a time of individual achievement and personal relationships. Politics will come later. Maybe. If they have time.[24]

While students socialize themselves into an apolitical college culture, some colleges and universities also work unintentionally against students' potential political participation. Indeed, in the modern

American university, college students learn to value higher education less for higher purposes like citizenship or sustainability, and more for higher status and pay. College is valued more for career than for citizenship, with educational institutions preparing students for private careers. There's more concern for the economy than the polity, as college and university leaders promise to keep the United States (and its students) "competitive in the global economy." Students and their institutions seem to believe in the invisible hand of "hire education," assuming that cohorts of self-interested careerists will somehow contribute to the public good. And despite the signs of imminent global weirding, virtually no colleges or universities have a sustainability requirement for their students.[25]

Compounding this marginalization of political purpose in the modern educational enterprise is the increased compartmentalization of the study of politics. Instead of assuming that *all* students need political skills and perspectives, universities seem to assume that some students will major in political science—and that will be good enough. Simply stated, political thinking isn't a part of the curriculum for most students. As a result, college students don't learn much about politics or the day-to-day practices of citizenship.

To some extent, this is because college is a head game. It's about information and knowledge, about research and writing, about theory and concepts. But it's not generally about practice. If you know your stuff, that's enough for most professors. And so students come to believe that knowing about environmental issues is inherently virtuous, even though nothing comes of it. Knowing the causes of global weirding becomes a substitute for doing something about it. Though students may learn more and more, they don't always *do* more.

Professors avoid practices and political issues partly because they fear the charge of bias. Instead of discussing issues honestly and letting the chips fall where they may, college professors—like the broadcast media—try to maintain their neutrality by presenting "both sides" in a way that causes no offense and no action. As a Minnesota student engaged in experiential education told the interviewers from the Center for Information and Research on Civic Learning and Engagement, "You sit in a classroom and you read your dusty books with your dusty professors about dusty things, and then you don't learn anything about what you can do with it, and then you go into the community and all of a sudden you're like, wow, this is who I am and this is where my skills can go." Some colleges and universities have begun to sponsor centers of civic engagement, hoping to catalyze student commitments to public affairs. These are good programs, but they tend to attract the already interested. And compared to the power of the privatized commercial curriculum, they're almost insignificant. In a time of planetary peril, American higher education still isn't teaching all students how to think and act politically.[26]

Exceptions

Even exceptions to the rule of political passivity can be problematic because some activists give activism a bad name. On any campus, there's a loudmouth activist who speaks so much that people stop listening, the confrontationalist who's against anything that anybody in authority is for, the debater intimidating other students with his wonky arguments. There's the purist, who believes that it's always all or nothing, and the leader who cares more about the line on his resume than about any real issues. Environmentally, the sentimental tree hugger is joined by the hair-shirt environmentalist, convinced that any suffering or sacrifice is redemptive, as well as the hypocrite who drives an SUV to the global-warming rally.

Such types are useful because they allow disengaged college students to distance themselves from responsibility for real environmental and social problems. In this way, the simplistic arguments of a few can excuse the simplistic response of the many. When student "passivists" can label people who care about the continuity of the Earth's ecosystems as "radical environmentalists," they can dismiss their own feelings of care for the planet. Mocking an environmentalist as a "tree hugger" allows skeptics to reject emotion and empathy as ways of knowing, locating themselves, ironically, within the instrumental rationality that has caused so many environmental problems. Careful criticism of activists is a good thing, but not when it keeps students from seeing the good models for thoughtful activism present on any campus.

In any case, the rule of political passivity is seldom violated in America, even among young and idealistic college students. As with other elements of their lives, college students see politics as optional. Busy students don't have time for politics. They study for good grades and good jobs, for the private pleasures of the American dream. In this world of credentialism, careerism, and presentism, college students unwittingly prepare a future for themselves that will be more difficult than it needs to be.

New Politics, Net Politics

Joe and Jo College come to politics with the political expectations of American culture, and in the early years of the twenty-first century those expectations are miniscule. Some Americans believe in small government, but almost all believe in minimal participation. So most college students do politics by watching TV and voting—if that. And yet, despite this inertia, some students are heading in a different direction, remaking American politics in their own image, which is increasingly high-tech. In *Millennial Makeover: MySpace, YouTube, & the Future of American Politics*, Morley Winograd and Michael Hais suggest that online politicking might change the character of American politics. Winograd and Hais see the generation of millennials—born between 1982 and 2003—as a "civic generation" of optimistic, communitarian, pragmatic problem solvers committed to finding political solutions for lingering structural problems. Millennials, for example, are generally inclined to support programs that alleviate poverty, make health care accessible, and advance economic equity. They believe in bipartisan politics and coalition building, rejecting the idea that "if you're not for us, you're against us." Especially in the wake of the financial collapse of 2008, they reject the market as the main mechanism of social improvement, supporting private-public partnerships instead. Millennials tend to be very tolerant and socially liberal, rejecting the use of abortion, guns, and gays as "wedge issues." More than any other generation, millennials also consider the environment an important issue: In a March 2007 poll, 68 percent said that protecting the environment was as important as protecting jobs (only 11 percent disagreed). Indeed, Winograd and Hais suggest that "when faced with a choice between exuberant economic growth and the preservation of the environment for future generations, millennials will choose environmentalism every time."[27]

Although some students still engage in the traditional politics of caucuses and canvassing, door knocking and phone banks, millennials do a lot of their politics online, sharing news items, blogs, e-mail, instant messages, and YouTube videos with each other. According to Nielsen NetRatings, for example, MySpace users of voting age were three times more likely than nonusers to interact online with politicians, and 42 percent more likely to watch political videos online. Politically-themed videos on YouTube were the second most popular topic cluster on the site in 2006. And a 2004 study suggested that "fully 69 percent of those involved in politics online met the Roper organization's definition of 'influentials,' opinion leaders, or trendsetters with their friends and neighbors." As "netizens," millenials don't mimic their parents' political participation, but they may drive a revolution in the way that Americans do politics. Winograd and Hais predicted in early 2008 that "the candidate who combines the newest in online campaign technology with a message that attracts Millennial voters will not only win the technology arms race, but also the presidency of the United States—and partisan dominance in the civic era that is just around the corner."[28]

Recent trends do seem to confirm that judgment about the engagement of college students. In 2006, college students told pollsters that political participation is an integral part of their lives, but it's not necessarily their parents' politics. When Harvard's Institute of Politics asked college students to define political activity, 88 percent listed "signing an e-mail petition about a social or political issue" and 77 percent included forwarding a political e-mail. Seventy-nine percent of students thought it was political activity to wear a T-shirt reflecting their political or social opinion, and 70 percent listed wearing a wristband, too. As consumers, 74 percent of students considered boycotts a political activity while 51 percent thought that purchasing from a company you like because of social or political values was a political activity as well. For a lot of American students, political involvement seems like no big deal—which may be why it's increasing.[29]

Voter turnout among those eighteen to twenty-four increased from 36 percent in the 2000 presidential election to 52 percent in 2008. By 2007, 35 percent of these young people considered themselves politically active. When asked what they had actually done, however, activities included, again, signing an online petition (50 percent), writing an e-mail or a letter for a political position or opinion (28 percent), contributing to an online discussion or blog (23 percent), attending a rally or demonstration (21 percent), and donating money (15 percent). Only 12 percent of young people had volunteered for a political campaign or other issue, and only 24 percent had participated in a government, political, or issue-related organization. Students don't go to a lot of face-to-face political meetings.[30]

Proof positive that college students are digitally political was the 2008 presidential election. In 2007 and 2008, many students gravitated to the politics of Barack Obama not only because of what he promised, but also because of *how* he promised it. Obama seemed to articulate the way that Americans are living lives of quiet desperation, not really happy despite all the affluence and advantages that we possess. He called us not just to a good life but to a better world. And he called younger people primarily over the Internet.

More than any other candidate, Obama paid attention to the culture of college students and younger voters, going to the Net roots to reach a generation of people who have grown up logged on. As we saw in chapter 6, screens can screen us from nature, but they can also connect us to each other, and they can connect us politically. The website Mybarackobama.com allowed visitors to do just that, encouraging Jo and Joe College to connect to the campaign by offering news feeds, issue positions, and blog posts. It invited people—incessantly—to donate money to the cause, and record-breaking Internet donations were a huge part of Obama's fund-raising campaign. Obama's website also connected students to their communities, suggesting ways to get involved in canvassing or phone banks, and providing immediate feedback by issuing updates on the effects of their activism. The campaign also sent frequent e-mail updates and YouTube feeds—easily forwarded—to promote Obama events, respond to Republican charges, and solicit donations. The Obama mania of America's young voters came, in part, from the Obama *media* of the campaign.

It's too early to tell what this means in the long run. College students still have good reason to be cynical, suspicious, and cautious about the quality of American politics. They still have dozens of distractions to keep them from understanding all the issues, and not enough time to do everything they'd like to do. But now they have their own good example of committed activism, and a little political experience to compensate for their poor political socialization. And they can see an administration more in tune with their own version of the American dream. The 2010 elections will be instructive: Will students maintain their political participation without the charisma of Barack Obama as a catalyst? Will their engagement continue, or will it be a situation of "one and done"?

The Individualization of Responsibility

Despite Obama's victory, it's still generally true that Joe and Jo College don't do politics in a normal day. The American political system runs without them, apparently beyond the need of active citizens. College students don't think about the politics of the planet very much either.

They've seen *An Inconvenient Truth*, but the truth is that it would be inconvenient to do much about it, and convenience is still one of the operative environmental values on campus.

In the face of all the environmental bad news, however, normal students are sometimes moved to individual actions like turning off lights they aren't using or buying compact fluorescent bulbs. Some committed students shop at a co-op and eat lower on the food chain by becoming vegetarians or vegans. Others park the car and ride their bikes to get around. These students try to consume with some ecological intelligence, exemplifying what Michael Maniates calls "the individualization of responsibility."

Many college students think that the environmental crisis is the result of their individual actions, and primarily their consumption patterns. In a 2004 survey of those eighteen to twenty-five, the top choice of volunteer activity was "buying products that are environmentally friendly." In a consumer culture, students are relentlessly taught to think that shopping choices make a difference—as indeed they do. As a result, ironically, they consume to reduce the environmental impact of their consumption.

This happens because commercial capitalism works by identifying our values and selling them back to us as commodities. Clever advertising and marketing literally capitalize on our deep anxieties about the plight of the planet to sell us things to make us feel better personally, if not to actually heal the planet. Looking at current trends of global warming, water shortages, deforestation, and agricultural mass production, we're sometimes near despair. But luckily, we can feel better by buying the new and improved greenwashed widget.[31]

As previous chapters have shown, individual responsibility is essential, and far better than individual irresponsibility, but it's only part of the solution. This faith in consumptive solutions to the problem of consumption confuses the symptoms of a problem with the *systems* of a problem. It makes us forget how much our choices aren't just ours because many of our options are structured for us by institutions. Consumers, for example, don't decide what to make or how to make it, so we don't know about the environmental impacts of extraction, production, transportation, or distribution. We don't make decisions about mining and agriculture. We don't burn fossil fuels to manufacture goods or to transport them to and from cheap labor markets. We don't decide how imports will move from docks to the stores where we first encounter them. As John Ryan and Alan Durning point out in *Stuff: The Secret Lives of Everyday Things*, Americans consume about one hundred pounds of materials a day, but

Citizen	Consumer
Self-sacrifice, community interest	Self-interest, interest groups
Collective deliberation and discussion	Individual choice (what to buy or not)
Social capital	Social standing
Public good	Private goods
Permanent community	Temporary transactions
Involvement in council of citizens	Involvement in buyer-seller relations
Political accountability— by election and persuasion	Market accountability— by competition and complaint
Voting with time (and money)	Voting with money
Commonwealth	Wealth
Politics as process of becoming whole person: non-instrumental	Instrumental attitude to politics: to get my rights and entitlements
General welfare	Customer satisfaction

we only generate about three pounds of garbage that we see. So 97 percent of our environmental impact is created by corporate America. And in our world, the government is responsible for keeping them accountable. As individuals, we do have responsibilities, but they're relatively small in a system of corporate power and decision making.[32]

The individualization of responsibility is a way of making us feel responsible for institutional choices that are seemingly beyond our control. It's also a way of teaching us to think of ourselves as consumers instead of citizens, as the chart above suggests.

The individualization of responsibility asks us, in short, to depend on individual ingenuity—and technological ingenuity—to solve environmental problems. It asks us to forget about our social ingenuity, the ways we can shape our social life and institutions so that they, too, provide a better life for people and the other inhabitants of the planet.

The Institutionalization of Responsibility

In a good society, institutions would do a lot of environmental thinking for the people. Incentives would be structured so that people wouldn't have to think so much about doing good for the environment. In a good society, our institutions would encourage and enforce environmental responsibility. Simply put, institutions would make it possible to live justly by just living. We don't yet live in that good society, but change is possible.

Americans have faced such challenges before. During the nineteenth century, for example, sanitation became a major problem in cities. Some people didn't think much about the mounting piles of garbage and sewage, but a few did. Those people shared and refined their thinking in print and in public meetings, and institutionalized that thinking both in laws and in institutions like municipal sewer systems and garbage collection. These days we don't think much about toilets or sanitary sewers, but that's because a toilet is a porcelain thought—an idea in action. When we flush, we are activating a thought pattern that was institutionalized for us long ago. Indoor plumbing is convenient in our private homes, but plumbing is also good public policy.[33]

It's beyond the scope of this book to describe or prescribe the environmental politics of the twenty-first century, but we might consider a few policies designed to institutionalize responsibility. The first is full-cost accounting to include the social and environmental costs of production in the price of goods and services. The power of the market depends on prices telling the truth, and individual businesses in a competitive market can't afford to tell the truth if other companies continue marketing misinformation and half-truths about the real costs of their products. Regulations can level the playing field for producers, and give consumers the information they need to be responsible. This is not new: We already have truth-in-advertising laws and requirements for nutritional information on foods. But one element of full-cost accounting will be new, and that's a price on carbon emissions to make people and businesses pay for the harmful greenhouse gases they generate. So a carbon tax or a cap-and-dividend program will be a top priority in making markets work efficiently for environmental quality.

A second sensible idea is to stop subsidizing environmental damage—as we do with industrial agriculture, automotive infrastructure, and energy-related extraction—and to start subsidizing scientific research, sustainable business practices, mass transit, sustainability education, green jobs, and ecological restoration. Government at all levels in the United States is increasingly participating in this ecological revolution, including—among hundreds of changes—improvements in energy conservation, waste management, transportation policy, and building codes. In the last thirty years, the state of California has provided numerous examples of good public policy that could be adopted or modified by other states or the federal government.

A related goal might be a tax shift, using the tax system to offer incentives for environmentally benign behavior and disincentives for environmentally problematic behavior. Reducing income taxes, payroll taxes, property taxes, and sales taxes, we could substitute pollution taxes, carbon taxes, traffic taxes, and resource-consumption taxes. We could stop taxing things we want more of, like income, and generate revenue by taxing things we need less of, like resource-consumption, greenhouse gases, and traffic congestion. Such a tax shift might eventually move us toward a "deep economy"—one that's good for people and the planet— rather than an economy that's good mainly for short-term profits and the bottom line.

A final goal must be environmental justice, making sure that the world's environmental resources are shared fairly, and that the world's waste isn't dumped disproportionately on poor people. So far, this has gotten less attention than other elements of a new green politics, but, as the Copenhagen summit showed in the fall of 2009, the world's developing nations are unlikely to participate in climate-change mitigation unless rich countries (who are responsible for most of the human-caused climate-related damage) attend to the ethics of climate change.

This may all seem pie in the sky, but it's worth noting that student activism in the 2008 presidential campaign has already paid off with substantive changes in environmental policy. In the first year of the Obama administration, despite focus on the economy, health care, and war policy, and despite stiff partisan opposition, Obama shifted the federal government from "*un*vironmentalism" toward environmentalism. He appointed the most powerful set of environmental administrators in history, including Nobel-Prize-winning scientist Steven Chu as energy secretary. He included $100 billion of green spending in the economic stimulus bill, and protected more than two million acres of wilderness land with the Omnibus Public Land Management Act. The Obama EPA reversed the policy of the Bush administration, declaring greenhouse gases a threat to public health that could be regulated under the Clean Air Act. The EPA also reversed the Bush administration by granting California and thirteen other states a waiver to enforce tougher vehicle emission standards than the federal government, while the president also announced new standards, first for the federal fleet of vehicles, and then for all cars sold in the U.S. Obama's commerce and interior secretaries negated a Bush administration policy that gutted the Endangered Species Act. And the president renewed the international role of the United States in environmental treaty negotiations by attending the

Copenhagen Climate Summit. Political activity of young people created real change.

Throughout all this, the president continued to make the case for a revived, renewable economy. On his first Earth Day as president, he toured an Iowa factory that had been converted from making Maytag appliances to manufacturing wind turbine towers. And he recast the conventional debate over environmental action: "The choice we face is not between saving our environment and saving our economy," Obama said. "The choice we face is between prosperity and decline. We can remain the world's leading importer of oil, or we can become the world's leading exporter of clean energy. We can allow climate change to wreak unnatural havoc across the landscape, or we can create jobs working to prevent its worst effects. We can hand over the jobs of the twenty-first century to our competitors, or we can confront what countries in Europe and Asia have already recognized as both a challenge and an opportunity: The nation that leads the world in creating new energy sources will be the nation that leads the twenty-first-century global economy. America can be that nation. America must be that nation."[34]

None of this has been easy, and it won't get any easier. There are lots of people with lots of money who are opposed to effective environmental policies, and the 2010 Supreme Court decision on campaign spending has made it even easier for corporations to get the best government that money can buy. In congress, the senate filibuster rules mean that small minorities can thwart the will of the majority. And outside of Washington, plenty of people who are comfortable with the status quo won't want to change their status. The environmental revolution of the twenty-first century will be contested and criticized. It will experience wins and losses, moving two steps forward and one step back—and vice versa. But if citizens speak their environmental concerns and organize effectively, the revolution will happen.

In the 2008 election, many voted for "change you can believe in." And yet it's not entirely clear what "change" really means. Do we mean to change politics to preserve the American way of life? Or do we mean to change politics to change the world? Sometimes, the more things change, the more they stay the same. And the American way of life— with all of its environmental implications—has been remarkably resistant to structural change. But looking at recent history it seems that politics can still help. As Daniel Patrick Moynihan said years ago, "The central conservative truth is that culture, not politics, determines the success of a society. The central liberal truth is that politics can change a culture and save it from itself."[35]

Training for an Ecological Revolution

If the climate of U.S. politics doesn't change radically, the climate of the Earth will. The world climate is changing already—and faster than scientists had predicted. But politics is changing in America and elsewhere. All over the world, people are making connections between the good life and a good planet. Some, like Wangari Maathai, Al Gore, and the Intergovernmental Panel on Climate Change, have won the Nobel Peace Prize for their work in saving the planet by saving people, but most of us aren't as notable because we're just doing what seems right, right where we are.[36]

Recent college politics has been part of this audacity of hope. Slowly but surely, students in the new century have been getting engaged both politically and environmentally. A few students have always been involved in environmental politics, generally through the youth outreach of organizations like the Sierra Club and the Campus Ecology program of the National Wildlife Federation. But in the first years of the new century, students have greatly expanded their political perspectives and participation in setting new rules for college political culture.

Tracking the political involvement of Jo and Joe College and their friends is almost impossible, in part because there are now so many organizations and actions, but also because so much of the organizing and action occurs on the Web. Early organizations included Sustainable Campus and Cool the Planet, a movement to stop global warming. Energy Action Coalition brought together some of the organizations for the first Fossil Fools Day in June 2004, and morphed into a collaboration of more than forty groups focused on campuses, communities, corporate practices, and politics. Energy Action Coalition promotes a politics that includes clean energy, green jobs, and clean politics. The coalition was also a catalyst for the Campus Climate Challenge, launched in October 2005 and now including over five hundred campuses committed to reducing carbon emissions. Energy Action was also a player in Powershift 2007, where more than six thousand young activists met in Washington, D.C. to learn and lobby for global climate change. The coalition also cooperated with the activities surrounding Focus the Nation, the largest teach-in in U.S. history, held in January 2008 on more than one thousand campuses nationwide with the express purpose of bringing environmental issues and young voters to the center of American politics. In the last few years, students have been invited to testify before Congress on their generation's commitment to a politics of permanence. Thanks to student activism, colleges and universities are primary drivers of the clean-energy market and the progressive politicians they helped to elect replaced environmental roadblocks in congress.

Some of the new student activism has been local, too, as collegians have mobilized otherwise apolitical student governments to focus on sustainability issues. At several schools, students have voted to put their money where their values are, taxing themselves to support college sustainability initiatives. Other students have lobbied college presidents to sign the Talloires Declaration or the Presidents' Climate Commitment. Still others have stood in solidarity with food service and facilities managers who are trying to green campuses. And at most schools, environmental organizations are enlisting friends and classmates in local learning and action.

It's not clear yet whether the new student activism marks a change in the political climate, or just a change in the weather. *Time* suggests, "For the Millennials, climate change is emerging as the defining issue of their time, just as civil rights or Vietnam might have been for the generation before." But it might be a surge of participation followed by a relapse to political passivism. As Rebecca Solnit says, "Many Americans seem to think that activism is an aberrant necessity brought on by a unique crisis, and then throw themselves into it with an unsustainable energy brought on by the belief that once they realize some goal or another, they can go home and be apolitical again." In the twenty-first century, that won't cut it. In the twenty-first century, the personal is political, but the planetary is political, too. So we need a culture to support the politics and policy of the ecological revolution. We need a political culture that's robust and resilient enough to maintain the Earth's vitality, biodiversity, and resilience.[37]

There's no place better than American colleges and universities for testing such a political culture. For the ecological revolution of the twenty-first century, we'll need citizens who understand the nature of global weirding, habitat loss, natural cycles, carrying capacity, cultural norms, and social movements. We'll need citizens skilled in the arts of conservation, preservation, and restoration. We'll need citizens who can put the new communications technologies to environmental and political uses. Right now, there aren't enough classes in the college curriculum to teach all these lessons. The college curriculum is a conservative force on every college campus because it is, at best, a twentieth-century artifact in a twenty-first-century world. The curriculum will eventually catch up to social needs, but the ecological revolution on campus will also have to be extracurricular. The revolution will entail substantial changes in the nature of college culture, including college political culture. And the faculty and administration can't do that. The old folks can help, but only college students can change the moral ecology of college culture.

Slowly but surely (or better yet, quickly and consistently), college students need to create a transformed college culture with a new "normal," a default setting in which everyday actions help the planet instead of harming it. Challenging the individualism and instrumentalism of college culture, as well as the *fun*-damentalism and escapism of breaks and weekends, they need to make politics an integral part of their lives, something *done* instead of watched. Marching to a different drummer, students can create sustainable models for the so-called "real world" right on campus. And Joe and Jo College can take those models with them when they graduate.

11

Making Environmental History

It seems pathetic that it has to be us, with all the other citizens of
the planet, and all the other resources out there, but since no one
else is doing anything about it, we don't really have a choice.
  Jerry Garcia, "Interview: Jerry Garcia (1989)," *High Times*

A new idea is first condemned as ridiculous, then dismissed as
trivial, until finally it becomes what everybody knows.
  William James

We cannot expect to be able to solve any complex problems from
within the same state of consciousness that created them.
  Albert Einstein

Never doubt for a moment that a small group of dedicated citizens
can change the world. Indeed, it's the only thing that ever has.
  Margaret Mead

▪▪▪▪▪▪▪

The nature of college is a part of the nature of American life, which is just
a small part of nature. Students live on specific college campuses, but
they also live in American environmental history. The ideas, institutions,
languages, and assumptions of our world, including campus culture,
come to us from the minds and the practices of the people of the past.
Institutions like capitalism and the corporation, advertising and marketing, religion and schools, malls and supermarkets, industry and industrial
agriculture all come from the people who preceded us. These traditions
are the default settings of American culture and its college culture.

On campus every day, students make environmental history by de-
ferring to these default settings or deviating from them. Repeating the
routines of their days and nights, students unconsciously make history
by voting for more of the same, living the common sense of their culture.
Until recently, common sense seemed to make sense because it contribu-
ted to "progress" and "success." Now, however, some of that progress
seems questionable, and some of our cultural successes are leading to

ecological failures. The assumptions and expectations of the twentieth century won't work in the twenty-first century.

It's time, therefore, to make a different kind of environmental history. Conscious of the complexity of our lives and our complicity with systems that we really don't support, we have a chance to change our ideas and institutions, our habits and our habitat. We have a chance to change the world into a place we will love to live in, a place we can proudly pass on to our children and our children's children.

Making History on Campus: What's Happening

Thousands of American colleges have already started to change the world by changing the standard operating procedures of their campuses. Pledging eventual carbon neutrality, for example, signers of the American College and University Presidents' Climate Commitment (ACUPCC)—have noted:

> America's higher education community can play a determinant role in addressing climate change. Leading society in this effort fits squarely into the educational, research, and public service missions of higher education. No other institution in society has the influence, the critical mass, and the diversity of skills needed to successfully reverse global warming.
>
> Tomorrow's architects, engineers, attorneys, business leaders, scientists, urban planners, policy analysts, cultural leaders, journalists, advocates, activists, and politicians—more than seventeen million of them—are currently attending the more than four thousand institutions of higher learning in the United States. Higher education is also a $317 billion economic engine that employs millions of people and spends billions of dollars on fuel, energy, products, services and infrastructure.[1]

Such commitments have made college campuses into a powerful proving ground for the ideas and innovations of the ecological revolution. From presidential suites to custodial closets, college personnel are proving that it's possible to institutionalize more sustainable solutions to perennial problems. Food services like Bon Appétit, for example, have committed to serving fresh, responsibly-raised food on its college campuses. Facilities directors all over the country are transforming campus infrastructure to save energy and money by establishing wind turbines, solar arrays, clean-energy purchases, and carbon offsets. They're commissioning green buildings from innovative architects and are looking for ways to heat and cool buildings more efficiently. For commuters, colleges are offering free transit passes, bike-sharing programs, parking preferences for hybrid or fuel-efficient vehicles (or both), and campus fleets that run on biodiesel or other alternative fuels. Many colleges are hiring sustainability coordinators to keep an eye on all the different possibilities for doing good by doing better, and to share successes both with the college community and other interested parties.

But presidents and administrators are not the only impetus for these positive transformations. Students and student organizations foment enormous change on almost every college campus, initiating and supporting a wide variety of projects and policies. Voting to increase student fees to increase sustainability efforts, creating CERFs—Clean Energy Revolving Funds—to capitalize on energy-saving projects on campuses, starting their own organic farms to supply the college food service, and banding together in college coalitions to sponsor recycling competitions or "energy wars," these students are revolutionizing college life and having a lot of fun doing it.[2] Additionally, organizations like the public interest research groups (PIRGs) and the Energy Action Coalition are equipping students with skills to enhance their political clout on and off campus.[3]

And yet, even this unprecedented positive activity it is not enough. For the most part, there's still more consciousness raising than cultural change. Even as environmental policies and participation change, there's still not much change in everyday life. The *culture* of college isn't changing much at all, and neither is American culture.

Making History on Campus: What's Not Happening

Despite all of this work, college students still live like most Americans, and they graduate into a world that's simply not sustainable. They live in climate-controlled dorms that still affect the climate, and they fill their spaces with stuff they "need," discarding it later as if it wasn't worth much—which, of course, it's not, in monetary terms. Like other Americans, they're nourished by nature and agriculture, but they don't return the favor. Driving their cars to a variety of destinations, they're also driving to a new world of reduced resources and enhanced environmental dangers. Students continue to pursue the pleasures of private life, opting for a world in which those pleasures will be increasingly rare. Watching TV and YouTube, checking Facebook and playing video games, they're screening themselves from the serious lessons the world might offer. Conforming to consumer culture, they're consuming the future. Campus life like this is dangerous because it teaches students to think that American consumer culture is normal, natural, normative, and inevitable. And if today's college students graduate with that understanding, the "real world" of our future will be hostile to many of their hopes and plans.

It's not entirely by accident, of course, that college culture is primarily consumer culture. Advertisers, marketers, and retailers work very hard to shape students' environmental values (and thus environmental impacts) by shaping their habits of consumption. They know that college is one of the best places to establish those habits for the rest of their lives. And as long as they continue to buy into conceptions of the good life that marketers supply, they'll keep filling students' minds with desire, their rooms with stuff, and their planet with problems.[4]

Ironically the problem isn't failure; it's a certain kind of success. The problem isn't evil people doing devilish things. It's normal people—us—living ordinary lives. We've succeeded in creating a consumer society that maximizes the pursuit of happiness—especially the material pursuits. But this success is also a failure, because, as Bill McKibben has suggested, "our environmental problems come from normal human life, but there are so many of us living those normal lives that something abnormal is happening."[5]

We're caught in what David Orr calls a "social trap," a situation in which people are drawn into individually rational behavior that is destructive to the planet. The environmental crisis is like a traffic jam. No single driver caused it, but every driver contributes. No one person can eliminate the problem alone, but a system of restraint and regulation can improve it. When individual actions—like driving—increase global warming, solutions must be both individual *and* social, both personal *and* political. Sustainability isn't a technical problem, it's a cultural problem, and we are that culture.[6]

Sadly, college culture is lagging behind the architectural and technological accomplishments on college campuses. In daily routines, students today still live pretty much like their predecessors a generation or two ago. So the challenge for students—and the challenge of this book—is to develop a college culture that's appropriate to the environmental realities of our time. There is a lot of serious thinking to do, and not just the standard thinking regarding schoolwork, jobs, family, and friends. In

American (Environmental) Values

Common Sense	Uncommon Sense
Individualism	"Land Community"
Anthropocentrism	Biocentrism
Just us	Justice
Freedom—independence	Responsibility—interdependence
Convenience—time poverty	Conviviality—time affluence, timeliness
Indoorness	Outdoorness
Resourcism	Ecosystem services
Domination	Right relation
Dominion	Stewardship
"Back to nature"	Always in nature
Homo economicus	*Homo ecologicus*
Life of abundance	Abundant life
Materialism—desire for stuff	Dematerialization—desire for fulfillment
Buyosphere	Biosphere
Quantity of life	Quality of life
Cheapness	Value
More for me	Enough for everybody
Neophilia—love of novelty	Biophilia—love of life
Democracy of goods	Democracy of common good
Me, the people	We, the people
Culture of distraction	Culture of concentration
Fun-damentalism	Fulfillment
Globalism	Localism
Human logic	Bio-logic
Hubris	Humility
Efficiency—doing things right	Efficacy—doing the right things
Presentism	Posterity
Nationalism—centralization	Localism—decentralization
Globalization—global capitalism	Planetization—natural capitalism
Out of sight, out of mind	On-site, in mind
Fossil fuelishness	Renewable energies
"The good life"	A better life
Progress	Progress

a world of myriad possibilities, students finally get to tackle some bigger questions, whether or not professors ever require it, including the difference between a good job and good work, and the relationship of fun and fulfillment. On campus and off, students can contemplate how college culture and consumption affects nature, and what they plan to do about it. Setting aside the technological determinism of American culture, they can think twice about tools and technologies, wondering whether cars, computers, and contrivances can ever get them where they really want to go. In their personal lives, they need to think about what they mean by love, *how* they mean to love, and whether their intimate love has any connections to larger human and natural communities. Sooner or later, too, they'll confront questions of ultimate meaning, their own spirituality, and the coping and hoping mechanisms that will help them brave the new world. Living away from home, students will have new resources to think about self and society and how individuals participate in communities, human and natural. In short, students get to think twice about America's commonsense environmental values and some *un*commonsense alternatives. This thinking will be work, but it will be good work, and as students convert ideals to action in their lives, it will free them to live the lives they want to lead in a society that supports their deepest values instead of undermining them.

Making Environmental History: What Could Happen

The culture we live in isn't appropriate for the twenty-first century. Unfortunately, cultures aren't like the new things we buy at the mall. Instead, like organisms, cultures evolve, with mutations here and there that are either accepted as a new common sense or discarded as simply deviant. Some of the mutations are almost accidental, as people adopt new technologies and adapt to them. Philo Farnsworth didn't intend to change American culture when he invented the first functional television system, but he did. Other mutations are very intentional. When Americans of the past argued for a new nation, an end to slavery, equality for women, or an end to smallpox or malaria, they fought hard for a better culture.

On our campuses, students have experienced changes in college culture that have arrived with technological innovations like computers, cell phones, and iPods, but they haven't seen many cultural changes that might support a sustainable society. So, as Gandhi is supposed to have said, "We must be the change we wish to see in the world." But students must also promote the change they hope to see on campus so that others will change as well. To that end, we need to think carefully about the roots and routes of cultural change, asking what makes people change their minds and their lives.

This won't be easy. Summarizing his research in *The First Year Out,* Tim Clydesdale reminds us:

> We are, in the end, deeply cultural beings. Mainstream American teens have largely become what popular American moral culture has shaped them to become. They form more or less successful patterns of navigating relationships and managing gratifications, they prefer consumptive leisure and willingly insert themselves into the work-and-spend cycle, they pursue the practical educational credentials necessary to sustain these patterns and preferences, and they give little attention to that which lies beyond their microworlds. Most teens, moreover, ignore (if not resist) all opportunities to critically evaluate these patterns or to understand the wider world. To do so, they use an identity lockbox.[7]

Opening that lockbox—the lockbox of the mind—is a challenge. It means being countercultural in the most profound sense. Fortunately for college students, college is a perfect place for learning a new rhetoric of hope and transformation, and learning how to transform that rhetoric into reality. Rhetoric is the art of helping people hear the truths they need to know, and living those truths day after day. And hope isn't just wishful thinking. Hope ends in action. Hope is not just something to have, it's something to *do*.[8]

Commons Sense for College Culture

There are many different ways of changing college culture and countless ways to do things right. There are books that offer advice on sustainable behavior. Some useful basic guides include *Wake Up and Smell the Planet,* by Grist, and *Green Living,* by E! magazine. Older (and wiser) is *The Consumer's Guide to Effective Environmental Choices,* by Michael Brown, which makes it clear that political choices *are* consumer choices because they set the parameters for production, and require the information that consumers need to make effective environmental choices. On the Web, there's useful and provocative information on almost any environmental topic: The Sierra Club maintains a "Green Tips Library," and *National Geographic* offers a green guide. The Worldwatch Institute offers *Good Stuff? A Behind-the-Scenes Guide to the Things We Buy*, and the Center for a New American Dream challenges us with a variety of green initiatives. There are also a number of green-living guides at particular colleges and universities.

Commons sense: The common sense of the twenty-first century, in which "everybody knows" that human life depends on other lives in the biosphere—and the health of the biosphere itself.

In looking forward to a new culture of college, there's no need to repeat here the good advice that's already available in abundance. But it might be worthwhile to consider a few general principles of a new common sense that would connect our lives to our deepest values. The new common sense of college culture will be a *commons* sense, a set of beliefs and customs that accustom us to our creative and conserving role in the global commons. In colonial New England, the commons was the area in which residents could commonly pasture their animals, the space that wasn't private property but was shared usefully by the people of the town. In the twenty-first century, our commons is the biosphere and its biodiversity, the source of the resources—earth, water, and air, interacting with the fire of the sun—that sustain us. In the twentieth century, we treated the commons like it was infinite—and infinitely resilient. In the twenty-first century, we'll need to treat it uncommonly well because unless we conserve and care for it, the commons will be exhausted. On college campuses, therefore, the new "commons sense" will help us live our lives so that the tragedy of the commons becomes the triumph of the commons. Here, then, are some guidelines for a "commons sense" of college culture:

1) College education isn't just classes, papers, and GPAs. It's also an open invitation to engage designing minds, first in understanding the designs of nature, second in understanding the culture of nature, and finally in designing a culture that enriches nature's health and our own deep fulfillment. William McDonough contends, "Design is the first signal of human intention. Our goal is a delightfully diverse, safe, healthy, and just world, with clean air, water, soil, and power—economically, equitably, ecologically, and elegantly enjoyed." College is where

we learn how to live well by design. It's where students can learn what in the world they're good at, and how they might be good for the world.[9]

2) John Dewey said, "Education isn't preparation for life. Education is life itself." At college, students practice academic disciplines in their classes, but they're also practicing human disciplines in everyday life. Because it's a culture committed at least theoretically to mindfulness, college is the right time to establish regenerative routines for the real world, developing habits that enrich habitats. It's a good place to make the mistakes that inevitably come with innovation, and to learn from them.[10]

3) Humans are solar-powered people on a solar-powered planet. College culture needs to show American culture how to adjust to that reality. On campus, students can begin to opt out of cycles that depend on the ancient sunshine of fossil fuels and opt in to designs that power life with current sunshine—solar power, wind power, and biomass. In their daily living they can develop models for a culture of permanence by purchasing megawatts of clean energy and generating negawatts of energy through conservation—almost always the most efficient energy strategy. The cleanest energy is still the energy we don't need, so we need to think carefully about the nature of needs and the nature of enough. As Bill McKibben says, "How much is enough?" is the most important question of our time—even if it's not on the final exam.[11]

4) Students are embodied beings in a material world, and therefore their materialism matters. Right now, most Americans practice a materialism that shows little regard for the materials we use in our lives or for the deep satisfactions that better designs might offer. We need a new materialism based on a reverence for the physical world and committed to using materials only for our essential human needs. And college, where all we really need is books, some food, a bed, and curiosity, is the perfect place to practice. This new materialism will let us dematerialize some of the satisfactions of our lives, and find more fulfillment with less stuff and a smaller ecological footprint. Etymologically, "thrift" and "thriving" are related, and they could be related again in a "commons sense" where the practice of restraint yields an increase in real satisfaction. Giving up,

after all, is a form of giving. It's a gift to the future and others in
the world because our restraint is somebody else's reprieve. Our
sufficiency provides for the future's sufficiency, too.

5) For many students, college is their first chance to budget money
on their own. As such, it is a wonderful opportunity to practice
putting their money where their values are. It's a chance to show
friends, family, and others how to buy environmentally responsible products and how to buy into systems of sourcing that
enhance the environment and the lives of the people we depend
on. Both college students and their institutions can leverage
purchases to change the nature of the supply chain. As citizens,
students can also work to put their taxes where their values are,
creating a government that supports environmental innovation.
At college, students have the luxury to advocate for programs
and policies that might make taxes more worthwhile, reversing
current subsidies for global weirding and biodiversity loss, and
advancing the energies of communities that are good for their
places and the whole planet.

6) The economy is for people, and not vice versa. Both "economy"
and "ecology" come from the Greek root "oikos," or household,
and both of them are meant to help us keep our households in
order, both in society and in nature. As it's currently configured
by commercial capitalism, however, the so-called free market
is an environmental catastrophe, making money by unmaking
the world. It promotes infinite consumption on a finite planet
and material production that produces, among other things,
pollution, biodiversity loss, and a radically changed climate
system that undermines the stability that's essential for good
business (among other things). But, with full-cost accounting,
the market *can* be configured to operate on the precautionary
principle, and to offer people incentives to find their satisfactions in goods and services that are good for the biosphere that
nourishes the economy. As an institution that stands partially
outside the profit economy, higher education provides both the
intellectual capital and economies of scale to change the nature
of markets in areas like food and energy.

7) In a culture of remote control, it's time to take control of the
supply chains that produce goods and services for us all over
the world. Right now, we can take real responsibility for our
lives by making sure that the corporations that make things

for us do it in socially and environmentally responsible and regenerative ways. In the long run, in a solar-powered world, global food chains and supply chains will disappear except for essentials. So some student efforts can be directed at reviving local production and local markets, cutting the carbon footprint of our food, clothes, cars, and other belongings.[12]

8) Cultures run on peer pressure, and peer pressure is us. Every spoken word and text message, every compliment and complaint, every activity—even inactivity—shapes college culture. Students who conform to the twentieth-century conventions of college culture encourage others to do the same. When they act to embody the new values of an emerging culture of permanence, they exert peer pressure for a more sustainable future. Peer pressure is the power of the people because each student shows every other one the meanings of "normal" and "cool"— which change over time—and which students can change in a more sustainable direction.[13]

9) We're *all* in this together. Exemplary influence doesn't only influence people nearby. People all over the world are looking to keep up with the Joneses in America—and, whatever their actual name, college students are the Joneses to global youth culture. As such, they have the opportunity to show people a new American Dream based on creative moderation and radical generosity. As citizens, students also have the opportunity to support national policies that show the world that the United States won't continue hogging the world's resources, as well as practical policies that support human development across the globe, so that everybody gets enough of the world's resources. Paraphrasing Martin Luther King, Jr., students can begin to bend the arc of the moral universe so that it tends toward environmental justice.[14]

The Joneses: The mythical other, responsible for motivating real people—us—to consume. The figurative family next door who put pressure on us to keep up with their appearance of wealth by buying things. Synonym: *us*.

---

10) Most importantly, if the pursuit of sustainability isn't also the pursuit of happiness, everyone will end up leading lives of quiet, or even loud, desperation. Environmentalism needs to be

fun and fulfilling, honoring the pleasures of the flesh as well as the joys of conviviality. It needs to remind us of the delights of getting back to nature and of getting back in harmony with nature. It needs to combine the *intensive pleasures* of good food, beautiful clothes, amazing architecture, deep spirituality, and human socializing with the *extensive pleasures* of knowing not only that we've done no harm to the planet, but that we've actually made it better.

■ ■ ■ ■ ■ ■ ■

This new "commons sense" can sustain an ecological revolution in the twenty-first century—starting here and now on campus. With such mindfulness, college students can transform college culture and the college culture of nature. Through individual actions, peer pressure, and institutional reforms, students can transform environmentalism into everyday life, creating a sort of "*in*vironmentalism" as an integral element of who we are and what we do. So far, most college students (and other Americans) have focused mostly on the "mental" part of "environmental." They've thought about their participation in environmental problems, but they have yet to make solutions to those problems part of the pattern of their daily lives. *In*vironmentalism needs to be ingrained in language and conversations, work and play, habits, routines, policies, and institutions. *In*vironmentalism needs to be "in," and it can't go out of style. Embracing the opportunities posed by our environmental problems, we *can* live happily ever after—which is, after all, the fundamental definition of sustainability.

American college students already make environmental history every day in classrooms and dorm rooms, computer labs and the cafeteria, bathrooms and kitchens. They're making history by their purchases of clothes and computers, iPods and cell phones, TVs and remote controls, cars, food, and fun, as well as with the established practices that govern their use of such things. Students always make history, but now they have the opportunity to make it by design. And all of us have the chance to shape our lives to shape the future of people and the planet. We have an opportunity to realize our best intentions by devising a culture that uses "commons sense" to solve its environmental problems. This history will also happen in Washington, D.C. and on the world stage, of course. The president and congress might make history by creating policies that make it easier to be good inhabitants of the planet. Other world leaders may do the same. But the ecological revolution of the twenty-first

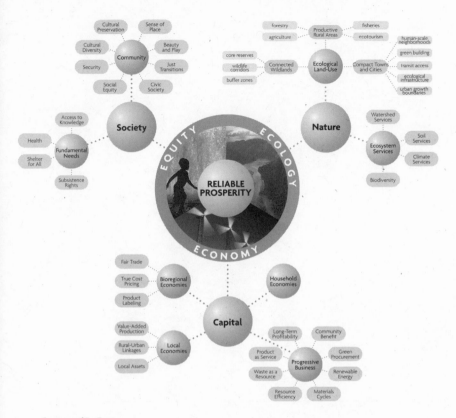

Courtesy of EcoTrust

century won't really happen unless we choose to *live* it where we are. It won't be easy, but it could be fun. It won't be smooth, but it will be fulfilling. It will move in fits and starts, and it will be contested fiercely. But that was true of the American Revolution, the abolition of slavery, and the movements for women's rights and civil rights. It's true of most great accomplishments. This challenge is the promise of our lives, of college culture, and—at its best—a new American Dream.

Notes

For additional notes and to continue the conversation, visit: natureofcollege.org

Note to Prelude

1. Paul Goodman, "The Duty of Professionals," *Liberation* 12 (November 1967): 39.

Notes to Introduction

1. David A. Morrison, *Marketing to the Campus Crowd: Everything You Need to Know to Capture the $200 Billion College Market* (Chicago: Dearborn Trade Publishing, 2004), 3–4; Peter Zollo, *Getting Wiser to Teens: More Insights into Marketing to Teenagers* (Ithaca, NY: New Strategist Publications, 2003), 197.

2. In "Varieties of Overconsumption," David Schmidtz and Elizabeth Willott note that "people overconsume when externalities are not internalized. For example, people overconsume nuclear power when the price of electricity does not include the price of proper disposal of nuclear waste." Schmidtz and Willott, "Varieties of Overconsumption," *Ethics, Place and Environment,* (October 2006), 359.

3. A summer school at Lancaster University in England followed a similar formulation in 2001. "Rather than concentrating on individual beliefs and attitudes or the behavior of 'green' consumers, the Summer School programme assumes that questions of sustainability and consumption have to do with the routine organization of everyday life and the mediation of lifestyles and 'choices' through social institutions and sociotechnical infrastructures. The programme takes consumption to be a collective enterprise held together by social expectations, cultural conventions, and material constraints." "Introducing Consumption, Everyday Life and Sustainability," Lancaster University, http://www.lancs.ac.uk/fass/projects/esf/online%20handbook.pdf (accessed June 13, 2010), 7.

4. Mariolina Salvatori, "Understanding the Students We Teach," *ADE Bulletin* 101 (Spring 1992), 69–75, reprinted at Associated Departments of English, http://web2.ade.org/ade/bulletin/n101/101069.htm (accessed June 13, 2010). For more on the importance of "free spaces" to social change, see Harry Boyte, *The Citizen Solution: How You Can Make a Difference* (St. Paul: Minnesota Historical Society Press, 2008).

5. The phrase "hoping mechanisms" comes from my friend Julie Madden, the social justice coordinator at St. Joan of Arc in Minneapolis.

6. Michael Pollan, *In Defense of Food: An Eater's Manifesto* (New York: Penguin, 2008), 28.

7. For more of the Ecologian's Dictionary, visit natureofcollege.org

8. Neil Postman and Charles Weingartner, *Teaching as a Subversive Activity* (New York: Delacorte Press, 1969), 121.

Notes to Chapter 1

1. The Environmental Protection Agency reports that buildings use 40 percent of American energy, and two-thirds of its electricity, and a large portion of that load is devoted to space heating, so these invisible environmental impacts are a big deal. *Buildings and their Impact on the Environment: A Statistical Summary*, compiled by U.S. Environmental Protection Agency Green Building Workgroup (2004), http://www.epa.gov/greenbuilding/pubs/gbstats.pdf. The comfort range of indoor air temperatures is, as Hal Wilhite points out, culturally determined. He notes that in Japan "the practice is still to heat the body, not the space." People use space heaters and blankets to keep warm in rooms that are, by Western standards, quite cool. Hal Wilhite, "The Socio-Cultural Construction of Comfort in Japan and Norway," in *Consumption, Everyday Life and Sustainability* (2001), Lancaster University, http://www.lancs.ac.uk/fass/projects/esf/onlinehandbook.pdf.

2. Tim Clydesdale, *The First Year Out: Understanding American Teens after High School* (Chicago: University of Chicago, 2007), 40.

3. For a lively history of time, see Jay Griffiths, *A Sideways Look at Time* (New York: Jeremy P. Tarcher, 2002). In *The Age of Missing Information*, Bill McKibben suggests that even after the introduction of the twenty-four-hour day, the hours seasonally varied in length. Bill McKibben, *The Age of Missing Information* (New York: Random House, 1992), 142.

4. Griffiths, *A Sideways Look at Time*, 196–204. Now, of course, almost all our appliances—cars, microwaves, cell phones, etc.—are embedded with clocks, and some of them are synchronized by satellite.

5. Alexis de Tocqueville, *Democracy in America* (Chicago: University of Chicago Press, 2000), 512. In today's America we work up to nine full weeks more per year than Europeans. Cash rich and time poor, we desire lifestyles so expensive that we can't afford the time to live them. For a good critique of the American culture of time, see John de Graaf, *Take Back Your Time: Fighting Overwork and Time Poverty in America* (San Francisco: Berrett-Koehler, 2003).

6. For a good introduction to environmental history, see Ted Steinberg's *Down to Earth: Nature's Role in American History* (New York: Oxford, 2002) or Carolyn Merchant's *American Environmental History: An Introduction* (New York: Columbia University Press, 2007). Anything by William Cronon is worth reading; I'm waiting anxiously for *Saving Nature in Time*.

7. The wind that drove the *Niña*, the *Pinta*, and the *Santa María* is a form of solar power, since the sun creates pressure gradients that cause the wind to blow.

8. Robert Paehlke, *Environmentalism and the Future of Progressive Politics* (New Haven: Yale University Press, 1989), 158. For America's systematic neglect of children, see the Children's Defense Fund website at http://www.childrensdefense.org.

9. Henry David Thoreau, *Walden* (New York: Harper Classics, 1965), 6.

10. Many American reformers have set their internal clocks to God's time, including Martin Luther King, Jr. King's merger of sacred and secular, of the

prophetic voice and civic republicanism, made him question the nature of American time, especially the doctrine of progress. In his magnificent epistle, "Letter from Birmingham Jail," he argued against "the strangely irrational notion that there is something in the flow of time that will inevitably cure all ills." "Actually," he insisted, in a passage that seems especially relevant to our times, "time itself is neutral; it can be used either destructively or constructively. More and more I feel that the people of ill will have used time much more effectively than the people of good will. We will have to repent in this generation not merely for the hateful words and actions of the bad people but for the appalling silence of the good people. Human progress never rolls in on wheels of inevitability; it comes through the tireless efforts of [people] willing to be co-workers with God, and without this hard work, time itself becomes an ally of the forces of social stagnation." Martin Luther King, Jr., *Why We Can't Wait* (New York: Signet, 1964). For a different sense of Sunday, see Winton U. Solberg, *Redeem the Time: The Puritan Sabbath in Early America* (Cambridge: Harvard University Press, 1977). For more on the possibilities of Sabbath, see Scott Russell Sanders, "Wilderness as a Sabbath for the Land," in *A Conservationist Manifesto* (Bloomington: Indiana University Press, 2009), 159–67.

11. Frederick Kaufman, "Wasteland: A Journey Through the American Cloaca," *Harper's*, February 2008, 46.

12. Steinberg, *Down to Earth*, 163–68. For a modern look at this business of reclamation, see Kaufman, "Wasteland," *Harper's*, 46–59.

13. Jamie Benidickson, *The Culture of Flushing: A Social and Legal History of Sewage* (Vancouver: University of British Columbia Press, 2007). The sludge that remains also receives additional treatment, using bacterial processes to reduce the number of disease-carrying organisms in the waste. After its purification, some sludge can be used as a fertilizer or soil amendment on agricultural lands. This isn't ideal, because human waste contains traces of all the chemicals that are in our system. And in an increasingly chemical culture, that can sometimes be a lot. Sewage routinely contains what the United States Geological Survey calls "emerging contaminants"—caffeine, antibiotics, antidepressants, tranquilizers, painkillers, and hormones—and not all of these substances can be filtered by conventional water treatment. Concentrations are generally low, but concerns still exist about the development of antibiotic-resistant bacteria in our water systems. See Andrew Revkin, "We Are What We Drink Is What We Are," Dot Earth (*New York Times* blog), http://dotearth.blogs.nytimes.com/2008/03/11/we-are-what-we-drink-is-what-we-are (accessed June 13, 2010).

14. Christopher Uhl, *Developing Ecological Consciousness: Path to a Sustainable World* (Lanham, MD: Rowman & Littlefield, 2003), 59. Stephen Salter, professor emeritus of engineering design at the University of Edinburgh, thinks the Swedish model of converting wastes into energy is promising. Wastes can generate power as syngas, biogas, or electricity, and heat pumps can extract energy for use in district heating or cooling projects. For a diagram of the possibilities, see "Waste Not: Making the Most of Our Sewage," *Times-Colonist* (Victoria, BC), http://www2.canada.com/victoriatimescolonist/features/sewage/2007-waste-not.pdf (accessed June 13, 2010).

15. We think of a shower as a necessity, but as Tim Kasser notes, "a hot shower is clearly a luxury, especially when we consider that most of the world's population has never experienced such a pleasure. What has happened is that this material pleasure has become the new baseline." As poet Randall Jarrell suggests, "the frontier of necessity" marches on. Tim Kasser, *The High Price of Materialism* (Cambridge: MIT Press, 2002), 58.

16. With its steady flow of warm water, the shower is a place for physical cleansing and psychological soothing, but it can also be a place for ideas. Studies show that showers can energize the mind and promote insightful thinking. Warm water stimulates nerve endings in the skin, releasing beta-endorphins to the brain, causing pleasure. At the same time, the soothing stimulation activates the brain. According to neuroscientist Frank Rice, such stimulation "can lead to something that is a new thought." And because we're not doing anything—or anything we need a lot of brainpower for—the seclusion of the shower is a good place "for ideas to form themselves into meaningful thoughts that we might not have otherwise." Almost literally, the shower is a flow experience in which our mind is free to make connections that otherwise elude it. If we were contemplating environmental issues—which mostly we're not—a shower could help lead us to new ideas and intuitions, like using less water or questioning our social conceptions of beauty. Tom Keyser, "Morning Shower Gets Under Your Skin," *Star Tribune*, April 27, 2007.

17. For more on these and other chemicals, see the Environmental Working Group's Campaign for Safe Cosmetics at http://www.safecosmetics.org.

18. Gus Speth reminds us that the world is experiencing a water crisis, and that it promises to get worse. More than a billion people worldwide lack easy access to fresh water; human beings already withdraw over half of available water. About half of the world's wetlands have already been lost, and people are "mining" finite supplies of groundwater like it is going out of style—which it is. Even in the United States, which is relatively wet, the EPA estimates that if water consumption remains at one hundred gallons per person per day, thirty-six states will face water shortages by 2013—just when today's first-year students graduate. James Gustave Speth, *The Bridge at the Edge of the World: Capitalism, the Environment, and Crossing from Crisis to Sustainability* (New Haven: Yale University Press, 2008), 32–34.

19. At Penn State in 1998, researchers found that "students consume about 60 gallons of water per person per day: 40 in showers, 10 in toilet flushing, 3 in the sink, and 7 in clothes washing. They seldom drink water." Christopher Uhl and Garrett Fitzgerald, "The Sustainable University," *Research/Penn State* Volume 20, no. 2 (May 1999), http://www.rps.psu.edu/may99/sustainable.html (accessed June 13, 2010). Both low-flow showerheads and timed showers, however, arouse students' sense of entitlement, the expectation that they can use as much as they want of any resource the college provides. Even so, college students and other Americans still use less water in the shower than in our food. In the aggregate, agriculture consumes 80 percent of America's freshwater resources (see chapter 4).

20. Elizabeth Shove, "Ratchets, Standards and the Reinvention of Normality," in *Consumption, Everyday Life and Sustainability*, Lancaster University,

http://www.lancs.ac.uk/fass/projects/esf/onlinehandbook.pdf. The St. Olaf bathtub story is recounted on the website of the Shaw-Olson Center for College History, St. Olaf College, http://www.stolaf.edu/collections/archives/scripts/oldmain/5.html (accessed June 13, 2010). Pricing ecosystem services like water can be a way of bringing our remote control of nature to mind. One problem for environmentalism is that many of our environmental impacts are out of sight and out of mind, and so they're not salient in our consciousness. We need ways to un-distance ourselves by finding ways of making our impacts sensual and salient.

21. Andrea Olsen, *Body and Earth: An Experiential Guide* (Hanover: Middlebury College Press, 2002), 84–85.

22. Uhl also reminds us that our bodies—like all other earthly bodies—are stardust, an evolutionary adaptation of matter that resulted from the Big Bang. Christopher Uhl, *Developing Ecological Consciousness*, 14–20, 52.

23. Rich Weiss, "Gut Reaction," *Washington Post Weekly*, June 12–18, 2007. See also Robert Krulwich, "Bacteria Outnumber Cells in Human Body," *All Things Considered*, National Public Radio, July 1, 2006, http://www.npr.org/templates/story/story.php?storyId=5527426 (accessed June 13, 2010).

24. Tara Parker Pope, "Germ Fighters May Lead to Hardier Germs," *New York Times*, October 30, 2007.

25. David E. Duncan, "The Pollution Within," *National Geographic*, October 2006, at http://ngm.nationalgeographic.com/2006/10/toxic-people/duncan-text (accessed June 13, 2010). Duncan points out that all of these chemicals have benefits, and that dosages are still low, but he reminds us that we are conducting a massive chemistry experiment on the planet and on our bodies. Other organisms are even more susceptible to our chemical experiments. Amphibians, for example, absorb our toxins through the skin so that we can see in frogs and toads some of the mutations that come from our chemical pollution of the world.

26. Carl Elliott, *Better Than Well: American Medicine Meets the American Dream* (New York: W. W. Norton, 2003). Women look for men who are tall and strong, with a facial structure uncompromised by diseases. And before the age of silicone, full breasts may have helped a man estimate a woman's age.

27. Eric Sorensen, *Seven Wonders for a Cool Planet* (San Francisco: Sierra Club Books, 2008), 35. For an instructive essay on the nature of habits and routines, see Bente Halkier, "Routinisation or Reflexivity? Consumers and Normative Claims for Environmental Consideration," in *Ordinary Consumption*, ed. Jukka Gronow and Alan Warde (New York: Routledge, 2001), 25–44. For more on the moral choices involved in global weirding, see Stephen M. Gardiner, "Ethics and Global Climate Change," *Ethics*, April 2004, 555–600, and "White Paper on the Ethical Dimensions of Climate Change," Rock Ethics Institute, Penn State University, http://www.psu.edu/dept/rockethics/climate/whitepaper/edcc-whitepaper.pdf (accessed June 13, 2010). Thanks to Maren Gelle for the connection between our conscious and conscientious lives.

28. John R. Ehrenfeld, *Sustainability by Design: A Subversive Strategy for Transforming Our Consumer Culture* (New Haven: Yale University Press, 2008),

147, 154–55. Ehrenfeld calls this process "presencing"—bringing the "out of sight and out of mind" into conscious consideration.

29. Anthony A. Leiserowitz and Lisa O. Fernandez, "Toward a New Consciousness: Values to Sustain Human and Natural Communities" (New Haven: Yale School of Forestry and Environmental Studies, 2008), 18, http://environment.research.yale.edu/documents/downloads/o-u/Toward-A-New-Consciousness.pdf.

30. Tony Cortese of Second Nature (www.secondnature.org) suggests that such systems thinking is essential as a common language in colleges and universities preparing students for the ecological revolution of the twenty-first century. He contends that "without such interdisciplinary systemic thinking, the net results to solve these problems are often narrow, ineffective solutions, or worse, actually increase the harm to people and the environment in another place or another time. Systems thinking is essential to developing a shared framework for understanding and dealing with complex, nonlinear systems that are characteristic of both society and the natural world." For a great (and free) introduction to systems thinking, see "Linking Thinking: New Perspectives on Thinking and Learning for Sustainability," World Wildlife Federation, http://www.eauc.org.uk/file_uploads/linkingthinking-302.pdf (accessed June 21, 2010).

Notes to Chapter 2

1. When anthropologist Rebekah Nathan first entered her dorm, she was "struck most by the sheer amount of 'stuff.'" Rebekah Nathan, *My Freshman Year: What a Professor Learned by Becoming a Student* (Ithaca: Cornell University Press, 2005), 19. For a short photo history of American college dorms, see M. J. Stephey, "The Evolution of College Dorms," Time.com, http://www.time.com/time/photogallery/0,29307,1838306,00.html?xid=newsletter-weekly.

2. When you look at them comparatively, college students (like other Americans) are extraordinary consumers. Jared Diamond notes that Americans consume more than twenty times more stuff than people in the developing world. He notes that people worry about population growth in the third world, but that smaller population growth in the first world has larger environmental impacts. Diamond, "What's Your Consumption Factor?" *New York Times*, January 2, 2008, http://www.nytimes.com/2008/01/02/opinion/02diamond.html (accessed June 21, 2010).

3. "Creating a consumer and a use for a product are central elements in the invention process—and not just at the end," says Mika Pantzar. "Steve Woolgar refers to this process as *user configuration*. User configuration leads to the formation of a 'script' (manuscript of correct use) which the consumer follows when faced with a novel product. From the manufacturer's point of view, creating a need and a market for the product is as important in the domestication of technology as is technical inventiveness." Mika Pantzar, "Designing Sustainability," in *Consumption, Everyday Life and Sustainability*.

4. The stuff in dorm rooms is pretty much the same things kids wanted at home. In *Getting Wiser to Teens*, for example, Peter Zollo notes that guys want

(in order) a TV, a CD player/stereo, a video-game system, a computer with an Internet connection, an alarm clock, a door that locks, a music collection, a hiding place (for belongings), a phone, and trophies or awards. Women want (again, in order) a CD player/stereo, photos, a phone, a TV, a door that locks, an alarm clock, a music collection, stuffed animals, a hiding place, and a computer with Internet access. "On the surface," notes Zollo, "these items seem to be nothing more than material possessions. But at a deeper level, they symbolize teens' underlying needs: entertainment, security, socialization, a sense of nostalgia (girls only), and sleep." Zollo also notes that both the paraphernalia and the underlying needs should be useful to marketers who want to sell *more* stuff to young people. Zollo, *Getting Wiser to Teens*, 194–96.

5. Barbara Kiviat, "Dressing Up the Dorms," *Time*, September 26, 2004; Sara B. Miller, "Home Decorating Craze Hits the College Dorm," *Christian Science Monitor*, August 17, 2005; National Retail Federation, "Back to College Spending Hits $36.6 Billion Due to Double-Digit Surge in Electronics Purchases," August 15, 2006.

6. "Off to College," Amazon.com, http://www.amazon.com/gp/events/back-to-school (accessed August 9, 2007).

7. Zollo, *Getting Wiser to Teens*, 46. Zollo contends that indi-filiation translates as, "I want to be an individual as long as that's what my friends are doing." The upscaling of dorm rooms is also a part of the process of ratcheting, whereby today's luxuries become tomorrow's necessities (Shove, "Ratchets, Standards and the Reinvention of Normality"). Fashioning the self with belongings also represents consumer conformity because the one choice we don't really get is to avoid the commercial expression of ourselves.

8. Barbara Kiviat, "Dressing Up the Dorms," and National Retail Federation, "Back to College Spending."

9. National Retail Federation, "Back to College Spending." See also "The Class of 2012 Grows Up Green," *Business Wire*, August 4, 2008.

10. As David Morrison says, "The market's eagerness to focus on products that self-express to others, commonly referred to as 'badging,' is often a highly motivating consumer behavior within the young adult segment." Morrison, *Marketing to the Campus Crowd*, 74. "Ensemble thinking" is often called "the Diderot effect," after an essay titled "Regrets On Parting with My Old Dressing Gown," by French philosopher Denis Diderot. For more on the Diderot effect, see the chapter titled "Diderot Unities and the Diderot Effect" in Grant McCracken's *Culture and Consumption: New Approaches to the Symbolic Character of Consumer Goods and Activities* (Bloomington: Indiana University Press, 1990), 118–29. And all of this is problematic because "as personal identity becomes further entangled with consumer behavior, it becomes harder and harder to challenge existing patterns of consumption." Anthony A. Leiserowitz and Lisa O. Fernandez, "Toward a New Consciousness."

11. One of the main reasons for all this stuff is what my students call "just-in-case consumption." They have all those clothes so that they're ready for any occasion. They have different shoes for different uses—running shoes, tennis shoes, cross-trainers, hiking boots, flats, heels, sandals, and

that ratty pair they've had since high school. They have a hundred DVDs just in case they need to watch one. They keep adding to their CD collections and playlists just in case they want to listen to a particular song. They keep a big car just in case all their friends want to go on a road trip. They need a lot of their belongings just in case they ever need them. Such defensive overconsumption, note Elizabeth Shove and Alan Warde, "has to be understood in terms of the management of social risk, the cost of failure and the sheer fear of being able to cope." And it helps consumers "redefine what is normal: expectations of peak load become ordinary and bit by bit new peaks appear." Elizabeth Shove and Alan Warde, "Inconspicuous Consumption: The Sociology of Consumption and the Environment," Department of Sociology, Lancaster University, October 1998, 12, http://www.lancs.ac.uk/fass/sociology/papers/shove-warde-inconspicuous-consumption.pdf. Or as David Schmidtz and Elizabeth Willott note, "When we feel insecure, we tend to consume more than is good for us." Schmidtz and Willott, "Varieties of Overconsumption," 11.

12. Randall Jarrell, "A Sad Heart at the Supermarket," in *A Sad Heart at the Supermarket: Essays & Fables* (New York: Atheneum, 1962), 66; Juliet B. Schor, *The Overspent American: Upscaling, Downshifting, and the New Consumer* (New York: Basic Books, 1998), 15–19; Pew Research Center, "Luxury or Necessity? Things We Can't Live Without: The List Has Grown in the Past Decade," December 14, 2006, http://pewresearch.org/pubs/323/luxury-or-necessity (accessed June 21, 2010).

13. For a general introduction to the meanings of art for Americans, see David Halle, *Inside Culture: Art and Class in the American Home* (Chicago: University of Chicago Press, 1993).

14. Deborah Du Nann Winter, "Shopping for Sustainability: Psychological Solutions to Overconsumption," in *Psychology and Consumer Culture: The Struggle for a Good Life*, ed. Tim Kasser and Alan D. Kanner (Washington, D.C.: American Psychological Association, 2004), 70.

15. For more on planned obsolescence, see Giles Slade, *Made to Break: Technology and Obsolescence in America* (Cambridge: Harvard University Press, 2006).

16. John C. Ryan and Alan Thein Durning, *Stuff: The Secret Lives of Everyday Things* (Seattle: Northwest Environment Watch, 1997). In 2006, Northwest Environment Watch became the Sightline Institute, now online at www.sightline.org. See also Annie Leonard, *The Story of Stuff* (New York: Free Press, 2010). For more on silicon chips, see "Computer Chip Life Cycle," Environmental Literacy Council, http://www.enviroliteracy.org/article.php/1275.html. For more on the nature of fast food, see Michael Pollan, *The Omnivore's Dilemma: A Natural History of Four Meals* (New York: Penguin, 2006), 109–19.

17. For a good introduction to the environmental impacts of globalization, see Corey L. Lofdahl, *Environmental Impacts of Globalization and Trade* (Cambridge: MIT Press, 2002).

18. John D. Adams, *Thinking Today as if Tomorrow Mattered: The Rise of a Sustainable Consciousness* (San Francisco: Eartheart Enterprises, 2000), 72.

19. The term "problem of invisible complexity" comes from Robert Bellah et al., *Habits of the Heart: Individualism and Commitment in American Life* (Berkeley: University of California Press, 1985), 207.

20. Hannah Arendt, *Eichmann in Jerusalem: A Report on the Banality of Evil* (New York: Viking, 1963). See also Thomas Merton, "A Devout Meditation in Honor of Adolf Eichmann," in *Raids on the Unspeakable* (New York: New Directions, 1966), 45–49.

21. For a detailed account of this shift in the shoemaking industry, see Alan Dawley, *Class and Community: The Industrial Revolution in Lynn* (Cambridge: Harvard University Press, 1976).

22. For more on "murketing"—the marketing of products with distraction or disinformation—see *Murketing [The Journal of]*, http://www.murketing.com/ journal.

23. Currently, some environmentalists are trying to assess the life-cycle costs of our belongings. See, for example, the Good Guide (www.goodguide. com) that Daniel Goleman sees as a form of ecological intelligence, but note that environmental costs aren't yet internalized in the prices. Daniel Goleman, *Ecological Intelligence: How Knowing the Hidden Impacts of What We Buy Can Change Everything* (New York: Broadway Books, 2009), 83–84.

24. John Fiske, "The Jeaning of America," in *Understanding Popular Culture* (New York: Routledge, 1989), 14.

25. Ryan and Durning, *Stuff*, 67. The term "the morality of spending" comes from Daniel Horowitz's *The Morality of Spending: Attitudes Toward the Consumer Society in America, 1875–1940* (Chicago: Ivan R. Dee, 1992). But see also Horowitz's sequel, *The Anxieties of Affluence: Critiques of American Consumer Culture, 1939–1979* (Amherst: University of Massachusetts Press, 2004), as well as William R. Leach, *Land of Desire: Merchants, Power, and the Rise of a New American Culture* (New York: Vintage, 1993), Gary Cross, *An All Consuming Century: Why Commercialism Won in Modern America* (New York: Columbia University Press, 2000), and Lizabeth Cohen, *A Consumers' Republic: The Politics of Mass Consumption in Postwar America* (New York: Vintage, 2003). And note how much consumer spending affected the economic collapse of 2008.

26. As Jukka Gronow and Alan Warde point out, it is precisely our routine and repetitive consumption—the commonsense consuming that is a habit of our hearts—that is difficult to change. When ordinary consumption becomes the default setting of college culture and American life, it's becomes "second nature" to us—even when it harms first nature. Gronow and Warde, eds., *Ordinary Consumption* (New York: Routledge, 2001).

27. Jane Hammerslough, *Dematerializing: Taming the Power of Possessions* (Cambridge: Perseus, 2001); "The Class of 2012 Grows Up Green," *Business Wire*, August 4, 2008. IKEA's environmental initiatives put American retailers to shame. See David Roberts, "Swedening the Pot: An Interview with IKEA Sustainability Director Thomas Bergmark," *Grist*, February 27, 2007. For some good reading on voluntary simplicity, see Duane Elgin, *Voluntary Simplicity: Toward a Way of Life that is Outwardly Simple, Inwardly Rich* (Harper, 1981); Stephanie Mills, *Epicurean Simplicity* (Washington, D.C.: Island Press, 2003);

and especially Jerome Segal, *Graceful Simplicity: The Philosophy and Politics of the Alternative American Dream* (Berkeley: University of California Press, 2003). Segal, unlike many advocates of voluntary simplicity, understands the political dimensions of changing consumption.

28. Information on dorm refrigerators can be found in *Consumer Reports*, September 2008, 8. "Less Stuff More Fun" is the slogan of the Center for a New American Dream (www.newdream.org).

29. "Green Buildings," Association for the Advancement of Sustainability in Higher Education, http://www.aashe.org/resources/building.php. For a slideshow, see Zach Miners, "10 Colleges with Green Dorms," *U.S. News and World Report*, http://www.usnews.com/education/best-colleges/slideshows/10-colleges-with-green-dorms (accessed June 21, 2010). For the monitoring at Central College, see http://pods.centralcollege.greentouchscreen.com (accessed June 21, 2010). Other colleges are going the other direction—building upscale dorms, with apartment-style suites and amenities like restaurants and coffee shops, exercise rooms and amusement areas, grocery delivery and laundry service. These residence halls are also a part of the environmental curriculum of the college. And they affect students' perceptions of the purpose of college. "The undergraduate university experience should be about getting kids to answer the basic question, 'What is a life worth living?'" contends Jonathan Zimmerman, director of New York University's History of Education program. "By making all these lovely things for the kids, we're answering that question for them." M. J. Stephey, "The Evolution of the College Dorm," *Time*.

30. For a good introduction to this tradition, see David Shi, *The Simple Life: Plain Living and High Thinking in American Culture* (New York: Oxford University Press, 1985). For a good account of why these reformers have been less than effective, see Gary Cross, *An All Consuming Century*, (New York: Columbia University Press, 2000).

Notes to Chapter 3

1. As this suggests, college students tend to wear clothes that seem natural. In addition to cotton, they also wear wool and leather. They generally like natural fibers next to their skin. They'll wear synthetic outerwear—nylon shells and Goretex jackets, or winter coats with Thinsulate—but, in general, they like to be close to nature—or at least natural fibers—in their clothes. For cotton marketing, see the website of Cotton Incorporated, at http://www.cottoninc.com.

2. As early as 1945, Henry Miller considered the United States an "air-conditioned nightmare." But the expectation of perfectly-controlled ambient air temperature has only increased since then. For a history of air conditioning, see Gail Cooper, *Air-Conditioning America: Engineers and the Controlled Environment, 1900–1960* (Baltimore: Johns Hopkins, 1998).

3. This specialization, of course, is a commercial strategy to sell more clothes—and it works.

4. The subculture of ripped and torn clothes in modern societies is fascinating. John Fiske suggests that such calculated carelessness is "excorporation,"

resisting the preferred meanings assigned to a commodity by its corporate sponsor in favor of subversive meanings shared in a subculture. "It is a refusal of commodification and an assertion of one's right to make one's own culture out of the resources provided by the commodity system." Fiske, "The Jeaning of America," 1–21. It's also, ironically, a way to speed the obsolescence of clothes, not for fashion reasons, but because, as the tag on a pair of distressed jeans notes, they might only withstand ten or fifteen washings.

5. The term "consumption community" comes from Daniel Boorstin, *The Image: A Guide to Pseudo-Events in America* (New York: Atheneum, 1987). For statistics, see Student Monitor, *Lifestyle & Media*, Spring 2006, 171, 173.

6. In 2008, according to the National Retail Federation, college students were planning to spend about thirty-five dollars on "back to school" collegiate gear. "Parents Holding on to Rebate Checks for Back-to-School Purchases," July 22, 2008. The World Wildlife Federation notes that some of these mascots are species endangered or threatened by habitat loss caused by human population pressures and by global climate change ("Help the Cats Behind the Mascots," March 14, 2005, http://www.worldwildlife.org/who/media/press/2005/WWFPresitem783.html). For more on the branding of colleges and universities, see James Twitchell, *Branded Nation* (New York: Simon & Schuster, 2004), 109–91.

7. What if institutions of higher education required students to master the ecological experience of the natural mascots? What if students learned to identify—practically and symbolically—with the natural world as intensely as with sports teams? It seems like a silly idea, but only in a society that systematically segments itself from nature. For more on our systematic, sensual, and linguistic separation from nature, see David Abram, *The Spell of the Sensuous: Perception and Language in a More-Than-Human World* (New York: Pantheon, 1996).

8. James J. Farrell, *One Nation Under Goods: Malls and the Seductions of American Shopping* (Washington, D.C.: Smithsonian Books, 2003), 42–45. Outfitters provide gear, but they also gear our minds for the experience of nature. Much of the marketing of nature by outfitters invites us to "get back to nature," which suggests that we're not in nature here and now. If we can get back to nature, we think, we can get back to our roots—to a genuine place, authentic life, our inner self. Historian William Cronon criticizes the American obsession with wilderness, especially when it leads us to think that our affection for wild nature absolves us of responsibility for the rest of it. William Cronon, "The Trouble with Wilderness; or, Getting Back to the Wrong Nature," in *Uncommon Ground: Rethinking the Human Place in Nature* (New York: W. W. Norton, 1996), 69–90.

9. "Levi's Fashions New Outlook in Ads, Jeans," *USA Today*, January 8, 2007.

10. "You Can Never Have Enough Jeans," Cotton Incorporated, http://www.cottoninc.com/Cotton-Commercials-Flash (accessed June 21, 2010).

11. Other popular college brands include Citizens of Humanity, Joe's Jeans, Rock & Republic, and William Rast (Justin Timberlake's brand). Roxana

Popescu, "Savvy, Jaded, Distracted and Loaded," *New York Times*, September 12, 2005); Louisa Thomas, "The Secret Language of Jeans," *Slate*, November 10, 2005, http://www.slate.com/id/2129956 (accessed June 21, 2010). Butt Lifters don't actually do any heavy lifting. A narrow fit in the seat pushes chubby cheeks up, like a push-up bra. But most of the lifting is purely perceptual. Sometimes a higher seam above the pockets draws the eyes upward. Pocket tops are angled in, making the ass seem ascendant, and side seams centered on the thighs can make the legs seem slimmer. Susan Phinney, "Bringing Up the Rear: Jeans that are Supposed to Give You a Lift," *Seattle Post-Intelligencer*, January 18, 2005.

12. For an account of these cultural meanings, see James Sullivan, *Jeans: A Cultural History of an American Icon* (New York: Gotham Books, 2006).

13. Summer Rayne Oakes, "The 'Green' Blue Jean: Market Trend Forecast," *S4: Sustainability Trends in Fashion* (Spring 2007—The Denim Issue); "Making Blue Jeans Green: About Cotton," Live Green, Live Smart. Fred Pearce, "Fred's Footprint: What Price Cotton?" *New Scientist*, June 18, 2008.

14. Estimate by Mindy Pennybacker, editor of the *Green Guide*.

15. Mindy Pennybacker, "The Hidden Life of T-Shirts," *Sierra*, January 1999, 8; "Making Blue Jeans Green: About Cotton." The jury is still out on genetic engineering.

16. World Wildlife Federation, "Agriculture and Environment: Cotton," http://wwf.panda.org/what_we_do/footprint/agriculture/cotton/environmental_impacts (accessed June 21, 2010).

17. "Blue Jeans Become Green Jeans," *New Scientist*, July 4, 2001. Scientists in England are working on a project called "Spindigo," trying to find a new all-natural process for making the blue dye in mass quantities.

18. The distressing process predictably shortens the life span of jeans. Gauray Doshi, "Stonewash Finish for Denim," http://ezinearticles.com/?Stonewash-Finish-for-Denim&id=388273 (accessed June 21, 2010).

19. Micha Peled's movie *China Blue* (2007) chronicles the making of blue jeans at a Chinese factory through the stories of three Chinese teenagers: Jasmine, a sixteen-year-old farm girl who works seventeen-hour days as a thread cutter for six cents an hour; Orchid, a nineteen-year-old zipper installer; and Li Ping, a fourteen-year-old seamstress. Revealing the stark contrast between what jeans symbolize to Americans, namely "a carefree, joyful life," and "the misery of the people that are practically enslaved now to make the product," the film puts a human face on sweatshops and globalization.

20. "Watch, Listen & Read," *USA Today*, April 2, 2007, 3B; "Slave to Fashion," *S4: Sustainability Trends in Fashion* (Spring 2007—The Denim Issue). For a more upbeat view of low wages, see James Fallows, *Postcards from Tomorrow Square: Reports from China* (New York: Vintage, 2008). For a shorter movie on the making of blue jeans, see "Making Blue Jeans," http://www.youtube.com/watch?v=-MTyEwUJPBA (accessed June 21, 2010).

21. For a thoughtful introduction to the ethics of globalization, see Rebecca Todd Peters, *In Search of the Good Life: The Ethics of Globalization* (New York: Continuum, 2004).

22. Shove and Warde, "Inconspicuous Consumption," 11.

23. Most American college students have grown up in homes with a "laundry room," or at least a laundry space, as domestic architecture shapes the expectations of consumers. Interestingly, in college, students adapt to a different domestic architecture, one that suggests an alternative to the single-family-home-with-all-of-its-own-appliances model. Even though it's environmentally advantageous, it's not a model that many students expect to follow after graduation, probably because it's more inconvenient than the resource-intensive alternative.

24. Kim Willsher, "Why Washing Your Jeans Can Cost the Earth," *Guardian*, June 12, 2006.

25. Cleanliness Institute," *Time*, December 23, 1929. For a modern version of the Cleanliness Institute, see the Soap and Detergent Association (www.cleaninginstitute.org).

26. Sarah Stillman, "Made by Us: Young Women, Sweatshops, and the Ethics of Globalization," Elie Wiesel Foundation, http://www.eliewieselfoundation.org/CM_Images//UploadedImages/WinnersEssays/Sarah_Stillman.pdf (accessed June 21, 2010).

27. Manufacturers, of course, might pass on increased costs to consumers—although they might simply reduce their profit margins. But paying more for clothes that don't compromise our principles could be well worth the cost.

28. Juliet B. Schor, "Cleaning the Closet: Toward a New Fashion Ethic," in *Sustainable Planet: Solutions for the Twenty-first Century*, ed. Juliet B. Schor and Betsy Taylor (Boston: Beacon Press, 2002), 54–59.

29. For the story of this powerful student movement, see Lisa Featherstone, *Students Against Sweatshops: The Making of a Movement* (New York: Verso, 2002).

30. "Top 100 Most Powerful Brands," BrandZ, 2008, http://www.brandz.com/upload/BrandZ-2008-RankingReport.pdf (accessed June 21, 2010).

31. Anna Kuchment, "Sense and Sensibility," *Newsweek*, August 5, 2008.

32. Reena Jana, "How Green Are My Blue Jeans," *Business Week*, September 18, 2006, 12; "Ms. Green Jeans," *Grist*, July 24, 2006; Wendy Von Buskirk, "Fashion Conscience Students Revitalize Denim in Earth-friendly Way," *Hometown Life*, May 31, 2007; "Rejeaneration," http://www.rejeaneration.com (accessed June 21, 2010).

Notes to Chapter 4

1. Waste isn't inevitable in cafeteria eating, although it certainly seems "normal." One of the most efficient food reforms is also one of the easiest: "Take what you'll eat, and eat what you take."

2. For an introduction to food cultures, see E. N. Anderson, *Everyone Eats: Understanding Food and Culture* (New York: NYU Press, 2005).

3. The cafeteria has become a metaphor for choice in other areas of American life. The college curriculum, for example, is often described as a cafeteria of academic choices, and in business we speak of "cafeteria-style" benefit plans. In many ways, the United States has become a cafeteria culture, replete with choices and pseudo choices.

4. Sidney W. Mintz, *Tasting Food, Tasting Freedom: Excursions into Eating, Power, and the Past* (Boston: Beacon, 1997), 13. For a collection of news reports on "freedom fries," see Brian Stross, Department of Anthropology, University of Texas, http://www.utexas.edu/courses/stross/ant393b_files/freedomfries.htm.

5. Joel Berg, *All You Can Eat: How Hungry is America?* (New York: Seven Stories Press, 2008). For a graphic look at disparities in food consumption, see Peter Menzel and Faith D'Aluisio, *Hungry Planet: What the World Eats* (Berkeley, CA: Ten Speed Press, 2005).

6. For a good treatment of work and inequality in America, see Christine Williams, *Inside Toyland: Working, Shopping, and Social Inequality* (Berkeley: University of California Press, 2006). See also Daniel Cogan, "Seeing Power in a College Cafeteria," in Ann E. Kingsolver, *More Than Class: Studying Power in U.S. Workplaces* (Albany: SUNY Press, 1998), 173–85.

7. For more on the Columbian Exchange, see Alfred Crosby, *The Columbian Exchange: Biological and Cultural Consequences of 1492* (Santa Barbara, CA: Greenwood Press, 1972).

8. Indian tribes were often hunters and gatherers, with incidental (and often moveable) agriculture. As colonists substituted the patterns of settled agriculture for the fields and forests of native America, they created a new landscape of small farms and woodlots. For more on the colonial ecological revolution, see Carolyn Merchant, *Ecological Revolutions: Nature, Gender, and Science in New England* (Chapel Hill: University of North Carolina Press, 1989) and William Cronon, *Changes in the Land: Indians, Colonists, and the Ecology of New England* (New York: Hill & Wang, 1983).

9. William Cronon, *Nature's Metropolis: Chicago and the Great West* (New York: W. W. Norton, 1991), 310.

10. Ibid., 256.

11. Michael Pollan, *In Defense of Food: An Eater's Manifesto* (New York: Penguin, 2008), 13, 105.

12. Jack Kloppenburg, Jr., John Hendrickson, and G. W. Stevenson, "Coming Into the Foodshed," *Agriculture and Human Values,* Summer 1996, 33–42. Michael Pollan, "Getting Over Organic," *Orion,* July/August 2003, 11; Joan Dye Gussow, "Can a Community Have a Food System?" *Open Spaces* 2, no. 2 (1999): 8–17.

13. Pollan, *The Omnivore's Dilemma,* 41–47.

14. Even the *Economist,* a conservative English publication that believes that free markets are the solution to most problems, contends, "If modern agriculture were invented today, it probably wouldn't be allowed. It pollutes the environment with pesticides, fertilisers and nutrients from feed and animal waste. Farming damages wild habitats. And domesticated animals are stocked at high densities and pumped full of growth hormones and antibiotics, with the result that they are often unhealthily fatty compared with their wild relatives." ("A New Way to Feed the World," *Economist,* August 9, 2003, 9.

15. As Michael Pollan points out, Americans eat very little corn that we recognize as corn, but we're each responsible for about a ton of it every year. "You are what you eat, it's often said, and if this is true, then what we mostly are is corn—or more precisely, processed corn" (Michael Pollan, *The Omnivore's*

Dilemma, 20, 85). Pollan's book is a brilliant explanation of the "cornification" of the American diet.

16. "Total Wind and Water Erosion, 1997," Natural Resources Conservation Service, http://www.nrcs.usda.gov/technical/NRI/maps/meta/m5112.html (accessed June 21, 2010).

17. Eric Schlosser, *Fast Food Nation* (New York: Harper Perennial, 2002). The speed of cafeteria culture is, of course, a reflection of a larger American fast-food culture—and not just at fast-food joints. Michael Pollan notes that the average American spends less than half an hour a day preparing food and just over an hour eating it. Human cultures have traditionally centered on food preparation and sharing, but we've saved time by eliminating those rituals from our lives (Pollan, *In Defense of Food*, 145).

18. Heather M. Jensen and Joseph F. Guenthner, "Historical Impact of Technology on the Potato Industry," paper prepared for the Idaho Potato Conference (2000), http://www.cals.uidaho.edu/potato/Research&Extension/Topic/Marketing&Economics/HistoricalImpactOfTechnologyOnThePotato Industry-00.pdf (accessed June 21, 2010).

19. Ryan and Durning, *Stuff*, 59.

20. Michael Pollan, *The Botany of Desire* (New York: Random House, 2002), 183–238.

21. Ryan and Durning, *Stuff*, p. 61.

22. Malcolm Gladwell, "The Trouble with Fries," http://www.gladwell.com/pdf/fries.pdf. For some of us, french fries are also a delivery vehicle for ketchup, but that's another story.

23. Ibid.

24. Ibid.

25. David Orr, *The Nature of Design: Ecology, Culture and Human Intention* (New York: Oxford University Press, 2002), 111.

26. Wendell Berry, "The Pleasures of Eating," in *What Are People For?* (San Francisco: North Point Press, 1990), 148. The pleasures of reading "The Pleasures of Eating" are considerable. The essay can also be found online at Center for Ecoliteracy, http://www.ecoliteracy.org/publications/rsl/wendell-berry.html (accessed June 21, 2010).

27. Ibid., 151.

28. Michael Brower and Warren Leon, *The Consumer's Guide to Effective Environmental Choices: Practical Advice from the Union of Concerned Scientists* (New York: Three Rivers Press, 1999), 58–64; Bryan Walsh, "Meat: Making Global Warming Worse," *Time*, September 10, 2008. Grass-fed beef is better for its carbon load; see Lisa Abend, "How Cows (Grass-Fed Only) Could Save the Planet," *Time*, January 25, 2010.

29. For more on college cafeteria initiatives, see "Dining Services," Association for the Advancement of Sustainability in Higher Education at http://www.aashe.org/resources/dining-services.

30. Walsh, "Meat: Making Global Warming Worse," *Time*.

31. "Local-Food Movement: The Lure of the 100-Mile Diet," *Time*, June 11, 2006. Ironically, though, it's not always the case that local foods are less energy

intensive. See Michael Specter, "Big Foot," *New Yorker*, February 25, 2008, as well as "Good Food?" and "Voting with Your Trolley," *Economist*, December 9–15, 2006, 12, 73–75. Bon Appétit food service has been a leader in promoting local foods in a "low-carbon diet." For a basic calculator of the carbon impact of your foods, see Bon Appétit's "Is My Lunch Causing Global Warming?" at http://www.eatlowcarbon.org (accessed June 21, 2010).

32. On the other hand, organic eating isn't entirely uncomplicated because organic production is often less intensive than industrial agriculture, with the result that more acres of farmland are needed. See "Ethical Food: Good Food?" and "Voting with Your Trolley," *Economist*.

33. Summer Banks, "Sustainable Food Confronts Elitist Past," *Yale Daily News*, February 12, 2008; Bruce Horovitz, "More University Students Call for Organic, 'Sustainable' Food," *USA Today*, September 27, 2006, B1–B2.

34. For a good answer to the last question, see David Orr, "Agriculture and the Liberal Arts," in *Earth in Mind: On Education, Environment, and the Human Prospect* (Washington, DC: Island Press, 1994), 117–21.

35. For more on St. Olaf's STOGROW farm, see http://www.stolaf.edu/orgs/stogrow. For more on Yale's farm, see Yale Sustainable Food Project, http://www.yale.edu/sustainablefood/farm.html.

36. Bill Mollison, *Permaculture: A Designers' Manual* (Tyalgum, NSW: Tagari Publications, 1988).

37. For more on Wes Jackson, see Craig Canine, "35 Who Made a Difference: Wes Jackson," *Smithsonian*, November 1, 2005, http://www.smithsonianmag.com/people-places/jackson.html (accessed June 21, 2010). For more on the Land Institute, check out their website at http://www.landinstitute.org.

38. Pollan, *The Omnivore's Dilemma*, 123–33, 185–273.

39. For one good example of such work, see the website of the The Leopold Center for Sustainable Agriculture at Iowa State University at http://www.leopold.iastate.edu.

40. In 2006, the number of fat and obese people superseded the number of hungry people in the world. But hunger is still a more important problem than obesity. LaDonna Redmond, "It's Not about the Seeds," *Orion*, January/February 2005, 11. The co-op in Northfield, Minnesota, is called Just Food, and it's a good name for the business of the cooperative commonwealth.

41. William McDonough and Michael Braungart, *Cradle to Cradle: Remaking the Way We Make Things* (New York: North Point Press, 2002).

42. For a good history of American agriculture, see Bruce L. Gardner, *American Agriculture in the Twentieth Century: How It Flourished and What It Cost* (Cambridge: Harvard University Press, 2006). For histories of food consumption, consult James E. McWilliams, *A Revolution in Eating: How the Quest for Food Shaped America* (New York: Columbia University Press, 2005); Harvey Levenstein, *Revolution at the Table: The Transformation of the American Diet* (Berkeley: University of California Press, 1988); and Levenstein, *Paradox of Plenty: A Social History of Eating in Modern America* (Berkeley: University of California Press, 1993).

43. For a lively introduction to the politics of food, see Daniel Imhoff, *Food Fight: The Citizen's Guide to a Food and Farm Bill* (Berkeley: University of California Press, 2007).

44. We celebrate the extinction of farmers with our pleasure in knowing that one farmer feeds one hundred fifty-five people. But farmers are the seed banks of agricultural practice, the genetic code for the future of farming. It may be "efficient" to have fewer farmers, but it's not wise. Katerina Athanasiou, "Seven Science Questions With USDA Secretary," *Cornell Daily Sun* (May 4, 2010).

45. R. Dennis Olson, "Farm Bill a Missed Opportunity," May 13, 2008, Institute for Agriculture and Trade Policy, National Campaign for Sustainable Agriculture, "2008 Farm Bill Wins," in *2008 Annual Report,* http://www.rafiusa .org/2008_annual_report.pdf.

46. Marion Nestle, *Food Politics: How the Food Industry Influences Nutrition and Health* (Berkeley: University of California Press, 2002). Critics of corporate food sponsorships usually focus on the indoctrination of children, but the politics of food also show up on college campuses. Coca-Cola, for example, paid the University of Minnesota $28 million for a ten-year deal.

47. For a delightful essay on the possibilities of a progressive politics of food, see Michael Pollan, "Farmer in Chief," *New York Times Magazine,* October 9, 2008.

48. For a glimpse of that new agriculture, see Thomas A. Lyson, *Civic Agriculture: Reconnecting Farm, Food, and Community* (Lebanon: Tufts University Press, 2004).

Notes to Chapter 5

1. Keith Naughton, "Cruising on Campus," *Newsweek,* August 22, 2005, 60; Rich Morin and Paul Taylor, "Luxury or Necessity: The Public Makes a U-Turn," Pew Research Center, http://pewsocialtrends.org/pubs/733/luxury-necessity-recession-era-reevaluations (accessed June 21, 2010). Other necessities include a landline phone (68 percent), a clothes dryer (66 percent), air conditioning (54 percent), television (52 percent), a computer (50 percent), and a cell phone (49 percent).

2. Sandra Block, "As Your Kids Go to College, Check Your Insurance," *USA Today,* August 27, 2001. Student Monitor, *Automotive,* Spring 2006, 9, 17, 62.

3. Naughton, "Cruising on Campus," *Newsweek* 60.

4. We assumed one round-trip a day, and didn't adjust for car pools or pedestrians (but we left out students and visitors, and the possibility of multiple trips).

5. Amy Best, *Fast Cars, Cool Rides: The Accelerating World of Youth and Their Cars* (New York: NYU Press, 2006), 5. American kids are also driven by cars in their playtime. Young boys especially get Matchbox cars and radio-controlled vehicles, while upscale kids get battery-operated SUV knockoffs. Once they can play video games, boys compete as racers in games like *Gran Turismo 4* and *Grand Theft Auto.* Kids watch NASCAR and other auto races on TV. No action

movie would be complete without car chases and crashes. At amusement parks, there are often rides like the Autopia at Disneyland, or go-kart tracks that give kids of all ages the kinetic pleasures of cars.

6. Richard Louv, *Last Child in the Woods: Saving Our Children from Nature-Deficit Disorder* (Chapel Hill: Algonquin Books of Chapel Hill, 2005), 62.

7. Peter Zollo points out that "the emotional benefit of obtaining a driver's license clearly transcends the functional." Zollo, *Getting Wiser to Teens*, 45–46. For an alternative rite of passage, see David Adam Lertzman, "Rediscovering Rites of Passage: Education, Transformation, and the Transition to Sustainability," *Conservation Ecology* 5, no. 2, http://www.consecol.org/vol5/iss2/art30 (accessed June 21, 2010).

8. At other times, however, cars are not an escape, but a way of driving to obligations—like jobs and extracurricular activities (including the ones that help you get into a good college)—in a culture that systematically marginalizes other forms of transportation. As Amy Best suggests, "the demands of work, urban sprawl, growing commuting distances, a general distrust of public transit, and the absence of government dollars for funding accessible transportation create a situation where kids increasingly need cars." Cars help families negotiate their increasingly complex schedules in a world of time poverty. And cars also help families negotiate good behavior in their kids. Car privileges are often the reward for good grades and educational achievement. So even though cars have an aura of freedom and escape, they can be ways of binding kids to certain social constructions. Amy Best, *Fast Cars*, 119, 125–28.

9. Cars, for example, keep us from being waiters. At college, there are two primary kinds of time. There's mandatory time—class time and library time, work time and homework time. And there's free time—sports time, TV time, video time, Internet time, Facebook time, party time, and time for hanging out. In a culture that runs in car-centric circles, all other forms of transportation take more time. You have to walk to the subway or the bus, and you have to wait for them to come. You might have to transfer, and then walk from the station or the corner to your destination. All of this takes time that could be free time. And we don't want to spend our free time waiting. So cars free our time for free time. Besides, as one of my students says, "cars are so much *cooler* than buses."

10. Zygmunt Bauman, quoted in Maggie Jackson, *Distracted: The Erosion of Attention and the Coming Dark Age* (Amherst, NY: Prometheus Books, 2008), 99. Mobility is a major American value. Historian George Pierson contends that mobility and migration have been the "M-factor" in American culture, shaping American values as much as the frontier or the revolutionary experience. George Pierson, "The M-Factor in American History," *American Quarterly*, Summer Supplement, 1962, 275–89; and *The Moving American* (New York: Knopf, 1973). For an alternative view, see Scott Russell Sanders, *Staying Put: Making a Home in a Restless World* (Boston: Beacon Press, 1994).

11. Griffiths, *A Sideways Look at Time*, 37; Pew Research Center, "Americans and Their Cars: Is the Romance on the Skids?" at http://pewresearch.org/assets/social/pdf/Cars.pdf (accessed June 21, 2010); Amy Best, *Fast Cars*, 163.

12. One complication of automotive status at college, however, is who actually owns the car. For many students, it's better to own your own car—even if it's a parental discard—than to drive a "cool" car that your parents provide. This fits closely with "the poor college student" syndrome, and with the ideal of independence in college. When you own your own junker, in fact, you can turn its liabilities into social assets, bragging about its shortcomings—the things that don't work, the rust that consumes the car, the unpredictability of the engine, the parts that fall off. In this case, ironically, status comes not from class, but from being déclassé.

13. Pew Research Center, "Americans and Their Cars." See also Stephen Dunn's poem, "The Sacred." Google it.

14. Beth L. Bailey, *From Front Porch to Back Seat: Courtship in Twentieth-Century America* (Baltimore: Johns Hopkins, 1989).

15. Amy Best, *Fast Cars*, 5.

16. For a delightful reading of SUV advertising and the environment, see Shane Gunster, " 'You Belong Outside': Advertising, Nature, and the SUV," *Ethics & the Environment* 9, no. 2 (2004): 4–26.

17. The road trip is also an American story, and sometimes, it seems, the story is the purpose of the trip. Ever since Jack Kerouac's *On the Road* (and probably even before), the trip to enlightenment (or at least to Florida) has been an important genre of student narrative. The Web, for example, is full of road-trip stories, and the car itself figures in many of them. Road trippers tell stories of speed, and of brushes with the law. Collegiate car trippers tell stories of endurance—the 26-hour drive, or the thousand-mile day. They tell stories of adversity, and of responding to adversity. They tell stories of human bonding— or at least hook ups. These automotive narratives are all variations on a theme of quest—testing the self by submitting to extraordinary tests of will, physical stamina, and social bonding. For a cinematic version of this narrative, see the Todd Phillips film *Road Trip* (2000).

18. Pew Research Center, "Americans and Their Cars."

19. For a general consideration of sex and cars, see David L. Lewis, "Sex and the Automobile: From Rumble Seats to Rockin' Vans," in *The Automobile and American Culture*, David L. Lewis and Laurence Goldstein, eds. (Ann Arbor: University of Michigan Press, 1983), 518–28. And for a contemporary view, see Amy Best, *Fast Cars*, 56–79. It's interesting that even though men drive kids to sports, there's no such thing as a "soccer dad."

20. One corollary of convenience is security. With a car, we're ready for whatever we might need a car for. As one of my students says, "I feel very content right now, knowing that my car is down in the parking lot . . . just in case I need to use it. You never know what might pop up." This is another example of "just-in-case consumption," owning things for all of life's contingencies.

21. Many of us also have more than a kinetic relationship with our cars. About 30 percent of Americans—and 40 percent of younger drivers (aged eighteen to twenty-nine)—think that their car has a personality of its own. Most of us think of cars as just a means of transportation, but about one in four Americans think of their car as "something special—more than just a way to

get around." Some people name their cars, or refer to them as "my baby," while others buff and shine them like trophies. Pew Research Center, "Americans and Their Cars." Karal Ann Marling suggests that our relationship with cars might even be called "auto-eroticism." Karal Ann Marling, "Auto-eroticism: America's Love Affair with the Car in the Television Age," in *As Seen on TV: The Visual Culture of Everyday Life in the 1950s* (Cambridge: Harvard University Press, 1994), 128–62.

22. It's not accidental that road rage often happens when our control is curtailed—when traffic keeps us from moving as freely as we expect, or the jerk in the next lane threatens our control of the highway.

23. Cars reinforce American individualism, but they are also a perfect example of "mass pseudo-demassification"—the process of making a mass-produced object seem like it was made just for you. Advertisers like to tell us that cars are an expression of the self, but it's a self that expresses itself mainly by making a payment. Lots of cars bear the name "custom," but few cars are actually custom-built. The car that defines you so well is one of a thousand that rolled off the assembly line on the same day. Stuart Ewen, *Captains of Consciousness: Advertising and the Social Roots of the Consumer Culture* (New York: McGraw-Hill, 1976), 45.

24. Griffiths, *A Sideways Look at Time*, 47.

25. David Schrank and Tim Lomax, 2005 *Urban Mobility Study* (Texas Transportation Institute, 2005), http://mobility.tamu.edu/ums/media_information/news_release.stm; Griffiths, *A Sideways Look at Time*, 47.

26. For a good look at the politics of SUVs, for example, see Keith Bradsher, *High and Mighty: SUVs: The World's Most Dangerous Vehicles and How They Got That Way* (New York: PublicAffairs, 2002), 238–70.

27. Ian Roberts, "Car Wars," *Guardian*, January 18, 2003; Jonathan Gaw, "By the Numbers," *Star Tribune*, January 14, 2007; National Defense Council Foundation, "The Hidden Costs of Oil: An Update," http://www.ndcf.org. For more on the real costs of cars, see Terry Tamminen, *Lives Per Gallon: The True Cost of Our Oil Addiction* (Washington, D.C.: Island Press, 2006).

28. For a brilliant analysis of how Americans treat the public sphere (including public transportation), see Jedediah Purdy, *For Common Things: Irony, Trust, and Commitment in America Today* (New York: Alfred A. Knopf, 1999), 77–128.

29. Gregg Easterbrook, *The Progress Paradox: How Life Gets Better While People Feel Worse* (New York: Random House, 2003), 94.

30. As one of my students said, responding to this passage, "It's more that we can't park on campus when there are *open* spaces—like over the weekend. Public safety [officers] are like Nazis, giving too many tickets. But here I'm showing our tendency to feel *entitled* to keep a car on campus."

31. Robert Wood Johnson Foundation, "A Matter of Degree: The National Effort to Reduce High-Risk Drinking among College Students."

32. With the cost of college tuition rising rapidly, many students work to make ends meet—and many of their jobs are off-campus, in the minimum-wage service positions that spring up around institutions of higher learning.

Working as retail clerks, cooks, waitresses, or baristas, students need to move from classes to the job expeditiously. More than 60 percent of college parents expect their students to work during college. The number of college students working full-time has increased from three hundred thousand in 1985 to nearly eight hundred thousand in 2005. And sometimes, of course, they need a car to get to work to make money to pay for their car. As one student said in 2006, "I work so I can pay for my car and go out at night." See Al Gore's movie, *An Inconvenient Truth* (2006), and the companion book, *An Inconvenient Truth: The Planetary Emergency of Global Warming and What We Can Do About It* (Emmaus, PA: Rodale Books, 2006) for more on convenient truths.

33. "Average Household Expenditures by Major Spending Category: 2003," Research and Innovative Technology Administration, Bureau of Transportation Statistics, http://www.bts.gov/publications/pocket_guide_to_transportation /2005/html/figure_10_table.html (accessed June 21, 2010). Cars seem cheaper than buses and trains, but that's often illusory. Their seeming inexpensiveness comes more from the *method* of payment than from the *amount* of payment. With public transportation, we usually pay for each trip (unless we buy a pass). With a car, we only seem to pay when we buy gas. In between pumping, we seem to be driving for free. Because we forget the fixed costs of owning a car, we underestimate their cost and convenience. In 1996, Northwest Environment Watch estimated the actual cost of driving a car at $1.05 a mile. Few trips on public transportation ever cost that much. Alan Thein Durning, *The Car and the City* (Seattle: Northwest Environment Watch, 1996), 47.

34. Griffiths, *A Sideways Look at Time*, 42.

35. Cambridge Energy Research Associates, "Gasoline Prices, Regulations & Demographics Transforming America's 'Love Affair with the Automobile,'" press release, November 30, 2006, http://www2.cera.com/gasoline/press/1,2231,00. html (accessed June 21, 2010).

36. World Carfree Network, "Some Statistics," http://www.worldcarfree. net/resources/stats.php#5 (accessed June 21, 2010). Mark S. Foster, *A Nation on Wheels: The Automobile Culture in America Since 1945* (Belmont, CA: Wadsworth, 2003), 132. Both Toyota and Honda have factories with nearly zero waste going to landfills (although this doesn't account for wastes produced before final factory assembly). Toyota added a 2.3-megawatt solar array to its factory in Ontario, California. But cars are still resource-intensive productions. Honda, for example, reports that producing an average car requires 800 gallons of water and 6.7 gigajoules of energy, with 747 kilograms of carbon dioxide emissions. Honda of America Manufacturing, "Honda Issues 2009 Environmental Report," press release, http://www.ohio.honda.com/pressroom /View_Release.cfm?articleid=213 (accessed June 21, 2010).

37. Andrea Coombes, "Teens a Sure Road to Higher Auto Rates," *MarketWatch*, November 6, 2005.

38. See Charles Perrow, *Normal Accidents: Living with High-Risk Technologies* (Princeton: Princeton University Press, 1999). We usually think of accidents as truly accidental, and, on a micro level they are. By definition, accidents are never individually intentional, but collectively they do seem that way. We know

that forty thousand people a year will die in car accidents, but we intend to drive our cars anyway. We may never hit another vehicle, but we drive the system of accidents just the same.

39. For roadkill statistics, see David Havlick, "Road Kill," *Conservation Magazine*, Winter 2004, http://www.conservationmagazine.org/2008/07/road-kill (accessed June 21, 2010), and Donna Daniels, "Vehicle-Deer Crashes," www.associatedcontent.com/article/94541/vehicle_deer_crashes_about_15_million.html (accessed June 21, 2010). See also Juliet Eilperin, "U.S. Wants Polar Bears Listed as Threatened," *Washington Post*, December 27, 2006.

40. James Gustave Speth, *The Bridge at the Edge of the World*, 76; Hannah Berg, "The Creation of Place: Context, Continuity and the Common Good in Northfield, Minnesota," unpublished ms., 2006; Michael Hough, *Out of Place: Restoring Identity to the Regional Landscape* (New Haven: Yale University Press, 1990), 100. See also James Howard Kunstler, *The Geography of Nowhere: The Rise and Decline of America's Man-Made Landscape* (New York: Touchstone, 1994).

41. John A. Jakle and Keith A. Sculle, *Lots of Parking: Land Use in a Car Culture* (Charlottesville: University of Virginia Press, 2005); Center for Land Use Education, "Rain and Snow—Where Do They Go . . . and What Do They Take with Them?" *Land Use Tracker*, Winter 2002, http://www.uwsp.edu/cnr/landcenter/tracker/winter2002/RainandSnow.htm (accessed June 21, 2010). Automobiles also change the character of wild and scenic landscapes. Many of the national parks in the United States predate the car culture, but motor vehicles have materially changed the nature of national parks. With cars, more people can get to the parks. But they get to parks that have been thoroughly modified by cars. Ribbons of asphalt and lots of parking subdivide the natural landscape. Car emissions affect the air that visitors (and resident plants and animals) breathe.

42. Thoreau's "Walking" is, by contrast, a celebration of pedestrianism. To Thoreau, walking was valuable because it connected people to the earth. Sauntering through the countryside, he established relationships with the plants and animals he passed. Thoreau mocked the people who were "going places," calling the railroad an improved means to an unimproved end. He wanted to experience places, not just traverse them. Imagine Thoreau on "Driving."

43. "Planet Gets a Lemon as Global Car Industry Revs Up," Worldwatch Institute, July 18, 2007, http://www.worldwatch.org/node/5197/print (accessed June 22, 2010).

44. "Air and Breathing," Environmed Research, http://www.nutramed.com/environment/carsepa.htm (accessed June 22, 2010).

45. Griffiths, *A Sideways Look at Time*, 42.

46. Speth, *The Bridge at the Edge of the World*, 75. Carbon calculations come from "How Can a Gallon of Gasoline Produce 20 pounds of Carbon Dioxide?" U.S. Department of Energy/U.S. Environmental Protection Agency, http://www.fueleconomy.gov/feg/co2.shtml (accessed June 22, 2010); on sinks, see Bill McKibben, *Maybe One: A Personal and Environmental Argument for Single-Child Families* (New York: Simon & Schuster, 1998), 92. Oceans aren't disappearing, of course, but their capacity to sequester carbon is declining due

to saturation. And the carbon already sequestered is threatening aquatic life at the base of the oceanic food chain.

47. For more on campus-transportation planning, see "Resources About Sustainable Transportation on Campus," Association for the Advancement of Sustainability in Higher Education, http://www.aashe.org/resources/transportation.php (accessed June 22, 2010), and Will Toor and Spenser Havlick, *Transportation and Sustainable Campus Communities: Issues, Examples, Solutions* (Washington, DC: Island Press, 2004).

48. Katie Alvord, *Divorce Your Car!: Ending the Love Affair with the Automobile* (Gabriola Island, BC: New Society, 2000); Chris Balish, *How to Live Well Without Owning a Car: Save Money, Breathe Easier, and Get More Mileage Out of Life* (Berkeley: Ten Speed Press, 2006).

49. For thoughtful perspectives on America's religion of cars, see *Word & World: Theology for Christian Ministry*, Summer 2008.

50. For a short introduction to such planning, see Alan Thein Durning, *The Car and the City: 24 Steps to Safe Streets and Healthy Communities* (Seattle: Northwest Environment Watch, 1996).

51. For a rich description of a new world beyond cars, see Elizabeth Farrelly, *Blubberland: The Dangers of Happiness* (Cambridge: MIT Press, 2008), 189–203. For a short introduction to land-use planning and automobility, see Alan Thein Durning, *The Car and the City.* And for an online introduction to car-free cities, see Carfree Cities, http://www.carfree.com/intro_cfc.html (accessed June 22, 2010).

Notes to Chapter 6

1. Victoria J. Rideout, Ulla G. Foehr, and Donald F. Roberts, "Generation M2: Media in the Lives of 8- to 18-Year-Olds" (Menlo Park, CA: Kaiser Family Foundation, 2010), at http://www.kff.org/entmedia/upload/8010.pdf (accessed June 22, 2010).

2. Rick Perlstein argues that college isn't college anymore, and that the reason for this is electronic connections. In the past, he says, college was a rite of passage because students distanced themselves from one set of connections to get perspective on the world and their lives. Now, with the connectivity of cell phones and the Internet, students move physically but not psychically. Perlstein, "What's the Matter With College?" *New York Times Magazine*, September 30, 2007.

3. For "Trends in Technology Use Among Entering College Students," see Pryor et. al., *The American Freshman*, pp. 15–17; Michael Snider, "Hey, Kids—Let's Play Adver-games!" *Macleans* (23 December 2002), cited on Word Spy at http://www.wordspy.com/words/screenager.asp.

4. Langdon Winner, *The Whale and the Reactor: A Search for Limits in an Age of High Technology* (Chicago: University of Chicago Press, 1988), 6. For an introduction to "invisible technologies," see Neil Postman, *Technopoly: The Surrender of Culture to Technology* (New York: Vintage, 1992), esp. 123–43.

5. Rideout, Foehr, and Roberts, *Generation M2*, 9, 16–17; Douglas Kellner, *Television and the Crisis of Democracy* (Boulder: Westview, 1990), 126; Zollo,

Getting Wiser to Teens, 192, 345–50. "Through repeated observations of real-life models and models portrayed in the media, as well as by reflecting on the consequences of their own behaviors in social situations, children develop normative beliefs about what social behaviors are appropriate." In other words, culture teaches us what's "natural." Eric F. Dubow, L. Rowell Huesmann, Dara Greenwood, "Media and Youth Socialization," in *Handbook of Socialization: Theory and Research*, ed. Joan E. Grusec and Paul D. Hastings (New York: Guilford, 2006), 405–6. Maren Gelle notes that we learn to watch television in our families, and for many of us, TV is almost a member of the family, which makes you wonder about so-called "family values."

6. Annie Dillard, *The Writing Life* (New York: Harper Perennial, 1990), 32–33. "Human contact with other species and wild nature is increasingly mediated through the television, constrained within the safe confines of the rectangular screen. There seems to be a growing societal blindness to the beauty, succor, and necessity of the more-than-human world." Anthony Leiserowitz and Lisa O. Fernandez, "Toward a New Consciousness."

7. Eric Weil, untitled charts and graphs, Student Monitor, 2008, at http://www.media-tech.net/fileadmin/podcast_source/download.php?select=Eric_Weil_PM%20Student%20Monitor.pdf (accessed June 22, 2010). Men and women watch the world differently. The top shows for guys were *Family Guy*, *SportsCenter*, *The Simpsons*, *24*, *Law and Order*, *South Park*, and *The Daily Show*. The top shows for women were *Grey's Anatomy*, *American Idol*, *Desperate Housewives*, *Real World*, *Friends*, and *Family Guy*. College men live in a world of cynical and satirical cartoons and comedy shows, along with sports, crime shows, and adventure shows. Coeds inhabit a different world of soap operas, talent shows, and sociability serials. Neither men nor women are watching many nature shows. Student Monitor, *Lifestyle and Media*, Spring 2006, 29–30.

8. Dubow, Huesmann, and Greenwood, "Media and Youth Socialization," 413–15; Marie Winn, *The Plug-In Drug* (New York: Penguin, 1985). Student Monitor sets the total TV time lower than Nielsen, at about eleven hours a week. Student Monitor, *Lifestyle and Media*, Spring 2006, 31. For the best recent cultural interpretation of television, see Jason Mittell, *Television and American Culture* (New York: Oxford University Press, 2009), even though it has very little on nature and TV.

9. Roni Caryn Rabin, "What Happy People Don't Do," *New York Times*, November 19, 2008; Robert Kubey and Mihali Csikszentmihalyi, "Television Addiction," *Scientific American*, February 23, 2002.

10. Mittell, *Television and American Culture*, 271–76. For a good introduction to cultivation theory, see "Audience Research: Cultivation Analysis," Museum of Broadcast Communications, http://www.museum.tv/eotvsection.php?entrycode=audienceresec (accessed June 22, 2010). For more on the effect of sexual content on young viewers, see Dubow, Huesmann, and Greenwood, "Media and Youth Socialization," 422–24.

11. Dubow, Huesmann, and Greenwood, "Media and Youth Socialization," 409–11.

12. Neil Postman, *Amusing Ourselves to Death: Public Discourse in the Age of Show Business* (New York: Viking, 1984), 3–4.

13. For a great (but dated) introduction to nature on TV, see Bill McKibben, *The Age of Missing Information* (New York: Random House, 1992).

14. For more on nature TV, see Gregg Mitman, *Reel Nature: America's Romance with Wildlife on Film* (Cambridge: Harvard University Press, 1999) and Cynthia Chris, *Watching Wildlife* (Minneapolis: University of Minnesota Press, 2006).

15. Alexander Wilson, *The Culture of Nature: North American Landscape from Disney to the Exxon Valdez* (Cambridge, MA: Blackwell, 1992), 117–56. This expectation of stimulation and entertainment also affects our expectations of college. If professors aren't as interesting or amusing as sitcom characters, we quickly consign them to the "bored room." See Mark Edmundson, "On the Uses of a Liberal Education: As Lite Entertainment for Bored College Students," *Harper's*, September 1997, 39–49.

16. On the aesthetic framing of nature, see Alison Byerly, "The Uses of Landscape: The Picturesque Aesthetic and the National Park System," in *The Ecocriticism Reader: Landmarks in Literary Ecology*, ed. Harold Fromm and Cheryll Glotfelty (Athens: University of Georgia Press, 1996).

17. McKibben, *The Age of Missing Information*, 77–79. Julia Corbett concurs: "The downside of such a focus [on individual species of animals] is the simplistic understanding of ecological systems. It seems to viewers that 'saving' an individual bear or wolf magically saves an entire ecosystem, and that saving only the big, dramatic, top-of-the-food-chain animals saves everything else." Julia Corbett, *Communicating Nature: How We Create and Understand Environmental Messages* (Washington, DC: Island Press, 2006), 127.

18. There's a new "green survivalism" to complement *Survivor*. See Alex Williams, "Duck and Cover: It's the New Survivalism," *New York Times*, April 6, 2008.

19. Alison Anderson, *Media, Culture and the Environment* (New Brunswick: Rutgers University Press, 1997), 107–170.

20. Postman, *Amusing Ourselves to Death*, 99–113.

21. Eviatar Zerubavel, *The Elephant in the Room: Silence and Denial in Everyday Life* (New York: Oxford University Press, 2008), 37.

22. Ross Gelbspan, "Snowed," *Mother Jones*, May/June 2005. See also Gelbspan's *Boiling Point: How Politicians, Big Oil and Coal, Journalists, and Activists Have Fueled the Climate Crisis—And What We Can Do to Avert Disaster* (New York: Basic Books, 2004).

23. See also Richard Doherty and Kevin G. Barnhurst, "Controlling Nature: Weathercasts on Local Television News," *Journal of Broadcasting and Electronic Media*, June 2009, 211–26.

24. Online there's even a Disaster News Network, at http://www.disasternews .net.

25. Americans are so accustomed to ads during the news that we take them for granted. But they tell us implicitly that this material isn't too important for

interruption. Try this thought experiment: What would you think of ads in the middle of a sermon at church, or a presidential address, or even a good heart-to-heart talk with your lover?

26. McKibben, *The Age of Missing Information*, 21. Purchasing power is why the Nielsen company began tracking college viewing in 2006. Advertisers want to reach students, and Nielsen tells them where they are. Mike Budd, Steve Craig, and Clay Steinman, *Consuming Environments: Television and Commercial Culture* (New Brunswick: Rutgers University Press, 1999), xiv, xvii.

27. Martin Green, "Some Versions of the Pastoral: Myth in Advertising, Advertising in Myth," in *Advertising and Culture: Theoretical Perspectives,* ed. Mary Cross (Westport: Praeger, 1996), 29–47.

28. For an example of the commercial sublime, see a "back to nature" Busch ad at http://www.youtube.com/watch?v=Pohw7dZRZk8. For the SUV sublime, see the Mercedes ad at http://www.youtube.com/watch?v=af7k4lpVFl4 (accessed June 22, 2010), or the Subaru commercial, "Ricky," http://www.youtube .com/watch?v=06Wkbi4dywk&feature=related (accessed June 22, 2010), or the Jeep ad where the SUV is "a force of nature," at http://www.youtube.com/ watch?v=L-veh6JN1Is&feature=related (accessed June 22, 2010), or the Nissan ad in which an SUV is transformed into wild animals in order to conquer nature at http://www.youtube.com/watch?v=fL38PFux6wE (accessed June 22, 2010). For a good parody of such ads, see the public service announcement at http://www .youtube.com/watch?v=4oNedC3joe4 (accessed June 22, 2010).

29. Richard White, "'Are You an Environmentalist or Do You Work for a Living?' William Cronon's Work and Nature," in *Uncommon Ground: Rethinking the Human Place in Nature* (New York: W. W. Norton, 1996), 171–85. Some students revel in the outdoor recreation represented on TV. In backpacking or camping, stripped of the superfluities of civilization, people discover a better sense of the bare necessities of life. They learn that the trappings of civilization are often just a trap, and that they can find exuberance and fulfillment without a lot of stuff or programming. But even in the wild, there's American materialism. As one student suggested, "You have to look, dress, and act a certain way to be involved in nature." Another observed, "Nature is portrayed as a lifestyle on TV. It is given a certain image with clothes and accessories and people who are hippies, wear Birkenstocks, and go camping all the time, sleeping in tents." If we don't have the right gear, it seems, our experience of nature would be less fulfilling. As one student suggested, "We develop product associations with nature and then we almost become product placements when we go into nature."

30. Shane Gunster contends that ads promising power, control, and menace are geared not just for driving, but for surviving in the increasingly hostile marketplace of neoliberal economics. "In this context," he says, "nature provides an ideal marketing signifier because it expresses the utopian desire to escape this environment into an Edenic paradise but *simultaneously* gives voice to the dystopian fear that retreat into a defensive shell is the only option left for comfortable survival. Desire and fear, utopia and dystopia, natural imagery sponsors the blending of these disparate emotions and ideals into a fluid, if schizophrenic,

promotional field that accommodates the affective mobility of consumers as they shift back and forth from one pole to another." Shane Gunster, "'You Belong Outside': Advertising, Nature, and the SUV," *Ethics & the Environment*, 2004, 18. See also Catherine M. Roach, "Thinking Like a God: Nature Imagery in Advertising." *Reconstruction* 7, no. 2 (2007), http://reconstruction.eserver. org/072/roach.shtml (accessed June 22, 2010).

31. For a great spoof of air freshener ads (and a critique of "clean coal"), see "Clean Coal Air Freshener," http://www.youtube.com/watch?v=W-_U1Z0vezw (accessed June 22, 2010).

32. See the ads on YouTube: "Ford Commercial Greenwashing," "2010 Toyota Prius 'Harmony' TV Commercial," "Energy Tomorrow Ad" (American Petroleum Institute), "Apple—MacBook Pro—The Cleanest Family of Notebooks," and "Clean Coal Technology." See also "The Seven Sins of Greenwashing," TerraChoice Environmental Marketing, http://sinsofgreenwashing.org/findings/ the-seven-sins (accessed June 22, 2010). For examples of greenwashing, see YouTube and "Greenwashing index," EnviroMedia Social Marketing, http:// www.greenwashingindex.com (accessed June 22, 2010). For a broader response to corporate greening, see Adrian Parr, *Hijacking Sustainability* (Cambridge: MIT Press, 2009).

33. "Orienting personal environmentalism around consumer choice . . . may as much as anything perpetuate the antiactivist thinking on which the system depends." Mike Budd, Steve Craig, and Clayton M. Steinman *Consuming Environments: Television and Commercial Culture* (New Brunswick: Rutgers University Press, 1999), 5. See also the discussion of "the individualization of responsibility" in chapter 10.

34. For a great critique of the imaginary and actual natures involved in American materialism, see Jennifer Price, "Looking for Nature at the Mall," in *Flight Maps: Adventures with Nature in Modern America* (New York: Basic Books, 1999), 168–206, and James Farrell, "The Nature of the Mall," in *One Nation Under Goods*, 33–52.

35. Bob Shanks, *The Cool Fire: How to Make It in Television* (New York: Vintage, 1976), 98.

36. Juliet B. Schor, *The Overspent American: Upscaling, Downshifting and the New Consumer* (New York: Basic Books, 1998), 78. For more on TV as a primary agent of materialism, see Tim Kasser, *The High Price of Materialism* (Cambridge: MIT Press, 2002), 53–57.

37. On desensitization, see Dubow, Huesmann, and Greenwood, "Media and Youth Socialization," 412. Bill McKibben suggests that TV makes the modern world seem ordinary and normal. But he also notes that the last half of the twentieth century was an unprecedented "binge" in which people used more natural resources than all the people who ever lived before then. But on TV, "this binge seems utterly standard, and it's exceedingly hard to imagine other models, societies, ideas." McKibben, *The Age of Missing Information*, 65. For a brilliant critique of mediation in America, see Thomas de Zengotita, *Mediated: How the Media Shapes Your World and the Way You Live In It* (New York: Bloomsbury, 2005).

38. "TV, Internet and Mobile Usage in U.S. Keeps Increasing, Says Nielsen," press release, February 23, 2009, http://blog.nielsen.com/nielsenwire/wp-content /uploads/2009/02/3_screen-press-release-4q08-final_022309.pdf (accessed June 22, 2010).

39. Wendell Berry, *Standing by Words* (San Francisco: North Point Press, 1983), 25–26.

40. Dubow, Huesmann, and Greenwood, "Media and Youth Socialization," 406; Rideout, Foehr, and Roberts, *Generation M2*, 20–23; Reynol Junco and Gail A. Cole-Avent, "An Introduction to Technologies Commonly Used by College Students," *Student Engagement: New Directions for Student Services*, Winter 2008, 4, 9.

41. "Press Room," Facebook, http://www.facebook.com/press/info. php?statistics (accessed June 22, 2010).

42. For a quick history of Facebook, see John Cassidy, "Me Media," *New Yorker*, May 15, 2006. Maggie Shiels, "Facebook Clocks Fifth Birthday," *BBC News*, February 4, 2009, http://news.bbc.co.uk/2/hi/technology/7868403.stm (accessed June 22, 2010); "Quick Facts," The Facebook Project, http://www .thefacebookproject.com/wiki/index.php?title=Quick_Facts (accessed June 22, 2010). ·

43. If given fifteen minutes of spare time, 17 percent of us would spend it on a social network compared to just 14 percent who would spend it with the television and 9 percent who would play a video game. In fact, social networking is so popular among those aged eighteen to twenty-four that it has overtaken pornography as the most visited category of site on the Internet. Bill Tancer notes that in the last two years, as Facebook has gained in popularity, the adult entertainment industry has seen negatively correlating declines in hits, dropping 33 percent. It seems that either social networks have so filled our days that we have stopped looking at pornography or that some of the same attractions are bringing us to Facebook, and the content there is perversely fulfilling some of the same desires. "Facebook: More Popular Than Porn?" *Time*, October 31, 2007.

44. In 2004 business manager Chris Hughes hoped that Facebook would be limited to small communities, saying, "We're trying to keep it to a realistic size so it's not completely disconnected from the everyday lives of people that are using it." While Facebook originally constrained contact to people in one's physically limited network, now it is decidedly global. The ideal of keeping connections between spatially near people has lost out to profit motives, as has always been the case with markets.

45. For a good introduction to identity issues on the Internet, see Danah Boyd, "Why Youth (Heart) Social Network Sites: The Role of Networked Publics in Teenage Social Life," in *Youth, Identity, and Media*, ed. David Buckingham (Cambridge: MIT Press, 2008): 119–42, as well as Buckingham's introduction to the volume.

46. Jean Baudrillard, "The Implosion of Meaning in the Media," in *Simulacra and Simulation* (1994), trans. by Sheila Faria Glaser, http://www.egs.edu/ faculty/baudrillard/baudrillard-simulacra-and-simulation-08-the-implosion-of-meaning-in-the-media.html (accessed June 22, 2010).

47. "Press Room," Facebook, http://www.facebook.com/press/info.php? statistics (accessed June 22, 2010).

48. Robert Bellah, *Habits of the Heart*, 115; Maggie Jackson, *Distracted: The Erosion of Attention and the Coming Dark Age* (Amherst, NY: Prometheus Books, 2008), 54–55.

49. Thanks to Brett Werner for help with this section.

50. Jackson, *Distracted*, 48.

51. Ibid., 84–87.

52. Eric D. Williams, Robert U. Ayres, and Miriam Heller, "The 1.7 kg. Microchip," http://www.it-environment.org/publications/1.7kg%20microchip.pdf (accessed June 22, 2010).

53. The website Wattzon.com estimates that a desktop computer includes 1,516,044,000 joules of embodied energy, while a laptop logs in at 1,136,097,000 joules.

54. For an introduction to electronic waste and e-cycling, see "eCycling," U.S. Environmental Protection Agency, http://www.epa.gov/waste/conserve/materials/ecycling/index.htm (accessed June 22, 2010).

55. Thomas L. Friedman, *Hot, Flat, and Crowded: Why We Need a Green Revolution—and How It Can Renew America* (New York: Farrar, Straus and Giroux, 2008), 333; "Down on the Server Farm," *Economist*, May 22, 2008; "Server Farms Becoming a Cash Crop in the Midwest," RedOrbit, May 7, 2008; Tom Vanderbilt, "Data Center Overload," *New York Times Magazine*, June 14, 2009. See also Jonathan Leake and Richard Woods, "Revealed: The Environmental Impact of Google Searches," *Times UK*, January 12, 2009.

56. Andrew Heining, "Facebooking the Biden-Palin Debate," *Christian Science Monitor*, October 3, 2008.

57. Eric Sorensen, *Seven Wonders for a Cool Planet: Everyday Things to Help Solve Global Warming* (San Francisco: Sierra Club Books, 2008), 98.

58. Ibid., 95.

59. Ibid., 94–95.

60. Jeff Young "Animated Polar Bear in Distress Pleads With Dartmouth Students to Save Energy," *Chronicle of Higher Education*, June 2, 2008.

61. Jackson, *Distracted*, 34, 175.

62. *Time*, (August 17, 1998) 1–2.

63. Wendell Berry, *What Are People For?* (San Francisco: North Point Press, 1990), 170–77. The question of human purpose is crucial. Berry wants to know what makes us human, and what makes us more human. In many ways, it's the unasked question of American technological innovation. We continually show that we have the know-how to produce inventive devices, but we're seldom as clear about the know-why.

64. The shift "From Consumers to Activists" is described more extensively in Mike Budd, Steve Craig, and Clay Steinman, *Consuming Environments*, 169–86.

65. Thoreau's *Walden* is, if you think about it, a perfect example of a plot project, making sense of his world by making sense of his place. Some other exemplary plot projects include William Least Heat Moon's *PrairyErth (A*

Deep Map) (Boston: Houghton Mifflin, 1991), Chet Raymo's *The Path: A One-Mile Walk through the Universe* (New York: Walker and Company, 2003), and Hannah Holmes, *Suburban Safari: A Year on the Lawn* (New York: Bloomsbury, 2005). For a book that integrates wisdom and practices, see Christopher Uhl, *Developing Ecological Consciousness: Path to a Sustainable World* (Boulder: Rowman & Littlefield, 2004).

66. John Cassidy, "Me Media," *New Yorker.*

67. Kathleen Dean Moore. *Pine Island Paradox*, 62.

68. We need appropriate technology, of course, but such technologies will only come from an appropriate culture—a culture designed to harmonize with nature's designs.

Notes to Chapter 7

1. As Peter Zollo suggests, "Teens are adept at shutting out classroom instruction. When a teacher is lecturing, chances are most students aren't fully listening—instead they're thinking about next period, the game after school, the weekend's festivities, or sex (you heard it here first!)." Zollo, *Getting Wiser to Teens*, 212.

2. Pew Research Center, "A Portrait of 'Generation Next:' How Young People View Their Lives, Futures and Politics," January 9, 2007, http://people-press .org/reports/pdf/300.pdf (accessed June 22, 2010); Zollo, *Getting Wiser to Teens*, 42, 47. For a summary of "What College Students Do for Fun," see Arthur Levine and Jeanette Cureton, *When Hope and Fear Collide: A Portrait of Today's College Student* (San Francisco: Jossey Bass, 1998), 98–99.

3. Michael Moffatt, *Coming of Age in New Jersey: College and American Culture* (New Brunswick: Rutgers University Press, 1989), 28–29.

4. "Inside College Parties: Surprising Findings About Drinking Behavior," *ScienceDaily*, January 6, 2008. Jodie Morse, "Women on a Binge," *Time*, April 1, 2002, 56–61. Beer Pong is now available for the Nintendo Wii. See "Beer Pong to WiiWare," May 21, 2008, IGN.com, http://wii.ign.com/articles/875/875849p1 .html (accessed June 22, 2010).

5. American College Health Association, *National College Health Assessment, Reference Group Executive Summary, Fall 2006* (Baltimore: American College Health Association, 2007), 9.

6. Researchers at Rutgers call this "socially situated experiential learning." For more, see Linda C. Lederman, Lea P. Stewart, Sherry L. Barr, Richard Powell, Lisa Laitman and Fern W. Goodhart, "The Role of Communication Theory in Experiential Learning in Addressing Dangerous Drinking on the College Campus," in Linda C. Lederman, W. David Gibson, and Maureen Taylor, *Communcation Theory: A Casebook Approach* (Dubuque: Kendall/Hunt, 1998), 329.

7. Koren Zailckas, *Smashed: Story of a Drunken Girlhood* (New York: Viking, 2005), 7.

8. Ibid., 113.

9. Mike Snider, "iPods Knock Over Beer Mugs," *USA Today*, June 7, 2006. Alcohol is widespread on campus, but it's not as widespread as Joe and Jo

College think it is. In 2006, the American College Health Association asked college students how many of them never used alcohol, and they asked students to estimate the number of nondrinkers. More than 20 percent of students reported that they never drank, but students estimated that number at about 4 percent. In the same way, while roughly 65 percent of students drank in the last month, students estimated that 85 percent did. And while only 0.4 percent of students drink daily, their peers estimated that almost 37 percent are daily drinkers. There's plenty of drinking in college, but there's plenty of imagination, too. And perceptions of drinking fuel peer pressure even more than peer behavior does. American College Health Association, *National College Health Assessment, Reference Group Executive Summary, Fall 2006* (Baltimore: American College Health Association, 2007), 7.

10. Few people have told students (and even fewer have *shown* students) that scholarship is intellectual play, and a delight to be doing. So students interpret schoolwork as drudgery.

11. Even before college, American teens feel stressed. When asked their biggest complaints about their daily life, 31 percent of teens said "stress," 29 percent said "not having enough time in the day," and 25 percent said "not enough sleep." A fifth of students cited school as a complaint, while almost a third suffered from "not enough money." Zollo, *Getting Wiser to Teens*, 295. Zollo also notes that teens "generally love their busy lifestyle . . . (it sure beats being bored)."

12. Zollo, *Getting Wiser to Teens*, 272. As usual, Zollo presents the cultural patterns of the weekend as a marketing opportunity, useful "for developing promotions that both motivate them and reach them where they play." The movie *Merchants of Cool* also shows brilliantly how advertisers and marketers appeal to the *fun*-damentalism of teens.

13. Ibid., 42–43. See also Kathleen A. Bogle, *Hooking Up: Sex, Dating, and Relationships on Campus* (New York: New York University Press, 2008), 51–52.

14. Boredom first emerged as a concept in the eighteenth century, when some people acquired enough leisure to be bored. It also coincided with individualism and the assumption that individuals had a right to happiness. It grew quickly with the rise of consumer culture, in which advertisers cultivate dissatisfaction. And it followed the rise of reflexive consciousness in a therapeutic society, as people learned how to focus on their own "inner experience." As a result, according to Adam Phillips, "we become more sensitive to our emptinesses, and more obsessed by what we lack." To some extent, too, the boredom of Jo and Joe College comes from their marginalization of meta-narratives, those cultural and institutional stories (often religious) that gave meaning and purpose to life. As people in the developed world focused more on their own stories than on the stories of their traditions and communities, the "Te Deum" of religion was replaced by tedium. Without the frame of a purpose-driven life, life sometimes seems to be just one damn thing after another. And that can be boring. Adam Phillips, "The Joy of Boredom," *New York Times*, December 18, 1994.

15. John D. Spalding, "Ah, Boredom!" SoMA (The Society of Mutual Autopsy): A Review of Religion and Culture, http://www.somareview.com/boredom.cfm (accessed June 22, 2010).

16. Part of the collateral learning of college is, in fact, how to cope with boredom. See, for example, CollegeBoredom (www.collegeboredom.com), the "home of bored college students," and CollegeHumor (www.collegehumor.com).

17. Mary Catherine Bateson, *Peripheral Visions: Learning Along the Way* (New York: HarperCollins, 1994), 56.

18. For a quick introduction to the brewing of beer, see the Wikipedia entry on beer: http://en.wikipedia.org/wiki/Beer (accessed June 22, 2010).

19. For a good introduction to environmental changes in brewing, see Kyle Cassidy, "Brewing Change: Why Craft Beer Makers Go Green," *Wend*, June 24, 2009, http://www.wendmag.com/greenery/2009/06/sustainable-craft-brewing (accessed June 22, 2010).

20. American College Health Association, *National College Health Assessment, Reference Group Executive Summary, Fall 2006* (Baltimore: American College Health Association, 2007), 9.

21. This is true of other forms of college fun, too. Dinner and a movie involve consumption, but people need to eat anyway. Intramural sports expend lots of energy, but it's mostly human energy. And sexual fun is a low-impact activity, unless there's a pregnancy.

22. Neil Postman, *Amusing Ourselves to Death*.

23. Thomas Pynchon, *Gravity's Rainbow* (New York: Penguin Classics, 1995), 251.

24. Maren Gelle, "Facets of Fun," unpublished ms., 2008.

25. Moises Velasquez-Manoff, "Why Your Happiness Matters to the Planet," *Christian Science Monitor*, July 22, 2008.

26. For an introduction to positive psychology and the science of hedonics (happiness), see Martin E. P. Seligman and Mihali Csikszentmihalyi, "Positive Psychology: An Introduction," *American Psychologist*, January 2000, 5–14.

27. J. A. Schmidt, D. J. Shernoff, and M. Csikszentmihalyi, "Individual and Situational Factors Related to the Experience of Flow in Adolescence," in *Oxford Handbook of Methods in Positive Psychology*, eds. A. D. Ong and M. H. M. van Dulmen (Oxford: Oxford University Press, 2006), 387–95.

28. Moises Velasquez-Manoff, "Why Your Happiness Matters to the Planet," *Christian Science Monitor*. See also Tim Kasser, *The High Price of Materialism* (Cambridge: MIT Press, 2002).

29. Laura Smith-Spark, "Schwarzenegger: Make Climate Hip," *BBC News*, April 11, 2007, http://news.bbc.co.uk/2/hi/americas/6546975.stm (accessed June 22, 2010).

Notes to Chapter 8

1. Deborah Roffman, "What Our Kids Know About Sex: All Mechanics, No Meaning," *Washington Post*, June 9, 2002.

2. Chris Harris, "Back to School, Back to Sex," *Hartford Advocate*, September 5, 2001. For a scathing fictional description of the new college sexual mores, see Tom Wolfe's awful novel, *I Am Charlotte Simmons*. For thoughtful, nuanced portraits, see Donna Freitas, *Sex and the Soul: Judging Sexuality, Spirituality, Romance,*

and Religion on America's College Campuses (New York: Oxford University Press, 2008) and Bogle, *Hooking Up*.

3. We get so focused on sex and love that we forget that there are larger issues, many of them environmental. How important is it, after all, to be "hot" on a warming planet? To screw around when we're systematically screwing up the environment? For more on the culture of distraction, see Postman, *Amusing Ourselves to Death*.

4. Moffatt, *Coming of Age in New Jersey*, 229, 254–55. Committed relationships, students think, "interfere with the goal of having fun" (Bogle, *Hooking Up*, 51). For a summary of how evolutionary biologists approach human sex, see Jared Diamond, *Why Is Sex Fun?* (New York: Basic Books, 1997).

5. Bogle, *Hooking Up*, 158–86; Freitas, *Sex and the Soul*, 136. TV affects the way we look at ourselves and at the opposite sex. A 2008 study shows that those of us who watch the sexiest shows on TV are more likely to act sexy, have sex, and become pregnant (or get a partner pregnant).

6. Yabroff, "Campus Sexperts," *Newsweek*, February 16, 2008; Pew Research Center, "A Portrait of Generation Next"; Levine and Cureton, *When Hope and Fear Collide*, 109; Bogle, *Hooking Up*, 165. According to the American College Health Association, about 44 percent of men and 43 percent of women had engaged in oral sex in the last thirty days, while 44 percent of men and 47 percent of women had experienced intercourse in the same time period. American College Health Association, *National College Health Assessment, Reference Group Executive Summary, Fall 2006* (Baltimore: American College Health Association, 2007), 10.

7. Freitas, *Sex and the Soul*, xviii, 5–6, 101, 126–36, 144–51; Norval Glenn, *Hooking Up, Hanging Out, and Hoping for Mr. Right: College Women on Dating and Mating Today* (New York: Institute for American Values, 2001), 13–23; Bogle, *Hooking Up*, 9, 27. "What fosters hookup culture . . . is not student culture alone," says Freitas. "Hookup culture is aided and abetted by all sorts of additional factors: administrators turning a blind eye, parents who don't know and perhaps don't want to know what their kids are really doing, the ongoing marginalization and trivialization of feminism by younger women and men, and a society that still treats men as gods and women as objects for male sexual pleasure and enjoyment." Freitas, *Sex and the Soul*, 213. On student misperceptions of the prevalence of hook-up culture, see Bogle, *Hooking Up*, 72–95.

8. Laura Vanderkam, "Hookups Starve the Soul," *USA Today*, July 25, 2001; *Hooking Up, Hanging Out*, 20–21.

9. Elizabeth L. Paul et al., "'Hookups': Characteristics and Correlates of College Students' Spontaneous and Anonymous Sexual Experiences," *Journal of Sex Research*, February 2000, 77; Bogle, *Hooking Up*, 47, 63–64, 166–68; Harris, "Back to School, Back to Sex," *Hartford Advocate*. In her research, Donna Freitas found that "the relationship between random hookups and sex while drinking to excess is *not* the norm" for about half the students at mainstream colleges and universities (Freitas, *Sex and the Soul*, 139–40).

10. David Knox et al., "College Student Attitudes Toward Sexual Intimacy," *College Student Journal*, June 2001; Freitas, *Sex and the Soul*, 142–58. Kathleen

Bogle's *Hooking Up* is also eloquent about the power that men have over women in hook-up culture. However, although men and women are different, they're not completely different. In "Why Humans Have Sex," Meston and Buss found men listed more physical and social-status reasons for sex, but they also found that men and women shared eight of the top ten reasons for having sex, and twenty of the top twenty-five. Cindy M. Meston and David M. Buss, "Why Humans Have Sex," *Archives of Sexual Behavior*, August 2007, 480–81.

11. American College Health Association, *National College Health Assessment, Reference Group Executive Summary, Fall 2006* (Baltimore: American College Health Association, 2007), 6. Men also experience sexual violation, but at much lower rates.

12. Freitas, *Sex and the Soul*, 145; Kathleen Fackelmann, "Study: Young Adults Now Find Porn More Acceptable," *USA Today*, December 13, 2007; Pamela Paul, *Pornified: How Pornography Is Transforming Our Lives, Our Relationships, and Our Families* (New York: Times Books, 2005), 1–11.

13. Freitas, *Sex and the Soul*, xv–xix; Bogle, *Hooking Up*, 59, 160. For one interpretation of what college students know (and don't know) about sex, see Joy Davidson, "Carnal Knowledge: 10 Things Most College Students Already Know about Sex and 10 Things They Should Know," *Men's Fitness*, September 1998. For more on why it's hard to express our deepest values, see the discussion in chapter 9 of this book.

14. Jean M. Twenge, *Generation Me: Why Today's Young Americans Are More Confident, Assertive, Entitled—and More Miserable Than Ever Before* (New York: Free Press, 2006), 165; Glenn, *Hooking Up, Hanging Out*, 23.

15. Jeffrey Kluger, "The Science of Romance: Why We Love," *Time*, January 17, 2008.

16. For more on the embodied nature of love, see Helen Fisher, *Why We Love: The Nature and Chemistry of Romantic Love* (New York: Henry Holt, 2004).

17. When Joe College hooks up with the babe from the fraternity party, their bodies aren't the only nature involved in intercourse. On the twenty-first-century college campus, sex is also an occasion for the transmission and proliferation of other organisms. To bacteria and viruses, human sex is an opportunity to travel, a way of reproducing during an act of reproduction. Gonorrhea and syphilis—and bacteria like chlamydia—love casual sex. Viruses like genital warts, herpes, and HIV flourish in cultures of promiscuity. And college students are active collaborators with sexually transmitted infections (STIs) because they are sometimes too drunk or too careless to take protective precautions. Sober students worry about STIs—they're a constant context for all of the coupling (and some of the abstinence) on campus. In a recent study, people aged eighteen to twenty-five worried more about getting a sexually transmitted infection than about finding a job, getting good grades, or caring for friends and parents. And these worries are warranted; almost two-thirds of all STI cases show up in people under twenty-five. Despite the efforts of the advertising industry to place romance in natural settings, not all

nature is friendly to romantic love. Anna Greenberg, "OMG! How Generation Y is Redefining Faith in the iPod Era," http://www.greenbergresearch.com /articles/1218/1829_rebootpoll.pdf (accessed June 22, 2010); Harris, "Back to School, Back to Sex." For a good introduction to STDs, see "Sexually Transmitted Diseases: Brochures," Centers for Disease Control and Prevention, http://www.cdc.gov/std/HealthComm/the-facts.htm (accessed June 22, 2010). Interestingly, college health services have emphasized safe sex, with more emphasis on the safety than on the sex itself. They seem to presume that casual sex is unproblematic, as long as couples use a condom.

18. Recently, it seems that unnatural processes may also be affecting the age of puberty in girls. Breast development, which historically coincided (more or less) with menstrual flow, seems to be happening earlier in American girls. And there may be environmental causes. See Sandra Steingraber, "The Falling Age of Puberty in U.S. Girls: What We Know, What We Need to Know," Breast Cancer Fund, http://www.breastcancerfund.org/media/publications/ falling-age-of-puberty.

19. Clydesdale, *The First Year Out*, 97.

20. For "romantic utopia," see Eva Illouz, *Consuming the Romantic Utopia: Love and the Cultural Contradictions of Capitalism* (Berkeley: University of California Press, 1997).

21. Ibid., 112–52.

22. Ibid., 91–95, 138–40; "EPA Warns of Dangerous Levels of Romance in Air," the *Onion*, February 8, 2006.

23. Tom Wolfe, "Hooking Up: What Life Was Like at the Turn of the Second Millennium: An American's World," in *Hooking Up* (New York: Farrar, Straus and Giroux, 2000), 6. See also Ariel Levy, *Female Chauvinist Pigs: Women and the Rise of Raunch Culture* (New York: Free Press, 2006); Patrice A. Oppliger, *Girls Gone Skank: The Sexualization of Girls in American Culture* (Jefferson: McFarland, 2008); and Susan J. Douglas, *Enlightened Sexism: The Seductive Message That Feminism's Work Is Done* (New York: Times Books, 2010).

24. Levy, *Female Chauvinist Pigs*, 30; Harris, "Back to School, Back to Sex." Not all colleges and not all students in America's colleges participate in raunch culture, of course. For a good description of the countercultural sexual ethos of America's evangelical colleges, see Donna Freitas, *Sex and the Soul*, 57–125.

25. Martha Irvine, "Who's A Grown-Up?" *Star Tribune*, May 16, 2003; *Hooking Up, Hanging Out*, 10–11; Bogle, *Hooking Up*, 172.

26. Inge Bell, Bernard McGrane, and John Gunderson, *This Book Is Not Required: An Emotional Survival Manual for Students* (Thousand Oaks: Pine Forge Press, 1990), 207; Glenn, *Hooking Up, Hanging Out*, 10–12, 50–58.

27. Wolfe, *Hooking Up*, 9.

28. Wendell Berry, "The Body and the Earth," in *The Unsettling of America: Culture & Agriculture* (San Francisco: Sierra Club Books, 1977), 97–140; American College Health Association, *National College Health Assessment, Reference Group Executive Summary, Fall 2006* (Baltimore: American College Health Association, 2007), 11. When anthropologist Michael Moffatt asked his students to write

sexual self-reports, he found that "no student writer of these papers said she or he was ready, even theoretically, to deal with pregnancy or childbirth." Moffatt, *Coming of Age in New Jersey*, 248. On American sex education, Eric Sorensen notes that in America "talk of sex is still taboo in most schools even as it saturates popular culture. Only 10 percent of U.S. students receive comprehensive sex education; one in four U.S. school districts has an abstinence-only curriculum. Through both direct funding and matching grants, the U.S. government steered some $1.5 billion to abstinence-only education programs between 1996 and 2006." Eric Sorensen, *Seven Wonders for a Cool Planet*, 35, 40.

29. John C. Ryan, *Seven Wonders: Everyday Things for a Healthier Planet* (San Francisco: Sierra Club Books, 1999), 21; United Nations, "Global Environmental Outlook," http://www.unep.org/geo/geo4/media (accessed June 22, 2010).

30. Sorensen, *Seven Wonders for a Cool Planet*, 34.

31. "Population Growth and Climate Change," *BMJ*, July 24, 2008. For a really readable introduction to this issue, see Bill McKibben, *Maybe One*.

32. Freitas, *Sex and the Soul*, 209–242.

33. Ibid., 218, 223.

34. Dorothee Soelle, *To Work and To Love*, (Philadelphia: Fortress, 1984) 129–39.

35. Ibid.

36. Ibid., 142.

37. Ibid.,130–33.

38. Ibid.,153. In her book *The Body of God: An Ecological Theology*, Sallie McFague provides a complementary way of seeing the spirit of nature. She suggests that another way to read Genesis is to think of creation as God's deep desire to create some bodies to love—planetary bodies, bodies of water, human bodies, animal bodies, bacterial bodies, etc. McFague describes the Earth as God's body, an expression of God, and suggests that all bodies—including our bodies—embody some of God's hope for the universe. "The world is the bodily presence," she says, "a sacrament of the invisible God." And if we see the world as God's presence, there are implications: "If God is in some sense body . . . then bodies would matter to God—God would love bodies—and salvation would be as concerned with such basic needs as food, clothing and shelter as with matters of the spirit. Salvation would be a social, political and economic matter and not just a matter of the spirit's eternal existence." If anybody's body is somehow also God's body, then it deserves our respect and devotion and love. If the Earth is God's body, then we need to be careful with our planet—genuinely full of care. Sallie McFague, *The Body of God: An Ecological Theology* (Minneapolis: Augsburg Fortress, 1993).

39. Glenn, *Hooking Up, Hanging Out*, 59–68.

40. William Cronon has been an eloquent spokesman for loving nature not just when we're "back to nature," but when we're confronted with nature in every moment of our everyday lives. See "The Trouble with Wilderness: or, Getting Back to the Wrong Nature," in *Uncommon Ground*, 69–90.

41. Moore, *The Pine Island Paradox*, 35–36.

Notes to Chapter 9

1. As Mary Evelyn Tucker and John A. Grim suggest in the introduction to a special issue of *Daedalus* on religion and ecology, "religion is more than simply a belief in a transcendent deity or a means to an afterlife. It is, rather, an orientation to the cosmos and our role in it. We understand religion in its broadest sense as a means whereby humans, recognizing the limitations of phenomenal reality, undertake specific practices to effect self-transformation and community cohesion within a cosmological context. Religion thus refers to those cosmological stories, symbol systems, ritual practices, ethical norms, historical processes, and institutional structures that transmit a view of the human as embedded in a world of meaning and responsibility, transformation and celebration. Religion connects humans with a divine or numinous presence, and with the broader earth community. It links humans with the larger matrix of mystery of life which arises, unfolds, and flourishes." Mary Evelyn Tucker and John A. Grim, "Introduction: The Emerging Alliance of World Religions and Ecology," *Daedalus*, Fall 2001, 14.

2. Craig Calhoun, "Preface," *SSRC Guide: Religious Engagement Among American Undergraduates*, Social Science Resource Council, http://religion .ssrc.org/reguide/index1.html (accessed June 22, 2010). For an account of a religious revival in college classrooms, see John Schmalzbauer and Kathleen A. Mahoney, "American Scholars Return to Studying Religion," *Contexts*, Winter 2008, 16–21. The phrase "from Protestant establishment to established nonbelief" is the subtitle of George Marsden's *The Soul of the American University* (New York: Oxford University Press, 1996).

3. *SSRC Guide: Religious Engagement Among American Undergraduates*, http://religion.ssrc.org/reguide. For more on faculty reluctance to discuss "the big questions," see W. Robert Connor, "Where Have All the Big Questions Gone?" *Inside Higher Ed*, December 12, 2005.

4. One good recent survey is Anna Greenberg, "OMG! How Generation Y Is Redefining Faith In The iPod Era." Although it studies all members of Generation Y (and not just college students), it offers important insights into the varieties of religious experience in this generation. I'll refer to this study throughout the chapter, and cite it below as "OMG!"

5. Clydesdale, *The First Year Out*, 4; Freitas, *Sex and the Soul*, 17–27. Distancing themselves from organized religion can be dangerous, since they lose a counterweight against the extremely organized commercial institutions that prey on them so effectively. For an introduction to "lived religion," see David D. Hall, *Lived Religion in America* (Princeton: Princeton University Press, 1997), and Robert A. Orsi, *Between Heaven and Earth: The Religious Worlds People Make and the Scholars Who Study Them* (Princeton: Princeton University Press, 2006). For a good introduction to American religious diversity, see Diana L. Eck, *A New Religious America: How a 'Christian Country' Has Become the World's Most Religiously Diverse Nation* (New York: HarperCollins, 2001). For the most recent work on college-age Americans, see Christian Smith and Patricia Snell,

Souls in Transition: The Religious and Spiritual Lives of Emerging Adults (New York: Oxford University Press, 2009).

6. David Brooks calls this personalized religion "flexidox" ("OMG!," 3, 6, 10). In many ways, their faith—and religious privatism—resembles the "Sheilaism" expressed in Robert Bellah's *Habits of the Heart*. At a Brookings Institution panel focusing on the "OMG!" research, William Galston noted that young people have grown up in "a high-choice society," and he said that "the rise of choice is associated with a kind of anti-insitutionalism" Brookings Institution, "Faith and Youth in the iPod Era," April 11, 2005, http://www.greenbergresearch.com/articles/1218/1213_transcript.pdf (accessed June 22, 2010).

7. Rebecca Kneale Gould, "Binding Life to Values," in *Ignition: What You Can Do to Fight Global Warming and Spark a Movement* (Washington, D.C.: Island Press, 2007), 120–22.

8. For a broad overview of recent developments, see Gary T. Gardner, *Inspiring Progress: Religions' Contributions to Sustainable Development* (New York: W. W. Norton, 2006).

9. Higher Education Research Institute [HERI], "The Spiritual Life of College Students: A National Study of College Students' Search for Meaning and Purpose," 3–4, 8, http://spirituality.ucla.edu/docs/reports/Spiritual_Life_College_Students_Full_Report.pdf (accessed June 22, 2010). Other studies of young people have found less religious commitment than the HERI research did. The "OMG!" study, for example, divided Generation Y (those eighteen to twenty-five) into three groups: 1) The Godly (27 percent of the sample), who make religion an integral part of their lives; 2) The Godless (also 27 percent), who may have spiritual interests, but no religious affiliations; and 3) The Undecided (46 percent), young people who reject traditional religious commitments, but maintain a modicum of belief and religious practice ("OMG!," p. 4). Even the HERI research shows an increase in students with no religious affiliation, from 13.6 percent of the sample in 1966 to 19.1 percent in 2006. John Pryor et al., *The American Freshman*, 4. Even 20 percent of "godless" young people say it's necessary to believe in God and have good moral values (Brookings Institution, "Faith and Youth in the iPod Era," 13, 18).

10. HERI, "Spiritual Life of College Students," 4.

11. Ibid.; Freitas, *Sex and the Soul*, 27, 39–41. The Greenberg "OMG!" study of Generation Y suggests that there is a gender gap in the religious practice of young people, with women much more likely to be "godly" and much less likely to be "godless" than their male peers. It also showed that religious identification tended to be stronger for young people—like African Americans or Muslim Americans—who are "outsiders." See "OMG!" 10–11.

12. Christian Smith with Melinda Lundquist Denton, *Soul Searching: The Religious and Spiritual Lives of American Teenagers* (New York: Oxford University Press, 2005), 129–30, 133–34.

13. Ibid., 161. Brookings Institution, "Faith and Youth in the iPod Era," 17. Donna Freitas finds a similar inactivity among college students: "Few do anything actively or practically to pursue a spiritual path."

14. Smith and Denton, *Soul Searching*, 162–63; Brookings Institution, "Faith and Youth in the iPod Era," 12.

15. Tim Clydesdale, "Abandoned, Pursued, or Safely Stowed?" Social Science Research Council (SSRC) Essay Forum on the Religious Life of American Undergraduates, February 6, 2007, http://religion.ssrc.org/reforum/Clydesdale.pdf (accessed June 22, 2010); Mark D. Regnerus and Jeremy E. Uecker, "How Corrosive Is College to Religious Faith and Practice," February 5, 2007, Social Science Research Council (SSRC) Essay Forum on the Religious Life of American Undergraduates, http://religion.ssrc.org/reforum/Regnerus_Uecker.pdf (accessed June 22, 2010), 4. Donna Freitas also finds that most students at America's mainstream colleges "divorce religious and spiritual questioning from their social lives" (Freitas, *Sex and the Soul*, 27, 35).

16. Clydesdale, "Abandoned, Pursued, or Safely Stowed?"

17. Brookings Institution, "Faith and Youth in the iPod Era," 4.

18. On the subject of compartmentalization, Smith and Denton think that when students say that religion is important to them, they mean that "religion is very important in the strictly *religious* sector of their lives" (Smith and Denton, *Soul Searching*, 138). Other students segregate religion in time, assuming that it's a life-cycle thing, appropriate for young children and their parents, but not for teenagers and college students. This "pediatric religion" is fairly widespread in America (Smith and Denton, *Soul Searching*, 158–59).

19. The Forum on Religion and Ecology has a Web presence—including essays and resources on each of the environmental resources of each of the ten religions—at http://www.religionandecology.org (accessed June 22, 2010). See also The Yale Forum on Religion and Ecology: http://fore.research.yale.edu/main.html (accessed June 22, 2010).

20. "FAQ," Religion and Environment Initiative, University of Chicago, http://rei.uchicago.edu/faq/index.shtml (accessed June 22, 2010).

21. For a short history of religious responses to environmental crisis, see Gary T. Gardner, *Inspiring Progress: Religions' Contributions to Sustainable Development* (New York: W. W. Norton, 2006).

22. Clydesdale, *First Year Out*, 197.

23. More than any other person, Larry Rasmussen has been my guide to thinking about religion as a natural resource for environmentalism. I recommend all his work, but especially *Earth Community Earth Ethics* (Maryknoll: Orbis Books, 1996). Beyond Rasmussen's work, a good starting point for understanding the range of religious engagement with the environment is Roger S. Gottlieb, ed., *The Oxford Handbook of Religion and Ecology* (New York: Oxford University Press, 2006), and Roger S. Gottlieb, ed. *Religion and the Environment*, 4 vols. (New York: Routledge, forthcoming). Other resources include Richard C. Foltz, *Worldviews, Religion, and the Environment: A Global Anthology* (Belmont: Wadsworth, 2003); David R. Kinsley, *Ecology and Religion: Ecological Spirituality in Cross-Cultural Perspective* (Upper Saddle River: Prentice Hall, 1994); and Steven C. Rockefeller, ed., *Spirit and Nature: Why the Environment Is a Religious Issue—An Interfaith Dialogue* (Boston: Beacon Press, 1992).

24. Bill McKibben, "Creation Unplugged," *Religion and Values in Public Life* 4 (Winter–Spring 1996). Native peoples tell creation stories that grow organically from the earth that sustains them. Through countless generations, Native people orally transmitted the stories of a spirit-filled creation. They revere the spirits that dance through all of creation and understand their use of the Earth as a sacred gift, a willing sacrifice of one spirit to another. Their stories reinforce a biocentric worldview, in which the teeming life of a bioregion and all its creatures is infused with spirits and meaning. As a result, Native peoples cultivate and celebrate a rich environmental knowledge. Their intimate relationships with the places they inhabit engage them in storytelling that names and celebrates every living thing with whom they coexist. See, for example, Jack D. Forbes, "Indigenous Americans: Spirituality and Ecos," *Daedalus*, Fall 2001, 283–300.

25. David Schmidtz and Elizabeth Willott suggest that when we habitually consume nature instrumentally, we miss out on other values of nature. By conforming to our culture's commonsense understanding of nature, we "are *under-consuming* nature's transformative value" (Schmidtz and Willott, "Varieties of Overconsumption," 6).

26. For a Christian expression of holy ground, see Gordon Lathrop, *Holy Ground: A Liturgical Cosmology* (Minneapolis: Fortress Press, 2009). For an interreligious dialogue, see Lyndsay Moseley, ed., *Holy Ground: A Gathering of Voices on Caring for Creation* (San Francisco: Sierra Club Books, 2008).

27. Advertisers, for example, try to distract us from the sacramental qualities of the world. Either that, or they try to sell it to us in the sacramental landscapes of SUV ads or in the little plastic serenity fountains that, we're told, "soothe the soul."

28. Mystics suggest that there's a deeper joy than the mere pursuit of happiness, and they advise us not to settle for less. Mystics invite us to imagine the world of our dreams and to work to make it real.

29. Buddhism, for example, teaches the interdependence of all parts of the natural world. And it knows that humans may only be at peace with the world after they have become inwardly peaceful. A peaceful self does not see the world through the eyes of dominance, exploitation, and greed; instead, it sees the world as a single fabric. Buddhist mysticism reminds Buddhists of their place in the world, of the ways in which all are woven together. Meditation and other practices bring Buddhists into a space and time in which they can re-center themselves with the world and search for a *right relation* with the universe. Mary Evelyn Tucker et al., *Buddhism and Ecology: The Interconnection of Dharma and Deeds* (Cambridge: Harvard University Press, 1998).

30. For a broad discussion of the possibilities of Sabbath, including "sabbath environmentalism," see Norman Wirzba, *Living the Sabbath: Discovering the Rhythms of Rest and Delight* (Grand Rapids: Brazos Press, 2006).

31. In *Sand County Almanac,* Aldo Leopold describes this expanding ethic of care.

32. Stephen Jay Gould, *Eight Little Piggies* (New York: W. W. Norton, 1992), 40.

33. While many college students experience worship as an insular and exclusive gathering—an escape *from* the world rather than an engagement *with* the

world—its intent is exactly the opposite. In his article "These Stones Shall be God's House," Troy Messenger writes how "worship is an act of world-making." In worship, religious people express the fullness and the mystery of the world. In prayer and in song, they identify the brokenness of the world and live out a desire to make it whole again. Singing in, through, and with all of creation, they ritually experience the creation restored. "Worship then," Messenger continues, "becomes not about the earth, but a co-creator with the earth." Troy Messenger, "These Stones Shall Be God's House: Tools for Earth Liturgy," in *Earth Habitat: Eco-Injustice and the Church's Response*, ed. Dieter Hessels and Larry Rasmussen (Minneapolis: Fortress Press, 2001), 173–84.

34. In *America: Religions and Religion*, Catherine Albanese contends that any religion includes four main components: creed, code, cultus, and community. The third component, cultus, refers to any particular set of rituals or practices that a religious community performs together. Because human beings are creatures of habit, we seem to do well with cultus, and liturgy is how we do cultus in our religious lives, formulating rituals for regular religious worship services—weekly, monthly, annually, depending on the tradition. Liturgy lets Christians, for example, know the shape of services every Sunday morning. Catherine Albanese, *America: Religions and Religion* (Belmont: Wadsworth, 1981). Religious rituals also offer a different way of joining past, present, and future, nurturing both communities of memory and communities of hope. Bellah et al., *Habits of the Heart*, 152–55.

35. Aldo Leopold, *A Sand County Almanac* (New York: Ballantine Books, 1966), 239.

36. Soelle, *To Work and to Love*, 83–114.

37. Curtis White, "The Ecology of Work," *Orion*, May/June 2007.

38. Thomas Berry, *The Great Work: Our Way Into the Future* (New York: Bell Tower, 1999), 3; Van Jones, *The Green Collar Economy: How One Solution Can Fix Our Two Biggest Problems* (San Francisco: HarperCollins, 2008). See also Alan Thein Durning, *Green-Collar Jobs: Working in the New Northwest* (Seattle: Northwest Environment Watch, 1999).

39. On downshifting, see Juliet B. Schor, *The Overspent American: Upscaling, Downshifting, and the New Consumer* (New York: Basic Books, 1998), 111–42. On the parameters of a new economy, see Juliet B. Schor, *Plenitude: The New Economics of True Wealth* (New York: Penguin, 2010).

40. Christian asceticism was started by people who understood religious practice as countercultural. When Christianity became the official religion of the Roman Empire, it sometimes got comfortable with practices of domination, exploitation, and the accumulation of wealth. A few Christians—known today as the Desert Fathers and Mothers—believed that the good life was more likely to happen on the margins than in the mainstream of society. In the desert, in the convent, in the monastery—basically in the boondocks—they came to value community, simplicity, and good work.

41. Schmidtz and Willott, "Varieties of Overconsumption," 5. Especially in situations of addiction—and there are plenty of them in American culture—people are overcome by their own preferences.

42. As Philip Cafaro suggests in *Thoreau's Living Ethics,* "The healthy side of all asceticism is its recognition of higher goals and its fostering of the discipline necessary to achieve them." Philip Cafaro, *Thoreau's Living Ethics: Walden and the Pursuit of Virtue* (Athens: University of Georgia Press, 2006), 84.

43. See Robert Wuthnow, ed., *Rethinking Materialism: Perspectives on the Spiritual Dimension of Economic Behavior* (Grand Rapids: William B. Eerdmans, 1995).

44. For a good discussion of religion and simple living, see Michael Schut, ed., *Simpler Living, Compassionate Life* (Denver: Living the Good News, 1999).

45. McKibben, "Creation Unplugged," 18–20.

46. Larry Rasmussen, "Drilling in the Cathedral," *Dialog: A Journal of Theology,* 2003, 202–25.

47. Nearly all of the mainline denominations call for policy changes in local and national government. The Shakertown Pledge calls us to "join with others in reshaping institutions." In most denominations, congregations are encouraged to work for change in their own local communities. A Baptist congregation in the South Bronx, for example, will likely respond to very different environmental issues than a Catholic congregation in rural Alaska.

48. Maren Gelle reminds me that weirdness might be just the right thing in a culture careening toward *global* weirding. Like the Beat poets of the 1950s, who claimed that madness (both anger and deviance) was the right response to an insane culture, college students might consider whether rationality is an entirely adequate response to collective lunacy.

49. In a related way, we tend to think of virtue as boring, imagining that vice is what makes life interesting. Within the epistemology of TV—where entertainment is the ultimate value—this makes sense. But in a real world that needs more virtue, it's absurd. We also seem to have a compensatory sense of virtue. If we put in any time at all doing good things, we feel justified doing anything else that's "not too bad." We don't practice a virtue ethic— we practice a minimalist ethic. We ration our goodness as if it were a limited resource. Both of these perspectives—and others current in American culture—come from our adherence to rule-based ethics instead of a virtue ethics. For an introduction to virtue ethics, see Ronald L. Sandler and Philip Cafaro, eds., *Environmental Virtue Ethics* (Lanham: Rowman and Littlefield, 2005) and Ronald L. Sandler, *Character and Environment: A Virtue-Oriented Approach to Environmental Ethics* (New York: Columbia University Press, 2007).

50. "Yearning for Balance: Views of Americans on Consumption, Materialism and the Environment" (Merck Family Fund, 1995).

51. Ibid., 5–8.

52. David Wann, *Biologic: Environmental Protection by Design* (Boulder: Johnson Books, 1990), 24–25.

53. Tucker and Grim, "Introduction," 19.

54. G. K. Chesterton, *What's Wrong with the World* (New York: Sheed and Ward, 1956), 29.

Notes to Chapter 10

1. "OMG!" 7; Clydesdale, *The First Year Out*, 51.

2. David Orr, "Orr's Laws," *Conservation Biology*, December 2004, 1458.

3. David Mindich, the author of *Tuned Out: Why Americans Under 40 Don't Follow the News*, says that "students who don't pay attention to politics cede their political power to their elders and their more-involved peers. And without political power they are screwed." David T. Z. Mindich, "Dude, Where's Your Newspaper?" *Chronicle of Higher Education*, October 8, 2004.

4. Since 1966, the Higher Education Research Institute (HERI) has conducted surveys of college frosh, as well as research projects on a variety of topics on campus culture. Since 2001, the Center for Information and Research on Civic Learning and Engagement (CIRCLE) has been studying the patterns of politics among young people and college students, and promoting programs of civic engagement. Since 2000, Harvard University's Institute of Politics (IOP) has also conducted biannual polls tracking trends in college political culture. The HERI website is at http://www.gseis.ucla.edu/heri/index.php (accessed June 22, 2010). CIRCLE's webpage is at http://www.civicyouth.org (accessed June 22, 2010). Although the webpage is filled with information about the politics of college students, the best single resource is "Millennials Talk Politics: A Study of College Student Political Engagement," Center for Information & Research on Civic Learning and Engagement (CIRCLE), 2007. Harvard's Institute for Politics can be found at http://www.iop.harvard.edu (accessed June 22, 2010).

5. Dick Meyer, "Politics Are So Lame," *CBS News*, February 3, 2006; Purdy, *For Common Things*, 38. For more on our apolitical socialization, see Nina Eliasoph, *Avoiding Politics: How Americans Produce Apathy in Everyday Life* (Cambridge: Cambridge University Press, 1998).

6. Callie Taggart, "Political Apathy Abounds at USU," *Hard News Cafe*, March 7, 2003, http://newscafe.ansci.usu.edu/archive/march2003/0307_politics.html (accessed June 22, 2010).

7. Moffatt, *Coming of Age in New Jersey*, 90–91, 132; "Millennials Talk Politics," 15–17, 29; Harvard University Institute of Politics, "Redefining Political Attitudes and Activism," April 2006, http://www.iop.harvard.edu/Research-Publications/Polling/Spring-2007-Survey/Fall-2007-Survey/Spring-2006-Survey/Executive-Summary (accessed June 22, 2010), 5.

8. Mariolina Salvatori, "Understanding the Students We Teach," *ADE Bulletin*, Spring 1992, 69–75, reprinted at http://web2.ade.org/ade/bulletin/n101/101069.htm (accessed June 22, 2010). In addition, American corporations established think tanks and political-action committees, and they sponsored scientists in raising doubts about established science. That story is told beautifully in Naomi Oreskes and Erik M. Conway, *Merchants of Doubt: How a Handful of Scientists Obscured the Truth on Issues from Tobacco Smoke to Global Warming* (New York: Bloomsbury, 2010).

9. Moffatt, *Coming of Age in New Jersey*, 90–95. For an extended discussion of cynicism, see William Chaloupka, *Everybody Knows: Cynicism in America*

(Minneapolis: University of Minnesota Press, 1999). Sometimes, sadly, to align our beliefs and behavior, we change our beliefs to fit our less-than-perfect behavior (Purdy, *For Common Things*, 18).

10. Martin Luther King, Jr., addressed this issue in his "Letter from Birmingham Jail": "We must come to see," he asserted, "that human progress never rolls in on wheels of inevitability. It comes through the tireless efforts and persistent work of men willing to be co-workers with God, and without this hard work time itself becomes an ally of the forces of social stagnation. We must use time creatively, and forever realize that the time is always ripe to do right."

11. "Millennials Talk Politics," 20. College students get great satisfaction from volunteering, but they're often satisfied with treating the symptoms instead of the systems of social problems. Paul Loeb recounts how one college student wished that the soup kitchen he worked in would still be there when his kids came to school, so that they could have the same experience. But if we ever adopted a comprehensive food policy in this country, we wouldn't need soup kitchens (Paul Loeb, "Against Apathy," *Academe*, July–August 2001).

12. The CIRCLE research discovered that fully 48 percent of students say they are not affiliated with either the Democrats or Republicans. They see political identification as a practice of conformity rather than a practice of collaboration. This fits perfectly, of course, with American ideals of individualism and independence ("Millennials Talk Politics," 4, 24). But students are not escaping the polarization of American politics. The Higher Education Institute's Cooperative Institutional Research Program (CIRP) freshman survey, for example, suggests that fewer students are identifying as moderates these days, and more are identifying as liberal or conservative, with conservative identification peaking at 33.8 percent in 2006 (Pryor et al., *The American Freshman*, 28).

13. Harvard University Institute of Politics, "Redefining Political Attitudes and Activism," 9. "Millennials Talk Politics," 20.

14. "OMG!" 7. In American culture, people generally foreground private life, and relegate public life and the common good to the background. It's the way we see the world and it is, in itself, a sign of the state of our political culture. It's our worldview—even though it obscures our view of the real world. See also Harvard University Institute of Politics, "Redefining Political Attitudes and Activism," 5, and Clydesdale, *The First Year Out*, 26, 197. Jedediah Purdy notes, "Contrary to the fantasy of the moment, public life and public institutions can never be obsolete. Our private lives—our work, our families, our circles of friends—are pervasively affected by things that can never be private: law and political institutions, economics and culture. We ignore these essentially public matters at the risk of misunderstanding our own well-being. And that misunderstanding invites us to neglect public concerns in ways that impoverish the public realm and, in time, erode the underpinnings of good private lives. Indeed, the interdependence of public and private is so great the speaking of them as separate is often misleading" (Purdy, *For Common Things*, 75).

15. Taggart, "Political Apathy Abounds at USU"; Meyer, "Politics Are So Lame."

16. Almost four in ten students spontaneously told the CIRCLE researchers that "they cannot be adequately informed about public issues because the news media is biased and untrustworthy" ("Millennials Talk Politics," 23).

17. Mindich, "Dude, Where's Your Newspaper?" *Chronicle of Higher Education.*

18. For a good introduction to the social organization of silence, see Eviatar Zerubavel, *The Elephant in the Room: Silence and Denial in Everyday Life* (New York: Oxford, 2008).

19. Jason Schwalm, "College Students Believe 'Voting Does Not Matter,'" *Louisville Cardinal,* September 19, 2006; "Millennials Talk Politics," 14–15; Pryor et al., *The American Freshman,* 75.

20. "Millennials Talk Politics," 22. The student focus on success, which they have learned at home and in school, also may not serve them well. David Orr suggests, "The plain fact is that the planet does not need more successful people. But it does desperately need more peacemakers, healers, restorers, storytellers and lovers of every kind. It needs people of moral courage willing to join the fight to make the world habitable and humane. And these qualities have little to do with success as our culture has defined it." David Orr, *Earth in Mind: On Education, Environment, and the Human Prospect* (Washington: Island Press, 1992), 12.

21. "Millennials Talk Politics," 21, 23; Meyer, "Politics Are So Lame"; Richard Flacks, *Making History: The American Left and the American Mind* (New York: Columbia University Press, 1988), 68–97; Both Flacks and Lizabeth Cohen show how Americans after World War II defined a new social contract with their government. They agreed that the government would promote economic growth and shield them from the vicissitudes of the marketplace. Experts would choose the best social policies. And citizens would consume the benefits of good government. As a result, the standard operating procedure of citizens would be inattention. Lizabeth Cohen, *A Consumers' Republic: The Politics of Mass Consumption in Postwar America* (New York: Alfred A. Knopf, 2003). For a sociological perspective on busyness, see Dale Southerton, "Feeling 'Harried': Hot Spots, Social Networks and Scheduling Practices," in *Consumption, Sustainability and Everyday Life,* Lancaster University, 2001, http://www.lancs .ac.uk/fass/projects/esf/online%20handbook.pdf (accessed June 22, 2010), 39–40.

22. Meyer, "Politics Are So Lame."

23. For an overview of citizenship, see Michael Schudson, *The Good Citizen: A History of American Civic Life* (New York: Free Press, 1998).

24. "Millennials Talk Politics," 25–26. For an early critique of the privatization of American higher education, see Wendell Berry, "The Loss of the University," in *Home Economics: Fourteen Essays* (San Francisco: North Point Press, 1987), 76–97.

25. Central College in Pella, Iowa, is one of the pioneers in this effort. See "Central Adds Sustainability to Core Curriculum," Central College, http:// www.central.edu/news/story.cfm?ID=201 (accessed June 22, 2010).

26. "Millennials Talk Politics," 8.

27. Morley Winograd and Michael D. Hais, *Millennial Makeover: MySpace, YouTube & the Future of American Politics* (New Brunswick, NJ: Rutgers University Press, 2008), 1–2, 6, 206–212, 250, 193, 210, 263. The Democratic tilt of millennials is also seen in polls. In May 2007, millennials preferred Democrats over Republicans by a 1.75-to-1.00 margin.

28. Winograd and Hais, *Millennial Makeover*, 167–71, 188. Approaching the 2010 elections, the prediction of "partisan dominance" seems unlikely.

29. Harvard University Institute of Politics, "Redefining Political Attitudes and Activism," 2–3, 8–9; Pryor et al., *The American Freshman*, 28.

30. Harvard University Institute of Politics, "2007 Youth Survey on Politics and Public Service" (December 2007), 4, 6.

31. Langdon Winner, *The Whale and the Reactor: A Search for Limits in an Age of High Technology* (Chicago: University of Chicago Press, 1986), 79–80.

32. Alan Warde, "Consumption and Choice," in *Consumption, Sustainability and Everyday Life*, 15.

33. See Martin V. Melosi, *The Sanitary City: Environmental Services in Urban America from Colonial Times to the Present* (Pittsburgh: University of Pittsburgh Press, 2008).

34. For a video of the speech, see "President Obama in Newton, Iowa, April 22, 2009, Earth Day," Iowa Public Television, http://www.iptv.org/video/detail.cfm/3683/tij_20090422 (accessed June 22, 2010).

35. Quoted in Lawrence E. Harrison, *The Central Liberal Truth: How Politics Can Change a Culture and Save It From Itself* (New York: Oxford University Press, 2006), xvi.

36. Andres R. Edwards, *The Sustainability Revolution: Portrait of a Paradigm Shift* (Gabriola Island: New Society, 2005); Paul Hawken, *Blessed Unrest: How the Largest Movement in the World Came into Being and Why No One Saw It Coming* (New York: Penguin, 2007); David Orr, *Down to the Wire: Confronting Climate Collapse* (New York: Oxford University Press, 2009).

37. Bryan Walsh, "Climate Change, One Light Bulb at a Time?" *Time*, November 8, 2007; Rebecca Solnit, *Savage Dreams: A Journey into the Landscape Wars of the American West* (San Francisco: Sierra Club Books, 1994), 14; Purdy, *For Common Things*, 160.

Notes to Chapter 11

1. American College & University Presidents' Climate Commitment, "Program Overview," http://www.presidentsclimatecommitment.org/html/documents/ACUPCCProgramOverview_000.pdf (accessed June 22, 2010).

2. For a list of places where students have instituted mandatory environmental fees, see "Mandatory Student Fees for Renewable Energy and Energy Efficiency," Association for the Advancement of Sustainability in Higher Education [AASHE], http://www.aashe.org/resources/mandatory_energy_fees.php (accessed June 20, 2010). For advice on creating a revolving loan fund, see Asa Diebolt and Timothy Den Herder-Thomas, *Creating a Campus*

Sustainability Revolving Loan Fund: A Guide for Students, Association for the Advancement of Sustainability in Higher Education, 2007, http://www.aashe .org/documents/resources/pdf/CERF.pdf (accessed June 20, 2010).

3. See, for example, RecycleMania (www.recyclemania.org) and the National Campus Energy Challenge (www.climatechallenge.org/ncec).

4. Morrison, *Marketing to the Campus Crowd*, 84.

5. McKibben, *Maybe One*, 93, 112 (emphasis in the original). I'm indebted to Alan Durning for writing that we live in "an economy whose success ensures its failure." Alan Thein Durning, *This Place on Earth: Home and the Practice of Permanence* (Seattle: Sasquatch Books, 1996), 30.

6. Schmidtz and Willott, "Varieties of Overconsumption," 3.

7. Clydesdale, *The First Year Out*, 211.

8. Rebecca Solnit, *Hope in the Dark: Untold Histories, Wild Possibilities* (New York: Nation Books, 2004), 5. See also Scott Russell Sanders, *Hunting for Hope: A Father's Journeys* (Boston: Beacon Press, 1998).

9. "Mission Statement," William McDonough + Partners, http://www .mcdonoughpartners.com/mission_statement.shtm (page discontinued June 20, 2010).

10. A good starting point would be informal discussion of Arran Stibbe, ed., *Handbook of Sustainability Literacy: Skills for a Changing World* (Totnes Devon, UK: Green Books, 2010), also available in an online edition; Poppy Villiers-Stuart and Arran Stibbe, eds., The Handbook of Sustainable Literacy, University of Brighton Faculty of Arts, http://arts.brighton.ac.uk/stibbe-handbook-of-sustainability/chapters (accessed June 22, 2010).

11. McKibben, *Age of Missing Information*, 122.

12. Purdy, *For Common Things*, 182–83. See also Peters, *In Search of the Good Life*, 192–210.

13. For a good readable introduction to social marketing, see Doug McKenzie-Mohr and William Smith, *Fostering Sustainable Behavior: An Introduction to Community-Based Social Marketing* (Gabriola Island: New Society Publishers, 1999).

14. For more on the idea of a new American Dream, see the Center for a New American Dream, http://www.newdream.org (accessed June 20, 2010).

Acknowledgments

A book like this may have only one person's name on the cover, but it's never a solo flight. Even though I'm usually alone when I'm writing, I'm always engaged in conversations with people, living and dead, whose words influence those I put on the page. I owe them all.

Innumerable thanks go to my students, who inspired this book and informed it, teaching me about their lives both in class and out of it. Thanks to Mark Werner, one of the liveliest minds I've ever encountered, both for his official collaboration on chapter 6, "The Nature of Screens," and for his careful reading of other chapters. Thanks to John Schwehn, who helped me write a chapter on religion and spirituality that was twice as long as the one in this book. The ideas that we cut out will be, I hope, the ideas he takes up later in his intellectual life. And thanks to Jens Mattson, whose artistic inventiveness is visible in most of the illustrations in this book.

My course Campus Ecology has been the fertile ground for most of my thinking on the nature of college culture. I owe a lot to the students who show up each year, willing to go deep in thinking about the moral ecology of everyday life. Special thanks go to Elise Braaten Nienow, who helped to create the class to provide "a space where imagination can happen." And thanks to Elise and the other students—Milena Klimek, Dayna Burtness, Mary Sotos, Kate Huber, Maren Gelle, and Kristin Johnson—who have team-taught Campus Ecology with me. They have been exuberant examples of how learning leads to teaching and vice versa.

My colleagues in History and American Studies have put up with my oddities and eccentricities for more than thirty years. And the Environmental Studies faculty, including pioneers like Bob Jacobel, Gene Bakko, Kathy Shea, and Gary Deason, have created and sustained a rich program that invites all of us to think comprehensively about environmental issues.

For a writer, time is of the essence, and I'm thankful for a St. Olaf sabbatical that allowed me time to pull together the most important ideas in this book. I'm also indebted to the Lilly Endowment for the gift of time during the 2006–2007 academic year, and to Bruce Dalgaard and St. Olaf's Lilly Program for Lives of Worth and Service. I also appreciate the conversations that are developing among Lilly Scholars and Teaching Fellows at St. Olaf.

Thanks for the critical and contrarian perspectives that arose in the faculty learning community on Sustainability across the Campus and Curriculum, sponsored by St. Olaf's Center for Innovation in the Liberal Arts. Conversations with Beckie Judge, Dan Hofrenning, Sherry Saterstrom, John Schade, Urmila Malvadkar, and Kris MacPherson were an interdisciplinary education in themselves, and helped me expand my horizons greatly.

I'm thankful, too, to all the people who sit on the St. Olaf Sustainability Task Force. Assistant Vice President for Facilities Pete Sandberg, who chairs the group, is an embodiment of the St. Olaf motto, "Ideals to Action." Gene Bakko, St. Olaf's first curator of natural lands, is a model both personally and professionally of how to live with "Earth in mind," and so is his successor, Kathy Shea. Hays Atkins, Katie McKenna, and Peter Abrahamsen, who have managed the St. Olaf food service for Bon Appétit, have taught students daily what the "good" in good food really means. Paul Jackson has been a lively leader of Environmental Studies on campus, and an engaged citizen off campus, too. In the Office of Residence Life, Pamela McDowell has worked with me and Campus Ecology students to make sure that environmental studies are taught not just in the classroom but in dorm rooms as well.

Beyond the St. Olaf campus, I'm grateful to people like David Orr, Bill McKibben, Michael Pollan, Christopher Uhl, Wendell Berry, Scott Russell Sanders, Kathleen Dean Moore, Jenny Price, Juliet Schor, Peggy Barlett, Geoff Chase, Nan Jenks-Jay, Tony Cortese, Judy Walton, and Eban Goodstein, who have influenced me deeply, often without even knowing it.

As always, I'm grateful for my membership (and my friends) in the community of St. Joan of Arc in Minneapolis, where I'm taught constantly that religion is practiced not just in places of worship, but in all the places of our planet.

My association with Milkweed Editions has been another pleasure in this process. My editor, Patrick Thomas, is both a former student and a fierce and friendly critic. I assured him at one point that the book was perfect. He agreed, but said that he hoped to make it "perfecter." He did, but I'm certain there are still flaws, and all of them are mine.

And finally, I'm grateful, more than words can say, to my family. Barb and I share coffee, cooking, conversations, and companionship every day. We go walking often, and our peripatetic pleasures are one of the high points of my life. It's also a delight to share time with John and Paul, Kristin and Benjamin, who show us every day that life is good.

JAMES FARRELL is the author of numerous books that examine the American way of life, from *One Nation Under Goods: Malls and the Seductions of American Shopping* (Smithsonian, 2003) to *Inventing the American Way of Death* (Temple University Press, 1980). He was the first Boldt Distinguished Teaching Professor in the Humanities at St. Olaf College in Northfield, Minnesota, where he teaches Campus Ecology, a course that makes students the subject of their own environmental studies. He also speaks to colleges around the country about "greening" college culture and the moral ecology of everyday life.

More Nonfiction from Milkweed Editions

To order books or for more information,
contact Milkweed at (800) 520-6455
or visit our Web site (www.milkweed.org).

The Colors of Nature:
Culture, Identity, and the Natural World
Edited and introduced by Alison H. Deming and Lauret E. Savoy

The Future of Nature:
Writing on a Human Ecology from Orion *Magazine*
Selected and introduced by Barry Lopez

Hope, Human and Wild:
True Stories of Living Lightly on the Earth
By Bill McKibben

Toward the Livable City
Edited by Emilie Buchwald

Milkweed Editions

Founded as a nonprofit organization in 1979, Milkweed Editions is an independent publisher. Our mission is to identify, nurture and publish transformative literature, and build an engaged community around it.

Join Us

In addition to revenue generated by the sales of books we publish, Milkweed Editions depends on the generosity of institutions and individuals like you. In an increasingly consolidated and bottom-line-driven publishing world, your support allows us to select and publish books on the basis of their literary quality and transformative potential. Please visit our Web site (www.milkweed.org) or contact us at (800) 520-6455 to learn more.

Milkweed Editions, a nonprofit publisher, gratefully acknowledges sustaining support from Emilie and Henry Buchwald; the Patrick and Aimee Butler Foundation; the Dougherty Family Foundation; the Ecolab Foundation; the General Mills Foundation; John and Joanne Gordon; William and Jeanne Grandy; the Jerome Foundation; Robert and Stephanie Karon; the Lerner Foundation; Sally Macut; Sanders and Tasha Marvin; the McKnight Foundation; Mid-Continent Engineering; the Minnesota State Arts Board, through an appropriation by the Minnesota State Legislature, a grant from the Wells Fargo Foundation Minnesota, and a grant from the National Endowment for the Arts; Kelly Morrison and John Willoughby; the National Endowment for the Arts, and the American Reinvestment and Recovery Act; the Navarre Corporation; Ann and Doug Ness; Jörg and Angie Pierach; the RBC Foundation USA; Ellen Sturgis; the Target Foundation; the James R. Thorpe Foundation; the Travelers Foundation; Moira and John Turner; and Edward and Jenny Wahl.

MINNESOTA
STATE ARTS BOARD

NATIONAL
ENDOWMENT
FOR THE ARTS
A great nation
deserves great art.

TARGET.

THE McKNIGHT FOUNDATION

Interior design by Wendy Holdman
Typeset in Arno Pro
by BookMobile Design and Publishing Services
Printed on acid-free 100% post consumer waste paper
by Friesens Corporation

ENVIRONMENTAL BENEFITS STATEMENT

Milkweed Editions saved the following resources by printing the pages of this book on chlorine free paper made with 100% post-consumer waste.

TREES	WATER	SOLID WASTE	GREENHOUSE GASES
47	21,550	1,308	4,474
FULLY GROWN	GALLONS	POUNDS	POUNDS

Calculations based on research by Environmental Defense and the Paper Task Force.
Manufactured at Friesens Corporation